PRACTICAL

Home Decorating
and Repairs

ILLUSTRATED

PAINTING THE HOUSE

Exterior painting is usually associated with ladder work. This illustration shows the correct method of mounting a ladder with paint-kettle and brush. Note also the hook by which the kettle is hung from a rung of the ladder while work is in progress.

PRACTICAL

Home Decorating and Repairs

ILLUSTRATED

*Professional methods simply explained
and illustrated for the home decorator
and handyman*

CONTRIBUTORS

ARTHUR BARRACLOUGH

JOHN W. DERRETT, F.I.B.D.

DENNIS LAYCOCK, M.Coll.H.

R. N. LE FEVRE, M.Inst.GasE., A.M.I.Mech.E.

JAMES PEERS, A.I.E.E.

ODHAMS PRESS LTD   LONG ACRE, LONDON

CONTENTS

4

SECRET OF THIS PROFESSIONAL FINISH

Careful treatment of all surfaces before painting is the secret of obtaining the beautiful smooth finish seen on this porch. Any difference between amateur and professional work is usually due to inadequate preparation and not to poor brushwork.

CHAPTER 1

EXTERIOR PAINTING

TREATMENT OF OUTSIDE WOODWORK AND METALWORK

THE main purpose of exterior painting is to preserve those parts of the structure which would decay if not protected by a paint film which is impervious to moisture. This paint also preserves the interior, for if the exterior woodwork decays moisture penetrates to the inside, while gutters which are badly rusted may allow water to enter rafter ends and wall-plates.

Paintwork is affected by varying atmospheric conditions—rain, strong sunlight, frost, wind, fog and dew. Even if the paint on the broad surfaces appears to be in perfect condition, there may be open joints and crevices through which dampness can enter and set up decay.

WHEN TO PAINT

The question is often asked: "How often should outside painting be done?" The right answer is: "Before the need for it has become very obvious." Experience shows that it is advisable to renew exterior paintwork at least once every three years.

When choosing a colour scheme remember that certain colours may fade in strong sunlight. Generally the more brilliant colours are most affected. Pale green of bright hue is particularly prone to fading. Apart from the question of fading some pigments are also more durable than others.

The number of coats of paint necessary depends on the condition of the work. Two coats is the minimum when the general condition is fairly good and no extensive stripping is necessary. Three coats produce a much better job as the filling and stopping may be sandwiched between the two undercoats. If the two-coat method is adopted bare patches should first be touched up with white- and red-lead priming, before proceeding with the undercoating. All paintwork which is stripped will need at least three coats.

EFFECT OF WEATHER

If weather conditions permit, the best time to do exterior painting is in the early spring or late autumn. Autumn is usually considered to be the best time because the weather is usually more settled, high winds are less frequent and the paintwork has time to harden properly before it is subjected to the heat of the summer. Success is largely dependent on the weather prevailing during the progress of the work.

Painting should not be carried out in wet weather or in a humid atmosphere. Mist and fog can be very harmful and several hours should elapse after such conditions have disappeared before painting is started.

High winds and dust storms may also be troublesome. If the undercoating should become dusty it can be rubbed down and touched up, but gloss paint is far more difficult to repair. Every effort should be made, therefore, to choose a fine day for finishing.

Let us first consider the nature of paints and the functions of the several components. Briefly, paint consists of powdered material in the form of pigments and driers incorporated in a liquid medium consisting of various drying oils and other diluents.

CONSTITUENTS OF PAINT

The purpose of the pigment is to obscure the surface and to provide the colour required. The medium is to bind the pigment to the surface and to form a protective film. It will also be obvious that the medium must dry after the paint has been applied and harden into an elastic and durable film.

The proportions of the constituents are varied according to the nature of the surface to be painted and the sequence of coats. A paint in which the medium is mostly turpentine will tend to dry flat, whereas a predominance of oil in the medium will produce a gloss.

No useful purpose would be served by considering this subject in great

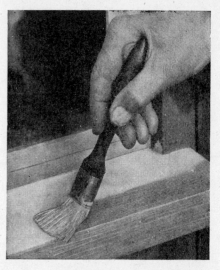

PRIMING

FIG. 2. *Applying a coat of priming to the bare woodwork of a window-sill. The priming should be spread evenly by brushing in order to force the paint well into the grain of the wood.*

detail; it is, therefore, proposed to deal only with the character of those paints which will be required on the average external painting job.

New woodwork requires knotting (Fig. 1) and an oily priming coat so

KNOTTING

FIG. 1. *Before applying the priming coat on new woodwork, any knots on the surface should be sealed with a form of spirit varnish known as shellac knotting.*

that the surface may be impregnated as deeply as possible (Fig. 2). It will be obvious that if turpentine should predominate, the wood would merely act as a strainer, leaving a film of pigment on the surface, and this would have very little adhesion after the turpen-

Dry red-lead should next be added to bring the colour to a bright pink; the colour is incidental to the correct amount of red-lead used. Red-lead is employed because it exerts a powerful drying effect on the oil and continues to operate when the oil has soaked into

BURNING OFF OLD PAINT

FIG. 3. *When old paint has been removed with a blow-lamp, part of the original priming remains in the wood and less oil will be required in the new priming coat. The flame is held ahead of the scraper, which should be moved continuously.*

tine had evaporated from the paint.

Woodwork from which the paint has been removed (Fig. 3) needs a less oily priming coat than new woodwork, because part of the original priming will remain in the wood.

Priming may be purchased ready-mixed or may be made from a good-quality outside undercoating. Take a sufficient quantity for the purpose and add 15-20 per cent of raw linseed oil.

the wood. Thus a sound protective film is formed which provides a good ground for the following coats.

For work which has only been washed and rubbed down, the first coat should contain more oil than is usually present in the average ready-mixed undercoating. To determine the need for additional oil, apply a little of the undercoating to a piece of glass. If it dries flat, without a gloss, about

STOPPING

FIG. 4. *Holes and crevices should be filled with genuine linseed-oil putty.*

10 per cent of linseed oil should be added. The second coat may be undercoating without any addition, other than normal thinning, and this forms a good ground for the finishing coat

of gloss paint. As a general rule a flat should follow an oily coat and a gloss should follow a flat. Remember that all paints are not suitable for exterior work. It is essential that all paints used for exterior work should be specially made for the purpose and recommended as such by the makers.

What diluents are necessary? If directions are given, always follow the manufacturer's advice. Undercoating is often very full-bodied and needs only the addition of a thinner to reduce it to a working consistency. Turpentine or good-quality white spirit may be used for the purpose. Gloss paints sometimes thicken on exposure to the air, particularly if the work extends over several weeks. In such cases a very little white spirit or turpentine may be added. It is best, however, to avoid the practice if possible. Oil should not usually be added to a proprietary gloss paint or varnish.

Finishing paints of the high-gloss variety, known as hard gloss, enamel

LEVELLING UNEVEN SURFACES

FIG. 5. *Fillers are used to level uneven surfaces. They are applied with a knife and set quickly. Only sufficient material should be mixed for the work in hand.*

paint, or varnish paint, are in effect pigments ground in varnish. Those recommended for exterior work contain oils and gums which provide an elastic film to withstand atmospheric conditions.

Varnish for exterior work should be a good-quality copal elastic varnish specially made for this purpose.

Putty for stopping (Fig. 4), the term applied to filling up holes and crevices, should be genuine linseed-oil putty. It consists of finely powdered whiting, ground into a stiff paste with linseed oil. White-lead ground in oil is also used in paste form with whiting for this purpose.

All paint should be thoroughly stirred before it is decanted for use. On opening a container it is helpful to pour off the thin liquid on the top into a spare pot. After breaking up the remainder and stirring well, the thin liquid can be replaced a little at a time until the whole mixture is of the same consistency. Replacing the lid

STRAINING PAINT

FIG. 6. *A piece of fine muslin or an old stocking tied over a paint kettle makes a good substitute for a paint strainer.*

Materials for filling (Fig. 5), the term for levelling uneven surfaces, include paste white-lead, whiting and gold size (a kind of quick-drying varnish). Their use will be described later.

Ready-mixed paints already have a proper proportion of driers in their composition and there is no need to add driers: indeed, if more driers are added there is a risk of causing the paint to crack comparatively quickly.

tightly and shaking the container vigorously should complete the mixing.

When painting operations extend over several weeks, especially when the work can be done only at weekends, skins may form over the top of the paint even though the lid is fastened down tightly after each use. If this skin cannot be removed in one piece it may be necessary to strain the paint each time it is decanted. If the skin is firm enough, it can sometimes be removed by cutting all round the edge with a knife and picking it up in the middle with the fingers.

If it is necessary to strain the paint, a piece of fine muslin or an old silk stocking tied over the paint kettle may be employed in place of a proper paint strainer (Fig. 6). At the end of the day all paint should be passed back into the stock pot and the paint pot wiped dry with the brush.

While not in use brushes can be prevented from becoming hard by suspending them upright in a pot of water (Figs. 7 and 8). A method of doing this is to bore a small hole

BAD PRACTICE

FIG. 8. *A brush should always be suspended; it may be ruined if the bristles bend on the bottom of a container.*

CARE OF BRUSHES

FIG. 7. *To prevent brushes from hardening, suspend them in a jar of water by passing a stiff wire through holes which should be drilled in the handles.*

through the handle of each brush and to thread the brushes on to a stout wire, the ends of which rest on the edge of the container. To prevent a dark brush from soiling a light brush, wrap it round with a piece of paper before placing it in the water. When a brush is required for use the water should first be well swished out, a piece of paper should then be wrapped round the bristles and any remaining water well squeezed out (Fig. 9). If possible keep separate brushes for each colour.

When a job is finished, the brushes should be well washed out in several changes of paraffin until they are quite clear of paint; they are then rubbed dry on newspaper and finally washed in hot water and soap. When putting the brushes into store, powder them well with insecticide to prevent them from being attacked by moths and spiders.

The equipment for outside painting should include: a blow-lamp with a pricker and a nipple key; stripping knife; stopping knife; shave-hook; ladderhook; paint kettles; dusting brush;

by capillary attraction (Fig. 10). This moisture may not only set up decay, but may soften the glue in the joints and cause them to open. In hot weather vapour pressure may cause the paint to blister and flake off.

Sashes which do not open and close easily are another source of trouble. If the hinges bind or the stop beads

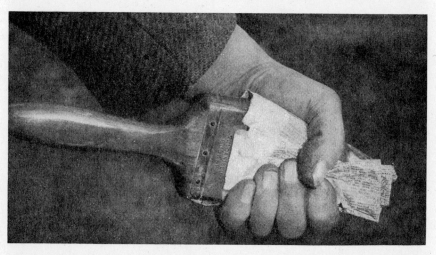

SQUEEZING OUT THE WATER

FIG. 9. *When a brush is removed from water, shake it out thoroughly and then wrap several thicknesses of newspaper round the bristles to squeeze them dry.*

flat brushes, 1 in., 2 in., and 3 in.; an old distemper brush; quirk stick; sponge, piece of hessian or cloth; pumice stone or waterproof glasspaper; buckets; soda, soap powder or sugar soap; a supply of paraffin; a pair of steps and suitable ladders.

Start by making a careful survey and note where the paint film has decayed, flaked or blistered, in order that the cause may be traced and, if possible, eliminated.

Tops and bottoms of sashes not properly painted may allow moisture to travel up and along the long grain

are too close to the sash, the leverage necessary to close the sash may exert a strain on the hanging stile, so causing the joints to open and, sometimes, the tenons to break. If this happens the wood will decay in an astonishingly short time. It is significant that double-hung sashes (sliding windows), which are not subjected to this strain, are not so liable to rot as are casement sashes.

Examination of the sashes can best be conducted from the inside. While doing this, any accumulation of paint round the hinges should be chipped

DEFECTIVE PAINTWORK

FIG. 10. *A paint film which is defective allows moisture to enter the woodwork and to weaken the adhesion of the coating.*

off and the hinges well oiled, taking special care to wipe off any superfluous oil which may have strayed on to the paintwork.

When the hinges are quite free the sash may be tested for closing. If the sash springs back even slightly, look for the cause. Intelligent observation will soon reveal the trouble. There should be proper clearance all round the sash and against the stop beads. On the hanging side the clearance should be equal to the thickness of a penny and at the top, bottom and meeting side the clearance should be twice as much. This is to allow for coats of paint and also for expansion at different times of the year.

WINDOW-SASH REPAIRS

If any major repairs are needed to the sash it is advisable to take it off its hinges. If only easing is required, this may be done without removing the sash, but in the long run it is best to take the sash off. Before doing so, a pencil line should be marked all round to indicate how much is to be shaved off. It is best to scrape the paint off the edge first and to put a

smear of linseed oil on the face of the plane to ease the working.

In the case of very open joints it may be necessary to hack out the glazing putty on the affected side in order to free the glass, and to cramp up the frame before fitting and driving in new wedges. As the stile is often quite loose it is advisable to knock it off the tenons and remake the joints with thick red-lead paint instead of glue.

If the window sashes are of the double-hung variety the first step is to examine and test the sash cords. It is dangerous to begin painting without first ensuring that the cords are in good condition. The usual method of testing is to pull the lines to their fullest extent and then to let them go (Fig. 11). If the cords stand the strain

TESTING SASH CORDS

FIG. 11. *Pull the cord to its fullest extent and release it. The cord should stand the strain of the falling weight.*

WASHING EXTERIOR PAINTWORK

FIG. 12. *Painted surfaces which are in reasonably good condition will need only washing and rubbing down before the new paint is applied. An old distemper brush and two buckets will be required, one containing water to which a little soda or sugar soap has been added and the other clean water. Note the scaffolding.*

of the falling weight and otherwise appear to be in good condition they will not need to be replaced. Badly frayed or broken cords should be renewed. The sashes should move freely, otherwise the painter will not be able to adjust them to the desired position for painting. An accumulation of paint on the parting beads (laths which run down the sides of the frame and separate the two sashes) is sometimes the cause of the sashes binding.

All the details mentioned should be dealt with before the normal preparation for painting is started. If any part of the work is left until the washing starts it may be neglected. During this preliminary survey, make a note of all parts which need stripping.

Stripping of old paintwork is necessary if it is flaking or badly blistered. If the trouble is localized, such as at the bottoms of sashes and in the area around joints, it will be sufficient if only these parts are stripped. If, however, the paint is flaking or blistered it is recommended that the whole of the paint coating should be removed.

RUBBING-DOWN

FIG. 13. *One of the purposes of rubbing-down is to provide a key for the new paint. The work is best carried out with water as a lubricant.*

PUMICE-STONE BLOCK

FIG. 14. *After dipping the face of the stone in water, each part of the surface to be treated should be rubbed down in the direction of the grain of the wood.*

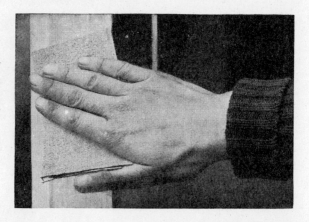

FIG. 15. *The method of folding shown in Fig. 16 provides a convenient piece of glass-paper for general use. The fingers cannot apply uniform pressure to a larger area.*

In old houses the woodwork has often been painted so many times and the mouldings are so gummed up with paint that their contour is disguised. In these circumstances it may be necessary to remove the paint in order to ensure a good surface.

In order to clean the surface thoroughly, level off irregularities, and provide a suitable key for the new paint, the surface should be washed (Fig. 12) and rubbed down. The rubbing-down should be done during the washing process. Rubbing-down wet is more effective than dry rubbing-down and avoids danger to health due

FOLDING GLASS-PAPER

FIG. 16. *Tear the sheet in two and fold each half into three to provide a convenient area for working by hand.*

to the inhalation of the paint dust.

Two small buckets should be used for washing and rubbing-down: one containing water to which a little soda or washing powder has been added, and the other containing clean water.

Pumice (Figs. 13 and 14), glass-paper, or steel wool may be used. Of these, the amateur will find that a fairly coarse grade of waterproof glass-paper gives the best results.

The method of folding the glass-paper is shown in Figs. 15 and 16. The paper is halved and each half is neatly folded in three. After a time the paper will begin to tear at the folds: when this happens the torn pieces should be folded again for use in awkward places.

Before washing, release all window fastenings and take down or otherwise protect the curtains from damage. It is advisable to close all inner doors to prevent the draught from carrying the dust inside or blowing the curtains about.

Prepare half a bucket of washing water and half a bucket of rinsing water. An old distemper brush is best for both laying on the washing water and for rinsing it off, but if a brush is not available a piece of hessian or a sponge may be used as a substitute. A knife and a dusting brush will be needed to clean out the crevices; an old table-knife can be used for this purpose and an old bannister brush with the nose sawn off makes an admirable dusting brush.

First rake out all corners, cut away all loose glazing putty and dust down. The next step is to lay-in all the window frame or door with the washing water, taking care not to let any water stray to the inside. Now dip the glass-paper in the water and proceed to scour the whole of the paintwork, including the remaining putty, not forgetting the tops and bottoms of the sashes.

When the rubbing-down has been completed the work must be thoroughly rinsed off with clean water. It is advisable to use two lots of clean water to make doubly sure that there is no soap or soda left behind.

USEFUL HINTS

When the washing has been completed, the next job is to burn off any defective parts; instructions for this work are given later. Rub down the burnt-off parts with coarse glass-paper and dust down well. All knots, and an area extending $\frac{1}{2}$ in. round them, should be given a coat of shellac knotting. The next step (Fig. 17) is to prime all bare wood, including any edges of sashes which have been eased and all rebates from which the putty may have been removed. Rusty ironwork, a subject which will be dealt with later, should also be given attention at this stage.

Painting is made easier and quicker if some attention is given to the correct technique. Never keep the paint kettle

PRIMING WOODWORK

Fig. 17. *The priming coat must provide a grip for subsequent materials and satisfy the suction of the surface. Tackle the upper part of the frame first.*

more than one-third full. When charging the brush, dip one-third of the length of the bristles into the paint and then press both sides of the brush on the side of the kettle to

18

distribute the paint evenly in the brush. If the brush is charged ·in this manner, wiping on the edge of the kettle should be unnecessary.

Use the brush best suited to the job in hand. A small one for small work such as sash bars and for cutting-in and a larger one for bigger areas.

The more the paint is forced into the pores of the wood the better the result will be and the greater the protection afforded. Keep the brush square to the surface (Figs. 18 and 19) and work it vigorously; this action will distribute the paint evenly. Brush marks can easily be eliminated by finally crossing and re-crossing with the tips of the brush, using very little pressure.

Cutting-in is the term applied to painting to fine limits such as painting up to glass, to a line, or to the edge of a moulding. A special size and type of brush is usually chosen for this work; a part-worn brush is most suitable.

There are two methods of using a brush when cutting-in; the first (Fig. 20) is that adopted by many good painters. It consists of drawing the brush along lightly several times until the few stray bristles at the

RIGHT

FIG. 18. *How to hold a brush when painting. By spreading the bristles and exerting uniform pressure the paint is forced well into the surface.*

WRONG

FIG. 19. *An awkward hold which restricts the painting action results in uneven distribution and prevents a good surface from being produced.*

CUTTING-IN

FIG. 20. *The brush is drawn along lightly several times as described in the text until a straight line can be painted.*

side of the brush have made a clearly painted straight line. The second method—usually employed with flat brushes—is to spread the brush sideways, applying more pressure (Fig. 21); in this way a perfectly straight line may be produced with one stroke.

The consistency of the paint should be such that it can be spread easily and left perfectly smooth and free from brush-marks. Two thin coats are better than one thick coat.

The procedure for exterior work is somewhat different from that adopted for interior work. The principles are the same, but on outside painting the order is often governed by the means employed in reaching the work.

Advantage should be taken when using ladders to do any part of the work within reach, even if it should

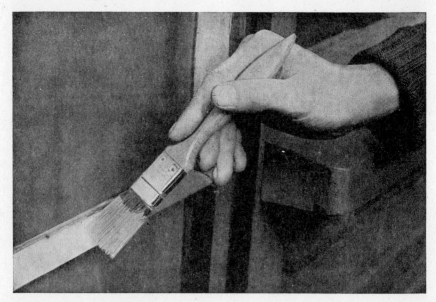

ALTERNATIVE METHOD OF CUTTING-IN

FIG. 21. *Many good craftsmen cut-in by using the flat of the brush, which is drawn lightly along the edge until the bristles, parted at one side, have made a clearly painted line. Repeated strokes may be necessary in order to achieve success.*

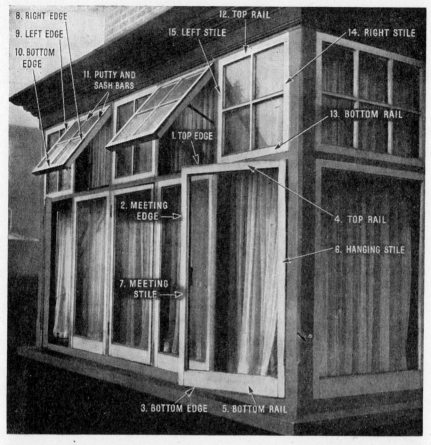

8. RIGHT EDGE
9. LEFT EDGE
10. BOTTOM EDGE
11. PUTTY AND SASH BARS
12. TOP RAIL
15. LEFT STILE
14. RIGHT STILE
1. TOP EDGE
13. BOTTOM RAIL
2. MEETING EDGE→
4. TOP RAIL
6. HANGING STILE
7. MEETING STILE→
3. BOTTOM EDGE
5. BOTTOM RAIL

SEQUENCE OF PAINTING CASEMENT WINDOWS

FIG. 22. *Numbers 1-7 refer to the lower window and 8-15 apply to one of the upper windows. The sequence of operations has been split for the sake of simplicity. When finishing in parti-colours allow the frames to dry before painting the sashes.*

not happen to be normal procedure. A little thought and organization will save much unnecessary movement of ladders.

The best plan when painting is to complete each section as the work proceeds and thus to avoid leaving an edge of paint so long that it partially sets and forms a ridge when the painting is continued. Thus with a case- ment window the top edge should be painted first, then the glazing putty of the top rail, and then the face, in the order shown in Fig. 22. The hanging stile should be treated next from the top downwards, in sections of about 9 in., glazing putty first and then the face. The bottom rail should follow next and finally the meeting stile. Do not forget the bottom edge.

21

The order of painting larger areas, such as front doors and garage doors, is shown in Figs. 23 and 24.

Faults to avoid in painting are fat edges, runs and curtains. The first is the term applied to an edge where the paint has gathered in a thick ridge. This will generally happen when two painted edges meet (Fig. 25); the last stroke of the brush, therefore, should

PAINTING A FRONT DOOR

FIG. 23. *After opening the door and edging it in a convenient position, the paint-work should be carried out in accordance with the sequence of numbers shown.*

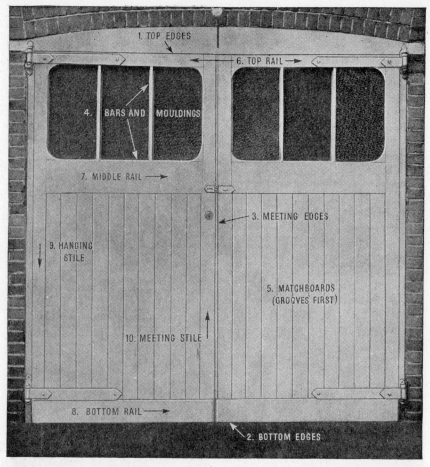

SEQUENCE OF PAINTING GARAGE DOORS

FIG. 24. *A convenient order for painting garage doors is provided by the numbers which refer to the same features on each door. Painters work in various ways and it should be realized that no hard and fast rules of sequence can be laid down.*

be down the edge to level it off. Runs and curtains seldom occur in under-coating but can be very noticeable in gloss paint. They are the result of too much paint being applied to mouldings and an uneven coat to flat surfaces.

Runs from the mouldings can be avoided by rubbing the mouldings with only a little paint on the brush. Curtains will not occur if the painting is finished with long, firm strokes in all directions. If the paint is left thicker in one place than another the thick part will run over the bare part. It will help considerably if, wherever possible, the paint is laid off downwards.

Unless one is left-handed, painting

23

is generally done from right to left. Steps should be on the left of the worker (Fig. 27); this gives freedom of reach for the right hand, a hold for the left hand and a resting place, if necessary, for the paint kettle. Never attempt to use a pair of steps as shown in Fig. 26.

Holes and crevices may be stopped with linseed-oil putty, putty and dry red-lead, putty and paste white-lead, paste white-lead only, gold-size and whiting. The latter is known as hard stopping and is most satisfactory. Stopping should be done between the first and second coats, using a stopping knife and a quirk stick (Fig. 28).

Filling is the term applied to levelling up irregularities in the surface. The best filler for outside work is certainly a mixture of paste white-lead, whiting and gold-size with a little turpentine. This mixture in the form of a paste is applied with a broad knife and when it is thoroughly hard is rubbed down with pumice-stone and water.

The preliminary survey, and all repairs and adjustments, must be carried out before beginning the

DANGEROUS PRACTICE

FIG. 26. *Apart from the difficulty of painting in such an awkward position, this illustration also shows a most dangerous method of using steps.*

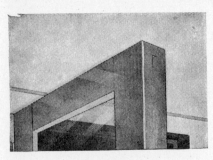

FAT EDGES

FIG. 25. *If too much paint is applied a thick ridge, known as a fat edge, may occur where two edges meet.*

painting proper. The importance of this preparatory work cannot be overemphasized.

If the whole of the paint is not to be burnt off, the sequence of operations should be: clean and rub down, burn off defective parts, touch in and apply the undercoating, stopping, second undercoat and, finally, the coat of gloss paint or varnish.

Assuming that the idea is to use gloss paint, the first step should be to clean out all gutters and rain-water heads; wire-brushing, dusting, and washing if possible. Rain-water pipes should be tested for clearance and gullies cleaned out and flushed.

Washing and rubbing-down should

QUIRK STICK

FIG. 28. *Filling in a crack with putty using a quirk stick. This useful tool can be made by the handyman from any small piece of wood. Note how the blade is shaped to force in the putty.*

be done from the top downwards; first the gutters, then the upper windows and finally the windows and doors on the ground level. This plan avoids dust and dirt being brushed on to work which has already been prepared.

Undercoating is the next job. If only one coat of undercoating is intended (two are advisable) it is best to add a little raw linseed oil or a small quantity of the finishing colour to it. When applying two undercoats, the second should contain a little more oil than the first, or should have a little of the finishing coat added to it.

FIRST COAT

The colour of the undercoating should approximate to the tone if not to the colour of the finishing paint. Thus, a broken-white would suit a cream finish. Generally it is best to have the undercoating a few shades lighter than the finish. Each coat should be lightly glass-papered with a fine paper before carrying on with the next coat. This step is important.

CORRECT PROCEDURE

FIG. 27. *The right method of using steps to paint the same metal down-pipe as that shown in Fig. 26. The steps are fully opened and placed on the left.*

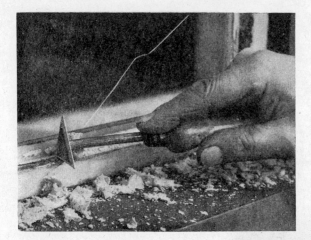

FIG. 29. *Scraping out defective putty with a shave-hook. Care should be taken to clean out the corners so that the whole rebate is clean.*

When the first coat is dry, it should be lightly glass-papered, well dusted and stopped. A mixture of paste white-lead and linseed-oil putty in equal parts is recommended for stopping: if too soft, add a little powdered whiting. Force the stopping well into the holes with a stopping knife, leaving the surface smooth and level. Cracks and crevices are best stopped by the use of a quirk stick. Glazing putties should be repaired at this stage as shown in Figs. 29-32.

FILLING

If the surface is uneven, apart from the need for stopping, filling up must be considered. Filling material may be made from one part of paste white-lead, from which most of the oil has been withdrawn by spreading it on and wrapping it up in paper, and two parts of powdered whiting. The mixture should be reduced to a smooth paste by adding gold-size and turpentine in equal parts.

In order to spread the paste easily with a broad knife or stripping knife it is essential to free it of lumps or pieces of paint skin. A good plan is to

FITTING THE GLASS

FIG. 30. *A thin layer of putty is run round the window frame and the lower edge of the new glass is inserted before the top is pressed home. The glazing putty is then applied and smoothed.*

26

to glass. When rain-water pipes are fixed close to the wall the use of a mask is very desirable (Fig. 33). A piece of cardboard or linoleum passed behind the pipe will enable the whole of the back of the pipe to be painted without disfiguring the brickwork.

The procedure for painting a double-hung sash window is as follows. Start the job by raising the lower sash and pulling down the upper sash so that they cross.

With the sashes in this position, the head and sill of the frame, the meeting bar, about six inches down the stiles of the lower sash and the top and bottom of the sashes, should be painted. The sashes are then closed and the remainder of the painting

APPLYING THE PUTTY

FIG. 31. *Glazing putty should be held in the hand and worked well into the angle. It is smoothed with the thumb as it is run round the edges of the glass.*

squeeze it through a piece of muslin. Sufficient pressure should be used on the knife to force the paste into the hollow places and skim it off the high parts.

When the filling is thoroughly dry and hard it should be rubbed down to a level surface with a piece of pumice-stone dipped in water. Wet or dry glass-paper can also be used for this purpose.

As an alternative to cutting-in when painting the putty use a mask consisting of a piece of thin card or zinc. Quite one of the best methods of masking is to use sticky tape, which may be left on until all the coats have been applied and then peeled off: this refers particularly to cutting-in

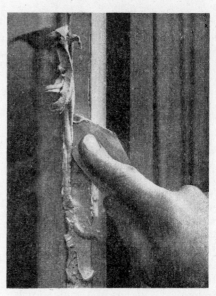

FINISHING THE JOB

FIG. 32. *The putty should be smoothed off with a knife. Although some workers apply pressure with the first finger, the thumb is more usually employed.*

27

METHOD OF MASKING

FIG. 33. *By holding a piece of wood or card between the pipe and the wall, the back of the pipe can be painted without defacing the surface of the brickwork.*

completed. Finally the sashes should be opened an inch top and bottom.

Paintwork which has disintegrated and is flaking can sometimes be removed with a scraper of the type used by floor-layers. This method is quick and efficient if there are only a few coats of paint to be removed. If the paint will not respond to this treatment it must be burnt off or removed by means of a paint solvent.

A blow-lamp is most commonly used for burning off. Of the two types of blow-lamp, one burning paraffin and the other petrol, the paraffin lamp is better for exterior work because it is more easily managed in gusty and cold weather.

Fig. 34 indicates the essential parts of a typical lamp. The principle is simple: first the coil is heated and the paraffin is then forced through the coil by means of the pump. Immediately the paraffin enters the coil it is vaporized and ejected through the nipple. The lighted jet passing through the coil serves to keep it hot and an occasional stroke of the pump is all that is necessary to keep the lamp going. Figs. 35-38 show how a blow-lamp should be started.

Blow-lamps must be handled with

the greatest care. In careless hands a blow-lamp is a potential source of danger and the following rules should be strictly observed:

1. Never operate the pump unless the coil is hot.

2. Shake up any paraffin which may be left in the container and turn it out into a pot for further use. If there is no paraffin in the lamp put some in the container and rinse it out well. Do this twice to make sure that the container is free from grit.

3. Remove the nipple and clean out the jet with a pricker. Nipples are not normally accessible without a special key, but if a key is not provided there is no alternative but to prick the nipple while it is still in place on the lamp. This is not entirely satisfactory as any obstruction which is dislodged may remain at the back of the nipple and may choke the hole again.

4. All paraffin, no matter how clean it may appear to be, should be strained. Use a funnel with a piece of fine silk tied over the top. Charge the container only one-half to three-parts full. Replace the filler cap tightly.

5. To heat the lamp, first release the pressure screw a few turns (this valve must always be open while pre-heating the lamp). Place the lamp at least 6 ft. away from any inflammable material. Fill the dish at the top of the container with methylated spirit, add a small piece of rag for a wick and light it.

BLOW-LAMP, PRICKER AND NIPPLE KEY

FIG. 34. *Shows the principal parts of a typical blow-lamp together with a pricker for cleaning the jet and a key to remove the nipple for cleaning purposes.*

HOW TO START A BLOW-LAMP

FIG. 35. *First a small quantity of methylated spirit should be poured in the dish below the heating coil. Care should be taken to avoid spilling it on other parts.*

HEATING THE BLOW-LAMP

FIG. 36. *Apply a match to the rag wick. The spirit should be allowed to burn out before any attempt is made to pump fuel from the container below.*

STARTING THE FLAME

FIG. 37. *Just as the spirit is beginning to burn out, the pressure valve should be closed. If the blow-lamp does not start, give a few strokes with the pump.*

MAINTAINING PRESSURE

FIG. 38. *As soon as the blow-lamp is alight, the flame may be brought to full brilliance by pumping firmly and briskly until the plunger becomes difficult to operate.*

31

METAL MASK

FIG. 39. *When burning the paint off a window frame an asbestos mask is used to protect the glass. The mask should not be held in contact with the glass, but about an inch away.*

10. Do not allow the flame to die away for lack of fuel. Try to anticipate the amount of fuel required before beginning the work, but have a small quantity of paraffin ready in a tin for topping-up purposes in case the lamp runs out of fuel. If the refilling is carried out quickly there will be no need to reheat the lamp. Remember to tighten the pressure screw before pumping and relighting.

When using the lamp, pass the flame up and down a small section of the work for a few seconds, until the paint is soft, and then strip it off with a suitable tool, a stripping knife, chisel knife or shave-hook. Except for very broad work, a triangular shavehook will be most useful.

When the flame is not in use, the lamp should be held so that the flame points away from the body. Make sure there is nothing inflammable within reach of the lamp. For example, when working on a front door, do not allow

6. As the flame dies down, close the pressure screw. Now give one or two strokes to the pump. The jet usually lights from the flame in the dish. Gradually increase the flame by pumping and pump occasionally while working.

7. If no gas is forced out of the nipple, use the pricker and be prepared to light up with a taper.

8. If, instead of gas, a long thin stream of liquid paraffin is ejected, the heating-up process must be repeated.

9. While the lamp is being heated, and while it is alight, it should never be left unattended. The lamp may be turned out simply by releasing the pressure screw.

the flame to pass through the letter box and set fire to anything on the inside.

When burning off the paint from sashes take care to avoid playing the flame directly on to the glass or it may crack. Some contact cannot be avoided if it is desired to remove the paint right up to the glass, but if care is taken just to soften the paint there should be no danger. The flame must not rest on the glass but be passed along an area about 6 in. in length at a moderate pace. Alternatively, an asbestos mask may be used to protect the glass as shown in Fig. 39.

Work in tidy patches and clean the surface well as the work proceeds in order to avoid unnecessary rubbing-down afterwards. Avoid scorching the wood unduly.

Dry, rotted wood is like tinder and smoulders readily; where it exists, therefore, the work should be carried out with great care. Any persistent smouldering should be damped immediately. Burnt-off woodwork should be well rubbed down with water, knotted and primed without delay.

PAINT SOLVENTS

As an alternative to a blow-lamp a paint solvent may be used, and in some respects it has advantages: there is little danger of fire and there is no risk of breaking the glass. However, the job takes longer, besides being messy, and the result is not always satisfactory.

For some work the use of a solvent is imperative: for example, when it is desired to retain the character of the wood. When stripping varnished or polished wood, the use of a lamp would spoil the surface owing to the charring and sealing of the pores of the wood.

Only the non-caustic type of paint remover is recommended. The alkali in the caustic variety is liable to be absorbed by the wood and may affect the new paint; it is also injurious to the hands. It should be remembered, however, that the non-caustic remover is often highly inflammable and should not be used near a naked flame.

Shake the container each time any of the paint-remover liquid is decanted.

UNDERCOATING

FIG. 40. *Paint used for undercoating should be of similar colour to that selected for finishing but, for preference, a few shades lighter in hue.*

Apply a full coat with a clean brush and then leave the job until the paint is soft enough to be scraped off, using the same tools as for burning-off. It may be necessary to give the work several coats and to remove one coat of paint at a time.

When all the paint has been removed, the treated surface should be thoroughly washed with turpentine or white spirit before any new paint is applied.

Surfaces which have been treated with solvent should need little rubbing-down and any rubbing-down which may be necessary can be done during the washing with turpentine. As with burnt-off woodwork, the surface should be knotted and primed as soon as possible.

In addition to the priming, stripped woodwork needs two undercoats (Fig. 40) and preferably a finishing coat of gloss paint. Stopping and filling should be done between the undercoats.

BLISTERING

Some doors are very subject to blistering: even experienced painters have at times been hard put to it to find a solution to the problem.

A relatively simple and widely used method of treating a door that is prone to blister and will not respond to any other treatment is first to burn off the paint bare to the wood; rub it down well with glass-paper, apply a thin coat of knotting to the knots and then apply two coats of good-quality washable distemper.

When dry the door should be rubbed down with fine glass-paper and then painted in the ordinary way with undercoatings and gloss paint. This treatment provides a somewhat less durable finish than that obtained when following a more normal procedure. Of course, distemper cannot be compared with a really good primer for durability. The distemper treatment is not always effective when blistering is due to the seepage of resin from knots, but it is satisfactory where the trouble is due to imprisoned air or moisture.

The advantage of plain painting, using one colour only, is that the work can be done more thoroughly, every part being well covered without the fear of encroaching on another colour. A popular method, however, is to use parti-colours, painting the sashes, say, in a light tone and using a darker paint for the frames and ironwork.

TWO COLOURS

Parti-colours are generally more attractive when strongly contrasted. For example, cream paint may be used for the lighter parts together with green, brown, black, blue or maroon for the darker parts. For undercoats broken-white may be used for the cream finishing paint. For the darker colours it is best to use an undercoating of the same colour but slightly lighter in tone, particularly in the case of blue or maroon, which may be somewhat transparent. An undercoating of a slate colour—made from white undercoating stained with vegetable black—is generally quite satisfactory for such colours as green, brown and black.

When painting in parti-colours (Fig. 41) it is best, when it can be conveniently done, to apply the finishing paint to the frames first and to allow it to dry before finishing the sashes. In the case of double-hung or sliding sashes it is best to finish the sashes first.

Before the use of hard-gloss paints

1. TOP EDGE

7. PUTTY AND MEETING STILE

3. MEETING EDGE

4. PUTTY AND RAIL

6. PUTTY AND HANGING STILE

5. PUTTY AND BOTTOM RAIL

2. BOTTOM EDGE

PAINTING IN PARTI-COLOURS

FIG. 41. *After painting the part marked A, then B, C and D should be treated, in this order, following the sequence shown numerically. It is best to allow this work to dry before completing the remainder in the second colour. Parti-colours look best when contrasted; for example, cream paint with dark blue or green.*

and enamel paints became popular, exterior painting was finished in ordinary oil paint or by applying a coat of varnish over a flatting coat of paint; both of these methods are good practice.

There is much to be said for the varnished finish as against gloss paint, and in spite of the greater time and the slight extra cost involved, the result will be well worth while. With this method the sequence of coats, after the usual preparation, would be: one or two coats of undercoating to which, if too flat, a little linseed oil has been added (the last coat approximating to the colour of the finish), one coat of semi-flat paint of the desired colour, and one or two coats of a good quality, copal elastic, exterior varnish. If two coats of varnish are to be given, the first coat should be allowed to dry thoroughly and be lightly rubbed down with fine glasspaper, or with pumice powder and water, before applying the finishing coat. Rubbing-down with pumice powder is very efficient. It is usually done with a felt pad, dipping the pad first into water and then into the pumice. After rubbing-down, the work should be well rinsed off. For very pale colours, white or pale copal-varnish should be used.

SPECIAL FINISHES

Grained work, as an alternative to plain colour, can be very pleasing and attractive when carried out carefully and with some artistry. It has a deservedly good reputation for durability. The durability is, of course, due to the fact that the work receives two or more coats after the surface has already been soundly painted and properly obscured. Graining is most suitable for finishing front and garage doors, and harmonizes with most colours. Readers who wish to attempt this class of work should refer to Chapter 9, which gives special consideration to this subject.

Spray painting is perfectly satisfactory for interior work, but for many reasons it is not entirely satisfactory for exterior work. Apart from other considerations, the amount of masking which would have to be done rules the method out as an economic proposition on most types of work.

ODD JOBS

Window-sills, in their original form, slope outwards to allow the rain to drain away. Oak sills, however, have a tendency to twist, often to such an extent that the original slope is altered. To remedy this fault, first burn off the paint from the top of the sill, then take a straight-edge and mark a line $\frac{3}{8}$ or $\frac{1}{4}$ in. from the top front edge, according to needs, and plane off the sill to this line. A steel plane, of the bull-nosed rebate type, and also a scraper will be needed for the purpose.

Front entrance gates, when newly painted, often become covered with dust before the paint is dry. It is therefore advisable to take the gates off their hinges and to paint them under cover, refixing them when the paint is thoroughly hard.

Windows should be cleaned before the finishing coat of paint is applied. There are two reasons for this: paint spots are more easily removed while the paint is still soft and some time should elapse after the work is finished before the glass is cleaned.

When stonework or stucco is painted it is customary to use paint of a stone

36

FIG. 42. *After removing any rust and preparing the surface, ironwork needs a priming coat containing plenty of red lead. Alternatively, one of the other forms of rust-inhibitive primers may be employed.*

or terra-cotta colour. Oil paint is usually employed, although oil-bound washable distemper may be used; it is not so durable as oil paint, but its matt effect is very attractive.

Paint will peel off waxed surfaces unless the wax is removed. Housewives are in the habit of wax-polishing such paintwork as they can reach. If this is suspected special care must be exercised to ensure that all the wax is removed. Most flat or egg-shell flat varnishes contain wax. A strong solution of soda or sugar soap should be used to remove the flat varnish before repainting. Flat varnish has little resistance to the weather and for this reason it is seldom used on exterior work.

Paint seldom fails to preserve iron or steel if the proper paint and methods have been employed in the first instance and the paint has been renewed at intervals. It is generally those parts which are difficult of access, and consequently neglected, which rust. This is likely to occur in the case of gutters, stack pipes and rain-water heads.

Gutters of the so-called ogee pattern have a flat back which is fixed tightly to the fascia board. The back of the gutter, therefore, receives only such

DOWELLED OUT

FIG. 43. *Short piece of tube placed between the pipe socket and the wall.*

paint as is applied before fixing. If left without further attention, in the course of time the backs may rust away completely. The only effective way of dealing with this problem is to take the gutters down periodically and to paint the backs with red-lead paint. When this is done an opportunity is also afforded to paint the fascia board. Rain-water heads also have a flat back and may be affected in a similar manner.

PIPES AND GUTTERS

Rain-water pipes, soil pipes, and ventilating pipes are often fixed so close to the wall that it is very difficult to paint the part nearest to the wall without disfiguring the brickwork. Far-seeing builders assist the painter in this connexion by dowelling out when fixing iron pipes. This means that a short piece of lead or iron tube is interposed between the lug of the pipe socket and the wall (Fig. 43). This plan allows plenty of space at the back for the whole of the pipe to be painted.

Generally far too little attention is given to the repainting of gutters. The inside is often neglected because

REPAINTING GUTTERS

FIG. 44. *When painting the outside of a gutter it is a good plan to treat the inside with a rust-resisting paint.*

USEFUL TOOL

FIG. 45. *An excellent tool for chipping metal-work can be made by grinding a sharp cutting edge on the end of a file. All rust must be removed and the bright metal exposed before repainting.*

it is out of sight or because there was water in the gutter when the painting was in hand (Fig. 44). The insides are just as important as the outside. Remember that a leaky gutter may result in dampness on the inside of the house and damage to the structure.

To prepare ironwork for repainting it should be thoroughly cleaned and all rust removed. Where washing is likely to cause water to collect in the crevices and cause further corrosion it is recommended that the remaining paint be well wire-brushed and dusted; but all the rust must be removed and the bright metal exposed. Wire-brushing

stripped off and the whole surface properly prepared.

The priming of iron and steel surfaces is an important matter; it is essential that the priming paint should contain rust-resistant pigments suspended in a durable vehicle. There are many specially made paints on the market which are claimed to possess these qualities, but the time-honoured custom is to use a paint containing as

BITUMINOUS PAINT

Fig. 46. *Manhole covers, gratings and smoke doors should be given a coat of bituminous paint. Such a finish will stand up to the weather.*

alone is not sufficient if the rust is deep-seated, but chipping with a sharp cold-chisel is very effective. One of the most useful tools for the purpose is a file, the end of which has been ground to a sharp cutting edge (Fig. 45).

If the paintwork generally is in good condition, look for local defects, particularly at welded joints. All such parts should be cleaned down to the bright metal before repainting. If the rust is extensive the paint should be

pigment a large proportion of red-lead.

Special ready-mixed priming for ironwork is supplied by most paint manufacturers, but a good alternative plan for the amateur is to take some dry red-lead and mix it into a paste with boiled linseed oil, to add a little white-lead paint and to thin out the mixture with a little turpentine for use. All exposed metal should be primed without delay.

When the priming is dry, ironwork should be given one or two coats of

CARRYING A LADDER

FIG. 47. *Gripping the ladder in one hand by one of the rungs at the point of balance, the other is used to steady it.*

undercoating and one coat of finishing gloss paint. Generally one 'coat of undercoating is sufficient.

Soil and ventilating pipes are usually coated with a special solution of a bituminous character before fixing. This coating cannot be successfully painted with ordinary oil paint, but should be given one or two coats of bituminous paint, which is readily obtainable. This substance must not come into contact with oil paint and it is wise to keep one brush for this type of paint. When the work is finished, the brush should be well washed out, first in paraffin or petrol and then with soap and hot water.

Manhole covers, gratings, gulley grids and smoke doors to flues are also best treated with bituminous paint (Fig. 46). Manhole covers should be taken up, de-rusted and given two coats inside and out. The sealing joint should be .cleaned out if necessary and filled with grease before re-bedding the cover.

Paint will not adhere to new zinc or galvanized iron until it has been exposed to the weather or has been specially treated. The best plan is to defer the painting for a few months.

USE OF LADDERS

It is wise for the amateur craftsman to consider his legal liabilities. Employers insure their workers against accidents; the majority also have third-party cover.

If the householder is insured under a comprehensive policy, he might be covered if a member of the public were struck by a ladder, but it is advisable to find this out. Of course, almost any insurance company would issue a short-term policy at a small cost to cover the period of the work.

WORKING OVER A PORCH

FIG. 48. *To reach the gutter over the lean-to, the erection of scaffolding, consisting of a board with one end resting on the window-sill and the other end lashed to an extension ladder, often provides the only means of dealing with awkward situations.*

As only a small part of the work can be performed without the aid of ladders, this very important matter should be given early consideration.

If the reader is not already in possession of the necessary ladders it will be necessary to buy them, to borrow from a friend or to hire from a firm whose business it is to hire out scaffolding.

In view of the danger of using a defective ladder it is most important to inspect all ladders thoroughly before use and to know the correct

SIMPLE EXTENSION LADDER

FIG. 49. *To raise an extension ladder of the push-up type, the lower section should be steadied with the foot and left hand, while the upper section is adjusted.*

way to handle them (Figs. 47 and 48).

There are two main types of ladder, pole ladders and extension ladders. All pole ladders are similar, but extension ladders vary considerably in general construction and in the method of raising, lowering and locking.

Pole ladders consist of strings (sides) formed out of a straight young tree sawn down the middle, with rungs of oak or other hardwood. The rungs pass through holes in the strings and are wedged. For greater security iron rods are passed through the strings under the rungs at intervals and riveted over on the outside. Before extension ladders came into general use it was common practice to lash two ladders together to reach a greater height or some point which could not be reached in any other way.

TYPES OF LADDER

Extension ladders are formed out of sawn timber of rectangular section with hardwood rungs mortised and tenoned into the sides. The sections are reduced in width to allow one piece to slide between the sides of the other. A desirable feature of high-grade extension ladders is a twisted wire rope which is embedded in a groove at the back of the strings: this makes it almost impossible for the strings to break and is a welcome assurance to the user.

The simplest form of extension ladder is that used by window cleaners. It consists of two pieces which can be secured in the desired position by iron clips and hooks (Fig. 49). For the average two-storey house a two-piece ladder with about twenty-six rungs in all is adequate unless complicated scaffolding must be erected to reach an awkward position as in Fig. 50.

WORKING OVER A BAY WINDOW

FIG. 50. *In the long run it is easier and quicker to erect a scaffolding, such as is shown here, than to adopt makeshift methods of reaching inaccessible parts.*

Longer ladders, of two or more sections, are raised or lowered by a system of cords and pulleys and secured by a locking device (Figs. 51 and 52).

All ladders should be carefully examined for possible flaws or other faults. If a defective ladder cannot be readily made safe, it should on no account be used. Pole ladders need little attention beyond occasional varnishing and usually remain sound for many years: extension ladders generally require rather more attention.

First see that the cords are sound and securely fastened. Examine the action and see how it works. The ladder should be perfectly rigid later-ally. The rungs should be sound and the strings free from fractures. All bolts and screws should be secure.

If the ladder is rickety, owing to lateral play, it may be found that the wedges have become loose. This may be due to the method employed by some makers when cutting the mortises. The wedges usually need attention every season.

If the wedges are loose, lay the ladder on its side on a level surface and tighten them with a piece of wood, of the same section as the wedges, and a hammer. Missing wedges should be replaced with new ones carefully cut to pattern. A job for the expert.

SAFETY MEASURES

FIG. 51. *To hoist the top section of an extension ladder the rope should be held, as shown, in the right hand, and drawn downwards. Grip the side of the ladder firmly with the left hand. Note how the rope is carried over the wrist.*

Short two-piece ladders can be easily manipulated without any trouble but with longer ladders assistance may be needed. The first step is to rear the ladder into an upright position using the method employed for raising a pole ladder (explained later) if necessary. One man stands at the back and holds the ladder, which is allowed to lean slightly toward the building. The other man places his left foot on the lowest rung and hauls on the cord.

Be sure that the locking device has fallen properly into place before releasing the cord.

The procedure for raising a pole ladder or one which has been spliced is somewhat different (Fig. 53). The butt should be placed at a distance of about one-third of the height of the ladder from the building. One man places both feet on the lowest rung, grips the third rung up with both hands and hauls backwards. The other

EXTENSION LADDER

FIG. 52. *Correct position for raising an extension ladder. Note the position of the hands and how the left foot is held on the lower rung to steady the base.*

44

RAISING A POLE LADDER

FIG. 53. *One man crouches at the foot of the ladder with both feet on the bottom rung and holding the third rung with both hands, while another raises it.*

lifts the top end and proceeds to raise the ladder with his arms extended, at the same time walking towards the building (Fig. 53). For those unaccustomed to this operation it is helpful to have someone at an upper window hauling on a rope attached to the top of the ladder (Fig. 54).

Ladders are lowered in similar fashion, except that the man standing erect walks backwards as the ladder is lowered. A method of raising a ladder single-handed is shown in Fig. 55.

Always make sure that the ladder rests on a suitable foundation, which should be firm and level (Fig. 57). On soft garden-earth it is best to stand the ladder on a piece of board. Packing pieces used for levelling up must be large enough to prevent them tilting or slipping out of position.

Ladders resting on the public way

45

should never be left unattended and a responsible person should always be standing by the butt when the ladder is in use. Secure the top of the ladder when possible. Always lower ladders at the end of the day and lay them flat on the ground if space will permit.

Sometimes it is necessary to fit a cross-piece (Fig. 56), to lash two pole ladders together or to add another section to an extension ladder. It is an important job which must be carried out meticulously and correctly. The additional piece should, if pos-

RAISING A HEAVY LADDER

FIG. 54. *By posting an extra helper at an upper window to pull on a rope attached to the ladder, assistance can be given in taking the strain from the men below.*

WORKING SOLO

FIG. 55. *By placing the butt against a wall it is possible to raise a medium-size ladder without assistance. Grip the sides and walk toward the building pushing the ladder from underneath as shown. This method is not recommended for dealing with a heavy ladder, particularly if the ground is uneven or if the eaves overhang.*

sible, be of a lighter section and it should lap the other piece by at least four rungs.

Experienced workers often splice ladders while they are erected and there are several ways of doing this, but it is not a method which can be recommended to the amateur. A better plan is to do the lashing on the ground. The method is illustrated in Fig. 58. Lay the ladders down in a convenient position and pack them up to allow free passage for the lashings. Let them lap for at least four rungs, with the rungs of one ladder just above those of the other.

The lashing should be done at four places: two at the top of the lap and two at the bottom. Contrary to common belief, the most important part of the lashing is that which binds the strings together and not that which happens to pass round the rungs.

Fig. 56. *A cross-piece, consisting of a stout piece of timber, secured behind the ladder head and lashed to it with strong cord, is invaluable when painting gutters and for resting a ladder against the surface of a large window frame.*

SECURING THE FOOT

Fig. 57. *When working on soft ground stand the foot of the ladder on a stout board and tie the lower rung to a stake which has been driven well into the earth.*

The most satisfactory lashing is carried out with stout sash cord. Two or four cords may be used, one at each lashing position, or one double-length cord at the top and bottom. The cord should be of sufficient length to make hitches on the rungs and at least six turns round the strings.

If two cords only are used they should be centred and started by passing them over the two rungs as shown. The hitches are then carried to each side close to the strings, and another hitch taken over the rungs. Next tighten up the hitches and proceed to bind the strings together, finishing with a magnus hitch. The lashing at the bottom of the lap is carried out in the same manner. Fig. 59 shows how to make a magnus hitch.

If four separate cords are used, begin with a magnus hitch over the two rungs close to the sides and continue to bind the strings as already described. See that the centres of the rungs are clear of any obstruction to the tread.

If the ladders are to remain lashed for any length of time, the lashing should be examined each day before use and re-tied if the lashing is at all loose.

When mounting a ladder keep upright, place the ball of the foot on the

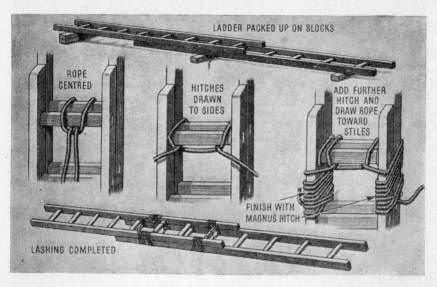

LADDER PACKED UP ON BLOCKS

ROPE CENTRED

HITCHES DRAWN TO SIDES

ADD FURTHER HITCH AND DRAW ROPE TOWARD STILES

FINISH WITH MAGNUS HITCH

LASHING COMPLETED

SPLICING LADDERS

FIG. 58. *After packing the ladders up on blocks and allowing an overlap of about five feet, the lashing should be completed as shown. The ropes should be drawn as tightly as possible and secured around the ladder stiles with a magnus hitch.*

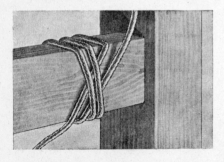

MAGNUS HITCH

FIG. 59. *This illustration shows how to tie a magnus hitch, a knot which is particularly useful for lashing ladders.*

rung and hold the sides of the ladder firmly in the hands; change the grip alternately as each step is taken.

Those who are unaccustomed to ladder work may feel somewhat strange at first, but confidence will come with practice. For those who need it, a good plan is to learn by easy stages. Try going up a few rungs and coming down, gradually increasing the number of rungs mounted until confidence is gained.

While working from a ladder concentrate on the job and keep a firm grip on the side with the free hand.

FINE PATTERN ON A LIGHT GROUND

*The delicate wallpaper gives this bedroom a particularly charming appearance.
Repetition of the background colour of the walls on the dressing table and bed
enhances the effect. The absence of heavy curtains gives a feeling of air and space*

CHAPTER 2

INTERIOR DECORATION SCHEMES

CHOICE OF COLOUR AND FINISH

THE amateur decorator has one great advantage over the professional. He may choose either simple or elaborate decorative schemes with little concern for the amount of work involved. The professional decorator must always be governed by cost. He cannot allow his men to spend more time on the work than the price warrants.

Furthermore, the amateur can finish the work exactly to his liking. Not being dependent upon a painter to put ideas into practice, it is possible to indulge in subtle colourings and harmony which cannot readily be explained in words.

QUESTION OF TASTE

There is no limit to the variety of interior decorations, so originality and individuality may be expressed without restriction. Not that outlandish, elaborate or costly decorations are always the most successful; on the contrary, it is often the simple background which proves to be most attractive. There are a few simple rules which govern the success of decorative schemes, and it is generally better for the amateur to learn these rules than to be given a limited selection of schemes from which to choose.

Unless complete refurnishing is contemplated, most interior decorations are governed by the existing furnishings. This does not necessitate adher-

ing to a rigid colour scheme. By all means use favourite colours; it is the correct use of them which is important. In general, really good furniture needs little more than a simple background, which may be matt (flat), glossy, or have any degree of gloss between the two; egg-shell for instance. The colour may be bright, dull, light or deep, and the finish may be rough or smooth. The materials used may be wallpaper, distemper, water-paint (oil-bound distemper), plastic paint (not a true plastics material by the way), or oil paint.

As the function of the decoration is, in this case, to enhance the qualities of good furniture, a suitable contrast should be made. It may be a contrast of colour and finish (for example, a matt, dull-green wall to contrast with the rich colour and high polish of mahogany), or it may be a contrast of texture, as when off-white, rough-cast walls are used as a background to finely carved and satin-like walnut furniture (Fig. 1). The object is to direct attention to the polished surfaces or to the fine shape of the furniture, by the contrast of widely different surfaces. The first rule is to allow furniture or furnishings of high decorative value to dominate the decorative scheme.

When the furniture is of poor quality or of inferior design the decorative scheme is greatly improved if the decorations are such as to direct attention to themselves. In such circumstances a patterned wallpaper, wallpaper panelling or striking colours may be employed as illustrated in Fig. 2.

Similar considerations should govern the amount of furniture which a room may contain. It is obvious that a room which is crowded with furniture demands a type of decoration which suggests extra space. Victorian drawing-rooms, so admirably reproduced in some film studio sets, provide examples of crowded furnishing and heavy decoration. It is generally accepted that these decorative schemes were gloomy and overpowering, yet in suitable surroundings some Victorian furniture, especially early pieces, assume an unexpected charm. It may surprise those who are so ready to dismiss everything belonging to the Victorian era to learn that collectors are now giving much attention to early Victorian pieces and good antiques.

WALLPAPERS

To give the appearance of spaciousness, all superfluous objects (meaningless ornamentation, picture rails, dado rails and the like) should be removed and the ceiling, walls and woodwork should all be in one colour, preferably a light tint. Compare the crowded appearance of the room in Fig. 3 with the same room as shown in Fig. 4. Interest need not be sacrificed by the exclusion of pattern. A powdered wallpaper decorated with spots or small figures may be used with advantage. Pale blue, pale grey and pale green are colours which look particularly attractive, and if the pattern is off-white or a lighter tone than the background, the wall colour seems to recede, thereby adding to the apparent space.

When choosing wallpaper bear in mind that it will not look the same on the walls as it does in the pattern book or in a small sample. Patterns will appear smaller and the texture will seem finer when the paper is hung. Even colour values will appear to be altered. A pale paper may seem to be almost colourless on the walls, and, conversely, one which appears rather heavy may be quite light when it is in position.

This is not a general rule, however, for richly coloured wallpapers in dark red, blue or green generally appear to be deeper when on the walls. This is due to the reflection of colour from

PLAIN BACKGROUNDS

Fig. 1. *A white, rough-cast wall provides a perfect setting for smooth furniture.*

one wall to another. Some wallpapers have an attractive sparkle from metallic powders which are incorporated during the printing, but as they lose much of this lustre when they are hung, it is as well to choose a wallpaper which and see as great a length of the paper as possible. Those papers which appear to be almost plain at close range may take on a pattern at a distance. Small patterns, which are often very attractive at close quarters

ORNAMENTAL BACKGROUNDS

FIG. 2. *Inexpensive furniture of simple design looks well against an ornamental background. Decorative panels and patterned papers draw the eye and make up for the lack of other interesting features in the room. Wall lamps add to the effect.*

has rather more gold or silver on the surface than is desired.

Wallpapers with a design in metallic print should be used with caution. They do not appear nearly as brilliant on a flat wall. Such paper has its proper use, and that is for small areas or for curved surfaces, which are known to reflect light well.

Never view a wallpaper too closely in a showroom. Stand a few feet away become indistinct, and small patterns of one colour on a background of another have a tendency to blend, thus giving a general colour quite different from that expected. Keep in mind the size of the room to be papered. Bold patterns may be used in a large room and look quite pleasing, but in a small room subtle clouded effects should be used, as such papers do not lose their appeal when they are viewed at close quarters.

Some notes on the reflection of colour and the effect of coloured lighting may be useful at this point. Reflection of light is generally understood by the amateur decorator. Most people overlooking a large lawn receives a considerable amount of green light which is reflected or absorbed by the walls and woodwork according to their colour. On a bright, sunny day this is particularly noticeable; but as a bed-

OLD-FASHIONED DECORATIVE SCHEME

FIG. 3. *Compare the heavy appearance of this room as it would have been decorated in the past with the conversion shown in Fig. 4 by a modern decorative artist.*

know that distemper or wallpaper will appear lighter in a room which is well lighted by either natural or artificial light. On the other hand, reflection of colour, which is only another form of reflected light and equally affected by reflecting surfaces, seldom receives the attention it deserves.

Colour is reflected in many ways and due consideration must be given to this fact when planning decorative schemes. The ceiling of a bedroom room is usually illuminated by artificial light, this factor is not so important as it would be for, say, a lounge in a similar position.

If coloured lighting or coloured lampshades are to be retained in a room which is to be redecorated, the effect of the coloured light on the colours of the decorations should not be overlooked. When illuminated, pink lampshades make pale-green walls appear to be grey, and amber shades have a similar effect on pale-blue walls. Incidentally, the grey so produced is luminous and attractive. Lampshades of strong orange colour make deep blue walls very drab, as do red shades which light deep-green suitability under different conditions.

Prolonged extremes of heat or cold are not likely to disturb normal domestic interior decoration, but ventilation and condensation must be taken into account. When rooms are

MODERN CONVERSION

FIG. 4. *The same room as that shown in Fig. 3 converted to suit modern tastes. The mirror hanging over the mantelpiece has been taken from above the sideboard.*

walls. These are but a few examples of the effect of mixing colours, a subject which is dealt with in more detail later.

Apart from their decorative values, the decorator's materials have been developed to suit various conditions. What is excellent for one room may be quite unsuitable for another. The materials may be divided broadly into paint, distemper and wallpaper and it is important to consider their badly ventilated or when a house is cold, condensation occurs on the ceilings, walls and woodwork.

If the walls are of bare plaster, or have been distempered or papered, the water is at first absorbed; it then dries out again gradually. But if the walls are painted or even distempered with a good-quality water-paint a small proportion of the water will not be absorbed, but will stay on the surface until it evaporates, or will simply run down the walls, according to the amount of condensation present. In a warm, dry climate, or in a well-heated and ventilated house, condensation will not occur. It should therefore be clear which class of material should long-term cost is the more important. Those who like a change of colour year by year, or alter their interior decorations at frequent intervals, will find a distemper made with whiting, size and dry powder-colour easy to

SPARSELY FURNISHED ROOMS

FIG. 5. *Wallpaper panelling looks particularly well in a sparsely furnished room, as the ornamentation contributes to the general effect. Cream-textured panels with rust-coloured borders and a plain buff surround look particularly attractive.*

be employed in any particular room.

Comparative costs must be taken into account. There is no doubt that size-and-whiting distemper is the cheapest form of decoration; water-paint comes next, then wallpaper, and lastly oil paint. When, however, the durability of these materials is considered it will be found that a papered room lasts longer than a distempered one, and a painted one outlasts both. This levels the comparative costs.

It is, therefore, necessary to decide whether the immediate cost or the wash off and to renew. Wallpaper may also be stripped and renewed cheaply and quickly. Those who prefer settled colour schemes and less frequent renovations may use washable water-paint of good quality, and those who demand a great deal of permanency in their interior decorations should use oil paint.

Size-bound distemper becomes dirty long before the oil-bound variety, owing to its extra absorbency. It cannot be washed, as the binding agent (size) is soluble in water. Only dry cleaning with a soft brush will prolong the useful life of this material.

Sparsely furnished rooms, especially those which contain furniture of indifferent quality, gain in appearance if suitable background ornament is allowed to remain. Decorations in wallpaper or other materials should augment the furnishings to give an impression of sufficiency (Fig. 5). Panelling with applied wood mouldings (Fig. 6) or wallpaper panelling (Fig. 7) provide means of achieving this effect. Other decorations which will serve the same purpose are graduated or clouded colouring in paint or distemper (Fig. 8), sponge-stippling with one or two colours on a background of another, glazing, scumbling (Fig. 9) or stencilling. Woodwork which is grained and varnished to match the furniture is attractive and connects scattered pieces

BACKGROUND ORNAMENTATION

FIG. 6. *In a room with very little furniture the use of panelling formed by wooden mouldings provides background ornamentation. This scheme is also suitable for halls.*

in a room, giving an impression of extra furniture.

Rooms which are amply furnished, but with widely different types of furniture, require an agent to give unity to the whole. Horizontal lines or

The following example may explain the idea. Suppose that the curtains are moss green, that the carpet is a rust colour, and that the upholstery is a tobacco brown. Yellow is analogous or bears a common resemblance

ORNAMENTAL BORDERS AND SET-PIECES

FIG. 7. *In general, ornamental borders broken by set-pieces have fallen out of favour, but they often improve the appearance of rooms furnished with worn pieces.*

bands of colour fulfil this purpose (Fig. 10). Further interest may be obtained if the lines, bands or borders employed are undulating, as shown in Fig. 11. If the furniture, upholstery, loose covers and curtains are of different colours, the walls should be of a colour which harmonizes. It may be possible to obtain some similarity by the use of a specially designed pattern, using a stencil for the purpose, but to employ suitable colours is far easier.

to all these, as each colour has a yellow content. A middle yellow (daffodil), therefore, should be the main colour employed for decoration. Green, brown or rust borders might be added with advantage.

Everyone is not fortunate enough to have rooms of good shape and fine proportions. Rooms may be either long and narrow, or too high in relation to the floor area, and they may contain ugly nooks and corners which make the room unsatisfactory in shape or size. It is customary for the amateur decorator to adhere to conventional decorations: ceilings distempered white, walls distempered or papered, and woodwork painted to match. This is all very well, but at the same time the decorator's materials may be used in a more flexible manner. By taking advantage of this fact, and using a little imagination, rooms may be decorated in the manner they appear to demand rather than in the timid style which is so often seen.

There is one rule to be observed which goes far toward the apparent correction of a room of ugly shape: this is to avoid separate treatment or colours for the various surfaces.

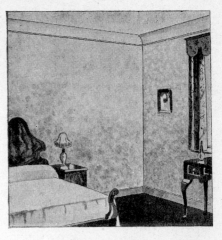

RESTFUL EFFECT

FIG. 8. *Clouded effects in pastel shades are most suitable for use in bedrooms.*

STENCIL PATTERN AND SCUMBLED EFFECT

FIG. 9. *A simple stencil pattern applied to a plain painted wall (left) is often improved by scumbling, which softens the effect as illustrated on the right.*

DISTINCTIVE DESIGN

FIG. 10. *Horizontal lines or bands of colour help to give unity to this room which is amply furnished but with different types of furniture. This decorative treatment is rather more formal than that shown in Fig. 11. Quiet, restful colourings are most suitable for such background effects, which look best in pastel shades.*

WAVY BANDS OF COLOUR

FIG. 11. *It should be quietly obvious that there is one "show" room in every home and this decorative background certainly affords relief from workaday surroundings. Restraint should be the keynote in selecting colours for the wavy bands and the larger their area the more subdued should be the colour employed. Although this scheme is somewhat unusual the idea may be modified to suit individual tastes.*

If one colour is employed throughout, the conflicting wall-planes will become less obvious. Similarly, also the eye may be attracted to a decorative feature which is judiciously placed. This feature may be a painted or stencilled spray of flowers, a single decorative panel of interesting shape, or even a large poster, such as the railway authorities supply, fixed to the wall and subsequently sized and varnished. It may be outlined with an appropriate colour. A wall painting (mural decoration) in oil paint or poster colour also provides a change.

Compare the effect of such decorations (Fig. 12) in an ill-shaped room with the less suitable type of decoration shown in Fig. 13.

OPTICAL ILLUSIONS

The use of pattern is effective for the apparent correction of unsatisfactory proportions. Vertical lines (of striped wallpaper, for example) give an appearance of extra height, especially if the effect is not contradicted by the horizontal lines of a picture rail or a similar feature. On the other hand, vertical lines have a tendency to reduce

A SUGGESTION

FIG. 12. *A plain wallpaper is most suitable for a room of this type. If desired a decorative piece may be added as shown on the right of the dressing table.*

AVOID THIS EFFECT

FIG. 13. *The lines on this wallpaper only draw attention to the defects in this room and accentuate its particularly awkward shape. Such effects are often difficult to visualize when buying paper in a showroom.*

the apparent floor area. Vertical lines give an appearance of strength; the mind associates them with columns and vertical supports of all kinds.

By similar associations—calm seas and the like—horizontal lines give a feeling of repose. They also have the effect of reducing the apparent height of a room, but compensate by making the floor area seem larger (Figs. 14 and 15). A wallpaper with a suitable design may be hung horizontally to serve such a purpose. Applied wooden mouldings or narrow wallpaper borders may be fixed to a wall at regular intervals, painted lines or stencilled borders may be employed, and existing horizontal features such as the frieze, the dado or the picture rail and chair rail can be emphasized by colouring.

Large patterns appear to reduce the size of a room, while small patterns

VERTICAL LINES

FIG. 14. *Walls decorated with vertical lines tend to make a room look higher, but the floor area will appear to have been reduced. In small rooms a narrow stripe is to be preferred to a wide one.*

HORIZONTAL LINES

FIG. 15. *Walls decorated with horizontal lines tend to make a room look wider, but there will be an apparent loss of height. This scheme should therefore be used in a high but narrow room.*

have the opposite effect. Square patterns and wallpapers with both horizontal and vertical lines are best employed for rooms with vertical walls, as confusion of line appears when they are used on sloping walls (Fig. 16). Diagonal patterns may be used when the walls are at various angles, as they have the effect of making the shape of such rooms appear to be more normal (Fig. 17). When the walls, or the angles between the walls, are out of square, a rectangular or vertical pattern emphasizes the fact. Distinct panels draw the eye from the angles, which may contain almost any pattern, but the panels themselves should always form true rectangles; otherwise the very fault which it is hoped to correct becomes more pronounced. A point to be watched.

CONFUSION OF LINE

FIG. 16. *Avoid the use of wallpaper with both horizontal and vertical lines in a room with sloping walls. The confusion of line will accentuate the defects.*

DISTEMPER AND PAINT

Scepticism is often expressed at the claim that oil-bound distemper can be washed successfully. The housewife knows that her linen is kept white by washing at regular intervals, and that when it becomes really dirty normal washing methods may not make it white again. The same consideration applies to a surface which has been distempered with water-paint. It must be sponged at sufficiently frequent intervals if it is to be kept immaculate. As the material is semi-absorbent, dirt is carried into the surface during the process of condensation and evaporation. If this is allowed to remain on the surface for a long period, no amount of sponging will remove the dirt without damaging the surface.

Although size-bound distemper is rather more difficult to apply than the oil-bound variety, it is generally more suitable for ceilings, as it may be

DIAGONAL PATTERNS

FIG. 17. *Papers with a diagonal pattern are excellent for improving the appearance of an awkwardly shaped room, and distract from the conflicting angles.*

washed off completely and renewed as often as desired at small cost.

Ceilings become dirty more quickly than walls, and as they are less likely to be sponged at frequent intervals it is perhaps as well to avoid treating them with water-paint. Oil-bound distemper may be washed off, but its removal is a laborious process even for the skilled worker.

When a surface is coated repeatedly with water-paint the material becomes brittle and starts eventually to shell and peel. This condition may be prevented by giving the surface an occasional coat of thin oil paint prior to re-distempering.

The choice of materials for the decoration of a room is largely governed by the purpose for which the room is to be used. When considerable wear is expected, it is advisable to use materials which will permit regular cleaning. Enamel, hard-gloss paint, and oil paint which has been subsequently varnished are examples of such materi-

CONVENTIONAL DADOES

FIG. 19. (*Above*) *Parallel lines painted at a suitable height with a deeper colour underneath.* (*Below*) *A wooden dado rail with imitation marbled slabs to the skirting is suitable for a bathroom.*

NOVEL DADOES

FIG. 18. (*Above*) *Bands of colour gradually increasing in depth toward the base.* (*Below*) *Vertical bands of graduated colour to give a fluted appearance.*

als. Flat paint becomes dirty more quickly than gloss paint and is not so easy to wash. Flat oil-finishes, however, are often more attractive than glossy finishes when used for decorating wall surfaces. They wear better than might be expected, and in some cases as well as enamelled surfaces.

Another consideration is the state of the surface to be decorated. The rough and bumpy state of some walls is accentuated when a gloss paint is used, but flat paint flatters bad surfaces. Closely patterned wallpaper, sponge-stippled effects in distemper or paint, and graining and marbling, have the important advantage of hiding faults.

So-called plastic paint, even when used thickly, does not hide defective surfaces as effectively as might be expected, but in certain cases—old plaster effects, for example—an uneven wall surface may add to the effect.

The use of dadoes, wallpaper panelling and applied wooden mouldings has been mentioned earlier, but only for the purpose of adjusting apparent proportions. Apart from this consideration, these items are of high decorative value. They may be used to break up large uninteresting areas; to allow various colours and finishes to be employed on one surface; to give dignity and richness to a room; to imitate wood panelling; and to give an architectural background for period decoration.

A band of colour, painted on the lower part of a room, is the simplest form of dado. This treatment is used

on that part of a wall which must stand up to hard wear while also preserving the decorative quality of the upper part of the wall. Such dadoes are usually completed by the addition of a painted line, or are bounded by a wooden moulding. They may be seen in hospitals and public buildings of all types and are usually painted with a glossy finish and in a deeper colour than the walls. Although the

PATTERNED BORDERS

FIG. 21. *Panelling formed with orna-mental borders. The pattern may be stencilled in gold bronze powder. Terra-cotta distemper in the panels with a gold surround form an attractive scheme.*

VARIATIONS IN DISTEMPER

FIG. 20. *A plain distemper background provides the setting for a two-colour effect in the panels produced by rag-rolling. Borders are in light distemper.*

decorative quality of any dado is negligible, it need not be so ordinary as it often appears. Perhaps the least offensive treatment is to paint the dado in gloss paint, but in the same colour as the upper part of the walls with a dividing line of slightly deeper colour. By painting the walls in one colour and varnishing the dado, a similar effect may be obtained, but the colour of the varnish may be unsuitable for pale tints such as light blue and pastel green.

Dadoes may be papered in one of the heavier types of wallpaper. This material may be bought ready-finished

LEAF PATTERN

FIG. 22. *Stencilled in leaf green on a light-brown distemper, this pattern also forms an interesting and charming border.*

in many colours, or it may be white if it is intended to be painted. Examples of decorative treatments for dadoes are provided in Figs. 18 and 19.

Imitation panelling may be carried out in wallpaper, distemper, paint, or with applied mouldings. Wallpaper panelling is dealt with elsewhere, so other forms will be considered here.

Suggestions for panelled effects in

distemper are given in Figs. 20–22. It is advisable to use the washable distemper for this type of work. The borders may be painted or stencilled, or narrow strips cut out of plain or decorated wallpaper may be used: the type of wallpaper specially designed for shop-window display is particularly useful.

Flat wall paint may be used in place of distemper, or combinations of wallpaper and distemper. Wallpaper and flat paint are also attractive alternatives.

SPECIAL EFFECTS

Applied wooden mouldings are excellent for setting out walls with good effect. Schemes which are suitable for glazed or scumbled effects are shown in Fig. 23. This illustration shows several moulding sections which are suitable for panelling.

An inexpensive and effective form of applied panelling may be carried out with plasterers' laths or similar thin strips of wood. They are first pinned to the wall, given a coat of plastic paint in, say, a ribbon pattern and subsequently finished in metallic paint. The use of such panelling is highly recommended. The laths look particularly attractive when painted dull green and flossed with gold metallic-paint, the panels being papered and the styles grained to represent walnut. Decorative corner pieces or ornament, as shown in Fig. 24, may be cut out of thick cardboard or plywood. They may be used in conjunction with the mouldings shown in Fig. 25, and decorated in the same manner.

Laths and small squares and circles of plywood, pinned to a ceiling, may be used to give the appearance of a cornice. An example which will, no doubt, suggest alternative designs is

DECORATIVE USE OF MOULDED PANELS

FIG. 23. (*Left*) *Cornice, walls and mouldings, painted white and glazed with the transparent colour.* (*Centre*) *Panelling suitable for a lounge in light-cream paint glazed with pink. Ribbons on moulding* (*shown inset*) *picked out with gold bronze.* (*Right*) *Cornice and frieze in cream distemper, panels painted apple green.*

shown in Fig. 26. This imitation cornice may be distempered with the ceiling and frieze, treated separately, or if there is no frieze, coloured to match the walls.

There is a paint or varnish suitable for any decorative finish, and a finish suitable for most decorative schemes. All these finishes may be bought ready-made. If, therefore, the home decorator knows exactly what to purchase, the chances are that his work will be more successful and time and expense will be saved.

For wall decoration in flat paint there are specially made flat enamels, flat wall-finishes and flat japans. They are all very easy to apply, they do not require stippling with a hair stippler and they seldom show brush marks. Most of these finishes go down in tone value (become deeper) as they dry, so

the paint in the tin may not appear to be the same colour as that on the pattern card. This is not a general rule, as some makes of these materials bleach as they dry. It is, therefore, advisable to try out the material, so

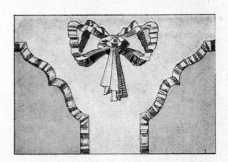

FINISHING TOUCH

FIG. 24. *An ornamental bow carefully placed in the space between two panels lends a pleasing touch to a simple design.*

as to allow for any colour alteration, before painting a large area.

Stock shades of paint may not appeal to everyone, so it is a great asset to have some knowledge of colour mixing and matching. Careful study of the subject will repay the home decorator from both practical and financial viewpoints.

CHOICE OF MATERIALS

Enamels and gloss paints have the disadvantage of altering in tone colour. There is an immediate alteration shortly after application, then a gradual change takes place until the material is quite hard. Some paints of bright colour lose their brilliance very quickly. Bright green sometimes turns blue, bright red may change to a dull pink, black may become grey, light blue may fade in sunlight to a pale grey, and bright yellow may gradually become dull, turning to a mustard and then to a buff colour.

Reputable paint manufacturers do their utmost to overcome this difficulty and many of them guarantee a reasonable permanency in their colours.

Scumbles, glazes and graining colours are also sold ready for use except for the addition of turpentine. Most of these materials are excellent and they are made with ease of application in view. They may be mixed or altered in colour by the addition of stainers; these are transparent, or semi-transparent, pigments ground in oil. Artists' oil colours may also be used for this purpose.

Priming paint containing red lead, oil paint (with or without a white-lead content), paint specially manufactured for painting ironwork, undercoatings for flat or gloss enamels, bituminous paint and metallic paints, are all available for their specific purposes and in every case it is wise to use the appropriate material.

Varnishes of all descriptions are obtainable: pale copal varnish specially made for front doors, and the like; oak varnish for real or grained oak; hard oak-varnish for such parts as

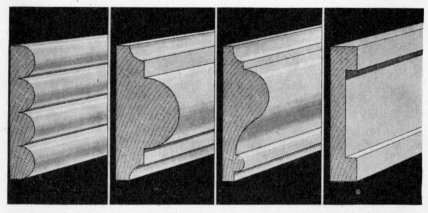

TYPES OF MOULDING

FIG. 25. *Four different types of moulding as used for the panels illustrated in Fig. 23. Mouldings should only be used in rooms of adequate proportions.*

NOVEL CEILING DECORATION

FIG. 26. *An attractive design for a ceiling decoration formed of plasterers' laths and differently shaped pieces of plywood, tastefully arranged to form a pattern.*

office doors or dadoes, where a considerable amount of handling can be expected; church oak-varnish for seats and floors; french oil-varnish for extra-pale colours; paper varnish specially made for varnishing wallpaper; dead flat, flat and egg-shell varnish for decorative use, and numerous other varnishes, such as general-purpose varnish, for other needs. Both inside and outside qualities of varnish are made. The inside quality is paler than the outside quality, but outside varnish is more protective. It should be obvious that when varnish is required, the type specially made for the work in hand should always be obtained.

Plastic paint may be purchased either in white or in colours. It may be subsequently painted or decorated in a number of different ways. If plastic paint is used exactly as directed, very long wear may be expected.

Cellulose finishes are made for application with the spray gun or with brushes. The brushing quality should be used only for such small jobs as the painting of kitchen or nursery furniture. It dries quickly and for this reason it is useful when two or more coats must be applied in one day. One advantage of these finishes is the purity and brightness of the colours they produce. Cellulose finishes (which usually have the smell of pear drops) should not be applied over existing oil paint.

However pleasing a proposed scheme of interior decoration may appear, some consideration must be given to its wearing qualities. It is a waste of effort to apply delicate finishes when their decorative effects will not last, and equally futile to spoil delicate finishes and subtle colourings by the application of heavy varnish with the idea of making the work wear longer.

Walls which are panelled and afterwards painted and grained to represent such woods as oak, walnut, mahogany, sycamore, pine or american walnut, are very attractive indeed and they constitute an extremely durable form of decoration (Fig. 27).

Another idea is to grain the woodwork in a room to match the furniture as shown in Fig. 28. It is said that attempts should not be made to depict woods in a paint medium, but when skilfully done the effect can be most realistic. The subject of graining is

ELABORATE IDEAS

FIG. 27. *Italian damask pattern wallpaper in panels, with the picture rail, skirting and background in grained walnut and the mouldings dull green.*

fully described in a subsequent chapter.

Circumstances may alter particular cases, but in general the bedrooms and the lounge receive less wear and remain clean for longer periods than the other rooms in a house. These rooms, therefore, may be decorated with delicate materials and fine colours. Some such finishes are: unvarnished, glazed or scumbled effects; plastic-surfaced wallpaper; whiting-and-size distemper; and unpainted plastic finishes.

The dining-room and the staircase are normally the next in order of wear, so the finishes employed should be rather more durable. Wallpaper, painted plastic paint, flat oil-paint, hard-gloss paint, enamel, varnished oil-paint, varnished scumbling or glazing or varnished graining are suggested. The varnish used may be glossy or matt, or, if extra wear is required from flat varnish, a first coat of gloss varnish followed by a coat of flat varnish may be applied with good effect.

WEAR AND TEAR

Bathrooms and kitchens require decorations which will stand up to steam and normal condensation. If fairly permanent decorations are required, hard gloss paint or enamel should be used or, if a matt finish is preferred, flat oil paint. Water-paint may be used but it tends to break down if condensation is excessive.

It is often imagined that dark colours and finishes such as dark-oak graining do not readily show dirt and finger-marks. This is a mistake. Dust will show on any surface and on black in particular. When an appearance of cleanliness is desired, it is best to choose surfaces which will show dirt but which are easy to clean. The cleanliness which follows is then real and not merely apparent. Dirt and grease, if allowed to remain, soon destroy a painted surface.

The choice of colours is a different matter. Those which discolour quickly should be avoided for rooms which are

once and for all. If such furniture (or skirtings), which is likely to be knocked, has been painted black or a deep colour, and is subsequently painted with a light colour, or vice versa, any small damaged part will show up.

MATCHED GRAINED SURFACES

FIG. 28. *By graining the door and skirting to match the cupboard and occasional table an effect of harmony is created. The appearance is improved by the plain walls.*

expected to be in constant use, or for rooms which receive a considerable amount of sunlight.

Most colours fade in intensity of hue but become lower in tone value (become darker). After a time, white and pale colours become more yellow and later tend toward brown. Regular sponging of paintwork, if only with cold water, will prevent discoloration to some extent. Colours which tend toward yellow (primrose, moss green, ivory, daffodil, pale orange and the like) are suitable when durability of colour is wanted; the tendency of colours to become yellow is not then so obvious.

When occasional furniture is painted it is wise to decide on a certain colour

If, however, a great change of colour is particularly desired, a coat of elastic varnish applied to the old surface before repainting, will act as a key for the new paint and will prevent it from shelling and flaking. Hard, smooth and impervious surfaces, as for instance marble, which are to be painted and which offer little adhesion to the paint, may be treated in a similar manner.

Work which has been previously painted with gloss paint or enamel does not require a coat of varnish, but the surface must be prepared by rubbing down with pumice-stone or glass-paper.

It is not advisable to treat handrails, door knobs, knockers and the like with oil paint. If such objects really must be painted, synthetic finishes will prove to be far more satisfactory.

It is not always necessary to prepare and repaint surfaces which are not satisfactory when washed. The old surface may provide a suitable ground for scumbling, glazing or graining.

Sponge-stippling with distemper on an existing discoloured distemper ground is a quick and effective method of renovation. A decorative scheme may be renewed in this way without the necessity for turning out the furniture or removing floor coverings. A narrow wallpaper border placed just above the skirting will hide discoloured edges and a new border to match the sponge-stippling gives the work a fresh and bright appearance.

Small stencilled patterns added to an existing plain wallpaper will often hide slightly damaged places. Dots, stars, fleur-de-lis or similar patterns are suitable. Distemper, poster colour or metallic paint may be used for stencilling on wallpaper (Fig. 29).

COLOUR SCHEMES

Apart from the use of appropriate materials, successful decoration depends largely on the employment of pleasing colour combinations. Although most people know instinctively which colours seem to go well together, they are not always capable of planning original colour schemes. Chromatics, the science of colour, is a fascinating study in itself.

The colour of an object is determined by the absorption or reflection of light on its surface.

Sunlight, as may be observed in a rainbow, is composed of red, orange, yellow, green, blue, indigo, and violet rays. An object which reflects all these

rays is white, but if all the rays are absorbed the object appears black.

When red, blue, violet and green rays are mixed in certain proportions so-called white light is produced, but when similar coloured pigments are mixed together they produce grey. This is due to the impurity of the pigments.

Briefly, each and every pigment which the decorator or artist uses contains a proportion of each primary colour. The following list gives the name of the pigment and the approximate percentage of each primary colour, red, yellow, blue.

Colour	Pigment	R.	Y.	B.
Red	Venetian red	80	15	5
	Indian red	80	10	10
	Scarlet lake	90	8	2
	Crimson lake	90	2	8
Yellow	Oxford ochre	15	75	10
	Yellow ochre	15	80	5
	Lemon chrome	2	95	3
	Middle chrome	3	95	2
	Raw sienna	15	70	15
Blue	Prussian blue	1	9	90
	Antwerp blue	3	7	90
	Cobalt blue	3	2	95
	Ultramarine	9	1	90
Orange	Orange chrome	35	60	5
	Burnt sienna	45	45	10
Brown	Raw umber	35	45	20
	Burnt umber	45	35	20
	Vandyke brown	40	35	25
Green	Brunswick green	5	50	45
	Viridian green	5	40	55
	Emerald green	5	45	50

It will be noted that the purest secondary colour may be obtained by mixing the primary colours with the highest readings. For example, a much purer violet may be mixed with crimson lake and ultramarine than with scarlet lake and prussian blue.

Unfortunately, it is impossible to obtain either pure black or pure white pigments. All the primary colours occur in them and one generally predominates. When black is mixed with white the mixture is not a true grey. There is always a blue or a green tinge which must be corrected by adding a little orange or red pigment. Similarly, coloured pigments, when added to a white pigment, alter slightly in colour value owing to the colour content in the white. As this content is usually blue, it is possible to mix pale-blue tints which are greater in purity than, say, pale orange tints.

The colours which are opposite on the colour circle (Fig. 30) are complementary to each other. For example,

red-orange is complementary to green-blue. Suppose that to a white paint, tinted greenish-blue, a touch of the complementary colour (a reddish-orange) is then added. The greenish-blue is at once neutralized and a duck-egg blue is produced. Or perhaps to a yellow-green a very little violet-red is added. The yellow-green is neutralized and it becomes olive green.

Ready-mixed paints which are too hard in colour may be improved by adding a touch of the complementary colour. For example, first find the approximate colour of the ready-mixed paint on the colour circle. The complementary colour will occur directly opposite. Then, from the list of pigments on page 72, find the pigment required.

Given white, venetian red, prussian blue, and lemon chrome, most tints required for normal decorations may

FLEUR-DE-LIS

FIG. 29. *A pattern sten-cilled on a plain ground adds to the apparent furnishing and relieves the monotony of a large room. The work may be carried out in distemper, poster colour or metallic paint. Stencilled patterns will also help to hide defects on wallpaper.*

be prepared. It must be remembered that the three pigments mentioned are all slightly yellowish. If softer colours are required, consult the list of pigments. It must also be borne in mind that prussian blue is very strong indeed, so it must be used with great care.

All the pigments may be bought in small tins from decorators' merchants. They are sold as colours ground in oil. If very small quantities are required, artists' oil colours may be used. They are supplied in tubes of various sizes, and are very finely ground.

COLOUR MIXING

Before adding pigments to white paint, first mix them with a little of the white paint on a palette (or on a flat piece of wood) and then add the mixture to the remaining white paint. It is advisable to save a small quantity of the white paint for correction in case the tinting has been overdone.

As most mixed paints go deeper in tone as they dry, it is wise to allow for this when the colour of dry paint has to be matched. If a little of the mixed colour is tried out on the paintwork which is to be matched, and the colour is allowed to remain for a quarter of an hour or so, the success of the colour matching may be judged accurately.

Colour mixing and colour matching is an interesting subject which requires careful study. Experience may be gained by mixing small quantities of colour on a palette to match various objects in a room, and the practice will be far more valuable than attempting to remember the various quantities of pigments required to produce various tints. It may, however, be useful to remember the pigments required for the production of the following tints:

Cream: white, orange chrome and a touch of blue
Ivory: white, raw sienna, lemon chrome
Parchment: white, oxford ochre, lemon chrome, blue.

When complementary colours of equal intensity are placed side by side, a rather unpleasant effect will be observed at the junction of the colours. This is due partly to the jump from one extreme to another, and partly to the effect each colour has of making the other seem more intense. If a black or white line separates complementary colours, the effect on the eye is spoiled.

When colours are placed on a black ground, the colours are intensified, but colours placed on a white ground become less bright.

Secondary colours when placed side by side (green and orange, green and violet, or violet and orange) are not pleasing to the eye unless one of the colours is very pale.

HARMONY AND CONTRAST

Combinations of primary colours (red, yellow and blue) are particularly attractive if the colours incline to each other, as in the case of scarlet and yellow. Such combinations are often used as military colours. When two primary colours are employed for contrasting harmony, the remaining primary colour should occur somewhere in the colour scheme. If the walls of a room are blue and the curtains crimson, a need will be felt for some bright yellow. Polished brasswork, a chinese-yellow vase, yellow silk cushions, or books with bright yellow jackets may satisfy the need.

When a room is painted all over in one colour and the furnishings are of a similar colour, the selected colour loses

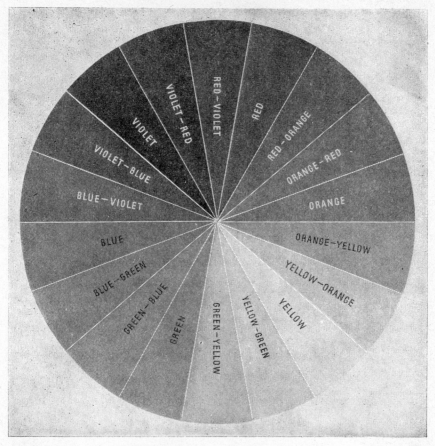

COMPLEMENTARY COLOUR CHART

FIG. 30. *A convenient method of selecting two colours which harmonize is to use one colour with its complementary, shown as opposites in the chart. For example, violet and yellow, or green and red are complementary and look well together.*

its appeal owing to the lack of another colour with which to compare it. As soon as other colours are introduced into the room the true colour value of the walls and furnishings will be seen to advantage.

Black and white should occur in all decorative schemes if only in the form of ornaments. The reason for this is that the eye may then observe the true colour values of the decorations in the room by comparing them with black and white.

Harmony of analogy occurs when one primary colour is dominant in each colour used. For instance, yellow-green, yellow-red and yellow-brown look well together, so do blue-green, blue-red and blue-grey and a great variety of similar combinations.

75

CHAPTER 3

DISTEMPERING

INEXPENSIVE DECORATION FOR WALLS AND CEILINGS

DISTEMPERING refers to any method of applying colours which are mixed with a glutinous substance soluble in water such as glue, gum, casein (milk powder) or white of egg. In this category are included washable distempers and water-paints which are bound with various silicates and oil emulsions.

There are two main varieties of distemper: ordinary or soft distemper, which is also sold ready-mixed in paste or powder form, and washable distemper, including water-paint, supplied in similar packing.

Ordinary distempers usually consist of a whiting base to which something in the nature of a glue size has been added as a binder. This form of distemper is generally used for ceilings in cheap or moderately priced work and for other surfaces which need periodical

ADVANCE PLANNING

FIG. 1. *If possible, all furniture should be removed from a room which is to be redecorated. This saves time by ensuring that there is easy access to walls and ceiling.*

READY FOR WORK

FIG. 2. *View of the same room as that shown in Fig. 1, with scaffolding in position for washing down the ceiling. Under the dust sheets are some pieces of furniture which have been stacked in the centre of the room as they could not be accommodated elsewhere. All work on the ceiling should be completed before treating the walls.*

renovation. Properly made and correctly used, it produces a perfect finish, often superior in appearance to that obtained by the use of more expensive materials. As ordinary distemper has comparatively little binder in its composition, it produces a perfectly flat surface without gloss or sheen. For ceiling work this quality is a very great advantage. Other advantages are its reasonable cost, the ease with which it can be made and applied, and the fact that it can be washed off for renewal. On the other hand, it is not very durable and dampness will cause it to change colour, flake and peel off. It cannot be washed

as can washable distemper or water-paint of reputable manufacture.

The base, or whiting, is prepared from chalk and is available in three qualities: paris white, gilders' whiting and town whiting. Gilders' whiting is most satisfactory for the purpose.

The binder can be almost anything of the glue family: scotch glue, french glue, jelly size, concentrated size or gelatine. Mural artists and other decorative painters sometimes bind their distemper with white of egg, parchment size or wax, and include other ingredients for which they claim special qualities, including long life.

WASHING-DOWN

FIG. 3. *Except when the ceilings and walls are new, all surfaces should be thoroughly washed before beginning to distemper. Work in patches as shown.*

Ready-prepared soft distemper in paste form, sometimes described as ceiling white, consists of a white base such as whiting, gypsum or clay or a mixture of each in varying proportions, together with a binder of glue size or casein. A preservative is added which keeps the mixture almost indefinitely; a distinct advantage over the home-made variety which turns sour in a few days. It is sold as a stiff paste which needs only the addition of water. In use these paste distempers are very economical, as any left over after com-

pletion of the work can be put back into the container for future use.

To prevent undue hardening of the material in the container it is wise to keep it well levelled and covered with a little water. This will avoid wastage and unnecessary straining.

Paste distemper is available in a variety of shades and colours. It is convenient to use ready-mixed distemper because it avoids the difficulty of matching if sufficient material is not made up, as might be the case if the home-made variety were being used.

SELECTING A BRUSH

Distemper brushes vary in different localities. In some parts the two-knot brush is in favour, in others the 6-in. flat brush, while some workers maintain that nothing but the four-knot or 8-in. flat brush will suffice. Similarly with distemper tools, that is, the small brushes which are used for enrichments; some still use string-bound tools, while others are content with an ordinary, small flat brush.

Brushes for distempering should consist of pure bristle of good quality and length, preferably set in vulcanized rubber.

When purchasing a brush it is wise to go to a long-established and well-known firm. Some people prefer a 6-in. flat brush to a two-knot brush, considering that such a brush will do more and better work than the two-knot type. Brushes made up in the form of knots bound with copper wire, and string-bound tools, should be soaked in water for a few hours before use. String-bound tools will need to be tied up, or bridled, before they are put into distemper. It is usual to bridle this class of brush owing to the length of the bristle from which it is made.

SPONGING THE SURFACE

FIG. 4. *After soaking the surface thoroughly with several changes of water applied with an old distemper brush, the job of washing-down is completed with a sponge and plenty of clean water.*

After use, brushes should be well washed out in warm water until no trace of distemper remains, and swished out as dry as possible. They should then be hung up or laid flat, care being taken to avoid damaging the bristles. Once the bristles are bent it is difficult to straighten them again.

PREPARATORY WORK

Start by preparing the room and treating all surfaces as illustrated in Figs. 1-4. New ceilings and walls will need little preparation, but it is advisable to go over the whole surface and remove any nibs or remnants of plaster with a stripping knife as shown in Fig. 5. Do not use glass-paper for this purpose, as any resulting scratches would be extremely difficult to remove.

If ordinary or soft distemper is being used, the porosity of the surface must be considered. If the surface is unduly

LOOSE PLASTER

FIG. 5. *New walls and ceilings should not require to be washed-down, but it is advisable to go over the surface with a stripping knife to remove any nibs of plaster. Never use glass-paper for this purpose as it will leave surface scratches which will be difficult to obliterate.*

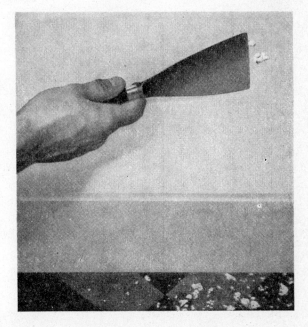

porous, the water content of the distemper is immediately absorbed, not only making the brushwork difficult, but rendering it impossible to join up one patch with another without showing coarse brush marks and a double thickness at the joint of the patches. The degree of porosity may be determined by moistening the tip of a finger and applying it to the plastered surface. If the moisture is absorbed within five seconds, a coat of clearcole (undercoat for soft distemper) should be given. If it remains wet for half a minute, a coat of clearcole should not be necessary.

As, however, the average amateur will be working single-handed and is unlikely to have the scaffolding facilities of the professional, it is recommended that a coat of clearcole be given in any case for easy working.

To overcome porosity it is customary first to apply a coat of clearcole, which consists of a medium-strength size to which a little whiting has been added. If size in the jelly form is used, it should be prepared as already described for making soft distemper. Concentrated size, which is really pulverized glue, should be mixed with cold water into a paste and reduced with hot water to the required strength. When cold, it should resemble a table jelly. If whiting is not available, a little of the distemper may be added to the size. Clearcole should not form an obliterating coat, only sufficient whiting or distemper being added to colour the size. For example, a cupful of distemper would be ample for a quart of size. Clearcole should be applied hot in

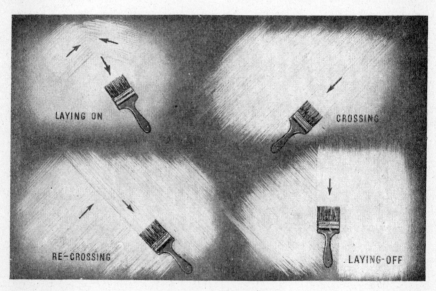

DISTEMPERING A WALL

FIG. 6. *Lay the material on quickly and evenly, covering an area about two feet in width from the top downwards. The material may be crossed, re-crossed and laid-off vertically. In practice there should be no brush marks such as are shown.*

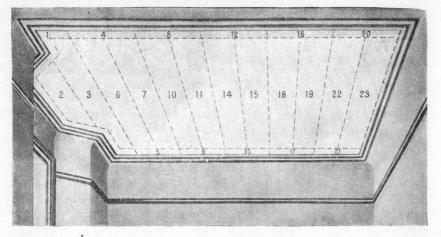

DISTEMPERING A CEILING

FIG. 7. *Start by the window at 1 and work in strips as indicated, taking in parts of the edge according to the sequence. The last edge is included in strip 23.*

order to penetrate the plaster as deeply as possible. Cold size, merely lying on the surface, is likely to be softened by the distemper, and when joining up one patch with another the distemper will slide off the surface, leaving bare patches. Always allow plenty of time for the size to harden before distempering: at least three hours after the size appears to be thoroughly dry.

STARTING THE JOB

When distempering, the aim should be to produce a solid, well-covered surface, free from brush marks, with full obliteration and no indication of the joint between one patch and another (Fig. 6). To achieve this end, suitable brushes must be used, the distemper must be of the correct consistency, the work should be done operating away from the light and carried out without delay. Professional decorators would use two pairs of steps and a scaffold board of requisite length. They would work in pairs, each

BRUSHWORK

FIG. 8. *Correct method of applying distemper to a ceiling. Keep the brush on the surface as described in the text.*

81

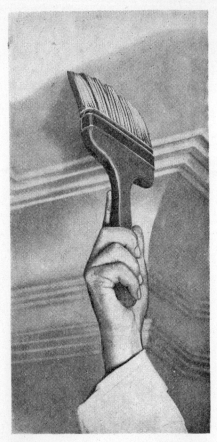

METHOD OF FINISHING

FIG. 9. *Correct way to hold the brush, with only the tip touching the ceiling.*

procure them, it is advisable to use two pairs of steps and a board. The position of the furniture and the type of scaffolding used will have some bearing on how the work will be done; whether it will be possible to do it in long strips or in square patches. In any case, the work should be started on the window side and carried along, in strips if possible, to the farther end. It should be noted that the width of the strips will be governed by how quickly the distemper sets. If it remains wet, with little indication of the edges drying, the strips may be wider; this will speed the work.

DISTEMPERING A CEILING

Assuming that the ceiling is one with a cornice and that the frieze is also to be distempered, the bed of the ceiling should be tackled first and the cornice and frieze done together afterwards; always work from the light (Fig. 7).

Arrange the scaffolding near the window. When beginning the work, charge the brush well with distemper halfway up the bristle and press it out on the side of the bucket. This distributes the distemper in the brush. To prevent the distemper from dropping, the brush should be turned upwards immediately after taking a dip from the bucket. Splashing only occurs when the brush leaves the work. When spreading the distemper, keep the tip of the brush on the work, turning the brush back on itself as the strokes are made from side to side (Fig. 8.)

Lay on about 6 in. from one side to the other, going on to the cornice slightly and making sure that the edge of the cornice is well covered. Now return to the start and cover a strip 1–2 ft. wide, according to the porosity of the ceiling. One dip of the brush will

doing half of the area and meeting in the middle. They would arrange the furniture beforehand so that the scaffolding could be easily and quickly moved from one position to the other.

The amateur should keep this plan in mind and endeavour to arrange the same facilities whether he is working from one pair of steps or from, say, a table. Easy movement of the scaffolding is important. If it is possible to

probably not do more than about half a square foot. It is important to put plenty on, to brush it out evenly, and to finish lightly, with the tip of the brush only, as shown in Fig. 9. Do not treat too large a patch before laying-off.

Apply the brush against the part previously treated, slightly overlapping, brush it out evenly (but not thinly) and finish as previously described. The finishing is the most important part of the technique; starting from the outer edge of the patch, the tip of the brush should be drawn towards the light and glanced off after having passed over the joint between the newly distempered portion and the previously treated portion. Try to avoid missing any

part of the ceiling, as subsequent touching up will show badly and spoil the appearance of the job.

When the bed of the ceiling is finished, the cornice and frieze may be worked together, treating the portion under the window first and finally the end portion of the room.

DISTEMPERING WALLS

The correct way to hold the brush for distempering walls is clearly shown in Figs. 10 and 11.

Soft distemper is seldom used for wall decoration. It is too easily damaged by abrasion, and, being easily removed by washing, dirty marks cannot be cleaned off without destroy-

RE-DECORATING A WALL

FIG. 10. *Distemper should be applied liberally and quickly in all directions. Every part should be evenly covered. Ordinary distemper dries too quickly to be worked like paint, but washable distemper and water-paints can be crossed and laid-off, or finished, provided that the work is done speedily. Note how the brush is being held.*

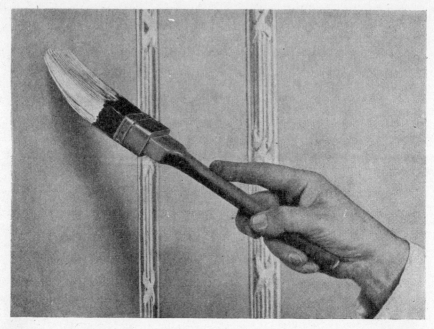

ADDING THE FINISHING TOUCHES

Fig. 11. *It is not always possible to lay-off ordinary distemper, but, holding the brush as illustrated, water-paint may be finished in a downward direction. It is unwise to apply a thick coat, as this makes good brushwork difficult.*

ing the distemper at the same time.

Washable distempers and water-paints are suitable for walls and ceilings, and when properly used over a suitably prepared ground, form a permanent coating which should not need to be removed when further decorations are contemplated; but the preparatory work must be thorough. If, for example, some soft distemper is left on the surface, any washable distemper applied over it would be most likely to flake off. Washable distemper is preferable, but not ideal, for bathroom and kitchen where humid conditions would cause a soft distemper to disintegrate and peel off. Never size the surface before applying washable dis-

MIXING DISTEMPER

Fig. 12. *Turn the distemper into a bucket and use a stout piece of wood for mixing purposes. Note how the bucket is gripped at the base between the two feet.*

temper; one thin coat followed by one full coat is all that is necessary.

Washable distemper is frequently used for coating exterior stucco and rough-cast. It produces an excellent effect and is a good treatment for such work. Special outside quality should be used and petrifying liquid should be

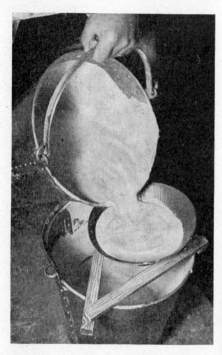

AFTER MIXING

FIG. 13. *Distemper may be passed through a paint strainer which should be supported on a triangle, made of three pieces of wood nailed together, on top of the bucket.*

employed for thinning the distemper.

Washable distempers are supplied in 4-lb. and 7-lb. tins, and in 28-lb., 56-lb. and 1-cwt. drums. The required quantity should be placed in a bucket and reduced with water or petrifying

liquid to a working consistency. It is denser than soft distemper and a much thinner coat, therefore, will produce obliteration. After being well stirred with a piece of wood (Fig. 12), the distemper should be strained to assist mixing and to remove any lumps (Figs. 13 and 14). All makers supply a petrifying liquid for use with their own brand of distemper, and it is unwise to use one firm's petrifying liquid with another firm's product.

Washable distemper is capable of giving a very fine finish and in this respect it has the characteristics of a paint. Indeed, it has much in common with oil paint. It is finely ground, the base is similar to that used in many flat paints and it needs careful brush-work. Two coats are usually sufficient. The first coat should be a moderately

STRAINING

FIG. 14. *It is advisable to stir the distemper gently with a brush as it is passed through the strainer.*

Fig. 15. *Used on paint or distemper to eliminate brush marks, a hair stippler produces a fine, even texture which can be very attractive.*

A strip about 18 in. wide from top to bottom should be coated, brushing the distemper out well, crossing and re-crossing to distribute the distemper evenly, and finally finishing with the tip of the brush downwards (Fig. 11). When laying-off from the picture rail, the brush should be allowed to rest lightly and for a split second

thin coat, followed by a full one. The material for the second coat should be of similar consistency to cream (not clotted cream). Both coats should be applied equally carefully.

If the brushes are of a sufficiently high quality, a fine finish may be obtained by brushwork only. It is best to keep the shortest edge; that is to say, if a wall is 12 ft. long by 7 ft. high, a vertical edge should be maintained working from right to left. Similarly, a recess 7 ft. high and 3 ft. wide should be started at the top and a horizontal edge maintained.

When starting a flank, cut in to the corner and for about three feet to the picture rail and the skirting. Some workers prefer to use a small brush for this purpose, but it is just as simple to do with the larger brush.

before drawing it downwards; this also applies when working from the skirting upwards. As applied to distemper, the term laying-off implies little more than adding the finishing touches to ensure even distribution.

STIPPLING

For good-class work it is customary to eliminate all traces of brush strokes by stippling the distemper while it is still wet with a hair stippler, treating each stretch as the work proceeds (Fig. 15). This method produces an even surface with a very fine grain. When working away from any edge, the stippler should be held diagonally to avoid straight lines showing the passage of the tool. Hair stipplers are expensive and for the amount of use it would receive it is hardly a good proposition for an amateur to purchase one. In practice, a more interesting effect can be obtained with two thicknesses of canvas or hessian tacked on to a wooden float (Fig. 16).

All splashes of washable distemper should be cleaned up before they are allowed to dry. Old newspapers spread about the floor will minimize the amount of cleaning necessary.

After the distempering has been completed, the material left over should be wiped back into the stock pot and the bucket and brush carefully cleaned. If the colour of the distemper has been changed, it should be kept separate for touching-up purposes.

Before re-distempering ceilings or walls which have previously been treated with washable distemper, the surface should be carefully examined for any signs of flaking. If there are no such indications, all that is necessary in the way of preparation is a sponge down with clear water and, after the surface is dry, a light rubbing down with fine glass-paper. Small holes and cracks should be filled with a good proprietary brand of plaster stopper, mixed with a little of the distemper. One thin coat followed by one full coat should then produce a perfect result

HESSIAN STIPPLER

FIG. 16. *A tool the handyman can make from a small block of wood and a piece of hessian. It may be used for distemper or plastic paint and gives an interesting texture which is rather more pronounced than that produced with a hair stippler.*

It is seldom necessary to remove old washable distemper entirely: if the surface is flaking, probably the original preparation was at fault and removal should be considered, as new coatings will not provide a cure. Some distempers can be removed by soaking the surface with hot water, scrubbing vigorously and by using a stripping knife. Obstinate surfaces may need a solution of common soda in water, but it is best to avoid this measure if at all possible as there is a danger of damaging the adjacent woodwork or polished floor.

After the distemper has been removed, the surface should be well scrubbed, the holes repaired and two coats of distemper applied.

PRECAUTIONS

Distempering over wallpaper is seldom a success and is, therefore, not recommended. Certainly if the paper is in a bad state it should not be considered. Occasionally, however, one is loath to strip a paper which appears to be in a good condition. Reasonable success may be gained only by carefully examining all edges and sticking down all loose parts with paste before the distemper is applied. Even so the distemper may loosen parts which previously appeared to be sound. Sometimes it is also extremely difficult to obliterate the pattern of the dyes used in the printing of the paper.

Before distempering over paintwork it is advisable to cut the hard glossy surface by washing it with a strong solution of common soda and by rubbing down with fairly coarse glasspaper. The surface should be thoroughly rinsed before applying the distemper.

The use of washable distemper provides ample opportunity for decorative effects such as stencilling, sponge stippling and the use of wallpaper borders.

Stencils for borders, corner ornaments and set pieces may be cut out of stout brown paper. To prepare them for use they should be coated on both sides with shellac knotting. Washable distemper is an effective medium for stencilling and may be applied over the stencil plate by using either a proper stencil brush (Fig. 17) or a small part-worn paint brush. The distemper should be used in paste form (or only slightly thinner), the brush being placed in contact with the stencil and wriggled until all the ornament is covered; the surface should then be lightly stippled with the brush before it is charged with distemper again.

Attractive effects may be produced by the combination of wallpaper borders and distemper. Walls may be panelled by the use of special corner-pieces with distempered panels. Ornaments placed in the angles of the panel add to the effect. Another scheme is to hang a border against the picture rail and the skirting. Further details of these methods will be found in other chapters. When borders are used, there is no need to cut in close to the limits with the distemper.

SPECIAL EFFECTS

Mottled effects in distemper can be produced in a variety of ways. The mottling may be done either while the ground is still wet or after it is dry. One method is to take three or four small brushes and tie them together so that they will go into separate pots simultaneously. The ground colour is usually of a light tone and the colours to harmonize are placed in the separate pots. While a section of the ground is

STENCILLING A BORDER

FIG. 17. *Holding the stencil flat against the wall with one hand, the brush is dabbed over the surface until all the ornament is covered. The distemper, which should be of the washable variety, is best used in paste form or only slightly thinner. If a proper stencil brush is not available, use a partly worn paint brush.*

still wet, the four brushes are dipped into their several pots and the wall dabbed about in a twisting fashion, the brushes being recharged as may be necessary.

Another method is to stipple the dry surface in one or more colours with a sponge. A piece of board is well charged with the mottling colour and the sponge is first dabbed on the board and then on the wall. The position of the sponge should be constantly changed to avoid regularity. A piece of crushed brown paper can also be used most effectively for transferring the mottling colour from the board to the wall.

Some ambitious amateurs may wish to attempt blended effects in distemper. A good obliterating coat should be given first and when dry the wall should be marked with chalk lines snapped in convenient positions to mark the division between the different shades.

Assuming that the idea is to shade the walls upwards from rose pink to cream, several pots are taken, one for cream, one for rose pink and others for the intermediate shades. By intermixing the distemper in the pots, the shades are carefully graduated. Separate brushes are needed with each pot, and some means must be provided for stippling after the shades have been blended with the brush. Starting at the top, a horizontal band of cream should be applied to the chalk line. When the next shade has been applied, the first brush is used to make a strong wavy

BLENDING DISTEMPER

FIG. 18. *Bands of different colour or different shades of the same colour are applied horizontally and blended by drawing the brush in vertical sweeps between, until the two bands are blended. The effect is completed with a stippler.*

line over the junction of the two shades in order to blend one colour into the other (Fig. 18). Horizontal brushwork will further assist the blending, which is completed with the aid of a hair stippler, hessian stippler or paper dabber. As hair stipplers are costly—and if only one is available it will need to be cleaned for the next shade—it may be wise to rely on paper dabbers to complete the final blending. As each shade is applied the previous brush is used for blending.

Floral-patterned effects in multi-colours may be obtained by the use of rollers which are covered with pieces of felt cut to a fancy pattern and so arranged that one working of the roller merges into the previous working.

A few special appliances embodying rollers with embossed floral or other patterns are available and give reasonably good imitations of wallpaper effects. They are primarily intended for use with oil paints and glazes, but quite good results can be obtained with a distemper medium. Although many householders seem to regard distemper as essentially a material for producing plain backgrounds, perhaps enough has been said to indicate that highly decorative effects are possible.

CHAPTER 4

INTERIOR PAINTING AND STAINING

THE MATERIALS TO USE AND HOW TO APPLY THEM

A KNOWLEDGE of painters' materials and their possibilities is half the battle in becoming an expert home decorator. It is a common mistake to imagine that there are only two types of paint—undercoating and finishing. On the contrary, there are many types made for special purposes and most of these require different methods of application.

Hard-gloss paints, enamels, flat enamels, flat japans, flat oil paints, synthetic and semi-synthetic finishes are comparatively recent introductions. Not so many years ago the painter and decorator had to be satisfied with paint which he made up himself from pigments ground in oil, linseed oil, dryers and turpentine. The excellent condition of paint surfaces which still exist in many town and country houses bears witness to the quality of the materials used and the craftsmanship employed in bygone days.

READY-MIXED MATERIALS

Enamels, gloss paints, ready-mixed oil paint, and all other patent finishes were put on the market in the first place to save the decorator time and trouble. Those of us in the trade who have been compelled to break up hundredweights of hard, paste white-lead appreciated the introduction of ready-mixed materials. The master painter was pleased to buy the newly introduced ready-mixed materials because he realized that he could be certain of a guaranteed standard of mixing, and he could allow his men to spend more time on application.

At first, ready-mixed paints resembled the product of craftsmen, but they developed gradually into paints which incorporated new white pigments and oils, until, at the present time, paint chemistry is a specialist occupation. Analysis only will prove what most ready-mixed paints are composed of, so the home decorator must buy many of his materials on trust. The safest plan is to buy paint of reputable manufacture and to obtain the type suited for the purpose for which it is intended.

PRIMING COATS

Ready-mixed, white-lead oil paint and oil paint with a zinc-oxide base are still manufactured and they are the most useful types of paint to buy for general use. It is far better for the amateur to buy ready-mixed finishing paints than to make them up himself. As each type of paint requires a different method of application, the treatment will be described as each type is mentioned.

New woodwork and bare plasterwork require a preliminary coat of thin paint known as the priming coat, or simply priming. It should be composed of white lead, raw linseed oil, patent driers and turpentine, or a ready-mixed paint could be used if it were known to contain such ingredients. The paint should contain approximately two parts of raw linseed oil to one of turpentine and be used thinly so as to penetrate the surface of the woodwork or plaster.

When burning off old paintwork it is often impossible to remove the priming coat. This proves not only that priming paint really serves its purpose, but also the excellent quality of the priming paint which was used in the past. It is sometimes thought that any old paint which has been thinned with turpentine is good enough for priming. This is a mistake. Half the troubles which occur to subsequent coats of paint may be traced to the use of an unsuitable priming coat.

DIFFERENT SURFACES

It is useless to add venetian red or red oxide to white lead to make a pink priming. These pigments only tint the lead and have no other value for priming purposes.

Priming paint should not dry quickly or, instead of penetrating the surface, it will simply form a surface skin. If priming paint is found to be drying too quickly, the addition of raw linseed oil will correct the fault. Do not forget to treat knots in woodwork with knotting varnish before the priming coat is applied.

Bare plasterwork does not require the use of pink priming, nor do walls which have been papered with white lining paper. White priming paint or white paint, tinted with pigments ground in oil, will serve the purpose. The only purpose of the pigments (stainers) is to allow the first coat of paint to be opaque. If pink priming is used for plasterwork an extra coat of paint may be needed if the finishing colour is to be white or a pale tint. Ironwork should not be painted with priming paint intended for woodwork.

Priming paint should be applied very thinly and rubbed well into the surface. One method, when priming a door, is to brush in all edges and mouldings, then the panels, next the centre stiles, follow with the rails and, finally, prime the outer stiles (Fig. 1). The separate parts of a wooden sash

PRIMING A DOOR

FIG. 1. *Treat the architrave first (stages 1-3), followed by the edge (4) and then the mouldings and panels. The rails and stiles should be painted last.*

2 SOFFIT AND BACK OF BEAD

3 BOTTOM-EDGE AND UNDER-SIDE OF LOWER RAIL

1 MEETING RAIL AND SASH BARS

PAINTING A SASH WINDOW

FIG. 2. *The positions in which sliding the sashes should be set when starting to paint. The parts marked 1 should be treated first, followed by those marked 2 and 3.*

should be primed (or painted) as follows: First open the window (both sashes), as shown in Fig. 2. Prime the meeting rail and the sash bars of the top sash which are within reach and proceed as shown in Figs. 3–5. If this order of work is followed there will be no need to handle wet paint and it will be unlikely that any part of the window is missed.

To prime a ceiling, a scaffolding

consisting of two pairs of steps and a scaffold board will be required.

Start work on the ceiling near the window. The first strip should normally be about 2 ft. wide and subsequent areas should be primed in similar lengths; that is, paint strips of about 4 sq. ft. at a time. After completing the first strip, start at the same end to paint a second strip. It will not be necessary to move the scaffolding. Proceed in similar manner until the whole of the bed of the ceiling has been painted. The scaffolding need be moved only for every two strips.

Walls are primed in the order shown in Fig. 6. Start at the top right-hand corner of the wall and prime a rectangle about 2 ft. wide and 3 ft. deep. Proceed as shown by the numbered rectangles. If left-handed, it will be best to start at the top left-hand corner, working in similar manner.

THE FIRST STAGE

FIG. 3. *After having set the sashes as illustrated in Fig. 2, the meeting rail and sash bars which are within reach, at the lowest point, are painted first.*

93

This order of painting does not apply to priming only, but to painting in general, although these strips are too wide for the application of hard-gloss paint, enamel or very quick-drying flat finishes. The strips should be about 10 in. wide for these materials.

Priming paint and ordinary oil paint should first be brushed on the

THE FINAL STAGE

FIG. 5. *Treat the pulley stiles last, but do not let the brush touch the sash cords, which may be pulled clear while the painting of these areas is in progress.*

PAINTING THE UPPER SASH

FIG. 4. *When the parts in Fig. 3 have been painted, the position of the sashes is reversed, as shown, for finishing.*

various planes evenly in all directions. First the paint should be brushed up and down and then crossed. For very fine work the paint may next be brushed in two diagonal directions, but this is not essential. During this process the brushwork should be very firm to begin with and lightened gradually as the paint is brushed in the various directions. Finally, lay-off the work; that is, smooth off the surface by drawing the brush over it in a series of strokes all in the same direction. No pressure is required, the weight of the brush being sufficient to draw the paint in the direction required (Fig. 7). By following these directions a fine, even film of paint will be given which will be free of brush marks.

This method of brushwork applies to each coat of oil paint, but hard-gloss paint, enamel, flat japan and varnish are applied in other ways. Woodwork should be laid-off in the direction of the grain in every case. Walls should be laid-off vertically unless, of course, they are set out in horizontal strips.

In the decorating trade, a priming coat of paint is not considered to be the first coat. A specification for painting work often reads: "Knot, prime, stop and paint . . . coats."

New woodwork and bare plasterwork usually require priming and three coats of paint. Four coats of paint are sometimes needed when, for instance, the finish is to be white or a very pale tint. By giving work four coats of paint alternate coats of oily and flat paint can be given. For example, the priming is oily, the first coat of paint is flat, the second coat is oily, the third coat is flat and the finishing paint is glossy (oily). The flat and oily sequence may be adhered to by priming, undercoating and finishing, but this is not sufficient if the work is to last. A good flat finish could be obtained by priming and painting the work with three coats of paint.

It must not be imagined that four coats of paint as well as priming call for an excessive amount of paint. Most people use paint much too thickly. They imagine that the more paint they can put on the better. This is true, to some extent, when gloss paint, enamel or certain flat-finishes are used, but for plain painting thin coats are better

SEQUENCE IN PAINTING A WALL

FIG. 6. *Unless naturally left-handed, it is most convenient to work from right to left in strips approximately two feet wide by three feet deep. Always paint from the top downwards as indicated by the numbers. The steps should be opened out to their full extent and should only require to be moved for every two strips.*

and are easier to apply than thick ones. In other words, it is the manner in which paint is applied, rather than the thickness of the coats, which gives the maximum protection.

It might seem that a thick coat of paint would obscure better than a thin one, but this is not always the case. A thick coat cannot be brushed out as evenly as a thin one, and the oil vehicle does not flow so readily. From the point of view of economy, three thin coats take no more paint than two thick ones, and perhaps even less. Of course, extra drying time is required, but the ease of application of three thin coats of paint actually cuts down the working time.

It is impossible to lay down a rule for the number of coats of paint required for various surfaces. Two coats of paint are sufficient only if the old work is in very good condition and similar colours are to be used again for the new decoration.

It is a mistake to depend on the finishing coat of, say, hard-gloss paint to obscure. Although some makes of this material have considerable covering power, it is only achieved at the expense of the glossy finish. The best results are obtained by using semi-opaque hard-gloss paints and enamels.

DURABILITY

The final undercoat should be opaque and similar to the finishing paint in colour. The finishing paint should be used as a protective coat and not as a means of obtaining colour and gloss in one operation. Black and deep colours may be obtained by the use of two coats of paint, one flat and one gloss. Three coats are better, as the solidity of two coats is more apparent than real (Fig. 8).

The use of paint, "knocked up" from white lead or other pigments ground in oil, driers, linseed oil and turpentine seems to have fallen out of favour. The advantage of using paste white lead, driers and the various vehicles and thinners is that the

LAYING-OFF

FIG. 7. *By holding the brush as shown only light pressure is applied to the bristles and the finishing touches, known as laying-off, are given so as to leave a surface free from brush marks. The weight of the brush alone is sufficient to draw the paint in the direction required.*

paint may be adjusted to suit any particular requirement. These materials, together with red lead and the various pigments ground in oil, and priming paint, allow paint for any purpose or finish, except high gloss, to be made up.

White lead or zinc oxide forms the best white base. White lead has superior wearing qualities and is recommended for exterior work, but it has a tendency to discolour. Zinc oxide does not wear so well, but it is much whiter than white lead and it does not discolour. It is suitable for all inside work and particularly useful for a variety of decorative finishes.

NUMBER OF COATS

For interior ceilings and walls which are to be finished in gloss paint, glazed, scumbled, or grained, and for woodwork which is to receive similar finishes, the first coat of paint over the priming should not contain an excess of oil. Do not use flatting or any of the patent finishes, but ordinary oil paint. Undercoating which is specially made for the job may be bought ready-made, and if it is not of the semi-synthetic variety it will usually be improved by the addition of a small amount of raw linseed oil.

If only two coats of paint are to be applied and the finish is to be glossy, the first coat of paint should remain rather flat. If, however, three coats are needed, the first coat should contain rather more oil and the second coat rather less.

The second coat of paint should never be applied until the first one is perfectly hard. Apart from this consideration, the rule to follow in all cases is flat on oily paint and oil paint on flat. Flat paint applied over another flat paint is sometimes permissible,

FINAL UNDERCOAT

Fig. 8. *The final undercoat should be opaque and similar in colour to the finishing paint. In this case ceiling and walls are to be the same colour.*

but gloss paint should never be applied directly over another hard glossy coat, unless the surface has been well rubbed down with glass-paper or steel wool to produce a surface with sufficient key for the reception of the next coat. There is one exception. Some synthetic paints, which are often of excellent quality, have no special undercoating. In this case, gloss on gloss is quite in order. The observations already made apply to the third and any subsequent coat of paint.

After each coat of paint has dried, it

SAVING PAINT

FIG. 9. *It may be found that a coat of paint can be saved by covering any marks on the surface with a little of the paint which is to be used for subsequent coats.*

must be rubbed down with glass-paper and dusted before the next coat is applied.

For outside work, middle-two grade glass-paper should be used, but number one or fine-two is more suitable for inside work. If the work has been properly prepared from the start, there will be no need to use coarse glass-paper.

The final coat of oil paint, applied prior to enamelling or painting with any kind of gloss paint, should be rubbed down with fine glass-paper, sponged with cold water to remove all traces of dust or grit which may remain in the mouldings, and well dried with a chamois leather. This operation should be done a few minutes before the application of the finishing paint

It sometimes happens that surfaces require an extra coat of paint if they are marred by small, uneven patches. Much paint and labour will be saved if the work is examined carefully before the first coat of paint is applied and any particular bad places touched up with paint (Fig. 9). Do not touch up such places with white paint, but match up the existing colour, otherwise the remedy will be almost as bad as the fault. Some such examples are doors which have been white-enamelled and show brown patches where the knots occur; walls with light rectangles where pictures have been removed and which have not faded to the same extent as the rest of the walls; stains on walls and ceilings, knocks and other damaged places on skirting boards, bare places near finger-plates and discolouring round electric-light switches.

When a room has received two coats of paint, most of the work should be in a fit state to receive the finishing coat, but it sometimes happens that window-sills or skirtings are unsatisfactory (Fig. 10). It should be obvious that it is not necessary to paint the whole of the woodwork again as so many enthusiasts do, but only those parts which require it. There is no virtue in applying an extra coat of paint if the existing surface is satisfactory.

When odd places require an extra coat of paint, adjustment of the colour may be necessary, otherwise the parts which receive the extra coat will be more solid than the rest, and these parts will show distinctly when the finishing colour has been applied.

PRESERVATION OF COLOUR

It will save both time and paint if, when particularly pure or bright colours are desired, the undercoats used are the same colours as the finishing paints. Coloured finishing-paints, especially the semi-opaque variety, will not cover well or evenly on white undercoating. They will appear streaky on walls and will show solid patches on such parts as door shoulders where the brushwork overlaps. Again, light tints of finishing paints or enamels will not dry the same

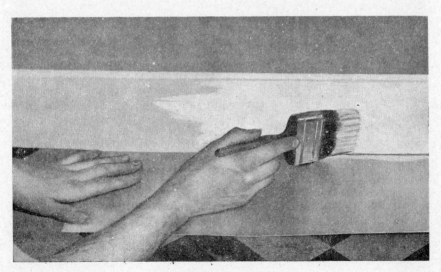

TO PROTECT THE FLOOR

FIG. 10. *When painting the skirting a sheet of card or a thin metal shield may be used to protect the floor. A mask can also be useful for the edge by the wall.*

CHOICE OF BRUSH

FIG. 11. *A 1-in. paint tool is a convenient size for painting a door, but after a little practice it will be found that a 2-in. brush can be used for larger areas.*

the present time, that varnish is rarely used in this way but is reserved for finishing grained, marbled, or similar types of work. The home decorator will, however, be able to turn out very durable work by preparing and painting work in the normal way, applying a coat of flat paint of the desired colour, and finishing the work with an appropriate varnish. The disadvantages are that varnish discolours more quickly than hard-gloss paint and enamel, and that very pale, subtle colours may be altered by the amber colour of the varnish. However, almost clear varnishes, such as french oil varnish, are manufactured and they alter colours so little that interior painting and subsequent varnishing is well worth considering for its superior lasting quality and its ease of application.

Dark colours, such as tobacco brown and brunswick green, and many colours used for exterior painting may be finished with more durable varieties of varnish, as the colour of the varnish will not affect the colour of the paint unduly. The application of varnish is dealt with later.

Enamels and hard-gloss paints are similar in composition and they are applied in the same manner. The amateur should buy those of reputable make, as there are, unfortunately, many hard-gloss paints on sale which are of inferior quality.

ELEMENTARY PRECAUTIONS

In the past, white and tinted hard-gloss paints could be readily mixed, but nowadays care must be taken to see that white hard-gloss paint will mix with the tinted paints by testing a small quantity. If the mixture jellifies or curdles it may be assumed that the paints will not mix satisfactorily.

colour as on the pattern card, if the undercoat has not been similar in colour. Professional painters and decorators make the final undercoat slightly deeper than the colour of the finishing paint, especially when enamel or similar semi-opaque finishes are to be used. The result is a better job and a satisfying richness of colour.

Before glossy paint appeared on the market, painted work was finished by applying a coat of varnish. It seems, at

Similar caution must be exercised before mixing different makes of enamel or gloss paint. Those with synthetic content will not mix with those having an oil content.

When a container of hard-gloss paint is opened, the medium will be found floating on top of the pigment. It need not be removed, but stir the ingredients well to mix them. This step is important and, if it is not done thoroughly, part of the work may lack the proper gloss and part may be transparent.

Apart from synthetic-resin enamels, the best makes of hard-gloss paint and enamel dry very slowly. It is necessary, therefore, to be sure the room is free from dust and dirt before painting is started; otherwise dust and grit will be carried on to the wet-painted surface.

BRUSHWORK

Hard-gloss paints and enamels are not easy to apply. When painting a large area, the beginner's wrist may ache before going very far, but if the following directions are followed, a first-class job will result.

Put a small amount of the paint into a clean paint-kettle and keep a varnish or enamel brush and a 1-in. paint tool at hand. A 2-in. varnish brush is quite large enough to handle for painting ceilings and walls and a 1-in. tool is a convenient size for doors, windows and skirtings. After a little practice, larger brushes may be used (Fig. 11).

Suppose that a door is to be painted: the edges are painted first with the 1-in. tool and each part of the door is enamelled in the sequence shown in Fig. 12.

Brush on plenty of the material, then work it in all directions, using very firm strokes. The full weight of the brush should be used all the time (Fig. 13) and no attempt must be made to lay-off the work. When the material starts to pull (becomes harder to work with the brush), brush it in the direction of the grain if painting woodwork, still using very firm strokes. The brush-marks may be ignored, as they will disappear automatically due to the characteristic flow of the paint.

When a door or a similar area of enamelled work has been completed,

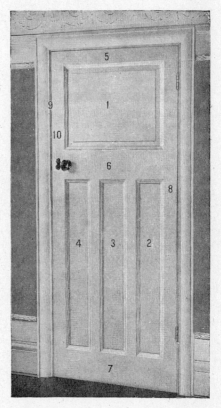

ENAMELLING A DOOR

FIG. 12. *When enamelling a door, brush on plenty of material and work it in all directions, using the full weight of the brush. Work in the order given.*

FIG. 13. *Using the full weight of the brush means bending the bristles against the surface as shown. This action forces the paint well into the pores of the material.*

examine it to see that the material is not running. Scallop-like runs may occur anywhere, but they are mostly found on work which has been brushed horizontally. Tears are likely to be found near the mitres of panel moulding.

If the paint has run, do not attempt to remove the excess, but with the dry brush work up the whole area until it is even again and finish the work with a firm stroke in one direction. Assuming that a paint of good quality has been used, surfaces painted with enamel may be worked for about half an hour after application. Hard-gloss paint usually sets rather more quickly. When surfaces have been worked up in this manner the final brushing may remain ropey (show ridges) for a considerable time, but do not be perturbed and do not attempt to soften the brushmarks. The paint will still flow and the brushmarks will disappear. Overbrushing should be avoided; once the paint has started to set, leave it alone.

When enamelling a small room such as a kitchenette, the ceiling should be enamelled first and any splashes which occur on the prepared walls should be wiped off with a piece of clean rag which has been damped with turpentine. Do not use dirty, dry rag or the tacky nature of the paint will transfer the dirt to the wall and the marks will be difficult to clean properly afterwards.

The walls should be finished next, followed by the windows and woodwork. It is best to leave horizontal surfaces such as shelves and windowsills until last. Do not stand on prepared surfaces to reach awkward places and do not rest heavy objects on them. The paint may not be hard enough to resist such treatment. Never stand or rest a scaffold board upon a marble or slate mantelpiece. They sometimes break very easily.

IMPORTANT CONSIDERATIONS

Always allow sufficient time for one coat of paint to harden before another coat is applied. It is not enough for the paint to be dry. If several coats of paint are given to a surface without allowing for hardening, and the hard-gloss paint is applied immediately the final undercoat is dry, there is a risk of the finishing paint cracking with a crocodile-skin effect. This is particularly likely when a quick-drying enamel is used. The reason is that the soft paint is sealed by the finishing coat, and in its attempt to absorb oxygen it expands and cracks the hard finishing-coat. When terebine, a powerful liquid drier, is added to oil paint to make the finishing coat dry quickly, there is an ever greater risk of subsequent cracking. Terebine must be used at times to hasten the drying of oil paintwork likely to be touched, but use terebine sparingly and be certain that the undercoats are really hard.

Enamels and similar finishing-paints are made up ready for use. Only in exceptional cases should anything be added to them.

Work in a clean manner. To prevent the paint-kettle becoming smothered with paint use one side of the kettle only. The way in which a brush is dipped into the paint may seem an unimportant matter, but there is a right and a wrong way. The brush should be dipped into the paint to about one-third the length of its bristles and one side of the brush allowed to touch the side of the kettle afterwards (Figs. 14 and 15).

Always touch the same part of the kettle with the brush. The paint-kettle should be held in the left hand with the brushes grasped as in Fig. 16 between the head and the handle.

CHARGING THE BRUSH
FIG. 14. *The paint-kettle should not be more than half full, and when charging the brush dip only about a third of the length of the bristles into the material. Although this advice may seem to be unimportant, experienced painters maintain that the quality of the finished work may quite well be affected by such trivial points. Incorrect technique may lead to uneven application.*

REMOVING THE
SURPLUS

FIG. 15. *After charging the brush, one side of it should be allowed to touch the side of the paint kettle. This action will distribute the material in the brush and avoid the wastage of paint.*

Finishing paints of the best quality take many hours to dry and many more to harden properly. It is wise to leave windows and doors slightly open after painting them and to use a newly enamelled room as little as possible, so as to keep the dust from rising and settling on the wet paint. It may happen that before the paint has dried, flies or other small insects alight on the wet surface and stick to it. If this occurs, do not attempt to take the insect off the half-dried paint, or more damage will be done to the paintwork than the insect could possibly do. Wait until the paint is quite dry and only then sponge off the dead insect and dry the paintwork with a chamois leather. The small amount of damage will be hardly noticeable.

USEFUL HINTS

When painting woodwork, take off all movable fittings such as window catches and door furniture before starting to paint. This allows the woodwork to be painted easily and prevents fittings from being daubed with paint. Strictly speaking, hinges should not

be painted. If they require protection a coat of aluminium or gold-bronze paint is recommended. If it is specially desired to paint them to match the door, the minimum number of coats of paint should be applied.

Wherever painting is carried out, all objects which may be easily spoiled should be protected. A newspaper slipped under a door will protect carpets or parquet floors and several pinned together serve well as a temporary dust-sheet. Paint splashes can be removed from windows with greater ease while the paint is still wet. Petrol and cotton-wool are best for removing wet paint from curtains or clothing. Turpentine and its substitute leave a greasy mark. If neither petrol nor turpentine is available, the wet paint spot should be rubbed briskly with a piece of the same material as that on which the mark occurs.

When two or more colours are used in juxtaposition, one colour must be allowed to dry before the other one is applied. Cut-in to outside angles when painting the mouldings round a panel. It is far quicker than attempting to cut-in to inside angles and a much cleaner cut is produced.

There are times when glossy surfaces are not desired, especially when they would show up uneven wall surfaces too much. On the other hand, flat-painted surfaces would not be quite suitable owing to considerations of wear. In such cases egg-shell finishes may be employed with success. The proprietary makes of this material are preferable to mixtures of flat and glossy paints.

Egg-shell finishes should be applied in the manner employed for the application of ordinary oil paint. Although some of these finishes are named enamels, they must not be worked too much with the brush. There are some exceptions, when the material should be applied as one uses flat japan. However, when special methods of application are required there is usually a special instruction on the label of the container.

A very hard-wearing egg-shell finish may be obtained by preparing, undercoating and enamelling in the normal way: when the enamel is quite dry and hard, the egg-shell finish is produced by rubbing the surface with a mild abrasive. Take a soft scrubbing brush or a well-worn distemper brush and dip it in dry pumice powder. Rub the enamelled surface with the brush, using a circular movement. Do not rub too hard, but allow the cutting action of the pumice powder to do the work rather than the friction of the

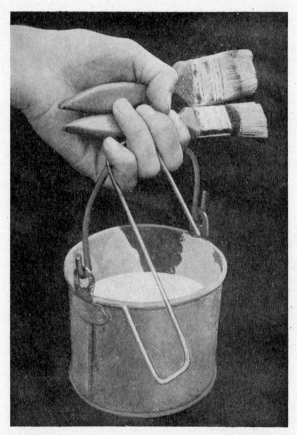

A PRACTICAL HINT

Fig. 16. *Hold the paint-kettle in the left hand with the brushes gripped between the hand and the handle of the kettle. If a ladder hook is required it may be held as shown. Either brush may be selected at will and, as shown in the frontispiece, the right hand is left free to grip the side of a ladder.*

brush. Finally dust the work down with a soft, dry brush or with a pad of soft rag. This finish is suitable for painted and decorated furniture on which a full gloss would be out of taste. The use of ready-made egg-shell finishes is advised for larger areas, such as on ceilings and walls.

CARE OF TOOLS

To finish painting for the day, brush down the sides of the paint-kettle and scrape out the brushes (Figs. 17 and 18); then cover the surface of the paint with a small amount of turpentine—just enough to prevent the paint from skinning. The turpentine used for this purpose will not be sufficient to thin the paint when it is mixed-in the following day.

Alternatively, brush the remaining paint back into the container, scrape out the brushes, clean out the paint kettle with turpentine, dry it with rag and be sure, of course, to seal up the container.

The brushes should not be cleaned out with turpentine, but simply stood in cold water. This excludes the air and allows the paint to remain in the

AFTER WORK

FIG. 17. *It is a good plan to brush out a paint-kettle at the end of a day's work. If this is done regularly, burning out will only be necessary about once a year.*

brushes without hardening (Fig. 19).

In the trade, painters usually stand the brushes in the material when using enamel or hard-gloss paint and cover both paint and brushes with cold water. A skin forms on the surface of the water, which is removed when the paint is to be used again. The water is,

SCRAPING A BRUSH

FIG. 18. *The back of an old knife is excellent for removing paint from a brush before it is washed out and put away after work. If the cutting edge is used there is a risk of damaging the bristles*

of course, poured carefully from the surface of the material.

Brushes need to be worked well into finishing paints. The material is very searching and often brings out colour from the head of an apparently clean brush. Dip the brush into the paint to the full length of the bristles, twirl it between the hands, then scrape out the colour. Repeat this operation several times before attempting to use the brush with the finishing colour.

CUTTING-IN

Glazing bars are painted with a 1-in. brush and are cut-in to the glass. Each pane of glass should be cut round separately so as to avoid missing any part. Hold the brush firmly and paint each bar with a single stroke of the brush. If the brush misses any part give an extra stroke. The work should not be done with short jabs of the brush, and although cutting-in may be difficult at first it requires only a little practice to become proficient. Confident brush strokes make for speed and less paint to clean off the glass. An alternative to cutting-in is to use a mask (Fig. 20).

Cutting-in to glass enclosed in iron frames is rather difficult owing to the extremely narrow, flat edges which occur next to the glass. The difficulty is usually caused by the glazier using an insufficient amount of putty when bedding the glass. If the narrow edges are well scraped and then made level with putty they will become almost twice as wide and quite easy to paint. Apart from this consideration, the even, flat surface which is then tight against the glass does not allow water from condensation to run down between the glass and the iron frame.

Some workers whiten the window glass when decorating a room. This may be done to convey that a room or a flat is not to let or to prevent inquisitive persons from peering into a room. It has no other purpose and whiting should always be removed before the final coat of paint is applied.

The proper sequence of work demands that the paintwork should be finished before the paperhanging. It is a practice to paint about half an inch of the plasterwork round all the edges of the woodwork: that is, round all architraves (door frames), the underside of picture rails, the top edge of skirting boards and all the edges round cupboards and mantelpieces (if painted). The purpose is to hide uneven cutting

TEMPORARY MEASURE

FIG. 19. *For very short periods only, brushes may be stood upright in water, which will exclude air and so prevent the bristles from hardening.*

of the wallpaper. If the edges of the woodwork are cut-in exactly to the plaster, the paperhanging must be done very accurately or edges will show between the wallpaper and the paint-work.

Before painting kitchens, bathrooms and lavatories, loose tiles should be replaced. It is useless to remove a tile and to attempt to stick it back with cement. There are several preparations on the market specially made for the purpose of refixing tiles. These are excellent as they allow the tiles to be refixed with the minimum of effort. A home-made adhesive, which is equally good, may be made with paste white-lead and japan gold-size.

REPLACING TILES

The material should be used in a rather stiff paste. When it is spread on the back of a tile with a knife (Fig. 21), it should remain as it is applied and not be wet enough to run over the edges.

Remove the loose tile and scrape the cement off the back. Scrape the place from which the tile was removed, then cover the back of the tile and the part of the wall with the paste. Allow a few minutes for the paste to set, then press the tile back into position. A small amount of paste will be squeezed from the joints, but it should not be removed until the tile is properly set.

White lead is a poisonous substance. When using it, even in the form of paint, cuts and scratches on the hands should be covered. After use, the hands should be washed thoroughly and particular care must be taken that no white lead remains in the finger-nails or in the cuticles.

Surfaces painted with white lead, like other preparatory paint-films, need glass-papering before other coats of paint are applied. As the dust of white-lead paint must not be inhaled, it is wise to damp the painted surface with water before glass-papering.

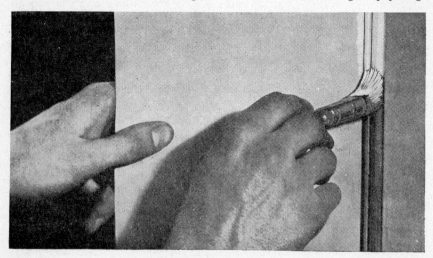

ALTERNATIVE TO CUTTING-IN

FIG. 20. *A simple and perfectly satisfactory alternative to cutting-in is to use a mask in order to protect the glass when painting a window frame.*

TILE ADHESIVE

FIG. 21. *A knife should be used to spread the adhesive on the back of a tile. The paste should be stiff and used fairly thickly. Allow a few minutes for the paste to set.*

Special wet-or-dry glass-paper is manufactured, but a fairly good substitute may be prepared by rubbing the back of ordinary glass-paper with linseed oil and allowing it to dry, or alternatively, giving the back of the glass-paper two coats of knotting varnish. Glass-paper so treated will not become limp and sticky when used on a wet surface.

Surfaces which have been damped with water and glass-papered must be sponged and dried before any further paint is applied. White-lead paint or paint containing red lead must never be applied with a spray gun unless a proper mask is worn.

All painters' materials must be used with due caution. They are not meant to be eaten. By taking reasonable precautions and observing normal cleanliness, any decorating process may be carried out without danger.

The inhalation of the fumes of turpentine is fairly harmless, but washing the hands in turpentine should be avoided. Soap and water with a mild abrasive will free the hands of paint quite effectively.

At the present time there are few baths which have painted surfaces, but they may occur in older houses. It must be remembered that such baths must resist extremely hot water. Several thin undercoats should be given and the paint used should contain the minimum quantity of oil. Special bath enamels are manufactured and this material only should be used for the finishing coat. A full coat of bath enamel should be given and the material should be allowed to harden properly. The method of application is shown in Fig. 22. The bath must not be used for hot water for at least one week after painting. Filling the bath with cold water after the enamel is dry speeds the hardening process.

PAINTING FURNITURE

When painting kitchen and bathroom furniture the surface should be prepared in the same way as for woodwork in general. Kitchen furniture may be greasy, and it is particularly important that all grease and dirt should be removed or the paint will not dry properly. Some quick-drying paints appear to dry on greasy surfaces, but they do not adhere properly.

The main problem in painting furniture is knowing where to start and how to proceed without handling the wet paint. In general, all undersides should be painted first, and the object should be examined from all sides to make sure that no part is missed. All parts of the work which are visible when the object is upside down should be painted first, with the exception of the sides, which should be kept free of paint to allow the painter to turn the object over.

The back of the object should then be painted, following with the sides, but places should still be left for handling. The front of the object should not be painted until it has been put into a position in which it can remain.

There are, no doubt, many objects which cannot be painted in exactly this manner. For instance, objects with many narrow flat edges should have the edges painted before the larger areas. By thinking before an object is painted, the proper order of painting the various parts should be obvious, the hands will not become smothered with paint (the identification mark of the amateur) and parts of the object will not be missed.

Finishing paint for furniture should be of a hard-drying quality, particularly for chairs. The object should be to cover the work properly but to use as little paint as possible. This means that several thin coats are preferable to one or two thick ones. If the work is carried out in this way there will be less likelihood of paint being chipped when the furniture is knocked accidentally.

LINOLEUM PAINT

There are special preparations on the market for painting old linoleum They are very effective for the renovation of shabby floor-coverings and they are quite successful if they are used exactly as recommended. The instructions usually appear on the tin.

All dirt and old wax-polish must be

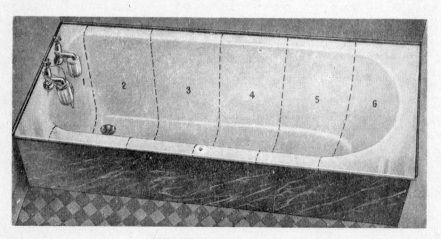

ENAMELLING A BATH

FIG. 22. *After fixing empty jam-jars under the taps to catch any drips of water, a bath should be painted in a series of strips, following the sequence indicated*

removed before the linoleum paint is applied. If soda or sugar soap is used to clean the floor, the material must be washed off properly with cold water. Allow the floor to dry, then rub it all over with a piece of rag which has been damped with turpentine. This removes all traces of polish and when the turpentine has evaporated the floor is ready to be painted. If possible, use the material specially manufactured for the job. If not, make up the paint with elastic varnish and add pigments ground in oil. White pigments should be used as sparingly as possible for this work and, in any case, the less pigment used the better the linoleum paint will wear. It is an added advantage if the colour of the linoleum paint resembles the colour of the floor-covering material. If the work can be completed in one application of paint so much the better, but if it is obvious from the start that two coats will be needed, thin the first coat with turpentine, but use the second coat as supplied.

When the linoleum paint is quite hard, give the floor a coat of floor polish and protect the surface with rugs for some time.

FLOOR DECORATION

Painted wooden floors are unsatisfactory. Surrounds which are not likely to be damaged may be painted in the same manner as other woodwork. Cement floors, however, may be painted with thin, flat paint made with pigments ground in oil, turpentine and japan gold-size. The work should be completed in a single coat and when dry given a good coat of floor polish. Suitable pigments are venetian red and chromium oxide. They may be altered in colour with raw umber, burnt umber, yellow ochre, burnt sienna, raw sienna or ultramarine. White pigments should be avoided.

Cement floors can be made far more attractive than they usually are. Checker-board patterns may be executed in alternate colours to give a tiled effect or borders and surrounds may be added. The floor should be ruled out with a lead pencil or chalk in the pattern desired and each part should be painted separately. White floor-polish should be used for floors painted in two or more colours, but tinted polishes may be used for floors in a uniform colour.

Do not paint tiles or vitreous enamel surfaces. They look well for a short time only, in fact until the paint starts to break down and to discolour.

STAINING A FLOOR

FIG. 23. *A mask should be used to protect the skirting when staining a floor. If any stain should stray on to the skirting it should be removed immediately with a small piece of clean rag.*

Properly stained and varnished work wears very well indeed and it may be executed at a fraction of the cost of ordinary plain painting. A disadvantage is that the grain of cheap woods is not hidden, but, of course, the grain of good-quality woods is shown to advantage.

There are three types of stain which may be used, namely, water, oil and spirit stains. The decorator is concerned with the first two types only.

Water-colour stain is best for clean, new woodwork. It is made up in the following manner: take dry colours which are obtainable at most oil shops or decorators' merchants, mix them with concentrated size powder to the proportions of one part size to six parts dry colour, cover with cold water and mix until a paste forms, then scald with boiling water. A list of dry colours suitable for various woods follows.

Pigment	Wood colour
Yellow ochre	Satinwood
Yellow ochre, 75 per cent } Burnt umber, 25 per cent }	Light oak
Yellow ochre, 50 per cent } Burnt umber, 50 per cent }	Middle oak
Yellow ochre, 25 per cent } Burnt umber, 75 per cent }	Brown oak
Burnt umber	Dark oak
Vandyke brown	Jacobean oak
Black (very thin)* ..	Grey sycamore
Vandyke brown, 75 per cent } Burnt sienna, 25 per cent }	Walnut
Vandyke brown, 75 per cent } Crimson lake, 25 per cent }	Mahogany

*A touch of ultramarine may improve the shade.

Stains should be used warm and brushed on the woodwork quickly. Go over the work once only and do not go back over places which have absorbed the stain, otherwise a dark patch will appear when the work is varnished. Do not use knotting varnish before staining, because the knotting varnish will not absorb the stain.

When the stained work is quite dry it may be varnished. Two coats of varnish are required; the first coat will be absorbed except on the resinous places. The second coat must not be applied until the first is perfectly dry, otherwise the second coat will also be absorbed. If a coat of clear size of medium strength is applied to the stained work, one coat of varnish may suffice for finishing purposes.

USE OF WATER STAINS

Water stain is suitable for large areas of matchboarding or new floors (Fig. 23). It is very transparent and will not, therefore, hide flaws in the woodwork. If nail holes are to be stopped, it is best to stain the woodwork first, and allow it to dry; then stop the holes with putty which has been stained with pigments ground in oil to a similar colour to the woodwork. A day or two should be allowed for the putty to harden on the surface before varnishing is attempted, otherwise the putty will smear as the varnish is applied.

The woodwork should be free of plaster or whiting before the stain is applied. Such materials absorb stain readily and result in dark patches on the finished work.

Oil stain is more suitable for old woodwork than is water stain. The material may be bought ready for use. Ready-made graining colours, scumbles or glazes are similar in composition and they may be used for staining with equal success. All these materials require the addition of turpentine only, although a little raw linseed oil may be added if the wood is very absorbent.

Oil stains should be thin, especially

for pale-wood tints such as waxed pine, sycamore or satinwood. It is permissible to apply two coats of stain to obtain a very deep colour, but, if possible, it is better to produce the full effect in one application. The first coat of oil stain goes into the wood, but a second coat is only partly absorbed and may produce unpleasant dark patches which will only show when the work is varnished.

Oil stain must not be confused with quick-drying, varnish stain. The latter, by reason of its quick-drying quality, forms a hard, brittle film on the surface of the wood. This material is only suitable for temporary work or for touching up damaged places on existing stained and varnished work.

SPECIAL CASES

Flat varnish and egg-shell (semi-gloss) varnish are excellent for interior use when a full gloss is not desired, but these varnishes will not stand up to exterior weather conditions.

Flat and semi-flat varnishes are used for the protection of grained and scumbled work or may be used to give a matt finish to existing glossy surfaces. On a grained surface a single application of flat varnish goes down quite flat. When extra wear is required, a coat of gloss varnish should precede the flat varnish. The flat varnish, in this case only, should be applied before the gloss varnish is quite dry. One coat is usually sufficient, but on existing glossy surfaces which have become hard two coats of flat varnish may be required. Flat varnish, when applied over an existing glossy surface, will not go down quite as flat as a coat which is applied directly to a newly-grained surface, but the extra protection given by the gloss varnish is worth while.

VARNISHING

FIG. 24. *This picture shows how a varnish brush is held. Fair pressure should be applied and no attempt should be made to lay-off the work as when painting.*

Old varnished-surfaces may be revarnished with flattering results, but all dirt and grease on the old surface must be removed prior to revarnishing, otherwise the varnish may not dry at all, or at least it will remain tacky for months.

When varnishing is to be carried out one important rule must be observed. The room must be free of dust and the surface to be varnished must be clean, dry and smooth. Absolute cleanliness is essential and all kettles and brushes must be free of dirt or old paint.

Varnishing magnifies uneven or rough surfaces. Gritty surfaces may be hidden by flat paint, so it is wise to rub the surfaces lightly with a fine glass-paper before the varnish is applied. It is surprising how even the smallest piece of grit becomes a disturbing blemish after it has been varnished.

Gloss varnish is applied in a similar manner to gloss paint and enamel. For good results be liberal with the material. Brush the varnish on in all directions until a reasonable area, say the surface of a door, has been covered. Now go over the work with the brush (without varnish) and work the varnish in all directions until it becomes difficult to brush. Finally brush the work in the direction of the grain (for woodwork) or in one direction for ceilings wand alls.

It is important that the work should be examined after a time to see that the varnish is not running into waves or into tears from the angles of the mouldings. If these faults occur, take the varnish brush and work up the surface. Give a firm, final stroke with the brush in one direction. Brush marks will disappear due to the flowing quality of the material: no attempt, therefore, should be made to soften or lay-off the work as when applying paint (Fig. 24).

PRECAUTIONS

Painters and decorators limit the varnish in their paint kettle to a small amount at a time, and they use that amount up before replenishing it. In this way there is less likelihood of the varnish becoming gritty. It is not always possible to keep the varnish perfectly clean as the brush is liable to pick up dust from walls and floors and this is transferred to the varnish in the kettle.

Painters also varnish large areas first, and window frames and skirtings next. Horizontal surfaces, such as window-sills and shelves, are left until last, when a small amount of varnish is put out specially for such surfaces.

If some varnish remains in the paint kettle when the varnishing is complete, it should be poured through muslin as it is returned to the container so as to remove grit. When stored, the container should be tightly sealed.

Never mix a container of varnish from the bottom as for a tin of paint. When the varnish is stored a sediment settles to the bottom of the container and clarifies the varnish. It is best, therefore, to disturb the container as little as possible. Varnish should be stored at a moderate temperature and not exposed to heat.

OTHER MATERIALS

Flat varnish is applied like flat japan and patent flat-finishes. Best results are obtained if the work is first brushed liberally and then treated with a hair stippler. However, careful application of flat varnish with the brush alone gives satisfactory results, especially on small areas.

Brush on plenty of flat varnish in all directions, taking care that it is distributed evenly. Do not brush the varnish unduly, but lay it off in one direction (or the direction of the grain) as soon as possible. After a surface has been flat varnished, leave it alone. When the varnish has been newly applied, it may appear to be unsatisfactory, but it will settle down quickly and produce a flat, even surface.

Flat varnish appears to be dry long before it really is so, and as fingermarks on the drying surface show when the work has set, newly-finished work should be protected.

Egg-shell varnish may be brushed rather more than the flat and dead-flat varieties. It requires stippling only in very exceptional cases, when, for example, a large area must be covered.

CHAPTER 5

SPRAY PAINTING

USING A SPRAY-GUN FOR PAINT AND DISTEMPER

THE application of paint or distemper by spraying has a special appeal to the amateur craftsman. Spraying has its limitations, but the quality of the finish and the speed of production can be counted as advantages over inexpert brushwork. It should not be imagined that brushes may be dispensed with altogether; how the brush can be usefully employed in conjunction with the spray-gun will be described in detail later.

Spraying is less tiring than brushwork, and eliminates the need for expensive brushes and expert brushing technique. Efficiency may be gained with surprisingly little practice.

The principle involved in spraying is simple. Briefly, the material to be sprayed is introduced into a powerful jet of air which ejects it through the nozzle of the gun in the form of a

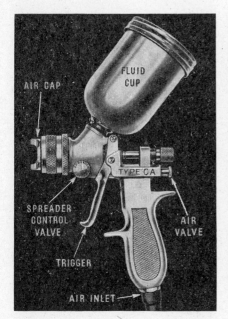

GRAVITY FEED

FIG. 1. *This gun is specially suitable for spraying heavy materials that must be applied at a relatively low pressure.*

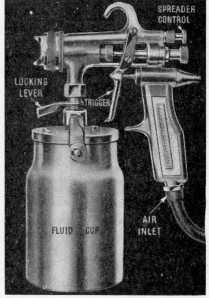

SUCTION FEED

FIG. 2. *As the cup can be detached and replaced in a few seconds this type of gun is excellent for colour changes.*

finely diffused spray. The material is supplied to the gun by gravity feed from a cup above the spray-gun (Fig. 1), by suction from an underslung container (Fig. 2), or from a pressure-pot connected by air-line to the compressor.

There are two main types of spraying machine, those using air pressure supplied by a compressor and those using air volume. The familiar bicycle pump will demonstrate both these principles. When the plunger of the pump is operated, air is pushed rapidly through the connector, but if the air flow is checked by placing the finger over the end of the connector, the air is compressed and on being released is ejected with much greater force.

In the compressor type of machine the air is stored in a tank where it is kept at high pressure by a motor-driven compressor. Such equipment will supply air for one or more spray-guns and is used extensively by painting contractors, motor-car manufacturers, furniture finishers, and in many other industries. In the machines using air volume there is no compressor or container for the air, the air-flow at the spray-gun being maintained by an electrically-driven blower.

AMATEUR EQUIPMENT

Spray painting is a method which until comparatively recently has not been within the reach of amateurs, as in the past spray-work called for complicated and expensive equipment. Today the power unit of most vacuum cleaners may be utilized (Fig. 3), in conjunction with a spray-gun; sometimes even the gun is included in the vacuum-cleaner kit.

For present purposes it is proposed to deal only with the air-volume type of machine. Included in this category are vacuum-cleaner blower units and certain inexpensive self-contained units. Many excellent and inexpensive spray-guns, especially made for easy attachment to the air tube of the blower unit, are obtainable.

When using the blower unit of a vacuum cleaner for spraying, the dust bag must be removed and the flexible air-hose attached to the blower end. Before attaching the spray-gun, the motor should be switched on to clear away any dust. It is essential that the air hose be perfectly clean, and this can be ensured by using the cleaner as a blower before attaching the spray-gun. Any dust left in the tube may result in the jet of the spray-gun becoming choked.

MATERIALS FOR SPRAYING

Almost any liquid which can be applied with a brush may be sprayed, provided that it can be thinned to a spraying consistency. Flat or gloss oil-paints, enamel, varnish, flat enamel, cellulose, lacquer, distemper, stains, creosote and metallic paints are a few of the materials which may be sprayed successfully.

While most paint manufacturers supply special qualities for spraying there is no reason why the amateur should not thin the material with an appropriate thinner. It is, however, important to use the correct thinners as recommended by the maker.

Most ordinary oil-paints, such as undercoating and oil finishing paints, enamels and varnishes, may be thinned with turpentine or white spirit Good quality, white spirit (commonly known as turpentine substitute) is perfectly satisfactory. Although the

VACUUM-CLEANER SPRAY-GUN

FIG. 3. *The power unit of most vacuum cleaners may be employed to operate a spray-gun which is often included in the kit supplied with the machine. The gun can be used not only for decoration purposes, but also for spraying insecticides and for shampooing carpets; but first it is essential to remove all dust from the cleaner.*

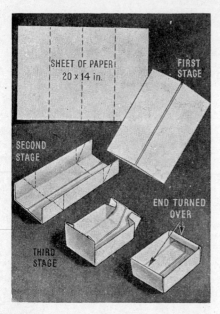

SHEET OF PAPER
20 x 14 in.

FIRST
STAGE

SECOND
STAGE

END TURNED
OVER

THIRD
STAGE

PAPER HAT

Fig. 4. *It is always advisable to cover the head and hair when spraying. A paper hat, as worn by the operator in Fig. 3, may be easily made as shown.*

smell of white spirit resembles that of paraffin, it should not be assumed that paraffin may be used as a substitute. Paraffin would be injurious to the paint.

Turpentine or white spirit is used in the composition of paints for the main purpose of enabling the paint to be applied to the surface with its proper content of oil or gum medium. During the drying process the whole of the turpentine or white spirit evaporates. For this reason oil should never be added to reduce a material to a spraying consistency; it would upset the balance of oil and pigment.

Special thinners, of the amyl-acetate variety, are necessary for all cellulose materials; no other thinners may be used. Ordinary distempers,

water-paints and oil-bound distempers may be thinned with water; for the two latter types petrifying liquid may be employed instead of water if the surface is unduly absorbent.

Materials partially composed of methylated spirit, such as french-polish and spirit varnishes, should be thinned with methylated spirit.

The room in which spraying is done should be kept well ventilated, but draughts should be avoided. The air will become more or less charged with vaporized thinner and pigment particles, but to a lesser extent with the air-volume system than when using compressed air.

Whether to wear a mask or not is for the individual to decide, but in certain circumstances it is imperative. It is advisable, for instance, always to wear a mask when using lead paint. Home Office Regulations forbid the application of lead paints by spray in interior work.

With the air-volume units the need for a mask is not so important, particularly as the work so carried out is seldom extensive or of long duration. In confined spaces good ventilation will do much to minimize any disagreeable effects from spray painting.

PREPARATION

When spraying cellulose in a confined space, a respirator should be worn. A convenient form of mask can be made from a length of tubular mutton-cloth, as supplied by motor-accessories firms, with a pad of cotton-wool in the centre. The pad is placed over the nose and mouth and the mutton-cloth tied at the back of the head. This type of mask is much less irksome to wear than the orthodox respirator available for the work.

Steps should be taken to protect furniture, hangings, floors and personal clothing from spray dust. Upholstery and floors can be covered with old newspapers. Unless the operator is wearing old clothes it is advisable to put on a boiler suit. To cover the head and hair, a paper cap, easily made from a sheet of paper measuring about 20 by 14 in. (Fig. 4), may be employed.

The preparation of surfaces for spray painting is the same as for brushwork. Washing and rubbing-down follow normal practice.

In certain cases it may be desirable to brush the first coat instead of spraying. Strange as it may seem, it is difficult to force the paint into the pores of such surfaces as new plaster, new woodwork, untreated cement-work, chip boards or hard-boards with a spray. The pressure of a brush is much more effective for priming these surfaces.

To obtain good results, it is important to understand the spray-gun and what happens when the material is ejected. Some guns designed for use with a vacuum blower unit are actuated by pressing a trigger; others by placing the thumb over a rear vent hole (Fig. 5). The material to be sprayed is drawn up from the container and blown through the jet in a finely diffused spray. Due to the specially designed jet and the impact of the spray on the surrounding air, the jet of material and air-flow increases in width, starting at approximately $\frac{1}{16}$ in. diameter and increasing to an effective spraying width of 3 to 6 in., depending on the distance the gun is held from the work (Fig. 6). In the centre the concentration of material is greater than at the edges. It will be seen,

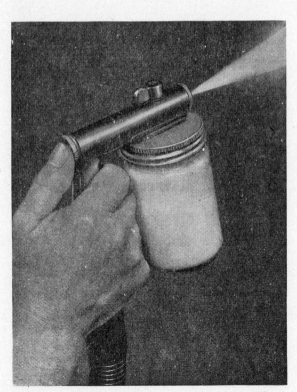

THUMB CONTROL

FIG. 5. *On guns which are not fitted with a trigger control, the spray is started by placing the thumb over a vent hole at the back. This is the type of equipment which is normally supplied for use with vacuum-cleaners.*

therefore, that while the centre of the part being sprayed may be well covered, the edges will have a lighter covering and the material will be blended into the ground. This spill-over, as it is usually called, varies with the type of spray-gun being used and the distance the gun is held from the work (Fig. 7). If the gun is held too close to the work, too much liquid will be applied and runs will result; if it is held too far away, only a mist or powdery coat will be applied. A little practice will soon determine the correct distance, which will vary from 8 to 12 in. according to the material being sprayed and the type of spray-gun in use (Figs. 8–12).

Whenever possible the spray should be at right-angles to the work, the gun being canted slightly inwards at the beginning and end of the stroke. In order to apply an even coat, the movement of the gun should be so regulated

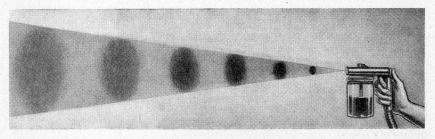

EFFECT OF DISTANCE

FIG. 6. *Shows how at short range the concentration of material is greater in the centre than at the edges. The effect varies with different guns and distances.*

SPILL-OVER

FIG. 7. *Outside the fine atomized spray around the centre, will be a lighter covering which blends towards the edges. This spill-over effect will be found to vary considerably on different guns and determines the method and speed of application.*

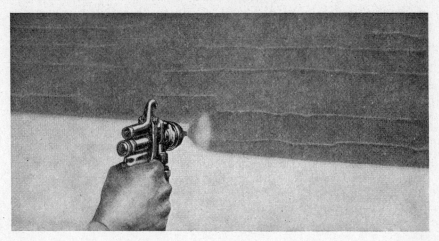

RUNS OR SAGS

FIG. 8. *If the gun is held too close to the surface an unduly heavy coat will be deposited which will result in runs or sags appearing on the finished work.*

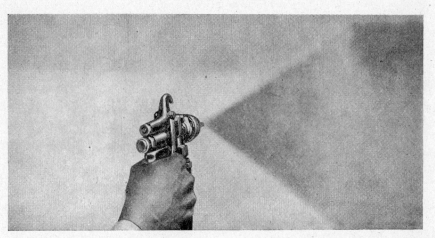

STARVED COAT

FIG. 9. *When the spray-gun is held too far away from the surface a thin, dusty coat will be deposited over a large area which will result in very uneven work.*

that the spray overlaps the previous application sufficiently to blend in and leave a similar amount of material on the surface.

When using a trigger-controlled gun, the amount of paint introduced into the air-flow is variable, so that a narrow band may be obtained by holding the gun closer to the work and applying a lighter pressure to the trigger. With guns having no means for regulating the paint flow, the same quantity of material would be applied over a smaller area, with the consequent need for a speedier movement of the gun.

The speed at which the gun should be moved depends on the consistency and viscosity of the material. Distemper or flat paint will allow a quicker movement than gloss paint, varnish or cellulose. The gun itself should be kept equidistant from the surface, for otherwise an uneven coat will be applied, with a consequent loss of paint as the spray blows past the object.

The gun should be moved evenly and at a speed which will result in the work being only just properly covered. Too slow a movement will result in runs and too quick a movement will make it necessary to go over the work again. Spasmodic movement of the gun leads to loss of time and patchy work.

When the paint has been suitably thinned and the correct working dis-

tance has been determined by tests, the gun should need no further attention and the operator can concentrate on the job. A good plan is to regulate the movement so that the work becomes wet—and only just wet. It is easy to see the difference between a wet coat and a powdery or mist coat.

GOOD PRACTICE

The degree of obliteration with sprayed work is remarkable, and it is often a temptation to finish with one coat. While this is sometimes possible it should not be attempted at the risk of having runs. As with brushwork, two thin coats are better than one thick coat.

On broad areas such as a wall or ceiling, work from the light and take care not to let the edges of each stretch become dry. Have the material ready thinned and strained, so that the container can be refilled without delay. When spraying woodwork having mouldings with deep hollows it is not

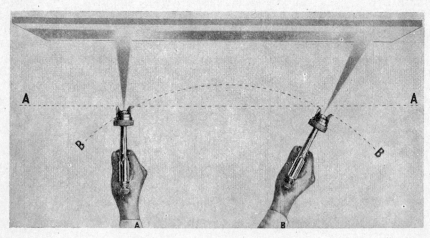

MOVING THE GUN

FIG. 10. *An uneven coat, heavy in the centre and tailing off at the ends of each stroke, results from moving the gun as B-B. Keep it parallel to the surface as A-A.*

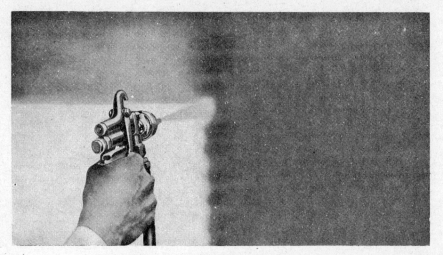

DOUBLE COATING

FIG. 11. *The spraying should be stopped at the end of each stroke, otherwise a double coating will be applied which gives the mottled effect shown.*

always possible to reach the lowest parts without applying too much material. A good plan is to give the moulding a light spray first and to work the paint into the hollows with a small brush. Another light spray will complete the moulding. It is important that the spray should not linger unduly on the mouldings, or tears of paint will appear across the rails.

The spray-gun should always be cleaned on completion of the work or if a job has to be suspended. Some materials set very quickly and a delay of an hour or so may cause the gun to clog. Cleaning is carried out by blowing the appropriate thinners through the gun. First empty the container and clean the gun as much as possible with a rag. Then put some clean thinners into the container and blow it through' the gun into a bucket or in the open air until the passages are clear. Finally wipe the gun thoroughly. Cellulose thinners should be used for cellulose

paints, turpentine or white spirit for oil paints, methylated spirit for spirit varnishes, stains or french-polish. Water should be used for distempers.

Paints which need much stirring or which have skinned over, and made-up paints, must be well strained through gauze or muslin before use.

MASKING

On account of the spill-over and resultant indefinite edge of the spray, it is impossible to cut-in as with a brush. It is therefore necessary to use a mask of some description to prevent the spray from passing beyond the object being painted and disfiguring the adjacent surfaces. A strip of zinc, tin, plywood or cardboard, about 18 in. long and 6 in. wide, will be found quite effective. When clearly defined limits are desired it is wise to do the cutting-in with a small brush. A mask is essential if any over-spray cannot be effectively wiped off, such as when spraying close to a finished ceiling.

Window glass may be masked with adhesive tape, the tape being left in position until the finished coat is hard. Another method is to cover the glass with a sheet of stout paper or cardboard. Alternatively, masking can be ignored and the glass cleaned with a razor blade when the paint is dry and hard. After each coat most of the glass can be cleaned with newspaper, leaving only a strip about 1 in. wide to be cleaned with the razor blade. When spraying distemper against painted work masking may be dispensed with if the paint is hard enough to be cleaned without damage.

All cleaning, except of the window glass, should be done immediately after each spray coat is finished. Spray dust will be more difficult to remove if it is allowed to harden.

When treating new interior woodwork, it is desirable to brush the first coat to ensure proper adhesion and filling of pores. New exterior woodwork, however, should always be given a first coat with a brush. Subsequent coats may be sprayed provided that the day is not too windy, that the work can be efficiently masked and that the brushed coat is not allowed to become too dry and hard before spraying.

The order of spraying woodwork, including deep-cut or carved mouldings, varies little from brushwork. Treat mouldings first, then panels, followed by rails and stiles from the top downwards. If the woodwork is reasonably plain it is possible to begin at the top and finish as the work proceeds.

LATER STAGES

Thin the undercoating with turpentine or white spirit until it sprays with a fine diffusion free from blobs. Thin a sufficient quantity for the job and strain it before use. Do not attempt to do too much with one coat.

When the undercoating is dry and

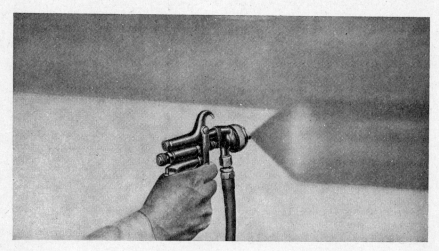

SPLIT FAN

FIG. 12. *A bare patch, as shown here, is usually caused by an obstruction in the fluid tip or air port. The fault can only be rectified by cleaning the nozzle.*

TAKING AN IMPRESSION

FIG. 13. *A piece of thin paper is placed over the border and rubbed with heelball or similar substance in order to reproduce the pattern on the surface.*

hard, take off any bits with fine glass-paper and stop all holes and crevices with putty or hard stopping made from whiting and paste white lead. If desired, coarse-grain or undulating surfaces may also be filled at this stage with a paste made of white-lead paste, whiting and gold-size, thinned to a working consistency with turpentine. Alternatively, one of the well-known proprietary brands of filler may be employed. The filler should be applied with a broad filling knife or stripping knife. Fillers which are mixed with water should be oiled-in, after rubbing down, with gold-size and turpentine applied with a rag; this prevents the filler from absorbing the oil of the finishing coat and leaving dull patches.

It sometimes happens that a wall has to be redistempered without removing the border. This may be done quite successfully by cutting a mask. Take a piece of thin paper about 3 ft. long and a little wider than the border. Lay the straight-edge against the top of the border and rub a piece of heelball, or similar substance, over the paper. This will indicate the pattern (Fig. 13). Now paste a thicker piece of paper on the underside and, when dry, cut out the shape with a penknife or scissors (Fig. 14). With an assistant to hold one end of the mask in position if required, spray about 4 in. (Fig. 15), after which the lower part may be completed without fear of damaging the border during the process.

When spraying a finishing coat of gloss paint, make several tests to avoid over-thinning. Greater care is necessary when spraying gloss paint to ensure that an even coat, free from runs, is applied to the surface.

advance by arranging the furniture in convenient positions. Make sure that the distemper is well strained, work away from the light, and apply two coats. Spray the bed of the ceiling first, then the cornice and frieze.

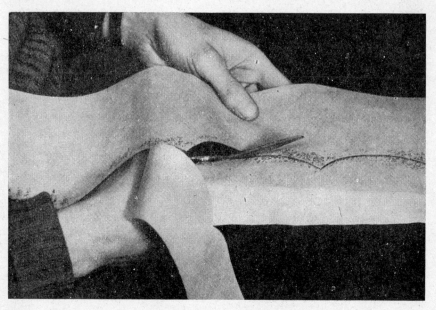

CUTTING THE MASK

FIG. 14. *The outline of the border on the paper is cut out with scissors to form a mask which is used to protect the border while spraying the wall below.*

When walls or ceilings are to be painted it is not advisable to apply a coat of size after the usual preparation. Surfaces which have been treated with washable distemper do not require sizing, and sizing is not required if washable distemper is being sprayed.

Spraying a ceiling is a welcome alternative to brushwork; apart from its speed and absence of brushmarks, the usual scaffolding of steps and board is not so essential. Often a pair of steps, or a box to stand on, is all that is necessary. Plan the work well in

Varnish may be sprayed with excellent results, but the special spraying-quality varnish should be used. The material should be thinned with turpentine or white spirit for all internal and external structural work. To obtain a full, lustrous effect it may be necessary to spray two coats. When dry and hard the first coat should be dulled by rubbing it with a wet cloth dipped in pumice powder. Rinse the surface well and allow it to dry before spraying the next coat.

Due to the rapid drying of cellulose

materials, spraying is often the only effective means of application for areas of any size. Cellulose materials are volatile and highly inflammable, and a naked flame should never be allowed near where cellulose is being sprayed. Much of the thinners used to bring the material to a spraying consistency is diffused into the air during spraying operations, and air, so charged, might constitute an explosive mixture. It is therefore essential to provide the best

SPRAYING OVER A BORDER

FIG. 15. *With the mask pinned or held in position over the border the wall can be sprayed in sections, the mask being moved from one position to another.*

possible ventilation when spraying cellulose in a confined space and whenever possible to spray in the open air. Without proper ventilation the fumes may cause headaches and sickness; a respirator is recommended.

Cellulose paints and fillers should be thinned only with the special thinners supplied by the manufacturers of the paint. It is inadvisable to mix different makes, or to use them together.

Although cellulose finishes may occasionally be applied directly on top of old, very hard oil paint, there is always a risk of causing the old paint to lift. If the oil paint is at all soft or elastic it should be stripped or treated with a sealer such as shellac varnish.

SPECIAL EFFECTS

After some practice with the spray its immense possibilities will be realized. Oil, water, and spirit stains may be sprayed with great success, wiping with a cloth to enhance wood grain when necessary. Metallic powders mixed with clear cellulose lacquer produces extraordinarily beautiful effects.

Graduated, shaded and mottled effects may be obtained by holding the gun at varying distances from the work.

Beautiful effects may be produced by the combined use of the spray and ornamental cut-out profiles. A clear-cut edge against the profile on the one side and a graduated effect on the other provides a unique opportunity for individual experiment. By adjusting and altering the position of the masks and superimposing one over the other a variety of beautiful effects can be obtained. The profiles, masks or stencils should be made of some stout material such as thin plywood.

CHAPTER 6

PLASTIC PAINTING

HOW TO PRODUCE TEXTURE FINISHES

Plastic painting is the term applied to a form of decoration in which the surface is patterned in a low relief. The charming effects which it is possible to produce in this medium provide a welcome change from painted or distempered surfaces. Its use provides unlimited scope for individual taste, imagination and artistry and the average amateur craftsman will find the work to be astonishingly easy. A selection of the simple tools required for plastic painting is shown in Fig. 1.

VARIETIES OF PLASTIC PAINT

There are several varieties of plastic paint on the market. The majority are in the form of a dry powder which only needs to be mixed with water, but some are in paste form and these are generally oil-bound. Most plastic paints are available in white and many pastel shades.

One of the advantages of plastic paint is that it can be applied to rough and undulating surfaces; there is, therefore, hardly any need for filling up, rubbing-down and surfacing. An outstanding advantage is that, as a permanent decorative base, plastic paint may be treated and re-treated at little cost to produce a variety of different colour schemes.

The delicate relief patterning obtainable provides a pleasant background for modern furniture and yet it harmonizes well with period or reproduction pieces and well-chosen

hangings. Some typical textures are shown later.

To some people it is a disadvantage if the plastic paint cannot be removed. Certain types are difficult to remove, particularly when they are oil-bound or have been painted, but material is available which can be removed (if not very easily) after soaking with water. There are advantages for the amateur in working with such materials, as the surface can be treated over and over again in a variety of different ways, including spraying with the paint suitably diluted, and yet the finished work can be removed when a change is desired.

PREPARATION OF GROUND

Almost any ground is suitable for the application of plastic paint, provided that it is sound and stripped of any previous decoration such as soft distemper, poor-quality washable distemper or wallpaper. The surface should also be reasonably non-porous and free from dampness. Preparation of the ground should be carried out on the same lines as for papering or distempering. Decayed plaster and cracks should be repaired, but it is not essential to level off undulating surfaces.

Plastic paint should not be applied over wallpaper, as the adhesion of the paper to the wall is seldom perfect and, in any case, the paper would not resist the soaking action of the compound and the subsequent pull of the material

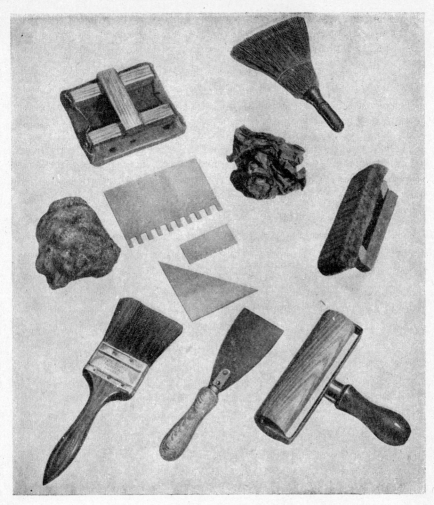

SELECTION OF TOOLS FOR PLASTIC PAINTING

FIG. I. *The very simple tools used for the manipulation of plastic paint include a flat brush, a stripping knife, a wooden roller, a float covered with carpet, various combs, a sponge, a ball of crumpled paper, a whisk and a hessian stippler.*

as it dries out on the surface of the wall.

Plaster surfaces generally need some treatment to render them non-porous. In most cases a coat of medium-strength size, applied hot, is sufficient. In cases of extreme porosity it may be necessary to apply a coat of a special sealer sold for the purpose, or a coat of oil paint.

Surfaces which have been treated with a good-quality washable distemper or water-paint, applied over a well-prepared ground, require no further treatment before the application of plastic paint, other than sponging down with warm water and lightly rubbing-down with glass-paper.

Painted or varnished surfaces should be washed with a strong solution of common soda, rubbed down with coarse glass-paper and well rinsed, to cut the hard film and provide a key for the application of plastic paint.

APPLICATION

If plastic paint is applied over match-boarding, it should not be expected that the paint will entirely eliminate the joints, no matter how well they are filled. The reason is that the boards are subject to expansion and contraction according to atmospheric conditions, and hair cracks are likely to appear at the joints when the boards move.

Plaster-boards, wall boarding and plywood may be successfully coated with plastic paint if previously treated for suction.

The consistency of the mixed material, the amount required and the method of application depend largely on the selected pattern of the texture and the depth of the relief. If a medium-fine-grain texture is desired, the material may be applied with a 4-in. or 6-in. flat brush. If a heavy relief is proposed, it may be quicker, easier and more economical to apply the material with a plasterer's laying trowel.

For average textures, the material should be mixed into a fairly stiff paste, free from lumps, according to the maker's instructions. Applied in

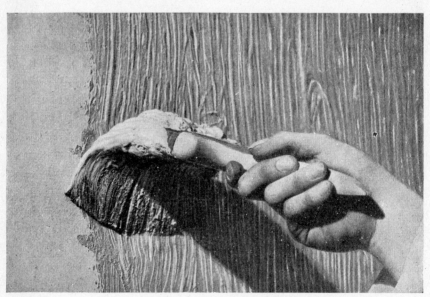

METHOD OF APPLICATION

Fig. 2. *For a medium-fine-grain texture the material should be applied with a 4-in. or 6-in. flat brush. To distribute the material evenly, it should be heavily brushed. For effects in heavy relief the material may be applied with a trowel.*

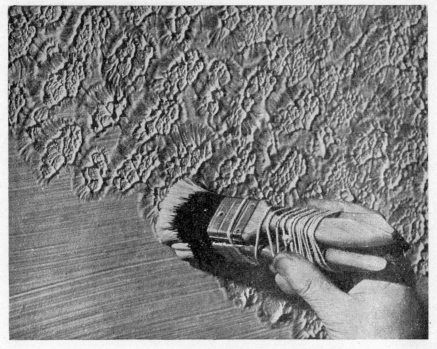

FLORAL PATTERN

Fig. 3. *Three paint brushes tied together with string form an interesting pattern when they are dipped in different colours and pressed into the paint. For this effect it is an advantage to apply the plastic paint fairly thickly and evenly.*

regular patches, preferably from right to left, it should be brushed heavily (Fig. 2) and vigorously so as to ensure even distribution of the material, if such a condition is necessary for the proposed texture. For some textures it is an advantage to apply the material unevenly.

Plastic paint is not particularly easy to cut-in to defined limits. Masking tape should, therefore, be used when the scheme includes panelling or mouldings. Gummed-paper tape is quite useful and should be wetted on both sides so that it may easily be removed on completion of that particular part of the work. Where it is not possible to use tape, it is best to use a small brush to cut-in, cleaning up with a sponge as necessary. Application of the ground coat should proceed fairly quickly in order to allow the texturing to be carried out while the material is still wet and plastic.

Texturing and patterning must be carried out while the material is still in a plastic state; a great variety of tools and gadgets may be used for the purpose. Special tools are available, but they are not essential. The tools required can be made quite easily at home or improvised.

As the plastic material is so responsive to manipulation it is advisable for one person only to carry out one method of texturing. But where, for example, a room calls for the use of two texturing methods, two persons could be employed provided that each confined his attentions to his particular texture. It is unlikely that two people would produce the same texture even though each used the same tool and method.

The variety of texture and patterns which can be produced is limited only by the imagination and manipulative skill of the worker. From the simple low-relief stipple to the heavy lace texture, and from abstract brushwork to more conventional forms of ornamentation, there are vast opportunities for experiment as shown in Figs. 3-10.

The most popular and easily ob-

DIFFERENT TEXTURES

FIG. 5. *It is often possible to combine different textures with good effect. In this case, sponge and comb work used together provide a fascinating contrast.*

tained objects for texturing include sponges, the brush used for application, wooden rollers and wooden floats covered with canvas or carpet. These, together with other useful tools, are shown in Fig. 1. The depth of the texturing can be regulated according to how the material is spread. Do not add more water to the paste to make it go farther; too much water is inclined to make the texture droop.

A popular method of texturing is with a sponge. After about 1 sq. yd. has been coated with the plastic paint, one side of the sponge should first be

SIMPLE IDEA

FIG. 4. *Stippling the surface with the same brush as is used for applying the material produces another texture which is also quite pleasing in a large room.*

dabbed on some of the material and then dabbed on to the wall, covering every part equally. A slightly different effect may be obtained by employing a twisting and lifting movement. For plain, stippled effects resembling fibre brushes are also useful for texturing, the fan-shaped clothes whisk being a notable example (Fig. 8).

When a self-coloured effect is proposed, the method of patterning and the tools should be carefully chosen so

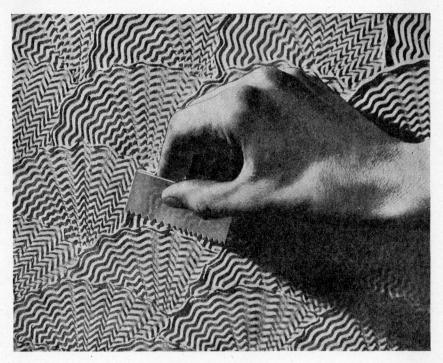

SHELL PATTERN

FIG. 6. *A piece of celluloid with a serrated edge, drawn over the material to form the shape of a shell, produces a novel effect for small decorative panels.*

pebble-dash, nothing is better than a hessian stippler. This is made of a square piece of wood with the edges and corners softened, covered with two thicknesses of canvas, and with pieces of wood nailed at the back to form a handle. Carpet will do just as well as canvas. This form of stippler is easy to use and allows the texture to be uniform throughout the job. Stiff that the ground is not exposed by too vigorous a treatment. Brushes, sponges, fibre brushes and stipplers do not present any difficulty, but stiff combs and the like may cut through the material and expose the colour of the ground.

Many textures, particularly those obtained by a lifting action, result in a number of sharp points. These sharp points may be flattened by dragging a piece of celluloid over the surface. A triangular set-square is ideal for this purpose. The material is allowed to set partially and the edge is dragged over the tops at a suitable angle and in all directions. The tool should be moistened at every stroke on a wet sponge. This treatment enhances the effect and gives the work a more regular appearance.

Highly decorative schemes may be carried out by painting and glazing the finished texture. Carefully chosen ground colours scumbled with delicate tints produce the most charming and colourful effects. With this method it is customary to use white or cream material for the texturing. When dry it may need glass-papering, according to the method employed for patterning.

FINE SCROLLS
FIG. 7 (*Above*). *Pleasant combination of sponge-stippling and ornamental scrolls for a setting over a mantelpiece.*

CLOTHES WHISK
FIG. 8 (*Left*). *How the scrolls illustrated in Fig. 7 are produced by means of a clothes whisk.*

FIG. 9. *A wooden roller, dipped into the plastic paint and passed lightly over the wall, gives this effect. When the material has set slightly, the result is improved by drawing a piece of celluloid over the texture.*

After dusting down well, the texture should be given a coat of paint or sealer, care being taken to ensure that every part is well covered.

The next consideration is the ground colour. If a plain-painted effect is desired, the work should be given two coats; an undercoating similar to the colour of the finishing coat, followed by one coat of gloss paint. If a glazed and scumbled effect is required, it is usual to follow the coat of sealer with a ground coat of semi-gloss paint of a light tone, and then to scumble with a thin transparent glaze of a deeper tone or different colour.

Probably the most delightful effects are obtained by scumbling over a broken-white or cream ground with transparent colours such as bright green, burnt umber, prussian blue, crimson lake, or raw sienna. For example, an old-parchment effect may be produced by preparing a ground of white paint to which a very little chrome yellow has been added and then scumbling with a transparent glaze tinted with raw sienna and black. Similarly, old ivory can be imitated by using the same colours in varying shades.

Proprietary brands of tinted scumble-glazes and transparent glazes are obtainable from most decorators' stores. The tinted glazes usually

LACE PATTERN

FIG. 10. *Example of the beautiful finish which is produced with the wooden roller shown in Fig. 9. The effect is enhanced by painting and glazing the surface after it has been allowed to dry and harden.*

require thinning before they are used.

Home-made glazes are seldom as satisfactory as the factory-made variety, but one to which colours ground in oil can be added may be made from two parts raw linseed-oil, two parts turpentine or white spirit, and one part of soapy distilled water. To each pint add some patent driers (the size of a walnut) and a little whiting. The mixture should be thoroughly shaken.

Although this formula is unconventional it will give excellent results.

The glaze should be applied fairly liberally and should be subsequently brushed out to an even film. It will be found that the general effect is considerably improved by wiping the work carefully with a cloth, to pick out the highlights and leave varying shades in the hollows. A rubber squeegee can be used on some textures to remove the glaze from the highlights; this has the effect of producing greater contrast.

FURTHER SUGGESTIONS

Painted and glazed surfaces are washable, but greater protection may be given to the glaze by varnishing. Flat or gloss varnish may be used. When flat varnish is used a more durable effect is gained by applying the gloss varnish first.

A pleasing leather effect may be obtained by rolling crushed tissue-paper or newspaper into a thin coat of the plastic paint. A thickness of about $\frac{1}{16}$ in. is applied and allowed to set slightly. The paper is then crushed into a ball, opened out to about half its original size, and firmly rolled into the material with a wooden roller. After about fifteen minutes the paper may be carefully peeled away, leaving a very tolerable imitation of a leather grain. When this is painted and glazed as already described, the result is truly remarkable.

Self-colour plastic paint cannot usually be washed, but instead of painting and glazing as a means of re-decoration, it may be renovated very simply by spraying it with a very thin coat of the same material.

There is wide scope for new methods of treatment, but they should first be tested on a wide board.

CHAPTER 7

PAPERHANGING

CORRECT PROCEDURE FOR WALLS AND CEILINGS

THE difficulties which the amateur craftsman may experience are usually due to his being unaware of the few simple rules on which success depends. While paperhanging is not particularly difficult, the beginner often adds to his difficulties by making shift and by trying out short cuts. This is seldom helpful, as a feature of paperhanging is that every part of the work is simplified by careful attention to detail in the preceding operation. This fact will be realized as the instructions develop.

As the average householder may not always have all the equipment used by the professional, alternatives will be suggested where possible.

Firstly, it must be pointed out that the practice of hanging new paper over

FINISHED RESULT

FIG. 1. *Part of the room in which the photographs illustrating this chapter were taken. Many of the features such as the bell-push, fireplace and electrical fittings, which are shown later in close-up, may be identified in this view. This picture was made after the papering had been finished.*

MEASURING ROUND THE ROOM

FIG. 2. *A simple method of finding the number of widths of wallpaper required, is to go round the walls with a piece of paper, marking each width with chalk.*

old cannot be too strongly condemned; not only is it unhygienic, but any irregularities on the surface of the old paper may show through the new. Edges which have come unstuck, but are not visible, may show as a result of the contraction of the new paste, which will pull the paper farther from the wall. Stripping the old paper, when carried out in the proper manner, is not an arduous task and the time and labour expended are undoubtedly well spent, if only to obtain a better finish.

CHOICE OF PAPER

There are two main considerations in choosing a wallpaper—cost and suitability. It does not always follow that the greater the cost, the greater the durability. Much depends on the toughness and texture of the paper and the character of the printing. Some of the higher-priced papers are more affected by abrasion and moisture than are the cheaper varieties. When considering the suitability of a paper, it is essential to take into account whether it is for, say, a dining-room, drawing-room, bedroom, or nursery, and to choose a paper which is not only in keeping with the room and its furniture as far as colour and design are concerned, but one which is also sufficiently durable to withstand the treatment it is likely to receive. Varnished papers, preferably varnished after hanging, are more durable for bathrooms, lavatories and kitchens, and probably a paper grounded and printed in oil colours is more suitable for a nursery where children's finger-marks might deface the walls.

Other considerations are the colours of the paintwork and distemper (if already decided) and the colour and style of the furniture, carpets and pictures, so that the whole may harmonize. It may be that the householder has very definite views about the paintwork and decides on its colour before choosing the paper. Generally, however, when the whole room is to be redecorated, including the paintwork and the ceiling, the paper is chosen first and the colours of the paint and distemper arranged to harmonize.

The main purpose of wallpaper is to provide a background which will provide a pleasing setting and which will tone with the general colouring of the room.

Rolls of wallpaper are technically known as pieces, but for the sake of simplicity they will be referred to as rolls or pieces according to the sense.

FINDING THE NUMBER OF ROLLS

In order to calculate the amount of paper required, it is necessary first to know the dimensions of a roll. Foreign wallpapers are made in various lengths and widths. English papers are supplied in rolls approximately 12 yd. long and 21 in. wide (when trimmed). Certain papers, of a better quality, are supplied in double and half pieces. For present purposes the English variety only will be considered.

The pieces of wallpaper which extend from the ceiling or picture rail to the skirting, technically known as long lengths, should be continuous. It therefore follows that the number of rolls required depends largely on how many of these long lengths can be cut from one roll. The first step is to determine how the roll will cut up.

In modern houses the measurement from the top of the skirting to the underside of the picture rail is usually about 6 ft. 6 in. in the lower rooms and 6 ft. in the upper rooms, depending, of course, on the height at which the picture rail (if any) has been fixed. It

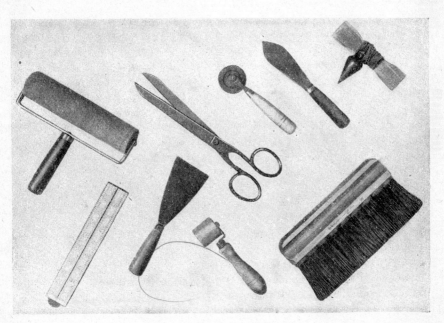

TOOLS FOR PAPERHANGING

FIG. 3. *Apart from a few items of equipment common to other work, the paperhanger will require the tools illustrated: a smoothing roller, rule, stripping knife, seam roller, scissors, casing-wheel, putty knife, plumb-line and hanging brush.*

is impossible to cut the paper to fit exactly, and in any case the paper stretches considerably when pasted. About 4 to 6 in. should, therefore, be added for final trimming to skirting and rail during the process of hanging.

Assuming that the drop measures 6 ft. 6 in., allow 6 in. for cutting-in to the tops and bottoms, and make the long length 7 ft. Out of a 12-yd. roll of plain paper it would be possible to cut five long lengths of 7 ft. each, leaving a short end of approximately 1 ft. With a patterned paper there would be a certain amount of wastage due to the need for matching the pattern and perhaps only four lengths could be obtained out of one roll.

FINDING THE NUMBER OF LENGTHS

After solving this problem, the next step is to count the number of long lengths required. This is easily done by taking a strip of paper 21 in. long and gauging round the room (Fig. 2), taking the chimney breast into account but not the doors or windows. Divide the result by the number of lengths obtainable from one roll. If the number of long lengths counted were twenty-four and the number obtained from one roll were four, six rolls would provide all the long lengths required. The spaces above and below the windows and over the door (technically known as unders and overs) are generally taken care of by using the remnants of the rolls. In the case of patterned paper the amount which will be left over is problematical and it is wise to allow an extra piece to permit of proper matching.

Another method is to calculate the entire area to be papered in square yards and to divide by seven, the answer being the number of pieces required. It must be remembered, however, that as the area of a piece of paper is exactly 7 sq. yd., an extra roll or so may be required, according to circumstances, for wastage and cutting. An extra piece in the ratio of one to each seven pieces is generally found to be sufficient.

For the average paperhanging job the equipment need not be very extensive. The following tools, some of which are in Fig. 3, will be required.

WETTING OLD WALLPAPER

FIG. 4. *Plenty of hot water should be applied with a brush before attempting to remove old wallpaper with a stripping knife. The wetter the paper, the easier it will be to remove from the wall.*

Paste brush. Usually a wide flat distemper brush. It may be slightly worn, but it is a mistake to use a half-worn brush if it can be avoided.

Scissors. Paperhangers' scissors have long blades which make for speed. Ordinary household scissors are quite satisfactory for the amateur except for trimming the edges.

Hanging brush. This is used for smoothing down the paper when applying it to the wall. A special brush is made for the purpose. It has long bristles which enable the paper to be tucked into angles. A reasonable substitute is an ordinary clothes brush; some hanging brushes resemble a clothes brush, except that the bristles are fuller and slightly longer.

Plumb-line. Used for testing the alignment of the paper; it consists of an egg-shaped piece of lead or brass attached to a thin twine. Any small, heavy object tied to a thin string will serve as a substitute.

Foot (or longer) rule. Necessary for measuring length.

Apron. This should have a large pocket for holding different tools.

Tear-stick. A bevelled wooden lath, 24 in. long and about ½ in. thick, used for cutting paper on the table.

In addition to the articles already mentioned, the professional paper-hanger usually employs a hand trimmer, casing wheel and rollers. These are not strictly necessary. Trimming of the selvedge can be done equally well with a knife and a straight edge, while a sharp, half-worn table knife or cobbler's knife is a good substitute for a casing wheel. If a hand trimmer is available, however, it is a very convenient tool and the instructions on trimming will include references to its use. Many home decorators will prefer

STRIPPING THE PAPER

Fig. 5. *When soaked, the paper should be easy to remove by running the stripping knife over the wall with a firm sliding action. If necessary, wet the paper again; let the water do the hard work.*

to have the paper trimmed by the supplier; the cost of trimming is trivial, but the result is not always satisfactory. Although the practice is unusual, some paperhangers maintain that it is quicker to trim the paper after the lengths have been pasted: whichever method is adopted, however, it is well worth while to become proficient in using scissors.

ANCILLARY EQUIPMENT

In addition to the tools already mentioned, the following will be required :

Trestle table. The professional uses a specially made pasting table, which consists of a pair of light trestles and a pair of boards, each measuring 6 ft.

FIG. 6. *Stripping should be done in neat square patches and particular care should be taken to avoid damaging the surface of the plaster. The paper should require little more than touching with the stripping knife.*

long and 11 in. wide, laid together on the trestles; the two boards being approximately the width of the paper. While it is convenient to have the proper paste-boards, it is possible to make do with a kitchen table of suitable size.

Steps. Ordinary household steps are quite satisfactory, especially the lattice type, which are strong and serviceable. Whether this type or builders' steps are used, it is wise to make sure that they are soundly constructed and that the cords are secure. Sometimes the hinges need attention and a screw must be tightened here and there.

Scaffold. A scaffold consisting of two pairs of steps and a scaffold board is necessary for such work as lining ceilings. A complicated form of scaffold may be necessary when papering a staircase. It is important that any such scaffold or other improvisation should be thoroughly sound. Any neglect in this respect may cause a serious accident and it is always better to be safe than sorry. Scaffold boards are $1\frac{1}{2}$ in. thick and of varying lengths. The boards should be lined, that is, placed one above the other, when the span is over 10 ft.

An improvised scaffold should be considered carefully from the safety aspect. A kitchen table may be used if the ceiling is not too lofty, but care must be taken not to walk off the edge while the work is in progress!

The importance of cleanliness cannot be too strongly stressed. Scaffolding which has been used for work prior to paperhanging may be thickly coated with plaster or distemper droppings and should be washed. Otherwise a good job may be spoiled by dirty marks. If the scaffolding is not cleaned the distemper or plaster may also drop in the room and be trodden into the floor covering; its removal is not easy.

It is advantageous to prepare the walls and ceiling at the same time, the upper stretch of the walls being more easily dealt with from the scaffold used to reach the ceiling.

STRIPPING WALLPAPER

Walls to be papered should be stripped bare to the plaster. First the paper should be damped several times with water, using a brush as shown in Fig. 4. When sufficiently soaked it can be easily removed with a stripping knife (Fig. 5). The stripping should be done in neat patches (Fig. 6), employing long firm strokes. When approaching rails, skirtings or other limits, the stripping knife should be moved parallel to the object, not at right-angles to it. The reason for this is that the plaster is often insecure near the skirting and, in the case of a picture rail, the stripped paper may be wedged between the rail and the wall.

If the paper to be stripped happens to be varnished or painted, some difficulty will usually be experienced in causing the water to penetrate the paper. The use of solvents such as soda or varnish removers is not always necessary. It is better to employ some method of scoring the surface to allow the water to penetrate. A sharp tenon-saw blade drawn over the sur-face in several directions will be found to be very effective. The water percolates through the scratches and softens the paste sufficiently to enable the paper to be removed in the usual way. A wire brush or a piece of large-tooth hack-saw blade may also be helpful.

When the stripping has been completed and the waste paper cleared away, the next step is to wash the wall thoroughly. Warm water is best for this purpose, using a scrubbing brush vigorously and then sponging off to clean the surface. A piece of hessian will serve just as well as a sponge. When stripping up to a cornice which has been distempered, care should be taken to scrape out any distemper which may have collected in the crevice. If this is not done there is a danger of the new paper peeling away. The wall surface should now be repaired, loose plaster being cut away and all cracks and nail holes filled. When the filling material is thoroughly dry, the whole of the wall surface should be rubbed down with medium-grade glass-paper, giving special attention to any repair work at the same time.

USE OF SIZE

Next, give the walls a coat of glue-size; the object is not entirely to prevent porosity but rather to present a surface which is only slightly but uniformly absorbent. Cake glue, concentrated powder size or vegetable size may be used. If cake glue is used it should be broken into pieces with a hammer, and soaked in cold water for twenty-four hours. It should then be heated gently and water should be added until the consistency is such that when cold it will set as a medium-strength jelly. Powder sizes generally have directions for use on the packet.

A good plan is to mix the powder with cold water into a paste and to add hot water according to requirements.

Whether the ceiling is to be papered or finished in soft (size-and-whiting) distemper, it should be treated in similar manner to the walls. If the ceiling is to be lined as a preparation for distempering, the procedure is somewhat different, sizing being deferred until the time of lining.

Walls which have been distempered with ordinary size-bound distemper should be washed bare to the plaster surface, but washable distemper need not be removed provided that it is adhering firmly. With all surfaces, whether plaster, plaster-board or wallboard, the golden rule is to stop abnormal suction by sizing.

DAMP WALLS

Dampness is one of the most serious causes of the disfigurement of walls and ceilings. The reader is therefore advised to consider carefully the advice given in other chapters on dealing with damp walls, their causes and cure, for if due care is not exercised, and the necessary preventive action taken, there is a danger of the new work being damaged.

When the cause of dampness has been removed, it is necessary to allow the affected parts to dry out in order to avoid damaging the new wallpaper. If the dampness is not of long standing, little else may be necessary other than allowing it to dry out naturally. It is better for the dampness to dry out naturally, but there is not always time for this before the re-papering is carried out. Apart from the unsightly patch on new paper caused by any damp parts not having dried out, there is a danger of the colour in the paper being bleached or otherwise changed. Some workers, therefore, paint the damp patches with a coat of shellac knotting or paint, but this practice is not recommended as a suitable treatment for dampness.

SHADING AND TRIMMING

It is impossible for manufacturers to guarantee that every batch of paper run off a machine is exactly the same shade. The variation may be almost imperceptible, or at times quite noticeable. If the rolls in a batch of paper vary in shade to a very marked extent, they should be returned to the merchant for exchange. Sometimes the difference is so slight that it could escape notice, until the paper had been applied to the wall and had dried out, when the difference in shade might be very noticeable. A slight difference, however, might not matter if the joint between the two shades were arranged to occur at an angle.

The method of shading the paper is shown in Fig. 7. About a yard of each piece should be run out on the table, one above the other, showing about an inch of the pattern. The table should be in a well-lighted position. By careful scrutiny and interchange of the position of the rolls it will be possible to detect any difference in shade and to segregate any faulty pieces. If there are two shades it is a good plan to mark the end of the rolls affected: A for one shade and B for the other. Later, by careful management, it may be possible to arrange for the change to occur at an angle.

All paper except lining paper should be trimmed, preferably on both edges. Some workers consider that a quicker and easier job is possible if one edge only is trimmed. This is not entirely

FIG. 7. *When dealing with most papers it is convenient to lay several pieces face up on the table as a guide for shading and matching. Careful study of any pattern will enable the paper to be cut with the minimum of waste.*

correct. Apart from the fact that it is impossible to hide the joints when the paper is lapped, it is easier and much quicker to work when both edges are trimmed.

The pattern on an English wallpaper is 21 in. wide. There is a selvedge about ½ in. wide on each side, and this must be trimmed off. This selvedge is not always of equal width on both sides—a point to remember when trimming.

Plain papers, or semi-plain papers which have no definite pattern to match, should be trimmed by at least 1 in. The method to be adopted when trimming depends on the character of the paper. In the past, paperhangers used long scissors (Fig. 8), but in recent years a number of trimming appliances have been put on the market, from the expensive rotary type of machine, which trims both edges at once, to the comparatively cheap hand trimmer (Fig. 9), which trims one edge

at a time. It is highly improbable that any professional paperhanger today trims his paper with scissors.

Most papers may be trimmed easily and well with these hand trimmers, but for the guidance of those who may be inclined to buy one, a type which has a cutting wheel, or more than one, is recommended.

Small pieces of wood fibre are used in the manufacture of certain papers. When trimming such a paper the hand trimmer is not satisfactory; the small pieces of wood catch in the wheels and cause the paper to tear. The best method in this case is to use a straight-edge and a sharp knife (Fig. 10).

Hand trimmers usually have a pair of cutting wheels and an adjustable guide which governs the distance from the edge of the paper to the cutting point. When this type of trimmer is properly adjusted, the paper can be drawn through the trimmer continuously. First take a ruler and lay it on the selvedge at the end of the roll, making a short pencil line where the paper should be trimmed. Now release the screw of the guide, pass the guide over the edge of the paper as far as it will go, adjust the wheels to the pencil mark and tighten the screw. Having adjusted the trimmer it is advisable to make a test before proceding to trim the whole piece. A few inches should be trimmed, and the result carefully examined to ensure that neither too much nor too little is being taken off.

To begin trimming, pass the trimmer on to the paper and rotate the cutting wheels with the thumb and finger, at the same time giving the trimmer a forward motion. Having pushed the trimmer to arm's length, the operation should then be carried out by drawing the paper through the trimmer as previously described. It is important that the trimmer be held in close contact with the edge of the paper. Before beginning to trim the other edge the trimmer must be re-adjusted, as the selvedge is rarely the same width on each side.

ACCURATE TRIMMING

Nothing helps so much in paperhanging as accurate trimming. The aim should always be to avoid showing the joints and this is impossible if the trimming is at all wavy. For this reason the guide of the hand trimmer must always be in close contact with the edge of the paper. If this is not done a wavy edge will result. Undoubtedly the best of all trimming is done with a straight-edge and knife, a method which can be well commended to the amateur. Three articles will be necessary for this

TRIMMING WITH
SCISSORS

FIG. 8. *By supporting the paper on the outstretched legs, the scissors can be held in one hand while the other hand is used to unroll the paper by pulling upwards.*

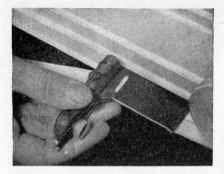

HAND TRIMMER

FIG. 9. *Close-up of a hand trimmer showing how it should be held. If the instrument is correctly adjusted and kept in contact with the paper close to the roll, it will operate efficiently.*

method: a perfectly true straight-edge, a sharp knife, and something on which to cut.

The professional uses a 3-ft. steel straight-edge and a strip of zinc about 3 ft. 6 in. long and 4 in. wide. Knives vary in pattern, each worker having his own favourite shape. Steel straight-edges are expensive and it may therefore be necessary to improvise. The

blade of a tee-square is a suitable substitute, or a carpenter could make a bevelled, wooden straight-edge to order. Instead of the zinc strip a piece of plywood could be used, or a strip of hard cardboard. A trimming knife can

USEFUL GADGET

FIG. 11. *An ingenious fitment, invented by the author of this chapter, for holding the roll of wallpaper while trimming it with any of the devices mentioned.*

KNIFE AND STRAIGHT-EDGE

FIG. 10. *An old table-knife and a steel straight-edge are the tools which many craftsmen prefer for trimming purposes. It is surprising how quickly and accurately an experienced workman can trim in this way.*

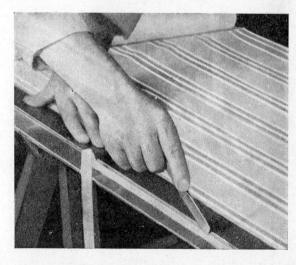

be made out of an old table-knife. It should be sharpened to a keen edge and kept sharp by an occasional rub on an oilstone. A pocket-knife is equally satisfactory if well sharpened.

The trimming operation is facilitated if a piece of thin card is gummed under one end of the straight-edge to act as a guide, the projection being equal to the width to be trimmed off. The best plan is to attach the slip and to cut it to length after adjusting the straight-edge to the correct position. As the selvedge is seldom the same width on each side, the gummed strip

USING A TEAR-STICK

FIG. 13. *With the roll in the right hand, position the tear-stick and pull the paper smartly towards the left shoulder.*

ASSESSING THE LENGTH

FIG. 12. *A most convenient method of finding the length of paper required is to roll it up the wall and to remove the end at the top with a tear-stick.*

may need some adjustment before trimming the other edge.

First lay the roll on the table with the end towards the operator. Place the straight-edge in position with the end of the gummed slip true to the edge of the paper and the straight-edge in line with the pattern. Make sure to hold the straight-edge down firmly while cutting. After the initial cut has been made, it will be seen that the adjustment of the straight-edge is a simple matter and that subsequent trimming can be carried out quickly and accurately. As the paper is trimmed, it should be rolled up and another length drawn out for the next cut. It is convenient to check the movement of the roll by passing a piece of string through the middle, fastening the ends with a small nail or drawing pin. Alternatively, a holder as shown in Fig. 11 may be employed.

Remember that it is possible to have paper already trimmed at a slight extra cost. Provided that the paper is properly trimmed this is an admirable scheme. Unfortunately, it is not always possible to rely on the paper being accurately trimmed.

The rotary machines which trim both edges at one operation need very skilful handling to give perfect results. Papers which are unevenly rolled must first be re-rolled loosely and knocked square before placing them in the machine or the paper will be trimmed unevenly. Often the retailer is reluctant to devote the extra time to the work. It is well to remember, though, that the man who trims the paper in the shop is not going to apply it. It is therefore advisable to consider the matter carefully and if at all possible to trim the paper oneself.

More care and attention are needed with a patterned paper than with a plain one, and some consideration should be given to this problem before cutting up the lengths. The pattern on a wallpaper is repeated at regular

CUTTING LENGTHS

FIG. 14. *After measuring the first length, it is placed on the paste-board to serve as a guide for cutting the remainder. The paper is rolled from left to right where it is torn with the straight-edge. Note how the rolls are stacked underneath the table.*

intervals, these intervals being known as repeats. Sometimes the match is square across the paper. This is known as a match-across or set pattern. If the pattern does not match square across, the match will be found half a repeat away. This is a half-drop pattern. In ordinary paper the length of the drop or repeat varies from 2 in. to as much as 15 in. For the sake of economy this will need consideration when cutting up the lengths, particularly when using a half-drop pattern.

The next step is to cut up the long lengths: the pieces which extend from the cornice or picture rail to the skirting. It is usual to cut up sufficient long lengths for the room at one operation. The first length is cut to the proper dimensions and the subsequent lengths are cut by using the first length as a

guide. If, however, the paper is of the patterned variety it should be arranged that the outstanding feature of the design is clear of the cornice or rail.

The most convenient method of assessing the length is to roll the paper up the wall (Fig. 12). If the end of the roll is at the top, the end of the paper may be taken off, using the tear-stick for the purpose, allowing 2 in. beyond the outstanding pattern.

To use the tear-stick, take the roll in the right hand, place the tear-stick in the desired position and pull the paper smartly against the bevelled edge, aiming at the left shoulder (Fig. 13).

When rolling the paper up the wall, allow a 2-in. overlap at the bottom and the top. This is for trimming-in when hanging.

If the paper is the right way up when

FOLDING AFTER PASTING—FIRST STAGE

FIG. 15. *When dealing with short lengths, fold the paper so that the two outer edges will meet. The first step is shown in this illustration. Avoid creasing the bend.*

STARTING THE SECOND FOLD

FIG. 16. *Pick up the left edge of the paper between the thumb and forefinger and lift it, as shown, to bring it towards the centre. Grip the paper lightly.*

it is rolled up the wall, it may be necessary to lower the paper a little on account of the pattern before allowing the extra length and cutting off. Afterwards it should be checked again for length to ensure that no more than 3 in. has been allowed at the top and bottom for wastage.

After cutting the first long length, it is laid on the table and used as a guide for the remainder (Fig. 14). The number of lengths required should have been assessed already by gauging round the room with a 21-in. stick, or a piece

of wallpaper as previously described.

At this stage it is necessary to refer again to the pattern. If it is a half-drop pattern it may be economical to cut alternately from two rolls. The right-hand end of the paper should be about 3 in. from the end of the table with the tear-stick lying on it. This would leave about a foot hanging over the left-hand end of the table. Now take the roll in the right hand and adjust the end to the end of the first length which is being used as a guide, then move the paper to the left until the pattern is in the correct position. The next step is to run the paper out and to tear off the length in line with the end of the first length. The position of the pattern during this operation depends on whether it is a match-across or a half-drop. If it is a match-across, the pattern should be immediately above the pattern on the previous length; if a half-drop it should be midway between the repeats. In the latter case the position of the pattern would be the same in each alternate length.

Having cut all the lengths required, the ragged ends of the left-hand side should be cut off. Making sure that the lengths have not moved out of position, grip the whole pack and draw it to the right so that the ragged ends lie on the table. The tear-stick is then laid on the pack level with the end of the first piece and held down firmly while the waste is torn off.

The best plan is to hang away from the light, that is to say, from the right and left of the window, meeting at some convenient point on the other side of the room—over the door is the

COMPLETING THE FOLD

FIG. 17. *Bring the left edge of the paper down to meet the right edge and smooth the join lightly with the palm of the hand. Let the paper soak for a few minutes.*

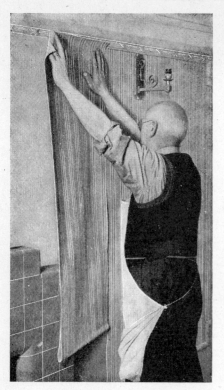

HANGING A LENGTH

FIG. 18. *After allowing about 2 in. to project at the top for trimming, the upper part is secured before the lower half of the paper is unfolded and smoothed into position with the hanging brush.*

usual practice. The reason for this is that the joints are less likely to show than if the hanging is done toward the light.

Before pasting the paper, the window frame should be tested with the plumb-line and arrangements made for the first length to be perfectly plumb. This precaution is important, otherwise it may be found that the pattern will recede from, or encroach on the rail, with resulting differences in the amount to be cut off. If the win-

dow happens to be out of plumb the difference should be trimmed off after hanging.

There are a number of cold-water pastes on the market, but most experienced craftsmen prefer to use paste made from wheaten flour as follows. Take $1\frac{3}{4}$ lb. of plain flour, beat it into a smooth batter with luke-warm water, add one gallon of boiling water, preferably from a saucepan, and stir well. A little cold water poured on top of the paste will prevent a skin from forming while the mixture is cooling. When the paste has cooled, it should be reduced to a working consistency with cold water.

Most proprietary brands of paste powder have directions for use on the packets; it is wise to follow them, reducing the paste to a consistency to suit the paper. Generally a fairly thin paste will be needed for a thin paper and a thick paste for the heavier types. For the average paper the paste

MARKING WITH THE SCISSORS

FIG. 19. *Use the tip of the scissors to mark the surplus paper to be trimmed off.*

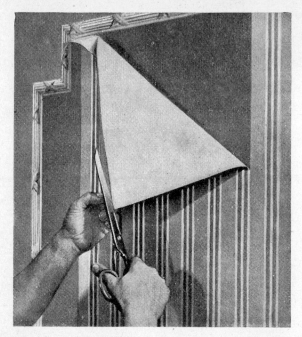

REMOVING THE
SURROUND

Fig. 20. *The paper may be gently pulled away from the wall, as shown, in order to cut along the line previously marked with the tip of the scissors at top and bottom of the length.*

to prevent the paste passing underneath and soiling the face of the paper. Before pasting the front edge, the paper should be drawn toward the operator until it overhangs the table by a fraction of an inch.

should be of such a consistency that it just drips off the brush.

Work in a good light and grip the paste brush as a distemper brush. Keep the brush upright with the tips of the bristles always in contact with the paper. When working on an ordinary table, choose one, if possible, with a square edge. A rounded or moulded edge makes it difficult to paste the edge of the paper properly without the paste straying to the underside.

The tops of the lengths should be on the right-hand side. The pack should be pushed away from the front edge and the top length brought forward again and placed in position for pasting, about 2 in. from the front edge of the table. Paste the top portion first, starting from the right and holding the paper down firmly with the outspread fingers of the left hand. When pasting, be careful to brush toward the edges

The top portion should next be folded in half and the remainder pasted and folded in a very similar manner. The subsequent folding must be accurate, edge to edge, with the ends meeting fairly close together in the middle (Figs. 15-17).

There are many reasons for folding accurately. The paste is enclosed and less likely to ooze out; the paper is more convenient to handle; soaking proceeds more evenly; the edges are less likely to dry prematurely and accurate cutting to varying width is facilitated.

To fold the paper, take the front, right-hand end of the paper between the thumb and finger of the left hand and make a semicircular movement, assisting it with the right hand placed flat (Fig. 15). During this operation it is essential to keep an eye on the two front edges. The folding should be done carefully, and without undue haste. When folding the bottom portion, the position of the hands should be reversed. If the edges do not fall perfectly true, they can be brought into alignment by gently sliding the top of the fold before finally smoothing it flat. Very thin paper may present some difficulty, particularly if too thick a paste has been used, and it may be necessary to fold it more deliberately and perhaps with some assistance.

If it is necessary to trim off the selvedge with scissors, it is not a bad plan to paste and fold first and then to trim length by length. As two thicknesses are being trimmed together it is particularly important that the folding be accurate at the edges.

Most wallpapers should be allowed to soak for a few minutes before hanging, and it is customary to paste several lengths before beginning to hang the first. Very thin and absorbent paper, however, can sometimes be hung as soon as it has been pasted. When using paste made from paste powder, it may be necessary to paste one length at a time, as there may be a tendency for the edges to dry and difficulty will then be experienced in unfolding if the paper is left too long before hanging.

HANGING THE PAPER

If the window frame is out of plumb it is best to pencil a vertical line about 20 in. away from the frame and to hang the first length to that line.

The pasted paper should be draped over the left arm and the top end of the paper gripped between the fingers and thumbs. The left knee should then be raised in order to break the fall as the paper unfolds itself. Adjust the top right-hand edge (Fig. 18), allowing 2 in. above the picture-rail, pass the hang-

ing brush down the middle of the paper and then from side to side. Finally crease the paper against the rail with the points of the scissors and trim off the waste. The lower part should then be unfolded, smoothed down and the waste cut off as illustrated in Figs. 19 and 20. The waste against the window frame may be trimmed off with the scissors.

When hanging subsequent lengths (Fig. 21), it may be necessary to match the pattern and carefully to butt the edges. Adjust the paper at the top left-hand side, keeping the right hand slightly away. Glance downwards to about knee level and adjust the paper by raising or lowering the right hand.

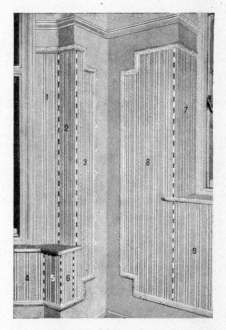

WHERE JOINS OCCUR

FIG. 21. *Sequence of dealing with awkward corners is shown numerically. Dotted lines indicate the joins. About* $\frac{1}{2}$ *in. of paper should turn each corner.*

If the paste has the right "slip," the paper may be butted to a nicety by gently patting it with the palm of the hand, using a sideways motion.

If the joints need any further attention after the usual smoothing down with the hanging brush, it is a good plan to place a strip of paper over the joints and to rub down gently with a small pad or roller (Fig. 22).

On approaching a corner, the paper must be cut to width, allowing no more than $\frac{1}{2}$ in. to turn on to the next flank. The cutting should normally be done after pasting and before hanging. Remember to plumb each corner when beginning a new flank and to hang the first piece upright.

When papering the chimney breast, the face should be done first, allowing

STRIPS FOR MATCHING

FIG. 23. *Any odd strips, which may be wanted for matching purposes, may be cut with the scissors after the paper has been pasted and folded ready for use.*

the paper to turn the corners for about an inch. The side pieces should be applied afterwards so as to lap the part which has been turned round the corner. Next trim-in to the mantelpiece and cut away all the waste, except for about 2 in., finally snip-in to the corners before marking.

Continue as already described until the flank opposite the window has been completed. Then follow on with the remainder, working from the left-hand side of the window, or the left-hand edge of the first length. If the paper is patterned with a large and definite

FELT ROLLER

FIG. 22. *Smoothing down with a felt roller after the paper has been applied with the hanging brush. Another method is described in the text.*

design (Figs. 23, 24), it is wise to adopt the latter course in order to match the pattern under and over the window. If the pattern is a small one, an error in matching may be disguised very satisfactorily by notching the last piece. Notching is carried out by allowing about 2 in. of the paper to hang over the edge of the boards and tearing out small pieces at intervals of 3 in. so as to leave a serrated edge.

Nothing spoils a good job more than dirty marks. During the process of pasting and hanging it is impossible to avoid putting paste on the fingers and the paperhanger should school himself to wipe his fingers on the apron immediately after touching the pasted side of the paper. If this is done regularly there is little risk of soiling the paper.

Cutting round fixtures such as brackets and bell-pushes, is shown in Figs. 25–27. The hanging should be completed at the top and the paper smoothed down, allowing part of the object to push through. The paper is then cut in a star fashion to enable it to fold round the block. After completing the lower part, the paper can be trimmed with a sharp knife or a razor blade. Whenever possible, of course, it is better to remove fixtures prior to hanging the paper and to replace them later. It makes the job easier.

PAPERING A CEILING

Ceilings which are badly cracked, stained or abnormally porous are often covered with white lining-paper before distempering. Friezes—the space between the picture-rail or border and the ceiling—are also usually

UNDER THE WINDOWS

FIG. 24. *Areas adjoining doorways and windows are usually papered last. It will be found that many short pieces which might otherwise be wasted can then be used up.*

lined, unless the wall is in a particularly good condition.

Lining paper is obtainable in rolls of varying widths and lengths. For normal purposes 12-yd. rolls, 22 in. wide, are most convenient. The usual practice is to cut up all the long lengths at the outset and to paste them one at a time. Pasting is carried out in the usual way, but the folding should be done in a "concertina" fashion in equal folds of about 18 in. (Fig. 28).

Although somewhat unorthodox, it will be found that lining is best done immediately after the sizing coat, sizing for about two widths and then applying the lining while the size is still moist.

Two pairs of steps and a scaffold board are necessary. Boxes of convenient height could be used instead of steps, but a proper scaffold board is an essential item of equipment.

When lining the frieze, keep a separate length for each flank and cut the paper to width after pasting, unless the amount to be trimmed off is only a few inches. Start from the right-hand side, holding the folded pack in the left hand and letting out one fold at a time. Adjust the top edge of the paper to meet the cornice and trim off any waste against the picture rail.

When lining the ceiling (Figs. 29-

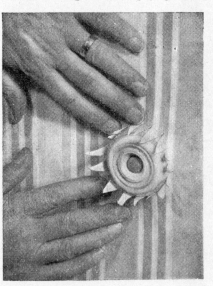

AWKWARD FIXTURES

FIG. 26. *To paper round a bell push or similar obstruction, a series of cuts is made in the shape of a star. The ends are removed later with a razor blade.*

32), it is helpful to measure out from the cornice 22 in. at each end and to mark the position for the paper with a chalk line.

The first length must be hung as near as possible to this line for about 2 ft., and then allowed to take its own course, alternately brushing down the middle and then from side to side. If this

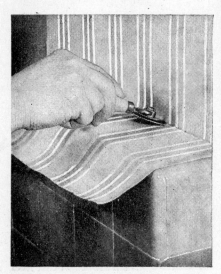

CASING-WHEEL

FIG. 25. *Trimming round the edges of a fireplace with a casing-wheel to remove the surplus length of paper.*

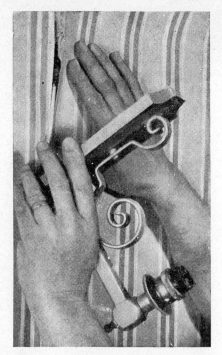

LIGHT FITTINGS

FIG. 27. *The easiest and neatest way to deal with a light fitting is to loosen it and pass the paper behind, making a small hole for the flex to pass through.*

procedure is adopted the following lengths will be easier to hang and butting to the edges will present little difficulty. In no circumstances should it be thought that it is easier to lap than to butt the joints. To attempt to lap the joint when papering a ceiling is usually to invite disaster.

The matching edge should always be on the left-hand side. The pack of folded paper, draped over a spare roll or a piece of broom handle, should be held in the left hand. Hold the paper well up to the ceiling and adjust about a foot of the paper into position with the right hand, accurately butting the

previous length and making sure that it does not fall away. Now take the hanging brush and keeping an eye on the meeting of the two papers, smooth down the centre and then side to side. Do not let the paper lap or open in the slightest degree. Immediately there is any indication that the joint is opening, pass the brush down the right-hand side instead of the middle. This will have the effect of turning the paper to the left and of closing the gap. Similarly, if the paper is inclined to lap, the brush should be passed down the left-hand edge. This method makes the work surprisingly easy, the butting being under full control. Brushing sideways to close a gap only accentuates the trouble. After cutting off the waste at either end, the whole of the paper should be smoothed over again with the hanging brush to make sure that every part is properly stuck down. When arranging the scaffold, the scaffold board must be parallel with the hanging line, with the left-hand edge of the board immediately underneath. When the lining has been completed, distempering may follow immediately. Nothing is gained by allowing the paper to dry first.

DECORATIVE FINISHES

There are many ways in which walls may be panelled, using one of the very wide range of highly decorative borders which are available. In some modern houses the panels are already formed with a small moulding, in which case the border is placed against the inner edge. The stiling—the parts outside the panels—is usually hung with a paper of a different tone or coated with a washable distemper.

Assuming that it is decided to form the panelling with a border, keeping the stile in distemper and the panel in paper, the first step is carefully to set out the panelling, indicating exactly where the border is to be. Measurements should be taken from the skirting for the horizontal lines, using a chalk line to strike the lines and finishing with a pencil and ruler. Chalk-lining is done by chalking a length of string, stretching it against the wall surface and "twanging" it so that a chalk impression is left on the wall.

It is advisable to have the stiling at the bottom about 2 in. wider than at the top. The top and upright stiling is usually of the same width; 8 to 9 in. for the bottom stiles and 6 to 7 in. for the

remainder will be found satisfactory. When marking for the upright borders it is convenient to use a plumb level instead of a plumb bob. The next procedure is to distemper the stiles, slightly overlapping the pencil line which indicates the outer edge of the border. Before proceeding with the panels the line which has now been obliterated by the distemper should be accurately marked in again.

The panel paper should be allowed to overlap the inner line for about $\frac{1}{2}$ in. If the paper has a large pattern it may be worth while centring the panel and working both ways in order to make the pattern symmetrical. All that remains is to hang the border to the line which

FOLDING CEILING PAPER

FIG. 28. *After pasting, long lengths of paper should be folded concertina fashion as shown. Note the way in which the paper is held at each side between the thumb and forefinger. The knack of folding paper in this manner needs practice.*

PAPERING A CEILING—THE START

FIG. 29. *With pasted length of paper supported with a spare roll, the loose end is fastened and smoothed down with the brush. The start is the most difficult part.*

has been pencilled on the distemper.

The border must be pasted and accurately folded before trimming or cutting. Never cut it into strips before pasting. It is usual to cut off about 6 ft. from the roll of border, cutting where possible on the point where one end of the strip will exactly match the other. The strip is then pasted, folded, trimmed and cut to widths, as shown in Figs. 33–36. Sometimes one edge is perforated round the ornament and the waste can be pulled off. This pulling apart can sometimes be done satisfactorily while the border is still folded, but if there is any risk of error it is best to unfold the strip for the purpose and to refold it afterwards.

When hanging the border it is scarcely necessary to mitre both ends. Start at the top right-hand corner and work to the left, finishing square. The vertical piece should next be cut at

45 deg. The professional will guess the angle, but a more accurate method is shown in Fig. 37. This consists of folding the border at right-angles and cutting through the two thicknesses close to the fold. The bottom mitre is dealt with in a similar manner, finishing square and starting again with the next piece cut at an angle. The next vertical piece will need to be cut at an angle at both ends.

The border should be applied to the wall as quickly as possible, otherwise the paste may dry and difficulty will be experienced in unfolding the paper. Never paste too much at a time, and use plenty of fairly thin paste.

Ornaments and set-pieces for use in conjunction with borders are available in a great variety and sometimes give a pleasing finish to the work. They are printed in colours and designed to harmonize with the border. In show-

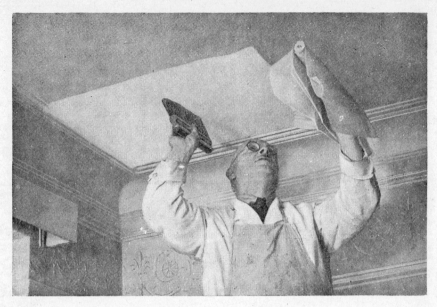

UNFOLDING AND BRUSHING

FIG. 30. *The smoothing brush is used to make all adjustments to the paper, which is allowed to unfold continuously while it is brushed centrally and from side to side.*

rooms and pattern books they are usually shown alongside the border for which they were designed. It is well worth while to visit a good-class show-room and to see these ornaments in position. Some of the ornaments include a part of the border, in which case they can be placed in position first and the border hung to them. Others are put on afterwards, lapping the border as required. Great care is necessary when separating the waste from the ornaments. The latter are usually perforated and do not need cutting with scissors. Paste the orna-ment before separating and lay it aside to soak before pulling off the waste. There is great scope for initiative and imagination in the use of these materials.

If one has already papered a ceiling with plain lining-paper the experience will be of great assistance when dealing with a patterned paper. The procedure is similar except that the paper will need trimming and matching, and more care is necessary to avoid soiling the surface with dirty finger-marks. In this case, as distinct from the method adopted when lining, the sizing coat must be allowed to dry before pro-ceeding to hang the paper.

SPECIAL PRECAUTIONS

To avoid showing the joints, it is best to begin hanging the paper from the light, that is, parallel to and against the wall in which the window happens to be. If reasonable care is taken when butting the edges, the joints will not be easily detected.

It will be wise to have some help, to

MAKING ADJUSTMENTS

Fig. 31. *Varying the position of the brush enables the paper to be pulled over to one side or the other. This means of adjustment may be used to correct a slight twist or to alter course. The pack of folded paper should always be held well up.*

assist in moving the scaffold or to hold the paper while doing some intricate cutting. It is strongly recommended that the customary scaffold be used. Two pairs of steps and a scaffold board are necessary. Unless the greatest care is taken, any makeshift, such as a table, will not only make the work difficult but may result in an accident. The scaffold board, which may be 3 ft. shorter than the room, should be at such a height that the head of the worker is about 6 in. from the ceiling.

It is best to have the room entirely clear of furniture. The pasting table should be placed in such a position that the scaffold may be moved freely. If there are any electric-light pendants, shades and lamps should be removed. For safety, globes or shades should also be removed from gas pendants.

Plasterwork on ceilings is seldom true enough to use as a guide for the first length. To make the work easy and to avoid disappointment, the best plan is to measure out 19 in. on the ceiling at each end and to snap a line from mark to mark with a piece of thin twine which has been chalked. At the end of this line, on the right facing the window, pencil over the chalk line for about 2 ft. Begin hanging the first length at the end; the pencil line will assist the initial adjustment.

The next step is to measure the length of paper needed, adding 6 in. in order to allow 3 in. at either end for trimming. It is usual to cut up all the long lengths at one time, although it must be remembered that the lengths around the chimney breast will be somewhat shorter. When the first

TRIMMING AWAY THE SURPLUS

FIG. 32. *The surplus paper left at the edge of the ceiling is marked with the scissors and then removed in precisely the same fashion as when working on a wall.*

length has been cut it is used as a guide to cut the remainder. Care should be taken to ensure that one length matches the other.

When pasting, the amateur is advised to have only one length on the board at a time, because with more than one it is difficult to avoid soiling the front of the paper with paste. Fairly thin paste is best for the average paper and a generous coat assists hanging. Make doubly sure of the edge, brushing away from the middle of the paper.

Folding is done in a concertina fashion as described for lining. As soon as the paper is pasted for the length of the board, it is folded in equal folds and drawn to the right in order that

the procedure may be repeated until the whole of the length has been pasted and folded. Do not on any account fold the paper from both ends.

APPLICATION

Keep the hanging brush and scissors to hand. Drape the folded pack over a hold-up stick held in the left hand and mount the scaffold. If unaccustomed to scaffold work, ask someone to hand the paper up after having mounted the scaffold.

Now face in the direction that the paper has to travel, undo the first fold and adjust its position with the right hand, true to the pencil line and allowing 3 in. to be cut off as waste. As soon as the end is securely stuck and in no danger of falling away, take the hanging brush and begin to unfold and smooth down the remainder. It is best to let this first length take its own course. If in the first place the paper has been set fairly true to the pencil line, it will run itself out accurately. Brush down the middle and then from side to side alternately. Cut off the waste at each end and go over it all again to make sure that it is stuck down, particularly at the edges. It will be recalled that 19 in. only was measured out on the ceiling. With this first length, therefore, will be a 2-in. strip to trim off, the paper being 21 in. in width. This trimming may be done with a casing-wheel, sharp knife, scissors or straight-edge.

After hanging the first length, the remainder is hung from the other end. Observe that by so doing the matching edge will be on the left-hand side of the operator. Match the pattern carefully and butt the edges. The hanging technique is the same as when using lining paper. If the instruction given is strictly followed, papering a ceiling will be found surprisingly simple. Trim true, paste and fold correctly, hold the pack well up to the ceiling with the left hand, watch the joints—these are the important points.

Gas pendants may present a little difficulty. The best plan is to cut-in from the edge nearest the pendant to the centre of the block and then to

PASTING BORDER PAPER

FIG. 34. *Use plenty of fairly thin paste, and spread it evenly. It is best to begin at the centre and to work outwards, applying full pressure to the brush.*

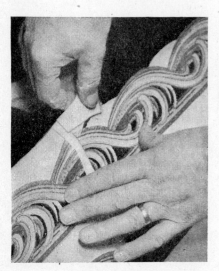

REMOVING WASTE

FIG. 33. *It is usual to find that the waste material on the outside of a border is perforated, so that it can be torn away.*

make the star cut. Some care is needed during this operation to prevent the paper from falling away and tearing. Before moving the scaffold to hang another length, make sure that all the edges are well stuck down. Remember to keep the face of the paper clean.

After the initial adjustment the paper should not be touched with the hands, all smoothing down and adjustment of edges being done with the hanging brush.

The most important matter when papering staircase walls is the scaffolding. Every care should be taken to ensure that the scaffolding used is sufficient, sound and secure. It is customary to hang the longest length first and then to work from left to right.

The extra-long lengths usually extend from the ceiling of the well, past the landing, to the ramp of the stairs. Two ladders are necessary, one longer than the other, and a good sound board.

The first step is to plumb and snap a chalk line 20 in. from the edge of the landing from ceiling to ramp. This is done, as before, by rubbing the line with chalk, suspending it from a picture rail, fine nail or other temporary support, holding it taut at the weighted end and then "twanging" the cord; a clean chalk line is thus

CUTTING AFTER PASTING

FIG. 36. *All borders are printed in 21-in. widths and will require to be separated after the material has been folded by cutting it with the scissors.*

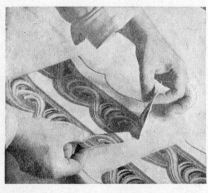

FOLDING BORDERS

FIG. 35. *As soon as the border has been pasted, it should be folded in similar manner to short lengths of wallpaper.*

made down the wall. Now take a roll of paper (re-roll if it is the wrong way up), hold it true to the chalk line and crease in to the top of the ramp. Allow 2 in. beyond this mark and cut off. Measure the length required and cut off, allowing a further 2 in. at the top for wastage.

All lengths over 10 ft. should be folded in concertina fashion as already described for ceiling work. Paste and fold from the top end of the paper.

Expert paperhangers cut all their lengths for each particular flight before beginning to hang. After cutting the first angle, the next piece is held to match and the paper nicked where the angle starts. It is then laid on the first piece and cut off at the same angle. Placing it back to the matching position, the new piece is then run out and cut off level with the top of the first piece. Note that each piece is shorter than the preceding one. The method, however, is somewhat involved and it would probably be best for the amateur to cut each length separately. The remainder of the work is similar to papering an ordinary room.

Among the special types of paper are the hand-made varieties. They are usually numbered at the end of each roll and it is important that the rolls are used in sequence of numbers.

All relief papers, which are heavily embossed, are best trimmed with a straight-edge and knife on a zinc strip.

The general principles to be observed are the same as when hanging ordinary wallpaper, but the application is somewhat different. Special care must be taken when folding not to bend the folds too sharply. Stretching must be avoided and care must be taken to avoid flattening the ornament.

Preparation of the surface is the same as for ordinary paperhanging. If the plaster is sound and well sized no further preparation is necessary. When the surface is old and disintegrating, it is advisable to apply a lining paper first, and to hang it horizontally.

HANGING SPECIAL PAPERS

Heavy papers should be cut to length and trimmed, after which the back should be sponged with water and put aside to soak for about ten minutes. Pasting should be done with fairly thick paste to which a generous proportion of dextrin has been added. It is a good plan to apply a thin coat of weak paste to the surface of the wall immediately prior to applying a relief paper. A felt-covered roller will assist in removing blisters. Borders and panelling strips which have to be superimposed should be applied with a paste of pure dextrin applied with a knife.

In the case of the hollow-back types of relief paper, it is a good plan to apply a coat of weak paste and water first and to allow the paste to soak in. As soon as the weak paste appears to have been partially absorbed, in, say, about ten minutes' time, apply a coat of heavier paste and hang the paper immediately. Do not use a roller, but dab the paper into position with the hanging brush.

Some relief materials are supplied plain and require finishing with a paint or glaze after hanging. Imitation-leather papers, which are a cheaper form of low relief, are supplied already finished in colour and need no further treatment after hanging.

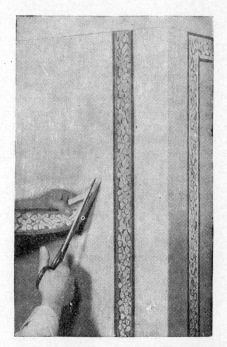

CUTTING A MITRE

FIG. 37. *Fold the border at right-angles and cut through the two thicknesses close to the fold, as illustrated. Only one end of the border need be mitred.*

CHAPTER 8

OBTAINING SPECIAL FINISHES

BLENDING, CLOUDING, GLAZING, SCUMBLING AND STENCILLING

THE home decorator should not expect to restrict his work to plain painting, distempering and paper-hanging. It often happens that special finishes are seen which he would like to incorporate in his own work, but he is not certain how such finishes are produced.

Decorators obtain many attractive finishes by blending, clouding, shading and stippling with oil paint, flat paint, glazes or scumbles.

Glazes are usually made of transparent or semi-transparent pigments ground in oil, together with turpentine, linseed oil, beeswax and a binding agent. They are used thinly and are similar to graining colours. Pigments ground in water with a binding agent (usually size) are also used for glazing.

Scumbles are made of opaque or semi-opaque pigments (usually white with other pigments added for tinting) and they are used to give a bloom or a fine, even, semi-opaque film to an existing colour. They are, in effect, little more than thin oil-paints.

USE OF SCUMBLES AND GLAZES

Artists sometimes make use of scumbles to soften colours and to suggest the effect of distance. They also use glazes to produce richness and depth of colour. The decorator produces similar effects on a larger scale. Where an artist glazes or scumbles an area of 1 sq. in., the decorator may

cover an area of 100 sq. yd.; the walls of a large room, for example.

Paint and distemper may also be employed for decorating ceilings, walls, woodwork or furniture by the use of shaped templets (thin metal or cardboard plates or shapes cut out of paper and used as shields to leave a pattern painted or unpainted) with which very effective shading and the production of abstract patterns may be obtained.

STENCIL DECORATION

Stencilling was used extensively by decorators some years ago to produce patterns and designs in paint or distemper. The use of stencils has fallen out of favour to some extent owing to the unsuitability of old designs for modern decorative schemes and neglect in preparing designs suitable for present-day use. However, it is an easy matter to design and to cut stencils and equally simple to apply them. It will be found that this form of decoration is by no means out of date, as the description of the work and the suggestions for the use of stencils should prove.

The mention of painted furniture may suggest white-enamelled bedroom suites or nursery and kitchen furniture, enamelled in bright colours. It is true that such painted furniture has its use, but it is not so well known that some of the finest rooms in town and country houses contain painted and decorated furniture. Desks, bedroom furniture, occasional tables, console tables, cocktail cabinets and the like are suitable for painting and decorating, and they may subsequently be glazed to give them an antique finish.

Such decorative finishes add interest to rooms which might otherwise be too severe in character and allow individual decorative schemes to be produced. The subtleties of colour and pattern and the uncommon, yet tasteful decorations which can be produced, allow decorative schemes to be built around the furniture. In this way colour contrast and harmony may be adjusted to fine limits which are outside the range of ready-made finishes in paint, distemper or wallpaper.

The finishes which are most quickly obtained are those which employ only plain oil-paint, and the easiest finish to carry out is that obtained by stippling a dry, painted surface with a paint of another colour or with paints of two or more different colours. Special rubber stipplers are available for this work, but no difficulty will be experienced in using a piece of sponge or, better still, a pad of old lace or net curtain for stippling on the colours. A few colour combinations are suggested in the following list.

Ground colour	Stippling colours
White	Light grey and light blue
White	Pink and delft blue
White	Sap green and light brown
Ivory white	Olive green
Cream	Light buff and cinnamon brown
Cream	Rust red and golden brown
Light green	Dark green
Middle green	Cream
Middle green	Daffodil yellow
Sunshine yellow	Pale violet

This list could be extended indefinitely. In general, it is better not to choose two strong, complementary colours for stippling on a background colour as the effect on the eye is to produce an unpleasant grey. However, light tints of complementary colours stippled on a pale neutral or slightly tinted ground will produce a delicate grey when the colours are seen from a distance. The individual colours will show when the work is examined more closely. Practise on a suitably prepared board before deciding on the colours which are finally to be used or on the amount of stippling to be done.

STIPPLED WORK

Flat (matt) colours for both groundwork and stippling are generally preferable for this type of work, although many interesting effects may be produced by stippling work with flat colours on glossy or egg-shell finished grounds. Stippling with glossy colours on either flat or glossy grounds is not advised.

When the ground coat on the surface to be stippled is quite dry, put out the stippling colours in two paint-kettles with a 1-in. paint tool in each, with which to transfer the paint to a palette. The palette should be fairly large; a piece of flat wood, measuring about 1 ft. 6 in. square, with a handle attached, is most suitable. Put a small amount of one of the colours on the palette, take a piece of sponge or a pad of old net curtain, dip it a little way into one of the colours, dab it on an empty space on the palette to free it of excess colour and then stipple the prepared surface. To stipple a whole wall or the walls of a room, go over the whole area once without making a great effort to keep the work even.

When the whole area has been stippled in this manner, go over the surface again with the sponge to fill up patches which have been missed in the first stippling. If a second colour is required, proceed in similar manner. When two colours are used, each one should be used rather sparingly so that there is sufficient space on the ground coat for the two.

Stippling in this manner produces a granite-like effect (Fig. 1), but if a piece of rag is screwed up into an uneven pad and used in place of the sponge or curtain material, a leaf-like pattern is produced (Fig. 2). Two colours have been stippled on a ground coat to produce the pattern shown in Fig. 1, but a single colour, more suitable for the pattern, has been used for the work shown in Fig. 2.

Further variety of pattern may be obtained by twisting the sponge or rag as the stippling proceeds. A slight dragging movement while stippling produces yet another pattern, but the dragging movement should be in one direction all the time. When stippling walls by the methods described, be sure to stipple right up to the corners or picture rail and right down to the skirting. A very small piece of sponge or rag will be needed for this purpose. If these parts are not properly stippled they will appear lighter or darker than the rest of the walls according to the colour of the ground coat.

COLOUR BLENDING

Graduated effects are produced by changing from one shade to another shade of the same colour, or by changing from one colour to another without showing a break or a sudden change. Ordinary oil paint is easiest to handle for this effect as it does not dry or set too quickly and therefore allows more time for blending the colours. Three lots of paint will be required whether one, two or three colours are being used, and at least three paint brushes

SPONGE-STIPPLING

Fig. 1. *This mottled, granite-like effect is produced by lightly dabbing a suitably prepared oil-paint surface with a sponge dipped in paint.*

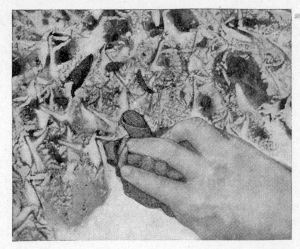

RAG-STIPPLING
FIG. 2. *Leaf pattern produced by stippling with a piece of crumpled rag. The effect looks best when used on small areas.*

will be needed, one for each colour or shade of colour.

When the walls of a room are to be painted in a graduated effect, each wall must be completed separately. For example, assume that a wall is to be graduated from a very pale colour at the top to a much deeper shade of the same colour at the bottom. The light colour and the deep one are made up first and a part of each is taken to make an intermediate shade. The wall should have been previously prepared and painted in readiness for the finishing coat of graduated colour. The oil paint should be of medium consistency and should contain approximately equal parts of turpentine and raw linseed oil.

The wall to be treated must be divided into three parts : the top being wider than the middle part and the middle wider than the bottom part. If the wall is, say, 9 ft. high, the proportions might be 4 ft., 3 ft., and 2 ft., respectively.

The top part of the wall is painted first with the lightest colour. Plenty of material should be used and the colour should be brushed on evenly, but not laid-off. Using the middle shade with the appropriate brush, the middle part of the wall is brushed-in similarly and

the joint of the two colours is blended with the brush which is used for the middle shade. The bottom part of the wall is then painted with the deepest shade of paint and the middle and deepest shades are blended in the same way with the brush used for the bottom part.

Next, a small amount of the lightest shade of paint is brushed on the bristles of a stippler. This is to prevent the dry stippler removing the paint from the part of the wall which is to be stippled first. Starting at the top of the wall, the work should be stippled in horizontal bands, taking care to overlap each band with the following one. Never stipple haphazardly or go back over parts which have been stippled already. If the work has been blended sufficiently with the paint brushes, stippling will blend the shades of colour perfectly. If the work is not perfect, do not attempt to stipple parts of the wall here and there, but, starting at the bottom of the wall when the stippler is in the deepest shade of paint, stipple the wall systematically upwards.

BLENDING WITH THE BRUSH

FIG. 3. *To blend one colour into another, or a dark shade into a lighter shade, the material should be brushed lightly in all directions and an attempt should first be made to obtain the effect as closely as possible with the brush.*

If the initial stippling has blended the wall perfectly, as indeed it should, a second wall may be brushed in the same manner as the first one, but when the stippler is in the deepest shade this wall should be stippled from bottom to top. A third wall would, of course, be stippled from top to bottom and so on.

When the walls of a room are being graduated in this manner the stippler should be beaten out from time to time to free it of excessive paint. An old newspaper, which can be opened to give a clean sheet on which to beat out the stippler, may be used. The stippler should not be washed in turpentine until the work has been completed.

It is possible to buy small stipplers specially made for treating small areas such as door panels and wall angles, but the amateur will find that a clean dusting brush is a good substitute for a small stippler and will be useful for stippling parts of the work where a large tool would be clumsy.

Two-colour and three-colour graduations are carried out in a similar manner. For two-colour graduations, a third colour is made by mixing the two colours in use. On a wall 9 ft. high, the middle band should be not more than 1 ft. wide for two-colour graduations, otherwise a three-colour effect will appear. The bands for three-colour graduations should be equal in width for most satisfactory results.

GRADUATIONS IN FLAT PAINT

Graduations carried out with flat paint may be executed in similar manner except that the work must be done very quickly. It is work for two men to graduate a large wall in flat paint and even then speed is essential. One man brushes on the colours and blends them roughly with the brushes and the second man follows with the stippler. Walls blended with flat paint must be stippled once only. If parts are gone over with the stippler while the flat paint is setting, the work will flash (shine where the extra stippling has been done) when the paint is dry. Fig. 3 shows a panel brushed-in and partly blended and Fig. 4 shows the finished work.

Walls which have been graduated in oil colour dry with a slight gloss, and may be finished with flat or glossy varnish. Graduated effects, carried out in flat paint, may also be varnished, but some change of colour must be expected. In the decorating trade surfaces finished in flat paint are usually left unvarnished. A thin coat of decorators' size, which has been strained through muslin, is sometimes brushed over the dry, flat-painted surface and is then stippled with a perfectly clean hair-stippler. When walls so treated become dirty, the size and the dirt may be washed off with warm water and a sponge, leaving the flat paint quite clean. The walls may then be given another thin coat of size.

USE OF TEMPLETS

Wall surfaces which are painted in flat finishes or distempered with water-paint wear well, and make good backgrounds for furnishings. But rooms decorated in this severe style often lack interest, especially when the furnishings are rather ordinary. One way out of this difficulty is to add interest by breaking up the wall areas with decorations carried out by masks or templets. Fig. 5 shows a wall treated to give a fluted effect.

The walls are painted first with flat finish of a light tint and are allowed to dry. Next a length of lining paper, the height of the walls and about 3 in. wide, with one edge straight, is given a coat of knotting varnish on both sides and allowed to dry. The walls are then marked out with chalk in strips about 10 in. wide. Slight variations in the widths for separate walls do not matter greatly, but each wall must be divided into vertical bands of equal

GRADUATED EFFECT

FIG. 4. *The area previously blended with the brush is now treated with a hair stippler, which eliminates brush marks.*

FLUTED WALL DECORATION

FIG. 5. *Decorative panels of this kind add interest to a plain distempered wall which might otherwise be rather severe in effect. The method of using an improvised templet and a stippler to produce this result is shown in Figs. 6 and 7. In the first instance, the bands, which should be of equal width, are marked out with chalk.*

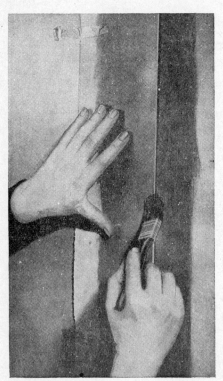

width. A kettle of flat paint is then tinted a shade deeper than the existing colour of the walls; the slightest difference in shade being sufficient for the most pleasing effect. Working from right to left, the paper templet is put into position against the first chalk line and secured with small lengths of transparent adhesive tape. With a 1-in. paint tool, the paint is brushed gently against the straight, right-hand edge of the paper templet, making sure that the paint does not stray under the edge of the paper. A strip of paint about 3 in. wide should be brushed on the wall, the right-hand edge of which is left rather bare to assist in the subse-

FLUTED EFFECT—FIRST STAGE

FIG. 6. *Paper templet in use when brushing on the paint for the fluted effect shown in Fig. 5. Note the adhesive strips at top and bottom of the mask and the position of the left hand.*

quent shading. This stage of the work is shown in Fig. 6. A small hair stippler or a clean dusting brush is then taken and the overlap of paint stippled into the existing wall-colour until a graduated effect is obtained. Fig. 7 shows the finished effect on one strip and another strip being stippled. The work is continued in similar manner until the whole area has been com-

Fig. 9 shows an ordinary door and architrave decorated with a painted surround applied by the use of a paper mask.

For the mural design illustrated in Fig. 10 the sky should be painted first, graduating the colour from strong sky blue at the top to pale blue at the bottom. The distant hills should be painted next, graduating the colour

FLUTED EFFECT— SECOND STAGE

FIG. 7. *With the templet still in position, a hair stippler is used to eliminate brush marks and to graduate the effect from a light to a dark shade.*

pleted. The curved head and foot of each vertical band may be added by the use of curved templets cut to suitable size and shape. The heads should be painted with the deepest colour and the feet with the lightest, thus adding to the convex appearance of the vertical bands forming the pattern.

OTHER EFFECTS

Templets may be used for many similar schemes (Fig. 8). It will be possible to carry out some of the suggestions made in Chapter 2, and many other interesting designs, by this means.

from dull violet to blue-grey. The middle distance, graduated from blue-green to yellow-green, should follow, and the foreground, graduated from bright green to pale, dull green should then be added. The silhouette of the trees should be painted last in deep grey-green with the exception of the pillars, which should be finished in white or cream. The whole of the work, excepting the sky, may be carried out by the use of simple paper templets.

One of the most charming decorative effects is obtained by glazing. Oil glaze is made by mixing 60 per cent turpentine, 25 per cent raw linseed oil, 10 per cent beeswax dissolved in turpentine, and 5 per cent japan gold-size, together with various transparent or semi-transparent pigments ground in oil.

Glazing is carried out in a manner similar to graining, but the medium is used with less pigment. It is applied to a previously painted, ground coat of suitable colour; usually white or a very pale tint is employed.

SIMPLE GLAZING

The simplest forms of glazing are those in which either rag-stippling or rag-rolling is employed to produce the effect. The glaze, which has been tinted to the desired colour, is first brushed on the dry ground-coat sparingly and evenly. A piece of clean, soft, cotton rag is then taken and, holding it as shown in Fig. 11, the work is gently stippled. For rag-rolling, the glaze is brushed on the ground in the same manner, but the rag is twisted into a roll and, holding it between the two hands as shown in Fig. 12, the rag is half pushed and half rolled down the work. If either of these effects appear too coarse or hard, they may be softened by stippling the surface with a hair stippler.

The following pigments, ground in oil, are useful for adding to a glaze medium : raw sienna, oxford ochre, burnt sienna, raw umber, burnt umber, vandyke brown, prussian blue, ultramarine, crimson lake, scarlet lake and viridian green. Lemon chrome, although a rather solid pigment, may be included for its brilliance and it may be added to glazes which contain the pigments already mentioned.

Rag-rolled or rag-stippled effects are very pleasant when carried out in ivory or parchment colours. The colours of the grounds

SPONGE AND TEMPLET
FIG. 8. *By sponge stippling along the edge of a paper templet many interesting patterns may be devised, as illustrated.*

NOVEL DESIGN

FIG. 9 *(Right) A scroll pattern, produced by means of paper masks. A white oil paint or washable distemper would be suitable for such a scheme, but a fairly dark background is essential.*

LANDSCAPE MURAL

FIG. 10. *(Below) Form of decoration in which features such as the pillars, tree silhouettes, hedges and surround have all been executed by means of stencil plates, patterns and masks. Although rarely suitable for the home, this form of mural decoration is quite frequently used in clubs and halls.*

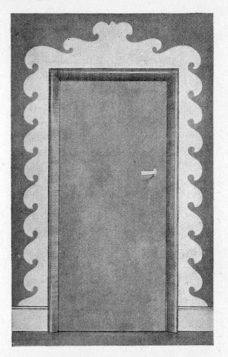

and the pigments required for the glazes are as follows:

Finished colour	Ground colour	Glaze
Ivory	White	Raw sienna, 90 per cent Lemon chrome, 8 per cent Prussian blue, 2 per cent
Parchment	Cream	Raw umber, 93 per cent Scarlet lake, 5 per cent Ultramarine, 2 per cent

These two glazes may also be used with good effect on the following ground colours : pale blue, pale green, apple green, pale tan, peach and apricot. They may also be used to glaze a surface painted with two or more colours. For example, the panels of a door may be pale cream, the stiles and rails pale green and the mouldings light brown. The whole of the door may be glazed and the effect will be mellow with a good colour combination.

Coloured glazes applied over white grounds produce very delicate tints which are suitable for bedrooms and drawing-rooms. Such glazes should be made up with high-grade pigments. Raw sienna with scarlet lake added makes a rose-peach colour when used as a glaze over white.

The amateur is advised to prepare a panel and to paint it white. It is then possible to experiment with various pigments made into glazes and to practise rag-rolling and various kinds of stippling.

A few hints on the mixing of pigments for staining glaze may be useful at this point. Ultramarine must not be

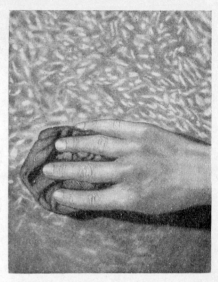

SHIMMER EFFECT

FIG. 11. *Delicate shimmer effect produced by rag-stippling in glaze, which is obtainable in a good range of colours or even in transparent form. It is best to try out the effect first on a panel.*

mixed with yellow pigments to make green glaze, unless an exceptionally dull green is required. Prussian blue and yellow pigments make green, but when used in a glaze over white a very hard green results, which usually requires the addition of a little red pigment to improve the colour. Orange glazes may be made with orange chrome, although this pigment is opaque.

Oxford ochre when mixed with scarlet lake produces a bright orange glaze which is more transparent than similar ones made with orange chrome. Raw sienna mixed with scarlet lake make a soft orange glaze. Neither scarlet lake nor prussian blue is suitable for making violet glazes as they both have a yellow content. Crimson lake and ultramarine, on the other hand, make a very pure violet.

Shading with glaze gives an ivory-like effect, but it must be carried out carefully or a coarse finish results. Two separate mixtures of glaze are required, the first is not stained with pigments but the second is coloured as desired.

The transparent glaze is first brushed over the area to be shaded and the tinted glaze is brushed round the edges (Fig. 13). A hair stippler as shown in Fig. 4 is then taken and the tinted parts are stippled from the edges to the centre. Mouldings should be brushed in with the tinted glaze, stippled with the hair stippler and, when the glaze has set a little, the face of the mouldings should be wiped clean.

Graduated effects are easy to carry out in glaze. First, the walls must be prepared and painted with a suitable ground colour. As when producing graduated effects in solid colours, a whole wall should be graduated at a time. The bands of colour are brushed on in the same way, but when glaze is being

used the colour must be brushed out well and evenly. Stippling is done in the same manner as for solid colour. If a graduated effect in one colour is desired, a method similar to the one described for shading is employed. The colour of the ground coat should be similar to the one required for the lightest part of the work. The top parts of the wall are then brushed-in with glaze, which should be transparent or very slightly tinted. Next the middle part of the wall is brushed-in with glaze which contains rather more pigment. The glaze which is brushed on the bottom band should contain more pigment still, according to the depth of colour required. Although the stippling which follows should be carried out in the same way as for solid colours, the material is more flexible and extra stippling may, therefore, be

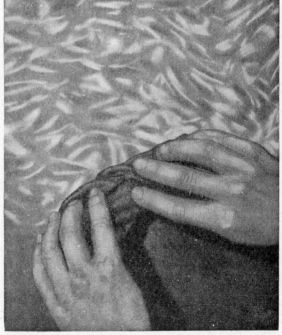

SATIN-FOLD EFFECT
FIG. 12. *A piece of rag irregularly folded and rolled over the surface of a wall which has previously been painted and glazed, gives this effect.*

given to parts which are unsatisfactory.

When glaze has once started to set, it must not be stippled, or, instead of the colour stippling out, the setting glaze on the wall surface will absorb any glaze on the stippler and result in the appearance of a dark patch which cannot be successfully removed.

CLOUDED EFFECTS

Clouding with glaze is an easy operation which is always effective, as it allows a margin of error and still looks well. As with other types of glazing, the surface to be clouded must be previously painted with a suitable ground colour. For clouding in a single colour, the glaze should be tinted and brushed over the whole of the area to be clouded. A piece of soft rag is then made into a smooth pad, and with a circular movement of the hand the clouded effect is produced by rubbing off parts of the glaze (Fig. 14). Note that all the glazing is joined if only by a thin strip. This prevents a patchy appearance in the finished work. When the whole of an area has been clouded in this way, the work is treated lightly with a hair stippler to soften the effect.

Clouding with glaze in two or more colours is rather more difficult. Separate amounts of tinted glaze are required and they are brushed on the area to be clouded in equal amounts. As far as possible, each patch of colour should connect with a similar patch. The patches of colour should not be made too small or,

VIGNETTE

FIG. 13. *For a shaded effect, light in the centre and graduating to a darker tone at the edges, glaze is applied with the brush.*

at a distance, a mottled rather than a clouded effect will be seen. The work is then carried out as described for clouding in a single colour. As a preliminary measure rag-stippling on the edges of the patches of colour makes the blending with the stippler a comparatively simple task.

GLAZING FOR BRIGHTNESS

Plain glazing is employed at times to give brightness or depth of colour. The glaze should then contain rather more pigment than usual. It is simply brushed on the surface of the dry ground-coat and finely stippled with a hair stippler. In this case lightness of touch is necessary and the stippler should be used quickly and lightly with a wrist movement only. The background for plain glazing should be rich in colour and the work is best confined to small areas, such as the woodwork of a room. A few suggestions for ground colours and glazes suitable for plain glazing follow.

Ground colour	Pigments for glaze
Pillar-box red	Scarlet lake
Rich red	Crimson lake
Orange	Orange chrome
Bright blue	Prussian blue
Cobalt (tint)	Ultramarine
Middle chrome	Raw sienna or oxford ochre
Copper (colour)	Burnt sienna
Bright green	Viridian green

The resulting colours are very rich or bright. They are suitable for interior work or for a front door. Pale carriage-varnish should be used to protect these finishes when they are used outside, but french oil-varnish is preferable for finishing inside work.

Vandyke brown is one of the most transparent pigments. When glaze is stained with vandyke brown only, very beautiful, subdued colours are produced if the glaze is stippled over rich ground-colours such as maroon, deep apple-green, dark tan, rich blue or autumnal tints. It may also be used to subdue and to give bronze effects to groundwork painted with gold, silver or copper metallic paint.

Glazing may be carried out in water-colour. Pigments ground in water are mixed with weak size and water, and the material is used in the manner described for oil glazing. Exceptionally soft shading and clouding are possible when water-colour glaze is used, especially when a badger softener is also used for the final softening. Surfaces which are to be decorated with water-colour glaze should be sponged with water to which a small amount of whiting has been added before the glazing is started. This provides a key for the water-colour which would otherwise be difficult to brush on the surface of dry oil-paint.

Water-colour glazing is more difficult to carry out than oil-colour glazing, but one advantage is that unsatisfactory areas may be sponged off and the surface can be reglazed.

SCUMBLING

Scumbling involves the application of a thin coat of opaque or semi-opaque paint over a ground coat. It produces the effect of a bloom as seen on grapes and peaches. Scumbles are made with high-grade, finely ground white and coloured pigments, thinned with different quantities of turpentine and linseed oil according to the finish required. Apart from the attractive finish given by scumble, it has the added advantage of giving unity to a decorative scheme by reason of the analogous harmony which is obtained by covering each colour used in the scheme with a thin film of a single tint.

Scumbles are rather more difficult to apply than glazes. It is essential to work quickly and efficiently on account of the speed with which this material sets.

When the walls and woodwork of a room are to receive a common treatment, the following decorative effect of scumbling could be tried. It produces a charming and uncommon effect. The whole area to be scumbled is prepared, painted with undercoating and given a coat of hard gloss-paint of a bright colour such as brilliant red, blue, green, yellow, violet or orange. This coat of glossy paint must be allowed to dry hard.

A scumble is then made up with flat white paint or flat cream paint and thinned with 85 per cent turpentine, 10 per cent raw linseed oil and 5 per cent japan gold-size. The mixture should be fairly thin; just thick enough to hide the colour of the ground coat. The area to be scumbled is brushed in quickly and stippled immediately with a hair stippler. When, say, a short length of wall has been covered in this way, the decorator takes a clean, stiff carpet-brush and stipples the scumble with it. The carpet brush removes the scumble in tiny scratches which remain glossy and bright in colour while the scumble dries matt. This method produces a fine, sparkling effect with very delicate colour. The carpet brush, used as a stippler, also removes the scumble from all the sharp edges of architraves, skirtings and mantelpieces. On no account must touching up be attempted while the scumble is wet. Any unsatisfactory places should be left until the scumble is dry, and only then touched up very carefully,

and a little at a time, by stippling on scumble with a small camel-hair brush or with a small decorators' fitch.

One man should be able to stipple up to 6 sq. yd. in this effect without help, but two persons will be required for larger areas. One person should brush on the scumble and stipple with the hair stippler, while the other should follow with the carpet brush. This scumbled effect must not be varnished or the effect will be destroyed.

Extremely thin scumbles, which are darker than the ground coat, may be rag-stippled or rag-rolled. In this way a more solid effect is produced than by similar stippling in glaze. The scumble to be used must contain more linseed oil than usual and the ground coat should be semi-flat. In this case the finished work may be varnished to leave either a glossy or flat surface.

OTHER EFFECTS

Old plaster effects are sometimes carried out in scumble. The ground coat should be of semi-flat, white oil-paint which has been stained with raw sienna and raw umber to a parchment colour. When the ground coat is dry, a scumble made with flat white paint and a touch of raw umber, and thinned with 80 per cent turpentine, 15 per cent raw linseed oil and 5 per cent japan gold-size, is brushed on the surface. A piece of clean canvas is then taken and the scumble is rubbed into the ground coat with a circular movement.

This effect is not recommended for modern decorative schemes or for smooth walls, but it is an excellent finish for period decorations when the plaster surfaces are old and rough, or when old ceilings incorporate plaster

CLOUDED EFFECT

FIG. 14. *Wiping a previously painted and glazed surface with rag, using a circular motion, gives a clouded effect which looks best when viewed at a distance.*

ornament or ancient beams and when old oak furniture, brasswork and pewter feature in the decorative scheme.

Plain scumbling may be employed for walls and woodwork if a delicate colour is required which has more interest than similar colours obtained by the use of solid, flat-paint finishes. The work is painted first with semi-flat paint, which should be of much stronger hue than that which is required in the finished effect. When the ground coat is dry, a thin scumble, made of flat white or flat cream paint and thinned with turpentine only, is brushed quickly over the ground coat and stippled evenly with a hair stippler as soon as possible.

If a door is to be scumbled in this way, it is best to brush on the scumble and stipple the work from the top to the bottom of the door, instead of treating each part separately.

Two people are needed to scumble large wall-areas. If one man should attempt such work single-handed it will be found that light joints will appear where the brushwork has been joined up. If the whole wall is brushed in first, the scumble will have set too much for effective stippling. It is easier to cover a large wall single-handed if extra linseed oil is added to the scumble, but a perfectly matt finish should not be expected.

BLENDED SCUMBLING

Scumbling will produce a charming effect of very delicate shading, clouding or blending, if a thin white or tinted scumble is brushed and stippled evenly over an area which has been previously clouded or blended with oil paint. Two or three colours of oil paint could be brushed on an area in patches and blended roughly with the paint brushes. The colours, which could be say, green, brown and pink, should be of medium hue; much stronger than those desired in the finished effect. The paint should contain equal quantities of turpentine and raw linseed oil. It should be of a consistency which does not set quickly, but such as to allow time to blend the colours.

The scumbling which follows should e carried out with the same materials,

or sap green, would look well. For this type of work both the ground coat and the stippling colour should be matt.

USE OF STENCILS

Stencilling is a convenient means of carrying out decorations which are intended to be fairly permanent. It is the method of applying patterns and designs to a painted or distempered surface by means of a stencil brush and paint which is dabbed over a design cut out of paper.

Decorators design their own stencils and cut them out of cartridge paper.

STENCIL DESIGN

FIG. 15. *Good cartridge paper is used in making stencils. The design may be drawn on it in pencil or a coat of linseed oil may be applied to make the paper sufficiently transparent for tracing a pattern through it.*

and in the same manner, as plain scumbling.

Sponge-stippling with thin, flat undercoating produces an effect similar to that of scumbling. It is a coarser effect but it is easier to carry out. The colour of the sponge stippling should be lighter than that of the ground coat, but brilliant coloured grounds should not be used. Flat, white scumble of medium consistency, sponged over a pale tint such as peach, duck-egg blue

The design is first drawn on the paper and care should be taken to leave sufficient paper ties to hold the paper together. Fig. 15 shows the construction of a design suitable for a stencil border. The heavy lines are those which are to be cut.

When the design has been drawn, the cartridge paper is turned over and the back is given a single coat of knotting varnish and allowed to dry. A sheet of thick glass is obtained which

CUTTING A STENCIL

Fig. 16. *Although special knives are made for cutting stencils, a safety-razor blade of the non-flexible type is equally good for the job. It will be found that a sheet of thick glass provides an excellent surface on which to cut the paper.*

APPLYING A STENCIL

Fig. 17. *The stencil tool should be carefully charged with paint as described in the text. Best results are obtained by dabbing the brush lightly and squarely over the stencil. Heavy pressure forces colour under the edges of the pattern.*

185

STENCIL BORDER IN TWO COLOURS

FIG. 18. *Two-colour stencil border in its simplest form. In this example, if small stencil brushes are used, the same plate can be used for the two colours.*

should be larger than the size of the stencil, and laid on a level surface. The cartridge paper is then placed on the glass right side up and the designs cut out with a stencil knife (Fig. 16). The coat of knotting varnish on the back of the stencil prevents the paper from tearing while the design is being cut. Stencil knives must be sufficiently sharp to cut through the paper without undue pressure. A single-edged razor blade makes a good substitute for a stencil knife. When the design has been cut out, the unvarnished side of the stencil should be given a coat of knotting varnish to prevent the oil and turpentine content of the paint from penetrating the cartridge paper when the stencil is used.

Note that guide lines have been drawn to the ends of the stencil and that snips have been cut out at the ends of the lines. Before the stencilling is begun, a chalk line is made on the wall corresponding to the guide line on the stencil. Fig. 17 shows the stencil border being applied. The cut-out snips have been placed on the chalk line to locate the stencil in the correct position. To avoid damage to the wall surface, small strips of transparent adhesive-tape may be used to keep the stencil in position. A stripping knife is used to keep the stencil flat on the wall so that paint does not creep under the edges of the cut-out design and spoil the outline.

Matt paint thinned to the required consistency with turpentine and a few drops of japan gold-size should be used for stencilling. The stencil brush should be dipped into the paint a little way only and then dabbed on a palette board to remove excess colour before applying the paint to the stencil. Use the stencil brush as dry as possible, and with short, straight, quick jabs. When one length of the pattern has been stencilled, the stencil should be lifted straight off so as not to smear the finished work and placed in the next position in such a way that the pattern at the end of the stencil covers a similar pattern of actual stencilled work, care being taken that the cut-out snips still coincide with the chalk line.

If a considerable amount of stencilling is to be done, it is best to stencil the design on one or two separate pieces of cartridge paper. These may be kept in hand and cut when the first stencil begins to wear. A copy of every stencil used should be kept for possible future use.

When a stencil has been used for some time the surface will become clogged with paint, and if it is used in this condition the stencilled pattern will not be as clear and sharp as it should be. The stencil should, therefore, be cleaned occasionally with turpentine and rag and dried well before it is used again.

Stencilling may be carried out in two, three or more colours. If the stencils are of simple design (Fig. 18), the separate colours may be applied with one stencil, using separate small stencil brushes; but complicated designs, which require two or more

TWO-COLOUR STENCIL DESIGN

FIG. 19. *Two stencils, as shown in the top and centre illustrations, are required to produce the elaborate decorative border depicted in the third. Before the second colour is applied it is important that the first should be thoroughly dry. Care must also be taken to ensure that the colours are in register.*

colours, are applied by means of two or three separate stencils which combine to form the complete pattern. Fig. 19 shows two separate stencils and the design produced by them. The second stencil must not be used until the colour of the first part of the design is dry. When drawing a design which is to be made into two stencils for the application of separate colours, sketch the complete design on tracing paper, rub soft lead-pencil on the reverse side and retrace the separate parts required on separate pieces of cartridge paper. The two designs may then be cut as previously described, and when they are applied a perfect design will be produced. At a convenient place on the second stencil, a small part of the design of the first stencil should be cut out. The exact relation of the second stencil to the first one will then be seen. Care must be taken that the guide is not stencilled again accidentally.

FURTHER SUGGESTIONS

Negative stencils enable the background of the design to be stencilled and the design itself to be left in the colour of the wall (Fig. 20). Note that the background has been cut out and not the pattern.

Stencilled borders have many uses. They may take the place of a wallpaper border under a picture rail or they may be used as panel borders, dado borders and the like. Poster colours are convenient for use with stencils which are intended to be applied on wallpaper. If an oil-paint stencil is applied to wallpaper, the parts to be stencilled must receive two coats of size before the stencils are applied, otherwise the oil content in the paint will spread from the edges of the design and discolour the wallpaper.

The amateur decorator has the advantage of being able to design and colour a border to suit the decorations of a room, and to apply many yards of stencilled border at negligible cost. Most stencil designs follow plant and flower forms, but an attempt should be made to design original stencils. Many ideas may be drawn from periodicals, advertisements and film studio sets.

Simple designs stencilled on a wall at regular intervals give very attractive

NEGATIVE STENCIL
FIG. 20. *Example of a negative or background stencil. In this case the ground is cut out and stencilled, leaving the design in the colour of the wall.*

effects. Small spots, dots, stars, diamonds, rings and conventional flower or plant forms, such as the fleur-de-lis, stencilled on a surface at regular intervals, come under what is known as powdering. Walls to be decorated in this manner are first marked out

BORDER WITH GRADUATED COLOUR

FIG. 21. *The effect of a moulding or cornice is produced by this stencil design for a border, the use of graduated colour giving an appearance of light and shade.*

lightly with chalk in the form of a grid. The small patterns are then stencilled on the wall surface at the grid intersections or at alternate intersections. Coloured patterns on a ground of a light tint or light patterns on a deep ground are equally attractive. A close pattern stencilled over a wall area could be the same colour but a lighter shade than the background. Another pleasing combination is produced by powdering the walls with a small design in flat paint on a background of glossy paint of exactly the same shade of colour. Glossy paint stencilled on a flat ground is similar in effect, but it is not so pleasant to use on account of the sticky nature of this type of paint when used for stencilling.

VARIEGATED COLOURS

Stencilled designs may be applied in variegated or graduated colours. Designs in variegated colours are only suitable for objects viewed at close range, as they lose their effect at a distance, but stencilling in graduated colour may be used for border stencils which imitate the effect of light and shade on mouldings. One such border is shown in Fig. 21, where the monochrome effect suggests relief. This type of border looks best if the lightest part of the stencilling is lighter than the background and the darkest part con-

siderably darker than the background. Such a stencil could be used to give the effect of a cornice. In this case the broad effect of light and shade should be emphasized, but intricate detail need not be included in the design.

Stencilling with gold or silver-bronze paint must be undertaken with caution. Remember that gold or silver will not appear to be bright on every wall at once. In fact, at least half the design stencilled with this material will look dull. In general, gold and silver look better on dark backgrounds such as crimson, powder blue or jade green. Gold looks well on any colour, but particularly on scarlet, purple and deep apple-green. Silver has a cooling influence and looks well on pale blue, pale green and crimson, but not on yellow or orange backgrounds.

As far as possible, the paper ties which hold the stencil together should be incorporated in the design. Painting out the blank spaces left by ties will then be unnecessary. Intricate designs which need ties on the stencil contrary to the design should have these ties painted out in suitable colours with a sable-hair pencil brush. Alternatively, a small stencil could be cut to fit the ties and to connect the design.

Painting (running) lines may be difficult at first. Decorators use a straight-edge and a lining fitch for such work. The position of the line is marked with a struck chalk line; that is, a length of string is chalked well, placed against the wall to be marked by holding the string tight at each end and, by lifting the middle of the string with the thumb and forefinger and releasing it suddenly, a perfectly straight chalk line is marked.

LINING FITCH

The straight-edge is placed on the wall in such a position that the top edge of the fitch reaches the chalk line. The bevelled edge of the straight-edge is placed against the wall so as to leave a space between the straight-edge and the wall, and the lining fitch is used from left to right (Fig. 22). Lines up to $\frac{1}{2}$ in. wide may be drawn with a single stroke of the lining fitch, but wider lines need marking out first with a double chalk line to show the correct width. Two lines are then painted with the lining fitch: the top line being painted as already described, with the top edge of the lining fitch touching the chalk line; but the straight-edge is held so that the top edge coincides with the chalk line for painting the bottom line. In other words, the bottom edge of the lining fitch touches the chalk line. Any space which is left between the two lines is filled in free-hand.

After use lining fitches should be washed well, first in turpentine and afterwards with soap and water. Soap should be left on the bristles to keep them straight and compact, but it must be removed before the lining fitch is used again.

The amateur may find it easier to paint lines by means of a stencil. Double lines and series of lines as well

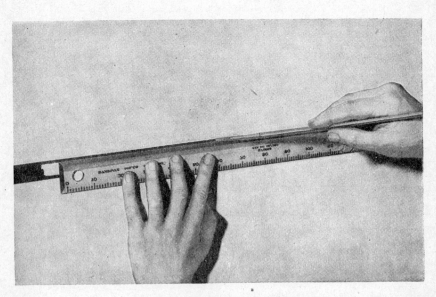

LINES AND BANDS IN COLOUR

FIG. 22. *Straight-edge and lining fitch used to draw lines on a wall. Note how the lines from the previously prepared band are used as a guide for the next stretch.*

DECORATIVE LINES

FIG. 23. *Line design for a plain corner. A few lines to form a panel or design on a plain wall often add character and appeal which is not always surpassed by more elaborate forms of decoration.*

as corner-pieces may be painted in this manner. Fig. 23 shows a border and corner-piece formed with lines only; this idea could be used as a panel border.

Very fine lines, such as those sometimes seen on carriages and painted furniture, are applied with specially fine brushes known as liners. The lines to be painted are sometimes lightly marked out, but more often they are drawn free-hand with the liner. The side of the hand or the little finger should rest on a moulding or the edge of a table while the line is being run. Paint is first put on a palette and the liner is then drawn through it. The full length of the hair of the liner is placed on the surface to be lined with a single, confident movement, and the liner is then drawn with a single stroke in the

desired direction to produce a line of even width. This is difficult work and skill in lining can only be acquired by practice.

Decorators often use gold leaf to decorate mouldings and the parts of an ornament which catch the light. The whole of a plaster ornament is rarely gilded all over. More often the larger part of it is painted a buff colour, which, at a distance, appears to be gold when the ornament is not catching the light. Only the tips of the ornament or a few narrow lines on the face of a plain moulding are usually gilded.

METHOD OF GILDING

The parts to be gilded are first painted with gold-size. When transfer gold is to be used, a mixture of japan gold-size, and yellow-chrome ground in oil, is applied, but when loose leaf-gold is to be used oil gold-size is applied.

The application of loose-leaf gold is very difficult at first. The oil gold-size, which must be prepared only a few hours before it is intended to be used, is painted on the parts of the work to be gilded and allowed to remain until it is almost dry. A few squares of gold leaf are then allowed to fall out of the book which contains them on to a gilder's cushion, see Chapter 11. The leaves should be allowed to float into the corner of the cushion against the parchment shield. A gilder's knife is then taken and one leaf of gold is picked up (with the knife and not with the fingers) and placed in the centre of the cushion as level as possible. The gilder then breathes gently on the centre of the leaf to open it fully and lays it flat and taut on the centre of the cushion. The knife is then used to cut the gold leaf into convenient sizes for the work in hand. For example, when gilding a line the gold would be cut into narrow strips just exceeding the width of the line to be gilded. The decorator then takes a gilder's tip and allows the camel-hair of the tip to touch his cheek or his hair. The camel-hair of the tip is then placed on one of the strips of gold. The gold, which adheres to the tip, is lifted, placed on the gold-size and pressed lightly in position with the tip. The gold which overlaps the part painted with gold-size will hang loose, but it should not be touched. When the gilding is complete, take a paper bag and a camel-hair mop and remove the excess gold, allowing it to fall into the paper bag. Any parts which have been missed are now gilded by stippling a little of the loose gold (from the paper bag) on the part missed, using the camel-hair mop as a stippler. The skewings (loose gold which remains in the paper bag) may be returned to the goldbeaters who will allow a refund according to the weight.

GILDING BY TRANSFER

No doubt the amateur will prefer the more simple method of gilding by transfer. The parts to be gilded are painted with japan gold-size which is allowed to become tacky. A leaf of transfer gold is then taken from the book and is held by the narrow strip which is not covered with gold. The leaf is then pressed against the part to be gilded with a small pad of cotton-wool. The gold adheres to the surface of the tacky gold-size and the leaf is then removed.

Gold leaf is expensive and it should therefore be used to the best possible advantage. If the leaf is dabbed on the gold-size haphazardly quite a lot of gold will be wasted and it is likely that parts of the work will be missed. Twist and turn the leaf to fit parts which are to be gilded; leaves of transfers on which scraps of gold still remain should not be thrown away but saved for touching up small parts which may have been missed. When the gilding is complete it should be lightly dusted with cotton-wool to remove any scraps of excess gold.

OLD FURNITURE

There are, no doubt, many people who have furniture which is no longer in the prime of condition. Packed away in boxrooms and attics may be pieces of old furniture which for reasons of design have been banished to those regions. Such furniture usually has one thing in common, and that is soundness of construction. With a little planning it is possible to alter such furniture. The removal of meaningless ornament, the replacement of ugly panels by plywood, the renewal or alteration of legs, and similar changes, may produce a useful piece of furniture which can be painted and decorated successfully. Indeed, it is just such furniture which is offered for sale at so-called fashionable prices.

PAINTED FURNITURE

It may be argued that painted furniture will not stand up to wear as well as french-polished pieces. On the contrary, decorated furniture will, in fact, last equally well, but only if particular care is paid to the preparation, the painting, the decorating and the finishing of the work.

Furniture which is to be painted and decorated and which has previously been french-polished must be washed with ammonia and water to break the surface of the polish and to provide a key for the first coat of paint. The french-polish could be stripped completely by the use of a paint-remover, but there is no need to go to such lengths unless the furniture has been polished again and again and the surface of the polish is cracked.

Very thin coats of flat undercoating should be used to build up the painted surface. As this type of work is likely to be undertaken as a hobby, there is no point in rushing the job by attempting to obtain solidity of colour in one or two coats of paint. Treatment with

metallic-paint, it may be grained to imitate antique finishes or modern veneering, table-tops may be marbled or two or more of these suggestions may be adopted simultaneously.

ORNAMENTATION

Much of the beauty of painted and decorated furniture lies in the hand-painted ornament so often included in the design. The amateur who does not feel equal to such work may substitute stencilled ornament. A study of antique painted furniture, much of which appears in our museums, will be most

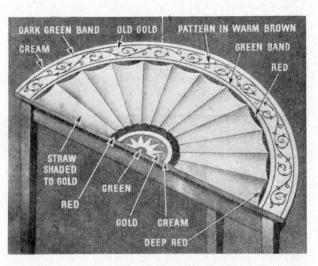

PAINTED FURNITURE

FIG. 24. *An interesting design and colour scheme for an occasional table. It is recommended that the finished work be given a coat of clear varnish.*

distemper filling should precede the second coat of paint. Rubbing-down with fine glass-paper should also precede each coat of paint. If this procedure is followed, a smooth, glass-like surface will result.

Decorating furniture is largely a matter of personal taste. Furniture may be glazed by one of the methods previously described, parts may be picked out in colour, mouldings may be gilded or painted with gold or silver

profitable in providing ideas. A semi-circular table-top, painted and decorated by means of templets (for shading the fan-like shape), stencilling (for the border) and lining is shown in Fig. 24. Furniture decorated in this manner may be glazed with a clouded effect after the painting has been completed. Raw sienna and a touch of black added to the glaze produce an excellent antique shade. A few suggestions for colour schemes follow.

Furniture colour	Ornament colour	Pigments used for glaze
Off-white	Dull green	Raw umber
Cream	Dull red	Raw umber and burnt umber
Green	Gold	Vandyke brown
Crimson	Cream	Vandyke brown
Biscuit	Rich, warm brown	Raw sienna
Pale yellow	Scarlet	Raw sienna

Painted and decorated furniture may be varnished with either gloss or flat varnish. If a gloss-varnished finish is desired, it is best to choose one of pale colour such as french oil-varnish.

Polishing with white or transparent french-polish gives a superior, hard-wearing finish. French-polishing is difficult, but the amateur will find that this work can be successfully performed in the following manner.

The painted work must be perfectly dry and hard and the polishing must be done in a dry, even temperature. A small quantity of white french-polish is put into a clean, dry container and one coat of the polish is applied with a large camel-hair mop. A new 1-in. paint tool is recommended.

When the surface is dry (in about an hour) a piece of cotton-wool is placed in the corner of a square of clean, soft, cotton rag (Fig. 25). The cotton-wool is saturated with french-polish, a few drops of raw linseed oil are added and the rag is folded as shown in Fig. 26. The rag is then twisted and held as shown in Fig. 27. By this time the french-polish will have soaked through the pad, which is known as a rubber.

The rubber is now placed on the surface to be polished and moved over

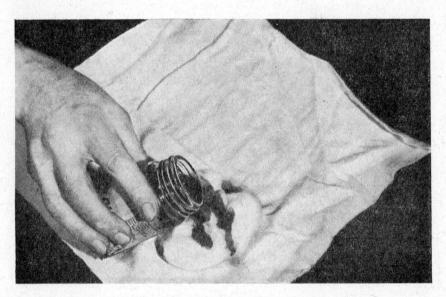

POSITION OF THE COTTON-WOOL

FIG. 25. *Place the cotton-wool slightly off the centre of the rag towards one corner and pour a small quantity of french-polish on the wool before folding over the corners to form the rubber shown in Fig. 26.*

and over it with a continuous circular movement and without lifting the pad. The polish gradually soaks through the rag and gives the surface a very thin film which dries quickly; in fact before the rubber goes over the same place twice. The movement of the rubber must be continuous, and it must not be lifted off the surface suddenly, or

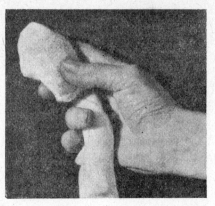

CORRECT HOLD

Fig. 27. *The correct method of holding the rubber when applying french-polish.*

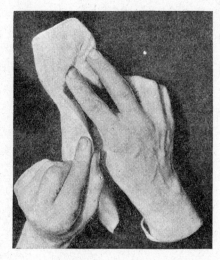

FOLDING THE RUBBER

Fig. 26. *Start by folding over the corner nearest to the pad, then fold in the sides and finally twist the surplus material to form the rubber shown in Fig. 27.*

the polish already on the surface will lift. When the rubber begins to pull, that is when it becomes difficult to work; it should be taken off the surface of the work with a sliding and lifting movement.

Adequate time must be allowed for the polish to harden between applications of polish. Extra french-polish must be added to the cotton-wool from time to time, and a few drops of raw linseed oil dropped on the rubber.

All parts of the work must be treated many times in this manner until a smooth shiny surface appears. This is known as bodying-up.

The final polishing, which gives the glassy surface typical of french-polished work, is carried out by using the rubber with a backward and forward movement. Practise on some unimportant object before attempting to polish a painted and decorated surface. It is important to get the feel of the work in order to know when progress is being made. The feel of french-polishing is almost impossible to describe in words, but will be gained by experience.

The final stage is to give the work a swift polish with the rubber which has been damped with methylated spirits only. This removes any trace of oil which may remain on the polished surface and gives a mirror-like finish.

If a dull finish is required, the work should be polished in the ordinary way, but when it is dry and hard the surface can be dulled with dry pumice powder and a new boot-brush.

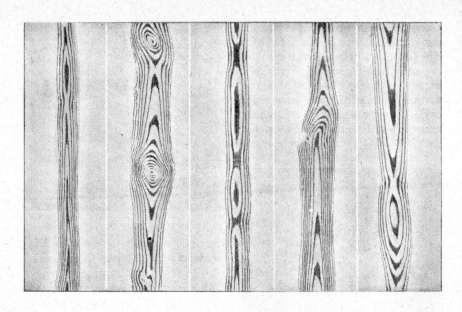

PINEWOOD AND OAK

(*Above*) *Examples of elongated hearts as seen in pinewood. Such figures should be painted on the surface with a sable-hair pencil brush after the graining colour is dry. The fine lines are added with a 1-in. paint tool and the work is finally softened with a pad of soft cloth. (Below) Some suggestions for imitating the coarse grain of hardwoods. The patterns are variously worked with comb and sable brush.*

CHAPTER 9

GRAINING AND MARBLING

IMITATION OF WOODS AND STONE IN PAINT

THE amateur decorator is usually confident of his ability to carry out plain painting, distempering and paper-hanging, but he rarely attempts to vie with the grainer. There is no reason why this should be so. Graining is not a difficult job, and once a few simple instructions have been mastered the handyman will find himself turning out excellent work.

Apart from its decorative quality, graining outlasts almost any other paint finish and has, therefore, an economic value when considerable hard wear is expected from decorations.

GROUND COATS

The grainer uses transparent or semi-transparent pigments ground in oil or water in a similar manner to stains. The great difference is that the grainer uses his stains on a previously painted surface and at such a consistency that they can be easily manipulated.

The painted surface on which the grainer works is known as the ground coat. As the grainer's pigments are transparent or semi-transparent, it is obvious that the colour of the ground coat plays a major part in the colour of the finished work, and the grainer, therefore, colours the ground so as to obtain the maximum help in the process of imitating the natural colour of various woods.

Ground coats should be similar in colour to the lightest part of the wood which is being imitated. The richness of colour of such parts should not be underestimated, and the finish of the ground coat should have just a little more gloss than flat undercoating. A little mixing varnish added to ordinary undercoating makes an excellent ground on which to work. Graining must not be attempted until the ground coat is perfectly dry and hard.

The most popular woods for imitation are oak, mahogany and walnut, but, as previously stated, any polished or natural wood may be grained. Ground colours for various woods and the pigments required for mixing them are given in the following table.

Wood	Ground colour	Pigments (*percentages*)
Light oak	Pale, bright buff	Yellow ochre 50, white 50
Medium oak	Medium buff	Oxford ochre 60, white 40
Dark oak	Warm buff	Oxford ochre 60, white 30, burnt umber 10
Jacobean oak	Dark buff	Oxford ochre 50, white 30, burnt umber 20
Natural oak	Pale, warm buff	White 80, oxford ochre 18, venetian red 2
Limed oak	Pale grey	White 96, orange chrome 3, prussian blue 1

Wood	Ground colour	Pigments (percentages)	Wood	Ground colour	Pigments (percentages)
Pale walnut	Medium warm buff	Oxford ochre 60, white 35, burnt umber 5	Satinwood	Pale yellow	White 70, yellow ochre 30
Medium walnut	Warm buff	Oxford ochre 60, white 30, burnt umber 10	Sycamore (grey)	Pale, silver grey	White 85, black 12, prussian blue 3
American walnut	Bright buff	Yellow ochre 50, white 40, oxford ochre 10	Sycamore (honey colour)	Very pale buff	White 85, yellow ochre 10, burnt umber 5
Burr walnut	Warm, medium buff	Oxford ochre 50, white 30, burnt umber 15, venetian red 5	Cedar (natural)	Medium brown-red	White 60, venetian red 20, oxford ochre 20
Pale mahogany	Pale, dull orange	White 60, venetian red 30, orange chrome 10			
Medium mahogany	Dull orange	White 50, venetian red 30, orange chrome 20			
Spanish mahogany	Dull, rich red	Venetian red 50, white 30, orange chrome 20			
Chippendale mahogany	Deep, rich orange	Venetian red 60, orange chrome 25, white 15			
Natural white mahogany	Pale orange	White 80, venetian red 15, yellow ochre 5			
Natural pinewood	Very pale pink	White 93, oxford ochre 5, venetian red 2			
Pickled pinewood	Off-white	White 95, oxford ochre 4, prussian blue 1			
Pitch pine	Warm, bright buff	White 50, yellow ochre 30, venetian red 20			
Teak	Warm buff	Oxford ochre 60, white 35, burnt umber 5			

If white-lead is used instead of a ready-mixed undercoat, a small proportion of patent driers will be required. Equal parts of raw linseed oil and turpentine should be used as thinners.

The ground coat should be applied on a previously prepared and painted surface and the work should be laid-off in the direction in which the grain is to run. For woods which have a coarse texture, such as oak and teak, coarse brushwork will help the finished work, but smooth woods, such as mahogany and walnut, require a smoothly finished ground-coat.

Oil graining colours, which may be bought ready-mixed, require thinning before they are used. The addition of turpentine is usually sufficient, but sometimes a little boiled linseed oil is also needed. Raw linseed oil may be employed, but its somewhat freer flow is liable to make the brushwork of graining run together.

Ready-mixed graining colour may be sold under the name of scumble or glaze, but the difference is in name only. However, ready-made scumbles are also sold for decorative finishes, so be sure to buy the type intended for graining. This is an important point.

Pigments ground in oil may be added to ready-mixed graining colours, or the colours for various woods may be intermixed. It is, therefore, a simple matter to adjust colours for any particular purpose.

Graining colours are composed of various transparent or semi-transparent pigments in a suitable medium. For those who prefer to prepare their own colours it is advisable to make up the medium first and to stain it with pigments afterwards. A medium which is suitable for almost any type of oil-colour graining is made up as follows.

To one quart of turpentine, add half a pint of boiled linseed oil and about two tablespoonfuls of japan gold-size. Next dissolve half an ounce of beeswax in turpentine and add the liquid to it. Pigments, ground in oil, may now be added to the medium a little at a time until the desired colour and consistency is reached. The more pigment colour which is added, the darker the graining colour will be.

It is better to use thin graining colour on a richly coloured ground than to use it thickly on a pale ground. In this way the transparency of the pigments is used to the best advantage. If thick graining colour is used for imitating woods such as sycamore and mahogany, an unsatisfactory, muddy appearance will result. A table of pigments required for graining various woods follows.

Wood	Ground colour	Pigments (percentages)
Light oak	Pale, bright buff	Oxford ochre 50, raw umber 50 (b)
Medium oak	Medium buff	Burnt umber 70, oxford ochre 30 (b)
Dark oak	Warm buff	Burnt umber 100 (c)
Jacobean oak	Dark buff	Burnt umber 50, vandyke brown 50 (c)
Natural oak	Pale, warm buff	Burnt umber 70, oxford ochre 20, ultramarine 5, crimson lake 5 (a)
Limed oak	Pale grey	Burnt umber 70, ultramarine 20, crimson lake 10 (a)
Pale walnut	Medium, warm buff	Burnt umber 70, raw umber 20, ultramarine 10 (b)
Medium walnut	Warm buff	Burnt umber 80, vandyke brown 15, ultramarine 5 (b)
American walnut	Bright buff	Burnt umber 50, raw umber 50 (b)
Burr walnut	Warm, medium, buff	Burnt umber 50, vandyke brown 50 (c)
Pale mahogany	Pale, dull orange	Vandyke brown 100 (b)
Medium mahogany	Dull orange	Vandyke brown 80, crimson lake 20 (b)
Spanish mahogany	Dull, rich red	Vandyke brown 70, crimson lake 30 (c)
Chippendale mahogany	Deep, rich orange	Vandyke brown 100 (c)
Natural white mahogany	Pale orange	Vandyke brown 50, burnt umber 20, ultramarine 20, scarlet lake 10 (a)

BRUSHING ON THE COLOUR

FIG. 1. *Panel partly brushed-in with graining colour. Note the brush marks, which should remain and not flow out as when working with ordinary paint.*

Wood	Ground colour	Pigments (*percentages*)
Natural pinewood	Very pale pink	Burnt umber 65, burnt sienna 30, ultramarine 5 (*a*)
Pickled pinewood	Off-white	Burnt umber 50, raw umber 45, ultramarine 5 (*a*)
Pitch pine	Warm, bright buff	Burnt umber 50, burnt sienna 45, ultramarine 5 (*b*)
Teak	Warm buff	Burnt umber 70, vandyke brown 20, crimson lake 5, ultramarine 5 (*b*)
Satinwood	Pale yellow	Raw sienna 70, oxford ochre 25, scarlet lake 5 (*a*)
Sycamore (grey)	Pale silver-grey	Black 75, ultramarine 20, scarlet lake 5 (*a*)
Sycamore (honey colour)	Very pale buff	Burnt umber 85, raw umber 10, ultramarine 5 (*a*)
Cedar	Medium brown-red	Burnt umber 75, vandyke brown 15, burnt sienna 10 (*b*)

NOTE.—The letters in italics after the names of the pigments denote the consistency of the graining colour, thus: (*a*) very thin; (*b*) thin; (*c*) medium consistency.

BRUSH-GRAINING

FIG. 2. *Drawing a brush-graining tool over the painted panel shown in Fig. 1 gives markings similar to wood grain.*

The simplest form of graining is executed by brushing the graining colour on the dry ground with an ordinary paint brush and then drawing a brush-graining tool or a clean dusting brush over the brushed-in work; markings similar to the texture of woods are obtained.

A panel partly brushed-in with graining colour is shown in Fig. 1. The material should not be spread on like ordinary paint, but well brushed out. Dip the brush only a little way into the graining colour and then brush the bristle as shown in Fig. 2. Although full pressure should be used all the time, a slight shaking movement of the wrist should be made so as to break up the straight lines made by the graining tool. It is a good plan to paint a panel with ground colour and, when this is dry, to practise on it until the technique is acquired. The panel will also be

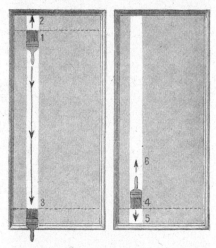

BRUSH-GRAINING PANELS

Fig. 3. *Push the brush upwards from (1) to the moulding (2) and down to (3). Change to (4), push down to the moulding (5) and back to (6) before lifting.*

on the material in all directions, finally brushing in the direction the grain is to run. If the graining colour is of the right consistency, the brush marks made by the paint brush will remain and not flow out. Now take a brush-graining tool or a clean dusting-brush and, with a fine stroke, draw it down the work. Use the full length of

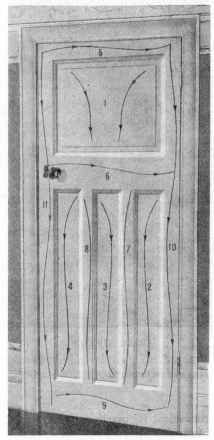

BENDS AND TWISTS

Fig. 4. *Suggested flow of grain on a door. The numbers indicate the order of work and the arrows show the direction in which the brush should be drawn.*

in with the colour and the graining brush is pushed upwards from the dotted line (1) to the moulding (2). Without lifting the brush, draw the brush down again to the dotted line (3), then lift the brush and place it on the dotted line at (4). Push the brush down to the bottom moulding (5), then, without lifting the brush, draw it well past the dotted line, lifting

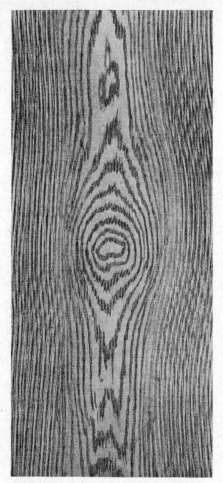

OAK HEART

FIG. 5. *Striking display of heart in oak, rendered in paint. Oak is widely selected for graining purposes.*

convenient for practising other types of graining later.

When brush-graining door panels it may be found that the graining brush leaves small parts at the top and bottom of the panels uncovered. This difficulty may be overcome by working as in Fig. 3. The panel is brushed

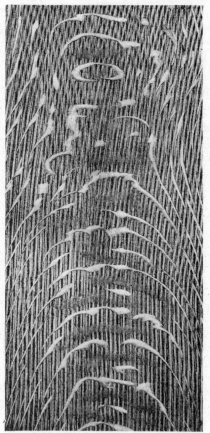

OAK FIGURE

FIG. 6. *Fine example of oak figure produced by wiping out a previously combed panel, with a graining horn and rag, as clearly illustrated in Fig. 12.*

the brush gradually from the panel (6).

Do not draw the graining brush straight all the time, but give variety to the work by making gentle bends and twists. Suggestions for the flow of the grain on a door are shown in Fig. 4. The numbers refer to the order in which the various parts are completed, and the arrows indicate the direction in which the brush should be drawn.

An impression of any wood may be produced by brush-graining. Although it does not copy the true character of the woods, it is useful when a quantity of work must be carried out in a short time or when the home decorator does not feel confident of his ability to carry

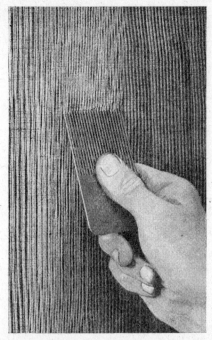

FINELY TEXTURED OAK

FIG. 7. *Applying the comb on a previously combed area to produce the fine texture in certain cuts of oak.*

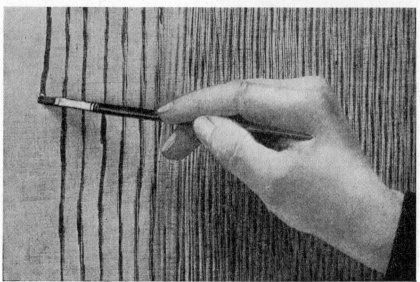

OPEN GRAIN IN OAK

FIG. 8. *Using a sable-hair pencil brush to paint in the open grain which is another characteristic feature of oak, and particularly effective if skilfully introduced.*

REALISTIC TOUCHES
FIG. 9. *Bends and twists in oak are also put in with a sable-hair pencil brush and such markings add further variety to the work.*

out figure graining with equal success.

Oak graining is very popular, and as it provides good practice in imitating the wood and gives some guidance in the graining of other woods, we will deal with it first.

Before proceeding, one particularly important point must be made. It is impossible to grain well unless one is familiar with the wood which is to be imitated. The amateur grainer must, therefore, study carefully the character, colour and texture of various woods.

The most striking characteristic of oak is the display of heart (Fig. 5) and figure (Fig. 6). When these character-

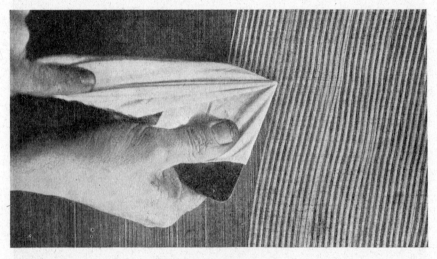

COMBING UNDER RAG

FIG. 10. *The plain parts of oak are grained by using rag and steel combs only. First, the coarse, steel graining comb is covered with rag and drawn down the brushed-in work as shown. A series of fairly thick, contrasty lines is produced.*

CROSS-COMBING

FIG. 11. *After combing under rag (Fig. 10) a finer comb is drawn over the work at a slight angle to the previous combing, to give a good imitation of oak texture.*

istics are seen against finely textured oak (Fig. 7), open grain (Fig. 8), and oak with bends and twists in the texture (Fig. 9), it is easy to appreciate the variety which can be introduced in the work.

The texture of oak may be imitated quite well with steel combs used in the manner described later. Steel graining combs are made in several grades, but the amateur will require three only: one fine, one coarse and one medium steel comb, each about 2 in. wide, will serve for most graining jobs.

Plain oak graining may be carried out by using rag and steel combs only.

WIPING OAK FIGURE
FIG. 12. *A graining horn or well-worn penny covered with a piece of clean rag is used for wiping out the figure on a combed panel.*

Brush in a panel as described previously. Do not use a brush-graining tool, but cover a coarse, steel graining comb with rag, and draw it down the brushed-in work (Fig. 10). Now draw a medium comb, without rag, over the work at a slight angle to the previous combing. This breaks up the lines made by the coarse comb and gives a good imitation of oak texture (Fig. 11). Various grades of texture may be produced by using different grades of comb. The cross-combing, however, must always be done with a finer comb

OAK HEART—STAGE I

FIG. 13. *Using a cloth pad to wipe out part of a panel for the insertion of a heart. Comb the part left in colour.*

DRAWING THE FIGURE—STAGE 2

FIG. 14. *Painting in the heart with a sable-hair pencil brush. After the figure has been completed, a dusting brush should be taken to brush the heart once only in the direction of the grain before combing (Fig. 15) to complete the effect.*

than the one used for the initial combing. Still further variety may be introduced by using the finer combs without rag.

When a panel has been crosscombed, a suggestion of figure will be seen. This may be developed into an oak figure by the use of a well-worn penny and rag. Take a strip of rag in the right hand and place the penny against it, holding the penny between the bent forefinger and the thumb of the right hand. Now take the loose end of the rag in the left hand and pull it over the penny. The figure may now be wiped out of the combed panel. Do not wipe out the figure suggested by the combing, but utilize it and add to it. This stage will be clearly seen in Fig. 12. As the figure is wiped out, pull the rag with the left hand so as to uncover clean rag from time to time.

To grain heart of oak, brush in the work in the normal way, then wipe out a part as shown in Fig. 13. Comb the part left in colour; then, with a sable-hair pencil brush, paint in the heart (Fig. 14). Take a dusting brush and brush the heart once only in the direction of the grain and finally comb the heart with a fine steel comb (Fig. 15). A few suggestions for coarse grain (which is painted on wiped-out strips in the same manner as hearts) are shown on page 196.

FIGURED WORK

Oak graining should not be overdone; plenty of rather plain work of various textures should be included in order to show the figured work to advantage. Give variety and interest to the work by contrasting close and open fibre.

All colours of oak may be grained in the above manner except limed oak,

COMBING THE HEART—STAGE 3

FIG. 15. *Drawing a fine steel comb over the complete figure breaks up the solid lines, shown in Fig. 14, and gives a realistic imitation of the natural wood.*

which requires a special treatment. The graining colour should be used very thinly for limed-oak imitation. Brush in the colour very sparingly and evenly, keeping the work as dry as possible.

For plain work take a steel graining-comb and draw it over the brushed-in work, making a slight shaking movement with the wrist to break up the lines of the comb (Fig. 16).

Hearts and open fibre are imitated by scratching them out with a sharp penknife (Fig. 17). When the heart or coarse grain is complete, fill up any remaining space with combing. Do not use cross-combing for limed-oak grain-ing, or the effect of lime remaining in the texture of the wood will be des-troyed.

Figure, which usually shows dark on limed oak, may be painted on the combed surface with a sable-hair pencil brush. This should be done when the graining is dry. After the figure has been painted and allowed to set a little, take a pad of soft rag and rub the figure lightly. The rag will not rub the figure out, but will take off just sufficient surplus graining-colour to give the figure its proper transparent quality.

Doors, architraves and mouldings are given a more realistic appearance if the graining colour is scraped out of all the angles as the work proceeds.

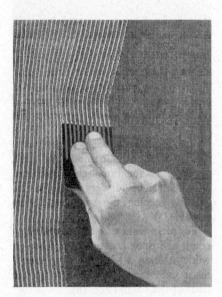

LIMED OAK

FIG. 16. *For plain work, a steel graining comb is drawn over the brushed-in work with a slight shaking movement in order to break up the lines of the comb.*

When graining mahogany, use rather more graining colour than when graining oak. After the work has been brushed-in, take a piece of cotton rag screwed up into a small pad and, hold-ing it between the thumb and fore-fingers, wipe out the light streaks (Fig. 18). When part of the work has been completed, add some further dark streaks with a fitch or a 1-in. paint tool. Now take a hog-hair softener (a soft dusting brush will do) and blend the work, taking care that only the ends of the bristle or hair touch the work. Soften first at right-angles to the grain and afterwards work with the grain. Finally flick the work briskly with the full length of the hairs in the softener, working from bottom to top to imitate the fine texture (Fig. 19).

The beautiful decorative feather of mahogany is produced in the following manner : Brush-in the work in the normal way, then add a dark streak of colour where the centre of the feather is to appear. Do not blend the work at this stage, but take the ball of rag in the fingers and wipe out the light streaks (Fig. 20). Next take a 1-in. paint tool and add dark streaks, following the run of the grain carefully. Finally, soften the work and produce the fine texture by flogging as previously described for plain mahogany.

MAHOGANY GRAIN

It is a great help to copy real pieces of polished mahogany. More about the real character of wood will be learnt in this way than from any description.

If real mahogany is examined, a con-siderable amount of mottling will be observed. This effect is often very pro-nounced on the backs of violins, and for this reason such mahogany is known as fiddleback. Mottling may be

LIMED-OAK FIGURE

FIG. 17. *Hearts and open fibre in limed oak are imitated by scratching with a sharp penknife. When the heart or coarse grain is complete, the remaining space is filled up with combing. It is usually better to avoid cross-combing for this wood.*

produced in oil-colour graining by the use of a hog-hair mottler or with a small piece of cardboard covered with a piece of soft rag. Fig 21 shows mottling being added to plain mahogany graining. The home-made mottler (rag and thin cardboard) is held in both hands and allowed to touch the wet, grained surface here and there as it is drawn over the work. Mottling should be softened with a hog-hair softener as soon as possible, otherwise it will set and will not soften without disturbing the graining colour.

After a certain amount of practice in graining oak and mahogany, very little difficulty will be experienced in graining walnut.

A characteristic of plain walnut is the way in which slender dark streaks broaden out at intervals. This effect may be imitated in the following manner. Brush in the work with graining colour, using rather more than usual. Take the paint brush without colour and, using the side of the brush in a scrubbing manner, remove the light streaks and leave the narrow ones. The latter will become darker by reason of the extra graining colour which is transferred from the flag (end of the bristles) of the brush. Soften the work in the direction of the grain, using a hog-hair softener or a soft dusting brush. Finally, give a medium-texture effect by flogging, as described for mahogany, but using the side of the softener as shown in Fig. 22.

Walnut sap is imitated by taking a dusting brush, or a softener, holding it as shown in Fig. 23 with the fingers separating the bristles into tufts, and

LIGHT STREAKS

FIG. 18 (*Above*). *A piece of rag screwed up into a small pad being used to wipe out the light streaks when graining mahogany. If necessary further dark streaks are added later.*

FINE TEXTURE

FIG. 19 (*Left*). *Flicking the work with the full length of the hairs in the softener, working from bottom to top, produces this fine mahogany texture in the paint, and a remarkable imitation of the natural grain.*

MAHOGANY FEATHER
FIG. 20 (*Right*). *By add-ing a streak of colour and wiping out light streaks on either side of it with a ball of rag, the beautiful decorative feather so characteristic of ma-hogany is created.*

MOTTLING
FIG. 21 (*Below*). *The mottler (described in the text) in use. It is held in both hands and allowed to touch the wet surface here and there as it is drawn lightly over the surface of the work.*

working from the centre outwards. Add a few dark streaks, taking care to follow the flow of the grain carefully, and finally flog the work very lightly. Mottling will improve the graining, but it must not be overdone.

Burr-walnut graining and the imitation of quartered work may be carried out as follows. On a brushed-in area, take a small piece of rag between the forefinger and thumb and, rolling it over the work and twisting it here and there, as the shape of the rag dictates, cover the whole area. Now add darker places and burr with a well-worn fitch or a 1-in. paint tool until a definite flow of grain is seen. Keep on wiping out with rag and adding finer veins with a sable-hair pencil brush until the work is satisfactory. Finish the panel by stippling very lightly with a dusting brush.

Matched panels or quartering, as

seen on bedroom furniture, may be imitated by taking a piece of rag between the fingers of each hand and allowing each hand to work opposite the other. Match up each side of the panel of the quartering in this way first, and complete the work by brush and pencil work as described for ordinary burr walnut. If one side of a matched panel, or two quarters of quartered work, are allowed to remain lighter

MAHOGANY TEXTURE

FIG. 22. *A medium-texture effect in mahogany is obtained by flogging the surface with the side of the softener only.*

than the rest, an effect similar to the reflection of light will be given.

American walnut, teak and cedar are all grained in the manner described for sap walnut. The grains of these woods are similar in character. American walnut sap is usually elongated, but apart from this feature, and the greater or lesser number of dark veins in this wood, the grain may be imitated with dusting brushes or hog-hair softeners only.

Pinewood graining, especially the pale varieties, has become very popular in recent years. It is most suitable for decorative schemes which call for the whole of the walls and woodwork to be grained, but it is also valuable as a quiet, neutral background for the display of period furniture. It is easy to imitate and the amateur should find little difficulty in producing work which is difficult to distinguish from the real wood.

As the decorative value of this wood is negligible when used for small areas, it is best to give instructions for graining a whole room.

IMITATING BOARDS

If the walls are panelled, so much the better, but if not the walls should be set out in vertical boards from 9–13 in. wide.

Set out the walls which should have been previously painted with the pale-pink ground coat, using a pencil line as a guide. Then score the wall lightly with a straight-edge and a blunt knife. If the room has a cornice, include it in the graining.

Take a large brush and paint a whole wall with the graining colour. Now take a pad of clean rag and wipe off as much colour as possible. Sufficient will remain to stain the ground coat

IMITATION OF WALNUT SAP

FIG. 23. *With a dusting brush or a softener, held as shown, with the fingers separating the bristles into tufts, work from the centre outwards. Follow the flow of the grain and add a few dark streaks before finally flogging the work.*

and a small amount will remain in the cuts made by the knife and show the position of each board. Vary the depth of colour of the boards, making sure that interest is given by contrasting light and dark boards by rubbing the edges of the imitation boards here and there. Leave some boards deeper and some lighter than the rest and vary the depth of colour of some of the boards at the top and bottom.

On a palette, or a piece of wood, mix a little burnt umber and raw umber with a few drops of linseed oil and turpentine. Dip the tip of the middle finger in the colour and twist the finger on the work to imitate the shape of knots. These knots may occur anywhere and they should vary considerably in shape and size. If ultramarine is added to a separate amount of the knot colour and burnt sienna added to another amount, knots of different colours may be produced. Next take a piece of rag, and, with the end of the finger, wipe out the centre of the knots with a rough circular movement. Leave a dark circle round some of the knots and wipe out highlights near others to give the effect of light catching the wave in the grain of the wood. Large knots should be light in colour but smaller ones may be left quite strong.

The elongated hearts of pinewood are added when the whole area has been prepared and is quite dry. Add a small amount of burnt sienna to some of the existing graining colour, then, using a sable-hair pencil brush, paint on the figure (Fig. 24). Do not attempt to paint all the fine lines seen in the actual wood, but only the amount of figure shown in the illustration. When several hearts have been painted in this fashion, take an almost dry 1-in. paint tool and, with little more than

SOFTENING THE FIGURE

FIG. 25. *After the figure has been completed with the pencil brush, take a soft pad of clean rag and rub very lightly.*

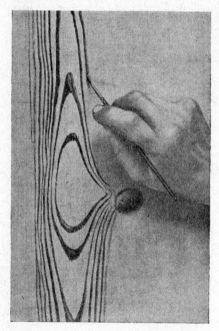

PINEWOOD FIGURE

FIG. 24. *Painting in the elongated heart of pinewood with a sable-hair pencil brush. Note that only the broad lines of the figure are put in at this stage.*

the weight of the brush, imitate the finer lines. Now take a soft pad of clean rag and rub the painted hearts very lightly. Instead of wiping off the graining colour as might be expected, the rag merely takes off the surplus colour and gives the graining a transparent, resinous appearance. Finally wipe out the inner edges of the hearts as shown in Fig. 25.

To grain satinwood, brush-in the work with thin graining-colour and draw a dusting brush down the work, as for rather coarse brush-graining. Finish plain work by flogging to give an extremely fine texture.

On panels and places where decorative grain may be seen to advantage, the work may be mottled. This mottling should be quite pronounced and rather wider than that of other woods (Fig. 26).

If the dusting brush is held at right angles to the run of the grain and the work is lightly stippled with the brush in this position, a fine, secondary mottling will be produced. The work

cardboard about 6 in. long and cover it with soft, cotton rag. Now mottle the work, holding the mottler at about ten degrees from the horizontal, and then go over the surface again, holding the mottler at about the same angle, in such a way as to cross the first mottling.

Allow the work to dry and, with a

SATINWOOD MOTTLE

FIG. 26. *It is necessary to employ thin graining colour for satinwood. The work is brush-grained, flogged and the decorative mottle is added with the dusting brush.*

should not be softened overmuch or the mottling will become smeary and characterless. Fig. 27 shows a panel being cross-stippled.

Both the grey and honey-coloured types of sycamore may be grained very effectively. First the graining colour is brushed evenly on the ground coat. Next make a mottler with a strip of

fine sable-hair pencil brush, add the spidery figure shown in Fig. 28. If the pencil brush is held almost perpendicular to the work, and the point of the brush is allowed just to touch the surface, very fine lines, characteristic of the grain of sycamore, will be produced.

Although the foregoing instructions

for graining in oil-colour will give satisfactory results for most jobs, and produce work of a high standard, the best imitations of the fine texture of wood are obtained by the use of water-colour prior to the oil-colour graining.

WATER-COLOUR GRAINING

Pigments ground in water are used for this process, and they are thinned with water and size, or water and stale beer. Vandyke brown, ground in water, is the most useful pigment to use for this work. It is suitable for the fine textures of nearly all woods.

The colour should be used very thinly and brushed on the dry ground-coat with a perfectly clean paint brush which is kept specially for water-colour.

When the work has been brushed-in, and before it starts to dry, take a grainer's flogger (or a long-haired dusting brush) and stipple the work, not with the end of the bristles, but by holding the brush flat and flogging with the full length of the bristles. The flogging should start at the bottom of the work and should be worked upwards (Fig. 29).

Go over the work once only and do not attempt to touch up any part which seems to be drying unevenly. After a little practice, the fine texture of any wood may be imitated. Close observation of the texture of various woods will be necessary before the true characteristics of any particular wood can be copied. In general, walnut, teak, cedar and mahogany have a fairly pronounced texture, but that of maple and sycamore is very fine. Flogging must not precede the graining of either limed oak or pinewood, and it

CROSS-STIPPLING SATINWOOD

FIG. 27. *Hold the dusting brush at right-angles to the run of the grain. Stippling the work lightly with the brush in this position produces a fine secondary mottling.*

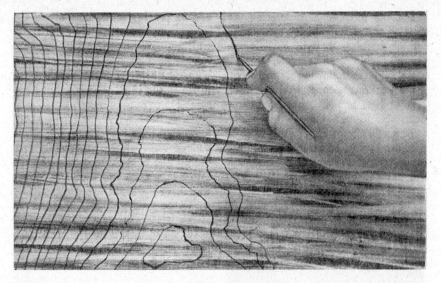

SYCAMORE GRAINING

FIG. 28. *After brushing on the graining colour evenly, the surface is mottled in two directions and allowed to dry before the spidery figure is added with the brush.*

is rarely necessary for oak graining.

Graining in oil-colour may be carried out as soon as the flogging with water-colour is dry, but better results will be obtained if the water-colour is allowed to dry and is then given a coat of a mixture of 50 per cent varnish and 50 per cent turpentine. This is known as binding-down and it must be allowed about twelve hours to harden before oil-colour graining is attempted.

MARBLING

The home decorator with a little artistic skill should be able to turn out very good imitations of marble. The process is fundamentally the same for almost all marbles, so all that is necessary, once the principle is known, is to become familiar with the varieties of marble and to know the appropriate pigments to use.

As in graining, marbling must be preceded by a coat of paint suitably stained with colours ground in oil. The following list gives the colours of the ground coats for the better-known varieties of marble.

Marble	Ground
Italian sienna	Cream
French sienna	Pale cream
Rouge roi	Pale pink
Swedish green	Oyster grey
Tinos (green)	Pale, dull green
Travatine	Pale neutral (putty colour)

There is no purpose in giving a longer list, as the simple rule to follow is to make the ground coat the same colour as the lightest part of the marble to be imitated.

To carry out marble imitation, make up a medium of 65 per cent turpentine, 30 per cent raw linseed oil and 5 per cent japan gold-size.

For the purpose of describing the method of marbling, which is the same for all marbles, we will take Italian sienna marble as an example.

Arrange the following pigments on a palette: raw sienna, burnt sienna, raw umber, vandyke brown, yellow ochre and ultramarine.

Brush in the ground with the clear medium, using sufficient to wet the ground well. Take a 1-in. paint tool, dip it in the medium first, then into

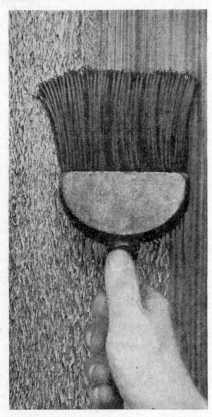

FLOGGING-IN WITH WATER-COLOUR

FIG. 29. *For this work the brush is held flat and the surface is flogged with the full length of the bristles.*

one of the pigments, and brush the colour out in a patch similar to that which appears in real marble. Use the remaining pigments in the same way, blending some of them with the brush as the work proceeds, but leave some places uncoloured.

Before the medium and the brushed-in patches have had time to set, take a pad of rag and dab the whole area evenly but lightly. Next fold the rag into a long strip and, standing a little way from the work, whip the surface sharply. This takes out light streaks in a very natural manner.

With a painter's fitch (a well-worn one is best), add the dark veins of the marble, using a mixture of raw umber and ultramarine. Finally soften the work with a hog-hair softener or with a soft dusting-brush.

SWEDISH GREEN MARBLE

To describe an effective part of marbling, that of obtaining incidental effects by turpentine splashes, the imitation of Swedish green marble will serve as an example. Note how a completely different marble may be imitated by the same technique by using different pigments.

On a pale, oyster-grey ground, brush in the medium which has been stained with a mixture of 90 per cent burnt umber and 10 per cent prussian blue. In this case the stained medium should be brushed out well and evenly. Now take a piece of screwed-up rag and dab the surface all over, afterwards softening the work with the hog-hair softener.

Put a little turpentine in a clean container and stain it with a small amount of raw sienna. Now take a clean 1-in. paint tool and dip the ends of the bristles into the turpentine.

COMPLETION OF MARBLING

FIG. 30. *Take a clean 1-in. brush and dip the ends of the bristles into turpentine. Hold the brush in the left hand, separate the bristles with the fingers of the right hand and flick spots of turpentine on to the work.*

Holding the paint tool in the left hand, separate the bristles with the fingers of the right hand in such a way that small splashes of turpentine fly on the surface of the work (Fig. 30).

After a moment or two the turpentine splashes will separate the brushed-in work and will leave small yellowish patches surrounded by dark outlines similar to those seen in Swedish green marble. Next take a small piece of old dry sponge, dip it in a little strong colour (burnt umber and prussian blue) and stipple the surface of the work, taking care to make the marks small and even. A few very light and bolder veins are added to give relief and interest. These veins may be wiped out in the same manner as the figure in oak graining; that is, with rag and a well-worn penny.

These examples should be sufficient to give the general idea of marbling, and it will be found that by combining them, and by using suitable pigments, any marble may be copied speedily and with excellent results.

It is hardly necessary to point out that work which is to be finished in an imitation of marble must be quite smooth, otherwise the finished work will always look very unnatural.

PATTERNED TEXTURES IN CEMENT

FIG. 1. *Apart from being weatherproof, textures such as the flattened stipple, fan pattern, finger-whorl pattern and rubbed texture form interesting backgrounds.*

CHAPTER 10

TREATMENT OF EXTERIOR WALLS

PURPOSE OF VARIOUS FINISHES

EXTERIOR walls may be of brick, stone, plaster, cement and sand, or cement, sand and lime renderings, concrete, roughcast or pebble-dash, glazed tiles, asbestos or even steel plates, and it is proposed to deal with the materials in that order.

In general, all such walls are sufficiently weatherproof and most of the subsequent treatments which they may receive (Fig. 1) are mainly intended either to preserve the initial surface or to refresh its appearance. As, however, weatherproofing is sometimes required, most of the materials which are used for treating exterior walls are of a weather-resisting nature. Gloss paint, oil paint, limewash, oil-bound distemper and cement paint all come in this category to a greater or lesser extent.

SOUND ADVICE

In some of our better town-houses the brickwork is really excellent. The bricklaying has been carried out with extraordinary care and correctness and may include shaped chimney stacks of great decorative value or ornament of carved brickwork or terracotta. Such brickwork should be allowed to remain in its original state, except, of course, for necessary repairs such as pointing.

A mistaken idea is that because bricks absorb water, interior dampness may follow. Rainwater which falls on brickwork is absorbed to some extent, but as soon as the rain stops the water evaporates and the bricks dry again. A brick will absorb a large amount of water, so even the most severe rainstorm will not saturate a double thickness of brickwork and penetrate to the interior surfaces of a house. A damp-course prevents the upper brickwork of a wall from absorbing moisture from the ground, but if the damp-proof course should happen to be damaged, water will be absorbed almost continually, resulting in decayed brickwork and, eventually, damp walls.

REFRESHING BRICKWORK

Brickwork which is of poor quality may be refreshed in colour, and yet retain its porous quality, if it is distempered with a mixture of size and dry venetian red, mixed as an ordinary size-bound distemper. The mortar joints (or pointing) may then be painted with a distemper made with vegetable black powder and size or with grey or white oil paint (Fig. 2). Although this treatment is quite common, it cannot be said to produce a pleasing or permanent result, as the colour of the brickwork gives an artificial appearance. If extra time is taken and the bricks are distempered in slightly different colours the work looks far more natural. The dry colours required are venetian red, yellow ochre, ultramarine blue and brunswick green. A pail of liquid size, a round distemper tool and a piece of wood about 18 in. square for a palette will be required. First dip the brush in the size and then into the colours; then rub the brush on the palette to mix the colours before attempting to distemper individual bricks. A good plan is to use pure venetian red for half of the brickwork and to colour the rest with venetian red mixed with one or other of the remaining colours (Fig. 3). Reddish tints should, of course, predominate.

COLOUR AND RENOVATION

Limewash (slaked lime and water) is useful for the brickwork of greenhouses and outhouses. It may also be used to colour the exterior walls of cottages when the brickwork is of poor quality. Limewash may be tinted by the addition of dry colours such as venetian red, yellow ochre and ultramarine blue. It is waterproof to some extent, but if extra waterproofing is desired boiled linseed oil may be added to the limewash. The walls to be treated should always be scraped or brushed down to remove any old, flaking limewash. A wire brush is useful when the surface is very loose. Two coats of limewash are desirable. The first coat should be rather thin and should be rubbed well into the work to make sure that all the joints and holes are covered. The second and final coat should be thicker and plenty of material should be used to fill up all cracks and holes. Embedded dirt need not be removed before limewashing.

Brickwork may be scrubbed with water and an old distemper brush for the purpose of cleaning and the result

PAINTING MORTAR JOINTS

FIG. 2. *When painting mortar joints with distemper or oil paint it is a good plan to hold a straight piece of wood against the edge of the brickwork as illustrated. Apart from protecting the bricks, a cleaner line is obtained along the joints.*

TINTING BRICKS

FIG. 3. *After dipping the brush in the paint-kettle containing liquid size, the colour is picked up from a wooden palette. In this illustration pure venetian red is being applied to "pick out" certain of the bricks and so produce a more pleasing effect than when all are the same colour.*

is often surprisingly good. The work should be started at the top of the wall and plenty of water should be used. When a part of the wall has been saturated the distemper brush is used in a downward, scrubbing manner; thus the surface water and the loosened dirt will be gradually brought down to the ground. Once a wall has been started it should be completed without a break. If it is left half-finished for any appreciable time the excess of dirt, which occurs where the work has been left off, will be difficult to remove later. Steam cleaning is carried out in a similar manner. The steam pressure loosens the dirt and pushes it downwards. On account of the plant required this is not a job for the amateur.

Brick walls, which have a great deal of embedded dirt, may be cleaned by the use of dry, wire brushes. If wire brushes are used, do not scrub as hard and quickly as possible or the brickwork will be damaged. Gentle and persistent scrubbing is far preferable.

Oil-bound distemper can be used to colour exterior brick walls. Outside-quality material must be used and the material should be thinned with petrifying liquid which is specially manufactured for the purpose. Two coats of oil-bound distemper will be required for brickwork. The first coat should be thin to penetrate the surface of the bricks and twenty-four hours should elapse before the second coat is applied. The final coat of oil-bound distemper should always be fairly thick or round. The substance spreads more easily than its thick appearance might suggest. On no account must a thin wash of oil-bound distemper be given with the idea of improving an unsatisfactory finish. The resulting finish will be more unsatisfactory than before. Colours should be chosen which the manufacturers recommend for exterior use.

PAINTED WALLS

Brick walls may be painted. Ordinary oil paint with a white-lead base and a reasonable oil content should be used. Flat undercoating or flat enamel is unsuitable, as it seldom withstands the effects of the weather. The first coat of paint should be in the nature of a priming coat. It should have a good oil content and should be used thinly. Unless the brickwork has been painted previously, at least three coats of oil paint will be required. Two coats may be sufficient if brick-red, brown or other deep colours are used. The mortar joints may be lined out with white or grey paint on dark painted brickwork or deep grey or black on light brickwork. Painted brickwork looks rather artificial, but it has the advantage of resisting the weather to a great extent and of appearing clean.

Stonework can be cleaned very well indeed by steam pressure, but washing down with water only, as described for brickwork, will prove satisfactory unless the work is situated in a smoky industrial area. If the walls are particularly begrimed, rubbing down with a piece of flat stone, similar to that used for the building, will loosen the dirt. The stone should be used in the manner described for rubbing down paintwork with pumice-stone. It is best to protect oneself with oilskins and to choose a wet day for washing down brickwork or stonework. Under such conditions the work can be carried out in under half the time required on a warm, fine day.

There are several stone preservatives on the market. They are applied with old distemper brushes. The stonework to be treated should be properly cleaned before any preservatives are applied, as the material binds dirt into the surface of the stone, making subsequent cleaning almost impossible.

Painted stucco walls, which are in

PAINTED WALL

FIG. 4. *Modern garden wall, with cement rendering and texture, painted cream. The finish is durable, resistant to moisture and of attractive appearance. It is important that outside-quality material only should be employed for this type of work.*

good condition, may be prepared for repainting by washing and rubbing down as described for ordinary paintwork. A rather strong solution of soda or sugar soap will be necessary if the walls are grime-encrusted. Dry brushing before washing makes the preparation easier.

Two coats of oil paint made with paste white-lead and patent driers, and tinted with the appropriate stainers (pigments ground in oil), are usually sufficient. The first coat should be mixed with equal parts of raw linseed oil and turpentine, and the second with rather more oil and proportionately less turpentine. A flat finish is not advised for this class of work or, indeed, for any kind of exterior surface since flat paints and enamels in general, with only a small amount of oil in their composition, have only a limited resistance to the weather.

If an imitation of stonework is wanted, it is best obtained by the use of one of the proprietary brands of imitation-stone paints of good quality.

SIMPLE REPAIRS

Stucco walls which are cracked, damaged or decayed require all faulty parts to be cut away. The roughing-in of the brickwork which is revealed should be painted with red-lead mixed with turpentine and boiled linseed-oil. Repairing with Keene's cement should follow. Do not attempt to make good very deep cracks or bare places with a single application of Keene's cement. Such parts should be built up to the surface of the existing walls gradually. In other words, the parts should be repaired roughly with Keene's cement to which a proportion of fine sand has been added.

This roughing-in should be left with

TYROLEAN FINISH

FIG. 5. *An open texture finish with a multiplicity of drip points which prevent rain-water from running down the wall in a sheet.*

a key (a rough surface) to which the final repair will adhere and it should be allowed to dry before the final repairing, with Keene's cement only, is attempted. Before they are quite dry the repaired parts should be painted with a non-oily lead paint. Alternatively, the repaired parts may be allowed to dry properly and then be painted in the normal way. It is, however, important to allow sufficient time for the repair work to harden right through before the first coat of paint is applied to the surface of the wall.

If the colour of the existing walls is matched in touching-up any repaired parts, a coat of paint for the wall area may be saved. If the touching-up is done with white paint, the repairs may show through several coats of paint and look clean and bright against the rest of the wall area.

Cement paint is unsuitable for the treatment of surfaces containing gypsum plasters or for existing oil-painted surfaces.

New stucco walls may be distempered with outside-quality oil-bound water-paint. The use of petrifying liquid for thinning is essential. Existing oil-painted stucco surfaces should not be treated with water-paint, but existing water-painted surfaces may be painted with oil paint. The initial coat of oil paint used in these circumstances should be thin and should contain equal parts of turpentine and raw linseed oil.

Cement and sand or cement, as well as lime and sand renderings, may be painted with oil paint, water-paint or cement paint (Fig. 4). Outside-quality water-paint, thinned with petrifying liquid only, must be used on cement, as for all other outside surfaces, treated in this manner. The first coat of the material must be thin and be rubbed well into the surface. Ample time must be allowed for hardening between the application of each coat.

CEMENT PAINT

The use of waterproof cement paint is excellent for walls rendered in cement. It prevents dampness, it is unaffected by rain, it is washable and it will not peel or rub off. The material must be mixed correctly or the result will be unsatisfactory.

All existing coats of distemper, oil paint or limewash and all loose material and dirt must be removed before cement paint is applied. If the surfaces to be treated are absorbent, they should be saturated with water and allowed to dry before the first coat of cement paint is applied. Add nothing but water to cement paint. One hundredweight of cement paint should be sufficient to paint 180 sq. yd. of cement and sand rendering with two coats of the material, if it is mixed correctly.

When applied by a distemper brush, the first coat of cement paint must be rubbed well into the surface. As with water-paint, twenty-four hours should be allowed for hardening before the second coat is applied. Two coats of cement paint or water-paint are usually sufficient, but an extra coat should be allowed if the existing surface is of a dark colour.

SPECIAL FINISHES

A light-textured effect may be obtained by using a dry hair-stippler. but extra-thick material should not be used with the intention of obtaining a heavy texture. Cement paint is not a substitute for plastic paint.

Oil paint and water-paint should not be applied to new cement-and-sand rendering, but both these materials may be used with success when the surface has had sufficient time to season. The preparation and painting of cement work should be carried out as described for plaster work, but repairs should be carried out with portland cement and sand, not with Keene's cement. Never attempt to rough-cast exterior walls with plastic

PEBBLE-DASH WALL
FIG. 6. *Cracks in pebble-dash walls should be repaired with a cement-and-sand mixture. A handful of pebbles should then be thrown sharply on to the wet surface, to which they will adhere.*

paint unless many subsequent coats of oil paint can be allowed.

Concrete walls may be treated in similar manner and with the same materials described for cement-and-sand renderings.

There is a tyrolean finish on the market which consists of white or coloured portland cement mixed ready for use with specially-graded sand. When applied by a special tyrolean machine it produces an open-texture finish, presenting a multiplicity of drip points which ensure that rain cannot run down a wall in a sheet (Fig. 5). It will be found that 1 cwt. of tyrolean finish will cover approximately 10 sq. yd.

ROUGH-CAST AND PEBBLE-DASH

Rough-cast walls may be treated as for cement-and-sand rendering. Extra materials must be allowed, as such a surface has a larger area per square yard than similar smooth surfaces. For instance, 1 cwt. of cement paint will only cover 90 sq. yd. of rough-cast,

against 180 sq. yd. of smooth rendering. Usually twice the amount of material required for smooth walls will be needed.

Pebble-dash should not require painting or distempering, although the materials mentioned for cement rendering may be used. In most cases, rain-water cleans the pebbles which adhere to the cement backing and produces a bright, sand-coloured and mottled surface. Once this natural colour is destroyed by painting—and quite a lot of paint is required to do so —it can never be regained and periodical renovating will then become necessary.

Pebble-dash walls should be examined at times to make certain that large cracks or crazing have not occurred which allow rain-water to penetrate to the backing. These cracks should be repaired with portland cement and sand and with a handful of pebbles thrown sharply on the wet surface to which they will adhere (Fig. 6).

Occasionally, exterior walls are

covered with glazed tiles. All that is required to keep them clean and bright is the use of water. If the tiles have become smoke engrimed, soda or sugar soap may be used in the manner described for washing paintwork. Tiled exterior-walls should be examined from time to time to make sure that loose tiles do not fall off and break.

TILES AND ASBESTOS

A loose tile must be carefully removed by slipping a stripping knife in the joint under it, holding the tile with the left hand and the thumb of the right hand while it is being removed. The tile may be refixed by the use of a special tile-cement or with white-lead and gold-size made into a paste. Both the back of the tile and the cement backing should be smeared with tile cement or white-lead paste and the tile should then be pressed firmly back into place.

If several tiles are loose, refix them one at a time, unless it is possible to number both the tile and the backing as each tile is removed. Tiles are not always interchangeable, on account of the mould on the back which leaves corresponding marks on the cement backing.

If tiles have become very old and discoloured and it is decided to paint them, the glazed surface should be given a coat of varnish before the first coat of paint. The varnish provides a key for the paint and prevents subsequent chipping.

Exterior surfaces of asbestos may be treated with paint, washable distemper or cement paint. A thin priming-coat of oil paint should precede distempering, but cement paint must be applied directly on the asbestos surface. Painting asbestos sheets with oil paint or flat paint is quite in order, but thin coats should be applied. Asbestos requires no protection and colouring is only applied for the sake of appearance.

When decorating asbestos surfaces, remember that the material is extremely brittle. Do not step on the roof of a shed which is covered with asbestos sheets or asbestos tiles. It is dangerous to paint corrugated asbestos roofing with black bituminous paint, as the material may be mistaken for corrugated iron until it is stepped on.

There are a number of houses with walls of steel sheets. Such surfaces should be treated as ironwork. Oil paint is the usual protective film.

METAL SURFACES

When repainting steel-wall surfaces, the preparation of the work must be carried out with care. It is no good painting over brown patches on the walls, as the paint will only hide the patch for a short time. Such places should be scraped free of paint and the rusty steel which will be revealed should be rubbed with a wire brush until it is quite bright. These bare places should be touched up as soon as possible with lead-oxide paint, which has a good oil content. Subsequent coats of paint should follow normal practice.

Bituminous paint is effective for protecting ironwork, and now that it is obtainable in light colours there is only one reason why it should not be used in place of oil paint. The objection is that once bituminous paint has been used on a surface, this material must be employed in future. Subsequent decorating with ordinary oil paint is out of the question, as the bitumen will bleed through any number of coats of oil paint.

CHAPTER 11

TOOLS AND MATERIALS

HOW TO CHOOSE THE NECESSARY EQUIPMENT

ALTHOUGH the average painter can manage with a limited number of tools, the equipment which a good, all-round decorator requires is considerable. Let us begin by describing the usual brushes and tools which should be available, and describe the purpose

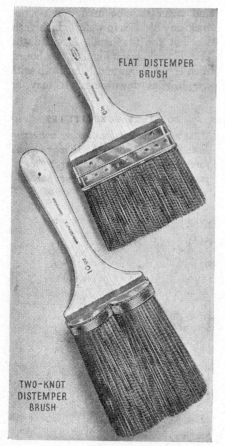

FLAT DISTEMPER BRUSH

TWO-KNOT DISTEMPER BRUSH

of the less familiar equipment later.

Whatever else the home decorator can dispense with, he will not go very far without distemper brushes and paint brushes. One really good distemper brush and a washing-down brush will be required. Different types of distemper brushes (Fig. 1) are favoured in various parts of the country. In the northern counties flat distemper brushes are preferred, but in the southern counties oval, two-knot distemper brushes are more popular. The latter are, perhaps, more suitable for amateur use.

Brushes are manufactured for the purpose of washing down (Fig. 2). These are really coarse distemper brushes and are much cheaper than good, all-bristle brushes. However, most painters and decorators prefer to use old distemper brushes for this work. A good distemper brush is an expensive item, and as there is no substitute for it, it is advisable to reject anything but the best if it is intended to turn out first-class work.

When buying a brush see that the bristles are set firmly and yet are soft and resilient. When the bristles are pressed back with the hand (Fig. 3)

CHOICE OF DISTEMPER BRUSH
Fig. 1. *Flat distemper brushes are preferred in northern counties while oval, two-knot distemper brushes are more popular in the southern counties.*

DUSTING
BRUSH

WASHING-
DOWN
BRUSH

and then released, they should fly back to their original positions. Shake the brush, and if a fine white dust emerges, the brush may be full of dressing which makes it appear to be of better quality than it really is. It is best to reject brushes which seem dry and brittle, as the bristles may suffer from dry rot. Examine the brush by holding it up to the light. Many of the bristles in a good brush may be split at the ends into two or three fine hairs (Fig. 4), but do not expect many of the bristles to be split.

Before use, a new brush should be washed out well in tepid water. Soap and water may be used, but do not wash any brushes in water which feels too hot for the hand. Suspend the brush in cold water for about six hours, then shake it out and hang it up with the bristles downwards. It may be

POSSIBLE SUBSTITUTES

FIG. 2. *These two brushes are not essential. An old distemper brush may be used for washing down and almost any soft brush may be employed for dusting purposes.*

TESTING A BRUSH

FIG. 3. *The bristles of a good brush should be springy, and should fly back to their normal positions after being bent over as shown here.*

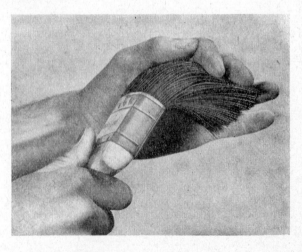

GOOD-QUALITY

FIG. 4. *A few of the bristles in a good-quality brush may be split at the ends into two or three fine hairs. Examine the bristles as shown in this illustration.*

necessary to bore a small hole in the handle through which to tie a piece of string. If the brush is used only occasionally, do not allow it to be put away in a damp condition as the bristles will be liable to rot, especially in a warm atmosphere.

Keep a distemper brush for its purpose. It may be used for washing down two or three times at first, to break it in and to rid it of all loose bristles, but thereafter it should be used for distempering purposes only.

PAINT-KETTLES

One or two paint-kettles will be needed. They are not indispensable, but are much more convenient to use than ordinary tins, empty salmon-cans and the like. They are thick and strong enough to be burnt out when they become thick with old paint. Burning out is done in the following manner: pour a little turpentine substitute or

petrol into the dirty paint-kettles, add a screw of paper or a small piece of rag to act as a wick, light the wick and retire a few steps (Fig. 5). Very soon the old paint will bubble, reach its flash point, burn itself out and leave a carbon deposit. Allow the kettle to cool (to avoid burnt fingers) and then scrape out the deposit with an old knife (Fig. 6), not with a good tool. Finish the cleaning with glass-paper, wipe out the paint-kettle with rag and then go round the joint and corners with a coat of knotting varnish.

Paint-kettles may also be cleaned by placing them in a solution of caustic soda and washing them out thoroughly with cold water afterwards.

Although two methods of cleaning paint-kettles have been described, there is no real need for such measures. Paint should be emptied back into the container immediately after use, and the paint-kettle should be wiped out.

Several paint brushes will be required. Although pound brushes (Fig. 7) are still used professionally, the amateur will find that flat paintbrushes are most suitable for home decorating. Fig. 8 shows two typical flat paint-brushes. It is advisable to have at least two sets of paint brushes : one set for white and pale colours and another set for dark colours. A minimum collection of paint brushes should consist of two 3-in. brushes, two 2-in. brushes, two 1-in. (known as inch tools) and one $\frac{3}{4}$- or $\frac{1}{2}$-in. tool.

REMOVING THE BLACK DEPOSIT
FIG. 6. *After a paint-kettle has been burnt out, allow it to cool and then remove the black deposit with an old knife. Never use a good tool for the job.*

BURNING-OUT PAINT-KETTLES
FIG. 5. *Pour a little petrol or turpentine into the dirty paint-kettles, pile them up as shown, add a screw of paper as a wick, apply a match and retire a few steps.*

Paint brushes should be examined in the same manner as distemper brushes. The bristles should be fine and long and they should hang well together. To buy cheap, inferior brushes is a waste of money. They will not last long, they are difficult to use and they will not allow painting to be carried out satisfactorily.

It is better to purchase a good dusting brush (Fig. 2) than to use an old carpet brush. Apart from its use for dusting off work after glass-papering, it makes a good substitute for a dragger (described later) when brush-graining is carried out, and it may be used as a stippler for glazing or scumbling. For these reasons, the additional expense may be worth while.

The following knives and tools (Figs. 9–11) will be required: a stopping knife, a stripping knife for removing paint and wallpaper, a broad knife for repairing cracks and damaged plasterwork, a filling knife for producing a good surface, a shave-hook for scraping mouldings and ironwork, and a chisel knife for use where a wider knife would be inconvenient. A hacking knife is useful for removing old putty when replacing broken panes of glass.

Metal paint-strainers (Fig. 12) with removable gauze are available and it is better to use one than to make do with muslin or old curtain material. Paint which has been exposed to the air and become full of skins should not be used until it has been strained.

The strainer is placed above the paint-kettle, as illustrated in Fig. 12, so that the paint can be poured into the strainer a little at a time. An old 1-in. paint tool is used with a stirring movement to work the paint slowly through the gauze mesh. Rid the strainer of skins from time to time as the job proceeds. If the skins are placed on an old newspaper they can be disposed of without trouble.

CLEANING THE STRAINER

If a large amount of painting is being carried out the strainer may be suspended in water when it is not in use, but if only occasional straining is needed the strainer should be cleaned out with turpentine substitute. Paint must never be allowed to dry in the strainer. If this has occurred, the gauze may be cleaned by holding it over a gas jet with a pair of pliers for a few seconds (Fig. 13), and then scraping the gauze lightly on each side with an old knife. Never use a good tool.

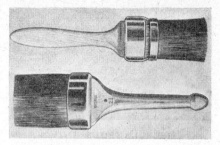

POUND BRUSHES

FIG. 7. *Some professionals consider that these oval brushes are superior to the flat brushes shown in Fig. 8 as paint spreaders.*

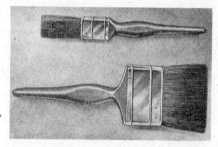

FLAT PAINT-BRUSHES

FIG. 8. *Available in various sizes and qualities, these flat paint-brushes are most suitable for amateur work.*

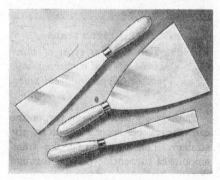

FILLING KNIVES

FIG. 9. *These tools are used for levelling uneven surfaces and are available in different widths. The blades should be flexible and of good quality steel.*

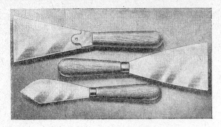

MISCELLANEOUS KNIVES

FIG. 10. *The two upper knives are strippers, for removing paint or wallpaper; the tool below is a putty knife.*

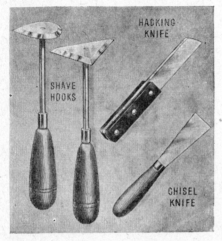

HACKING KNIFE

SHAVE HOOKS

CHISEL KNIFE

FURTHER ESSENTIALS

FIG. 11. *Two different types of shave hook, a chisel knife and a hacking knife for such jobs as chipping-out old putty.*

Painters say that enough turpentine can always be spared to clean the strainer. This means that the small amount of turpentine poured through the strainer, after the last of the paint has been strained, will not be sufficient to thin the paint unduly. Paint straining helps to remove skins, and to amalgamate any colours ground in oil which have been added to the paint.

It is difficult to decide whether a blow-lamp for burning off old paint should come under the heading of essential or desirable equipment. It depends on the volume of work the home decorator intends to carry out. If consideration is given to the use, apart from that of burning off paint, to which a blow-lamp may be put, it is probably as well to have one.

There are several types of paraffin and petrol blow-lamp. If the lamp is to be used solely for burning off paint, a light, paraffin blow-lamp is recommended. Remember that a cumbersome lamp is difficult to use from a ladder.

Besides the brushes and tools already mentioned, the home decorator will need one or two pails, a sponge, a 2-ft. rule, one or two screwdrivers, a pair of pincers and a light claw hammer.

If it is not possible to hire or borrow scaffolding, an extension ladder is

PAINT-KETTLE AND STRAINER

FIG. 12. *The best form of paint strainer is that fitted with a removable gauze on a collar which can be easily cleaned.*

FIG. 13. *By holding the paint strainer with a pair of pliers over a gas flame, any paint which may have dried and hardened on the interior may be scraped away with a knife. Of course, it is better to clean the strainer with turpentine immediately after use.*

essential. A small, single ladder of about ten rungs, two pairs of six- or eight-tread steps, and one long and one short scaffold board are also required for most jobs.

DESIRABLE EQUIPMENT

Under the heading of desirable equipment come all the brushes and tools which a capable decorator uses and which have not yet been described.

Badger brushes (which are very expensive) are used for softening and blending when certain types of graining and marbling are being carried out. Badger softeners should be used for water-colours only. Hog-hair softeners are similar to those made from badger hair, but they are used for softening and blending oil colours. They are rather expensive, but considerably cheaper than badger softeners (Fig. 14).

A flogger (Fig. 15) is used to imitate the texture of wood prior to graining mahogany or other close-grained woods. It looks like a very thin, flat distemper brush, and its use is described under graining. A long-haired dusting brush makes a passable substitute.

Fitches are small brushes with long shafts (Fig. 16). They are used for working into awkward corners, for painting very narrow iron sashes, for picking out colours on cornice members or similar mouldings, for mural decoration and for scenic painting. Decorators' fitches are similar to artists' oil-colour brushes. The lining fitch is used with a straight-edge for painting straight lines.

Sable-hair pencil brushes are used for signwriting and fine decorative work. They are made both flat and round and in several sizes. The round ones are useful for graining (Fig. 17).

Hair and rubber stipplers (Fig. 18) are used for a variety of purposes in the decorating trade. They are made in several sizes. Some have fixed handles at the back while others have adjustable handles. The main use of a stippler is to produce an even surface on flat paint. One man brushes the flat paint on roughly (but evenly) while another man follows with the stippler. The stippler is used to produce graduated effects in paint or distemper, and to beat out glaze (transparent oil-colours). Many of the effects obtained with plastic paint (such as imitation stonework) require the use of a hair stippler.

Rubber stipplers produce coarse, medium or fine textures when used on plastic paint or paint glaze. They may also be used to give pattern effects in two- or three-colour distempering.

Brushes are made especially for varnishing (Fig. 19). They are oval in section and the bristle is firmer than that in paint brushes. They are ideal for the application of enamels and hard-gloss paints. Various sizes are obtainable in many different qualities.

The dragger (Fig. 20) is a small, flat brush which produces clean, sharp brush-graining. It has a very limited use.

Piped overgrainers (Fig. 21) are made with four, five or more separate pencils. Those made of sable are suitable for graining and overgraining such woods as oak, sycamore, maple, mahogany and pinewood. Hog-hair overgrainers are similar but produce a

FLOGGER

FIG. 15. *This brush has a single line of black bristles and is used to imitate the texture of wood in graining mahogany and other close-grained woods.*

SOFTENERS

FIG. 14. *Used to remove evidence of brushwork, especially in graining processes. Badger-hair brushes are used for water-colour and hog-hair for oil colour.*

coarser effect. They are used in the main to grain walnut.

Mottlers (Fig. 22) are small, flat, hog-hair brushes which are used to produce mottled effects when graining mahogany, sycamore, maple and walnut. They may be used in oil- or water-colour.

Steel graining combs (Fig. 23) may be bought singly at so much per inch, or in sets. Their use is limited to oak-graining.

Gilder's tips are small, flat, camel-hair brushes which are used solely for the application of loose-leaf gold. The camel hair is set in cardboard.

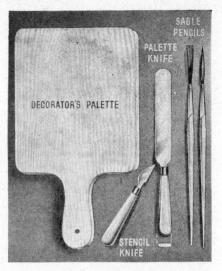

SPECIALIST TOOLS

FIG. 17. *Some of the items which will be required for touching-up and adding lines, scrolls and other decorative effects. The palette knife is used for mixing pigments and the sable pencils are used for graining.*

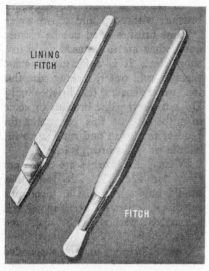

FITCHES

FIG. 16. *These brushes are used with a straight-edge for painting lines and for picking out mouldings and similar objects. The best bristles are pure white.*

A gilder's cushion is a type of palette covered with cotton-wool and chamois leather (Fig. 24). It is used by gilders and decorators to cut loose-leaf gold. When the gold is transferred from the book to the cushion it is prevented from blowing away by a parchment shield.

A gilder's knife has a long, stainless-steel blade with a blunt edge. It is used to cut loose-leaf gold.

Grainers and marblers usually carry a few feathers in their kit. They are used to add the veins to imitation marble in the most natural manner.

Liners (Fig. 25) are brushes made for painting narrow lines on wheels or furniture. A brush specially made for stencilling is shown in Fig. 26. The bristles should hang well together.

An artist's palette should be used for signwriting, but a home-made palette is preferable for a convenient surface on which to mix pigments before adding them to paint (Fig. 17).

Palette knives are used for mixing pigments before adding them to paint. The blade should be soft and springy, and when bent should spring back to its original position. Stencil knives are used for cutting stencils out of cart-ridge paper and for graining limed oak.

It is important for the decorator to carry a plumbline and a chalk line.

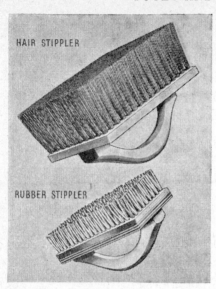

STIPPLERS

FIG. 18. *Coarser effects are given with the rubber than with the hair type.*

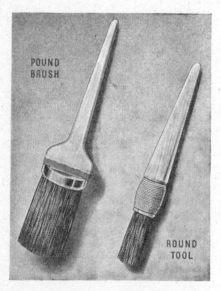

VARNISH BRUSHES

FIG. 19. *One brush has a pressed metal ferrule and the other is bound with string.*

The use of these items is essential for many types of work.

One general rule which must be observed is to keep all tools clean. Distemper brushes should be washed out immediately after use. If washable (oil-bound) distemper has been used it is advisable to wash the distemper brushes with soap and warm water.

Paint brushes need not be cleaned out if they are to be used again in a short time. It is sufficient to stand them in cold water, making sure that the water covers the bristles only. Do not allow paint brushes to stand in turpentine as this penetrates the head of the brush and runs down the handle when the brush is in use.

When paint brushes are to be put away for a considerable time they should be washed first in turpentine substitute or paraffin, dried on rag, and afterwards washed with soap and water.

Varnish brushes may be suspended in linseed oil, or in a solution containing equal parts of linseed oil and turpentine, but the brushes must be cleaned before they are used again for varnish work. All knives should be kept clean and bright, particularly filling knives and gilder's knives.

CHOICE OF MATERIALS

There is not only a wide choice of paint, distemper and wallpaper, but considerable variety in these materials; it is therefore useful to be familiar with the purpose of each. Although these materials are fully described in other chapters, a summary will be useful at this point.

In general, oil paint is used for exterior and interior woodwork and ironwork, distemper or wallpaper for ceilings and walls, and varnish for the protection of paintwork or stained floors. Oil paint is composed of pigments ground in oil to which linseed oil, turpentine and driers (either in paste or liquid form) have been added. It is used for undercoating work which is to be finished in hard-gloss paint or enamel, or for ground coats which are applied prior to graining, scumbling or glazing. Oil paint may be used alone for the preservation of woodwork or ironwork or, with a minimum oil content, for wall and ceiling decoration.

DISTEMPERING

Distemper may be of the size-bound or oil-bound variety. Size-bound distemper may be made at home with whiting and size or may be bought in powder or paste form requiring the addition of either cold or boiling water, as the instructions on the packing direct.

Size-bound distemper is used mainly for ceilings or for walls where an inexpensive finish is required. One advantage is that this material may be washed off completely at any time, when dirt and distemper are removed together, leaving a clean plaster surface. It is not suitable for surfaces which may be quickly soiled or for walls which are likely to be rubbed.

Oil-bound distemper (also known as water-paint) is suitable for work which is expected to receive a fair amount of wear. It is washable to some extent and may be used for most ceilings and walls, but oil-bound distemper must not be applied over an existing size-bound distemper. One coat of size-bound distemper is usually sufficient. In any case, a second coat is difficult to apply and is likely to prove unsatisfactory. On the other hand,

DRAGGER

FIG. 20. *This tool is commonly used in brush-graining, being drawn through the wet colour to produce woody effects.*

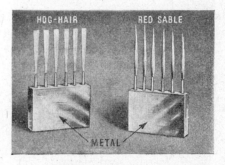

PIPED OVERGRAINERS

FIG. 21. *These are for producing regular and evenly spaced fine lines when graining. There may be four or more pencils.*

MOTTLERS

FIG. 22. *Thin brushes of hog bristles set in a metal holder of convenient width.*

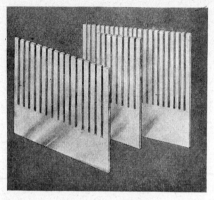

GRAINING COMBS

FIG. 23. *These are available in various sizes. A 3-in. comb is recommended.*

usually two coats of oil-bound distemper are required.

The main use of varnish is for its great protective quality. It is used to protect plain paint, graining or decorated surfaces, and may also be used directly on natural or stained-wood surfaces. Varnish is also used merely to produce a glossy finish.

Stains and graining colours are made of transparent or semi-transparent pigments ground in oil with the addition of linseed oil, turpentine and driers. They may be used for new woodwork or floors and may be subsequently varnished. The types made for decorative finishes (scumbling and glazing) and graining are intended to be applied over a previously prepared and painted surface.

COUNTING THE COST

The expenditure on materials for various types of decoration should be compared. Limewashed or size-bound-distempered surfaces are the cheapest to carry out, both as regards the cost of material and the expenditure of time; the use of oil-bound distemper comes next, wallpaper follows, and painted

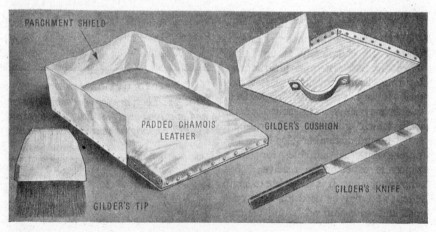

GILDER'S KIT

FIG. 24. *The small board padded with cotton-wool and covered with chamois leather is known as a gilder's cushion. The parchment shield is to prevent draughts while gold is being handled. The knife has a flexible blade with a fine edge which is smooth, but not sharp. The gilder's tip is employed for lifting the gold from the cushion.*

wall surfaces are the most expensive to complete. On the other hand, a painted wall in a good condition can be refreshed by the application of a single coat of paint. But the foregoing remarks do not mean that painted wall-surfaces should be employed only as a luxury.

The useful life of the materials must be taken into account, and if hard wear and long life are required of a surface, in the long run paint may be cheaper than frequent redecoration. Furthermore, painted surfaces may be washed from time to time and, if this is carried out regularly, the surfaces will always appear fresh and clean. However, painted wall-surfaces are not to everybody's taste. In other chapters the decorative use of distemper is dealt with and, as oil-bound distemper lasts as long as most people require of a decorated surface and re-distempering is a comparatively cheap opera'ion, this material may well be chosen is an alternative to painted or papered walls.

EXTERIOR FINISHES

Limewash (slaked lime and water) has little decorative value, but it is a useful material when large areas of, say, rough brickwork are to be made white and clean. It does not rub off easily and is a cleansing material in itself. Cellars, outhouses, greenhouse brickwork, chicken houses and the exterior walls of cottages may be limewashed. Limewash may also be used for whitening exterior walls, as a means of reflecting light into a dark room.

When starting to decorate a newly built house, the occupier should be satisfied with modest decorations at first. It is a waste of time and material to carry out expensive schemes for at least one year. The woodwork should

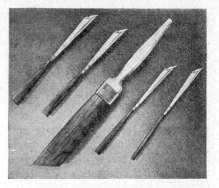

LINERS AND SWORD STRIPER

FIG. 25. *Tools for water and body colour work. The sword striper (centre) is used for special finishes and lining purposes. The liners are set in quills.*

STENCIL BRUSH

FIG. 26. *Available in different sizes, the best types have white bristles which are set in cement with casings of tin.*

be protected, but the use of high-glossy finishes should be postponed for a time. The use of good elastic oil-paint is to be preferred as this will harden slowly and provide an excellent base for subsequent finishes.

Beware of staining the floors of a new house until the right type of material to use and the correct method of applying it are known.

The ceilings of a newly built house may be distempered at once, provided that size-bound distemper is used. As the ceilings are fairly white when left by the plasterers, a coat of clearcole is unnecessary. Use the distemper thinly.

CHAPTER 12

PAINT DEFECTS

COMMON CAUSES OF FAILURE

SUCCESSFUL results in painting and decorating depend in the main on thorough preparation of the surface and the skilful application of suitable materials. Any negligence or error of judgment in these respects may substantially affect the appearance and durability of the work. There are also other factors, for instance, the atmospheric conditions to which the decorations are subjected in service, which may exert their influence. Thus, though it may seem that every reasonable precaution has been taken, defects will occur at times. The most common forms of failure, their causes, and the steps which can be taken to avoid or remedy them, are considered here.

COMMON DEFECTS

Since there is a natural inclination, when a job goes wrong, to blame the material, it may be said at once that, provided this has been made by a reputable firm and has been properly used, the product is seldom at fault. Modern finishes produced by any good factory are scientifically prepared and such close supervision is exercised over every stage of manufacture that very few faulty materials ever come on to the market; as a general rule, therefore, we must look elsewhere to account for failure.

One of the commonest of painting defects is blistering (Fig. 1), and it is also one of the most annoying, since it may take place for no very obvious reason. It is largely confined to exterior work and is due, in most cases, to the presence of either moisture or imprisoned air under the paint film, to resinous deposits on the surface of woodwork, or to rust on iron or steel surfaces (Fig. 2).

Very little moisture or trapped air is needed to bring about this form of trouble, which will often occur on unseasoned timber or on surfaces

PAINT BLISTERING

FIG. 1. *Blistering of paint over galvanized iron: magnification × 35. Such a defect might result from moisture or air trapped under the paint film.*

recently exposed to rain, dew or even fog, though superficially they may look quite dry. When they are subsequently subjected to heat, as from the rays of the sun, the moisture or air expands, forcing the film away from the surface in the familiar blister form. If there are unsealed knots or sappy places in the wood, the heat will soften the resin and draw it upwards, pushing away the paint in the process (Fig. 3).

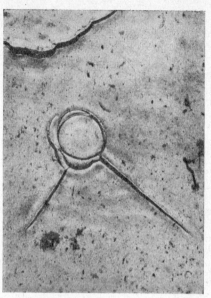

UNTREATED KNOT

FIG. 3. *Spiral cracking of paint film on wood: magnification* × 12. *The presence of an untreated knot might cause this defect to appear in quite a short time.*

EFFECT OF RUST

FIG. 2. *Blistering of paint applied over rusted steel: magnification* × 13. *All traces of rust should be removed from the surface before painting, by wire brushing or by the use of an abrasive.*

In the case of iron or steelwork, any traces of rust will spread beneath the paint film and, as they occupy more space than the original metal, will cause blistering and even fracturing of the film in a relatively short time.

When a considerable number of blisters develop, the only satisfactory course is to strip the paint, either with a blow-lamp or paint-remover, and to start again. If there are only one or two isolated blisters, it may be worth while cutting out the affected area, priming, stopping and touching up, though it is not easy to make such repairs inconspicuous, and the result is not always satisfactory.

While it would be rash to guarantee complete immunity from blistering, the risk of it taking place can be reduced if the following precautions are observed :

(1) See that the surface is as dry as possible, allowing ample time for moisture from rain, dew or any other

source to evaporate before attempting to paint.

(2) Brush the primer well into the surface to avoid possible trouble from air pockets.

(3) Take care that all knots are properly sealed with shellac varnish (knotting); in the case of bad knots, scorch with the blow-lamp and scrape out as much resinous matter as possible, seal with shellac and make good the cavity with white-lead stopper.

(4) In preparing iron or steel for painting, remove all rust with emery cloth, or by scraping or wire-brushing, and apply a coat of rust-inhibitive primer (for example, red-lead paint), without delay.

(5) When mixing paints, avoid adding too much oil to the undercoat for

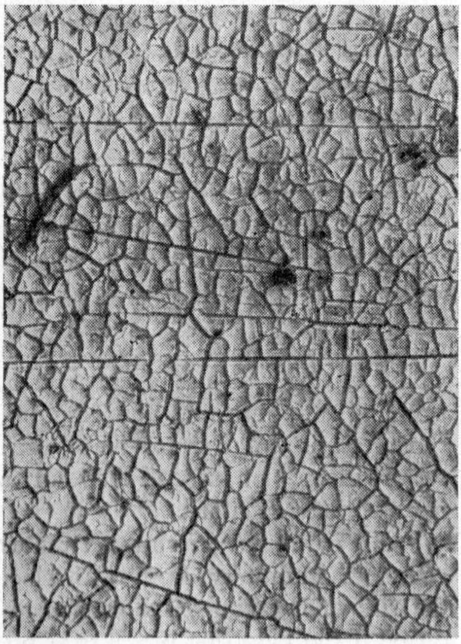

CRACKING

FIG. 4. *Paint should always be renewed long before it gets into this condition if damage to property is to be avoided.*

surfaces which will be exposed to the sun; undercoats which are too soft and elastic tend to promote blistering.

Even the best outside paintwork must break down in time and in one of two ways—by chalking or powdering, or by cracking, depending on the nature and formulation of the paint. When the paint fails by chalking, it first loses its gloss and then, owing to the disintegration of the binder, releases particles of pigment as well. If the process is gradual, it is the least objectionable way in which the breakdown can occur, because, although the film becomes progressively thinner, there is no fracture and it thus retains its protective property to some extent. Another advantage is that it leaves an excellent ground, requiring only a minimum of preparation, for repainting.

When chalking develops within a few months, it may be because of the use of an inferior paint. Some cheap paints, for instance, contain appreciable proportions of rosin, which gives a good initial gloss but has very little resistance to the weather. It may also be caused by applying the finishing coat over an undercoat which is too porous and contains insufficient oil, so that it absorbs too much binder from the finishing coat, leaving this deficient in gloss and underbound.

CHALKING AND CRACKING

Chalking is mainly limited to white and pale-coloured finishes and some pigments (for example, white lead and titanium) are more subject to it than others. It frequently occurs on paintwork exposed to sea air, and for such surfaces there is some advantage in using, as a finishing coat, a paint containing a combination of white-base

FIG. 5. *Only at* 60 × *magnification can the full effect of the cracking in a weathered paint film be seen, and the need for early renewal be appreciated.*

pigments as, for instance, 75 per cent white lead and 25 per cent zinc oxide. The last-named pigment reduces the risk of chalking, while the white lead decreases the danger of cracking, to

which a "straight" zinc-oxide paint is often inclined. Such paints are available from most of the leading manufacturers.

Cracking, in outside paintwork (Figs. 4 and 5), which has weathered for some time, is a prelude to flaking and denotes that the film has lost its original flexibility. It can no longer accommodate itself to the expansion and contraction, due to atmospheric changes, of the surface. This defect is more serious than chalking, for it allows moisture to penetrate; this weakens the adhesion of the coating and brings about flaking.

FINDING THE CAUSE

When cracking takes place prematurely, it may be due to the use of an inferior paint or to an incorrect coat sequence. Low-grade paints soon lose their elasticity on weathering. As regards the coat sequence, if a hard-drying finish is applied on top of a coat which, because it is rich in oil, has more flexibility, cracking may follow, since the undercoat will expand and contract to a greater extent than the finishing coat, as illustrated in Fig. 13.

WRINKLED SURFACE

FIG. 6. *Extreme example of distortion of the paint film as caused by too heavy a coating or by applying a second coat of paint before the first coat is dry.*

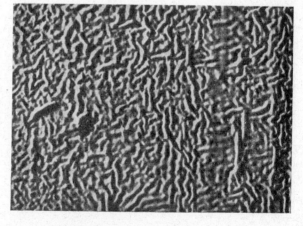

Extensive cracking is nearly always a sign that the adhesion of the paint film in general is weak and will not make a reliable foundation for new paint. It is therefore safer to strip the existing coating before re-painting. If only the top coats are affected, however, and the cracks are widely dispersed, it may be practicable to remove all loose portions by rubbing down. The surface should be made good with hard stopper forced well home with the knife, rubbed down again thoroughly when this material is dry in order to remove any excess and re-finished in the normal way.

When paintwork dries with a wrinkled surface (Fig. 6), the painter is nearly always to blame. Either the paint has been applied in too thick a coat or sufficient drying time has not been allowed between coats. Ordinary paints and varnishes dry by absorbing oxygen from the air : if the coating is too thick, the drying of the upper portion of the film shuts off the supply of air from the lower, which remains soft and, being subject to more movement, distorts the face of the film into wrinkles. Similar action takes place if inadequate drying time is allowed between coats.

The discoloration of paintwork may be due to various causes, ranging from simple dirt deposition to complex chemical action. In industrial districts, where the air is charged with impurities, outside paintwork may be blackened or discoloured in a very short time. As the dirt, thus deposited, may be acid or alkaline and may affect the durability of the film, periodic washing is advisable where this is practicable. In manufacturing areas, sulphurous compounds in the atmosphere may have the effect of turning white-lead finishes brown.

There is also the action of light to be considered. The majority of coloured pigments used in paint are reasonably fast to

MOULD GROWTH
FIG. 7. *Discoloured patches, usually black or purple, caused by mould growth on a white hard-gloss painted wall. This defect is most likely to occur on walls which are subject to damp or very severe condensation.*

FIG. 8. *An isolated brick from which the paint has been thrown off owing to efflorescence. The surrounding brickwork which was painted at the same time remained in perfect condition.*

light, but a few, particularly some types of green, are not. Permanent greens and other colours are available and, although the paints containing them may be rather more expensive, the extra cost of such materials is well worth while.

A common form of discoloration is that known to the painter as bleeding. This effect often takes place when a white or pale-coloured paint is applied directly on top of a ground containing certain pigments—mostly reds—which are soluble in the oil or turpentine in the new paint. The result is that the new paint is tinged and this bleeding effect will persist even if additional coats of paint are superimposed.

ELEMENTARY PRECAUTIONS

Before painting in white or pale tints on top of any old red or pink paint or distemper it is as well to make a preliminary test on a small inconspicuous part of the work, with the finish which it is proposed to use. Leave this for about a week and if no discoloration has taken place by the end of this time, it should be safe to paint without fear of bleeding. If there are any signs of bleeding, seal the old surface with a coat of shellac varnish before painting.

There will be similar trouble if an attempt is made to paint directly on top of woodwork which has been previously treated with creosote, preservative stain or any coal-tar derivative; in this case the discoloration will be a dirty brown. A coat of shellac will prevent this from happening. Where the creosote or stain is very old, a coat of aluminium primer may be effective.

Paintwork may be discoloured by alkaline action: this form of trouble is largely encountered when painting over new cement, certain types of plaster gauged with lime, new asbestos sheeting and other substances containing portland cement, which is strongly alkaline. Some pigments, particularly prussian blue, chrome yellow and brunswick green, are readily attacked by alkalis and the use of paints incorporating them should be avoided for grounds of this description.

Alkaline action may also be responsible for the failure of paint to dry properly or, more often, to re-soften after it has dried. The alkali in new cement and similar surfaces has the effect of saponifying (turning to soap) the linseed oil in the paint film, which remains permanently sticky. There is always some risk in painting such surfaces until they have aged for a year or so, and it is safer to distemper them. If, for some reason, painting must be done while they are still new, allow them to dry out for as long as possible and apply a coat of special alkali-resisting primer, made by most paint manufacturers, before putting on the undercoat.

⟩ Paint may also fail to dry if it is applied on top of a greasy or waxed surface. Special care should be taken in preparing kitchen walls and woodwork which is subjected to frequent handling or likely to collect grease. Thorough scrubbing with a warm solution of sugar soap will generally be effective. Treat surfaces which

have been wax-polished witn turpentine or white spirit to remove any wax residue before attempting to paint over them.

Do not forget that, unless a room is properly ventilated, the drying of new paintwork may be unduly delayed. Lack of adequate ventilation, if prolonged and combined with a damp atmosphere, may encourage the development of mould on paint, distemper or wallpaper. There are various forms of mould (Fig. 7), but the most common type appears in clusters of black spots which may spread rapidly and, as the spores are air-borne, may infect other surfaces. Since the spores feed on oil, size, paste and other organic matter, redecorating on top of work affected in this way only serves to encourage their development.

At the first signs of mould, strip all

PEELING OF PAINT FILM

FIG. 9. *Paint peeling from a heavily trowelled surface of Keene's cement. The hard, almost impervious, surface which this plaster acquires when over-trowelled makes good adhesion, even of oil paint, particularly difficult to guarantee.*

affected paintwork, distemper or paper and destroy it by burning. Scrub the plaster with soap and water and then apply an antiseptic wash; a solution of zinc silico-fluoride (6 oz. to 1 gal.) is effective for this purpose. Allow the work to stand for about a fortnight and then examine the surface for any recurrence of the trouble; if the surface is clear, redecoration can be safely carried out, but if not, repeat the treatment.

Both interior and exterior surfaces will sometimes be disfigured by a whitish crystalline deposit, known as efflorescence (Fig. 8). This is caused by moisture which has found its way into the wall. The trouble may be due to penetration from the exterior, to a defective damp-proof course, or to faulty guttering. Soluble salts, dissolved in the brickwork of backing, are brought in solution to the face of the wall where, when the water has evaporated, they crystallize out. The salts may pass through the finish or may partially dislodge it as in Fig. 8.

FINDING A REMEDY

There is no speedy and effective remedy for this form of trouble, to which certain types of brick are more liable than others. The fault will continue either until the supply of salts in the wall is exhausted, or until steps are taken to prevent the ingress of moisture to the wall. All that can be done in the meantime is to remove the deposit as it forms by dry scraping. If water is used, the salts are dissolved, but they crystallize out once more when the surface has dried out.

When a finish in flat oil-paint is required, it will occasionally be found that in some parts there is a slight sheen which mars the uniformity of

PLASTER DEFECT

FIG. 10. *Delayed expansion of a gypsum plaster, showing characteristic swelling and disintegration of the finish.*

the work. This is technically known as flashing; it may be due to the paint not having been stirred properly before use, so that all its various ingredients are not adequately combined, or it may be caused by the use of a brush previously employed for gloss paint or varnish and not washed out thoroughly enough afterwards. The most likely explanation, however, is that the brushwork has been too vigorous in some areas, with the result that a slight excess of oil is brought to the top of the film.

It is not easy to remedy this defect, but, if noticed in time, it may be possible to effect some improvement by placing a wad of clean white blotting-paper, saturated with the flat paint well thinned out with turpentine, against the surface, allowing it to remain in contact for a few minutes.

DISTEMPER

So far, we have been mainly concerned with defects on paintwork, but trouble is more likely to be encountered with water-paint or distemper, and particularly from flaking. Distemper is rather more liable to flake than paint because its film is thicker, more brittle and not so well bound or naturally adhesive.

Flaking may take place for a number of reasons. On bare plaster, there may be too much or not enough suction. In the former case, the brush will drag as the distemper is applied and too much of the binder will be absorbed, leaving an excess of underbound pigment on the surface. In the latter case, the distemper, or certain paints for that matter, brushes on easily, but, owing to the density of the plaster, it will not key properly and its hold will be precarious (Fig. 9). Certain types of hard-faced plaster have a very smooth surface, particularly when, as often happens, they are over-trowelled by the plasterer. It is sometimes difficult to obtain good adhesion of the distemper on such surfaces (Fig. 10) and it is advisable to apply a coat of special primer (supplied by most of the leading paint manufacturers) to the surface.

In rooms which are poorly ventilated and where there is a good deal of condensation, as in kitchens and bathrooms, premature failure of distemper is a frequent occurrence. The coating, being porous, absorbs the condensed moisture, which shows far less than on a more impervious film such as that of paint. But the alternate wetting and drying soon weakens the binder of the distemper, and, having little or no elasticity, cracking, followed by flaking, will occur (Figs. 11 and 12).

Soft (size-and-whiting) distemper must always be removed before redecorating; it washes off with warm water easily enough. Washable distempers or water-paints are more difficult to strip, and for this reason it is fairly common practice merely to remove all loose matter and to apply a fresh coat on top.

In many instances this is successful, but it involves a certain amount of

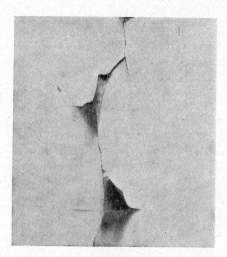

FLAKING

FIG. 11. *Example of water-paint flaking on plaster caused by inadequate preparation of the surface before application.*

DISTEMPER FLAKING
FIG. 12. *Flaking of distemper from a plastered ceiling as caused by heavy condensation of moisture or faulty preparation of the surface before application.*

risk of failure. Coat after coat of oil paint may safely be applied on top of each other, but there is a limit—though, unfortunately, not a definable one—to how many coats of distemper can be superimposed without fear of trouble. Each time a fresh coat is applied, the underlying film is wetted by the water it contains, and contracts strongly in drying out, thereby encouraging cracking. When these fractures occur, the edges tend to curl outwards, and it is not long before flaking takes place.

Washable distempers vary considerably in formulation and one brand sometimes quarrels with another, if their rates of contraction are substantially different. Although this seldom happens, it is worth bearing in mind when the renewal of a distemper finish is under consideration.

Even if it is only very slightly cracked or flaking, the strength of the bond of a distemper finish, which has been on a wall or ceiling for some time, is always problematical. It is safest to strip down to the plaster before redecorating, but if this seems to

involve too much labour, the next best course is to remove all loose or weakly adhering matter, rubbing the limits of all patches thus formed to a feather edge. Then apply a coat either of thin oil paint or of varnish-size (equal parts by volume of oak varnish and white spirit); this serves to reinforce and to bind down the existing coating and makes a good foundation.

VARNISH

Broadly speaking, most of the defects described in connexion with paint apply equally to varnish. The latter is, however, a somewhat sensitive material, more easily affected by atmospheric conditions than is paint; it is consequently important that it should be stored at an even temperature and not subjected, in the container, to extremes of heat or cold.

The form of trouble most likely to be encountered with varnish is that known to the painter as blooming. This defect is also liable to occur at times in enamel work, but it will not be so marked as in a varnish coating.

Blooming shows itself as a whitish

cloudiness on parts of the varnish film and may develop within a few days, weeks or even months after application. The cause is obscure and no one type of varnish appears to be more susceptible to it than another. Its occurrence is probably due more to the conditions in which the varnish is applied or to which it is subjected in the early stages of the life of the film, than to the material itself.

In many cases blooming is undoubtedly caused by the deposition of moisture on the varnish before it has had time to harden. For this reason, precautions should be taken to avoid exposing the work to draughts, since these are accompanied by a lowering of the temperature which involves a certain amount of condensation, though in microscopic form. For similar reasons, varnishing should not be carried out in the late afternoon in

early spring or autumn, or during a spell of very wet weather (Fig. 14). Fumes from gas or coke fires are also apt to induce this defect, but an even temperature should be maintained.

Blooming may take the form either of a fine cloudy deposit on the face of the film or, when examined through a microscope, may be seen to consist of

EFFECT OF RAIN

Fig. 14. *Photomicrograph showing the effect of rain spotting on wet varnish.*

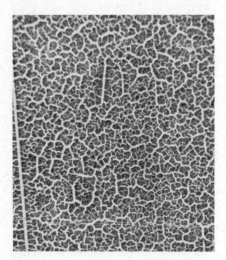

DEFECT IN LACQUER

Fig. 13. *Microscopic checking on lacquer film, as might be caused by the application of an inelastic finish over a flexible ground.*

tiny pits within the structure of the coating. The cloudy deposit will generally yield to rubbing with a soft leather or with a pad slightly moistened with sweet oil; nothing will remove the pits, and it is necessary to flat down and re-varnish.

Since the risk of blooming is greatest during the drying period, the more this is prolonged the greater likelihood there is of trouble. It is significant that, generally speaking, quicker-drying varnishes are less liable to this fault.

CHAPTER 13

INSPECTING THE PROPERTY

WORK PREPARATORY TO COMPLETE RENOVATION

THE handyman should be capable of carrying out all but major alterations to his property. Of course, there are occasions when only the skill of the craftsman will suffice: in the case of extensive damage, for example, or when a dangerous structure must be made safe. But the normal repairs, renovations and decorations which are required about the house may be carried out with success if willingness and enthusiasm are combined with the knowledge of how best to start and finish the work.

Experience is the best of all teachers, but there is no reason why the experience of others may not be turned to advantage. In this book the handyman has the benefit of the experience of craftsmen in painting, decorating and household repairs to guide him.

PRELIMINARY EXAMINATION

The purpose of painting and decorating is to clean, to protect and to beautify the surfaces of plaster, woodwork and ironwork. Although the most important of these is that of protection, the other purposes should not be overlooked.

Property decreases in value unless renovations are carried out regularly. Woodwork rots and needs to be replaced and ironwork soon rusts if its surface is not protected. When such deterioration has once occurred no amount of subsequent painting will put matters right, but suitable treat-

ment will give a longer lease of life. It is, therefore, far better to maintain property in its original state than to attempt repairs and renovations only when an urgent need arises.

When about to decorate a house, it is important to examine the property

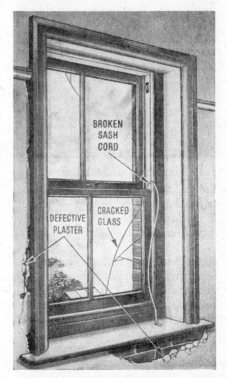

BROKEN
SASH
CORD

DEFECTIVE
PLASTER

CRACKED
GLASS

URGENT WORK

FIG. 1. *Broken sash cords are dangerous and should be repaired as soon as possible. Note the defective plaster.*

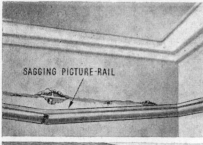

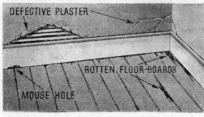

SAGGING PICTURE-RAIL

RAINWATER LEAK

DEFECTIVE PLASTER

ROTTEN FLOOR-BOARDS

MOUSE HOLE

INTERIOR DEFECTS

FIG. 2. *Selection of faults which may be found in various rooms of a house. It is particularly important to rectify such defects before redecoration begins.*

methodically and to make notes of the most urgent needs. Start on the top floor and trace marks and stains on the ceilings, which may suggest leaky roofs, directly to their source. Look for the cause of draughts which may come from defects under window-sills, badly fitting windows, broken sash cords, broken or decayed woodwork or broken or cracked glass (Fig. 1). Inspect the plasterwork, paying special attention to ceiling and wall angles and looking for clues which might suggest

insects or vermin (Fig. 2). The plaster-work around mantelpieces should be examined. If the chimney breast has a smoked appearance it may be that there is a leak in the brickwork or that the mantelpiece is loose (Fig. 3). Unless these trifles are attended to before redecorations have been carried out there is a likelihood that the new decorations will suffer.

A thorough examination should be made of all the woodwork, looking for defective mouldings, cracked door-panels and ill-fitting doors. The electric-light switches should be firm and safe (Fig. 4).

This examination should be carried out in every part of the house and particular attention should be paid to the state of dark passages, where damage might otherwise be overlooked. North and east walls may, on account of the exposed nature of the outside walls, be damp or have decayed plaster. Bumps on walls should be tapped lightly. If they should sound hollow, or if the surface moves, it is probable that some decay exists. This is not usually a serious matter, as in most cases it will be confined to the superficial plasterwork. Wallpaper peeling off the ceilings or walls (Fig. 5) usually indicates dampness. If there is damage of any kind, do not be satisfied with the thought that it can be put right quickly, but find the cause, which may be more serious than is often imagined; an examination of the corresponding wall on the outside of the house will probably reveal the cause (Fig. 6).

Loose or rotten floor-boards should not be overlooked; and a note should be made of broken or missing tiles in kitchens, bathrooms and lavatories. Examine the condition of taps and wastes and look for cracks in lavatory pans, basins and sinks; lavatory cisterns which will not flush properly or which show patches of rust may need to be replaced. Door furniture (handles and other fittings) should be in good order, the doors should close properly and the hinges should be firm and free of excessive rust. All windows should be tested by opening and closing them. If some of them will not open easily, they may be merely held fast by paint, in which case a sharp tap with the ball of the hand should free them; but there may be more serious defects. Finally, see that window catches are intact and that they operate freely.

EXAMINING THE EXTERIOR

The outside of the house should receive equal attention. Start on the roof. Take safety precautions and do the job properly. Never be satisfied with a cursory glance from the top of a ladder (Fig. 7). Look for displaced or missing tiles, and displaced or damaged lead flashings of gutters and chimney-stack angles.

Before descending the ladder, examine the rain-water troughs or gutters. They may be full of rubbish. They may have broken away from their supports or may be rusted through. A cracked downpipe may be noticed or a bird's nest blocking the head of such a pipe (Fig. 8). See that the brickwork of the walls is in good condition and note where the pointing needs to be repaired (Fig. 9). When exterior walls are covered with ivy or similar creeping plants, make sure that the plants have not damaged the walls.

The exterior woodwork should receive particular examination. See that rotten wood has not been hidden with a recent coat of paint and that newly applied paint is not blistering or peeling. Make sure that the joints of the woodwork are reasonably free of putty and that the putty of window glass is complete and neat (showing that the windows have been glazed previously by a capable man).

SMOKY FIREPLACE

FIG. 3. *A black deposit around the mantelpiece usually indicates a defective chimney. Note the condition of the plaster and the missing tiles. All of these faults should receive attention before the room is prepared for painting or distempering.*

If part of the cement work has been distempered, see that the distemper is not flaking and that it does not rub off easily: a sign either that the coating is old and weathered or that an inferior distemper has been used.

Wooden gates and railings may be in poor condition. Rotting may have occurred on the posts, especially near ground level, or on any part of such woodwork which has not been properly protected. In severe cases a concrete post (Fig. 10) may be employed.

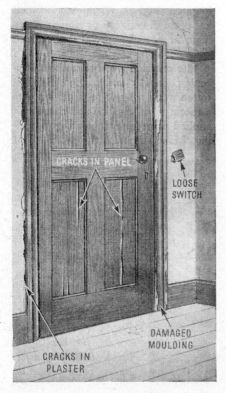

WEAR AND TEAR

FIG. 4. *Doorways are liable to deteriorate more quickly than the other parts of a room. The defects indicated are those which are most likely to occur.*

See that the grates leading to the drains are effective, and that they are not clogged (Fig. 11), and look for cracks in the inspection covers of the main drains (Fig. 12).

It should be remembered that any extensive repairs carried out on woodwork or plaster will necessitate redecoration, so a list should be made of the essential repairs and preparation which must be carried out first, and then of the decoration which must follow.

When a house is being decorated from top to bottom by tradesmen, it is the duty of the foreman painter to make sure that all ceilings and distempered walls are washed off, that all the old wallpaper is stripped, that the woodwork is washed and rubbed down, that any rubbish is cleared away and that all the floors are washed, before any coats of paint or distemper are applied. This plan should be followed, as closely as possible, by the amateur decorator. By working in the correct manner, the work is easier and no risk is taken of the finished work being damaged by subsequent cleaning. Moreover, the finish of the work will not be spoiled by dust settling on the surface before the work is dry.

PROTECTIVE MEASURES

Chimney flues should be swept before any work is begun. It is no joke to be compelled to wash a whole room again after the preparatory work has been carried out.

If a new close-cover carpet is to be fitted to a room, make sure that the door clearance is sufficient. Doors which have to be removed, adjusted and refixed after they have been decorated are likely to be damaged. Even if no damage should occur,

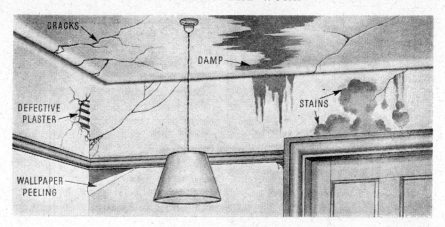

EFFECTS OF DAMPNESS

FIG. 5. *More damage can be attributed to dampness than to any other single cause. Cracks and other defects in plaster are but a few of the consequent effects.*

touching up the hinges will be necessary and dirty finger-marks will have to be removed. For the same reasons, broken sash cords and cracked and broken windows should be replaced before decorating.

Floors, especially those which are stained and varnished or those of polished oak, should be well protected. Dust sheets are best for this purpose and they should be pinned down to save time in adjusting them while work is in progress. Old newspapers or sheets of brown paper may be used as substitutes for dust sheets. It is also wise to take up linoleum, to tie it up in rolls and to replace it only when the decorations of the room have been completed.

In order that no part of a job is forgotten and that the work proceeds in the correct order, it is a good plan to make out a list of the various jobs which need to be done in the manner of a painter's specification. The following is an example: "Take up the linoleum, stack and protect furniture

EXTERIOR DEFECT

FIG. 6. *Typical crack in an exterior wall which allows dampness to enter.*

CAREFUL INSPECTION

FIG. 7. *Do not be content to inspect property from the ground. Get a ladder and do the job properly. It is often surprising what defects can be found.*

and floors, sweep chimney, repair sash cords, replace broken glass, ease door for carpet, attend to small repairs to woodwork, wash old distemper off ceiling and frieze, repair cracks, strip wallpaper, sponge walls, repair walls, remove rubbish, distemper ceiling and frieze, size walls, wash woodwork, paint woodwork first coat, stop woodwork, paint woodwork second coat, wash windows, paint woodwork final coat, paper walls, add border."

Dampness on walls must be treated

before decorating is attempted. There are special preparations on the market which overcome this difficulty. Their use is explained in later pages.

The less furniture which a room contains, the quicker and easier it will be to decorate. If the furniture cannot be removed to another room, it is best to stack it in the centre of the room, island fashion, and to cover the whole with a large dust sheet. Sheets of newspaper pinned together form a good substitute for a dust sheet or a lining, to give extra protection to an actual dust sheet. When the furniture is stacked in this manner, the walls and woodwork are clear and work may proceed without having constantly to

REMOVING A BIRD'S NEST

FIG. 8. *It may be found that birds have nested in different parts of a building or that leaves from near-by trees have blocked the gutters or downpipes.*

MISSING TILES

DISPLACED RIDGE-TILE

DEFECTIVE POINTING

DEFECTS IN ROUGH-CAST

CRACKED DOWNPIPE

RUBBISH IN GUTTER

LEAD FLASHING DAMAGED

BROKEN GLASS

BULGE IN ROUGH-CAST

EXTERIOR EXAMINATION

FIG. 9. *Some of the faults which may develop on the exterior of any house. It is a good plan to make a list of such defects while inspecting the property, so that no essential repairs are forgotten later.*

move things from place to place. Ease of working should receive every consideration. For example, when a considerable number of materials are to be used for the decoration of a room, it is far more convenient to construct a temporary paint bench than to have the materials lying about the floor. Alternatively, the materials may be kept in a large wooden box, so that everything is moved at one time.

PLANNING THE JOB

Decorating work is much easier if the proper scaffolding is used. For normal house decorating two pairs of steps and a scaffold board are indispensable equipment. If necessary, a wooden box could take the place of one pair of steps (Fig: 13). The height of the steps and the length of the scaffold board must depend upon the size of the rooms. A short ladder is

also very useful for work on staircases.

Pails of water should not be left about when there is no further need for them. A pail of water knocked over accidentally is almost certain to cause trouble and may spoil the ceiling of a room below.

If glass or mirrors are stacked in the centre of a room they should be well protected; if a mirror or a plate-glass table top must remain in position and is covered with a dust sheet, the word GLASS should be chalked on the outside of the sheet.

There is no need to consider different types of wallpaper here, but the possible uses of lining paper may not be sufficiently understood. White or tinted lining paper often provides the only means of ensuring a reasonably good surface on which to apply distemper. It strengthens old plaster ceilings and walls which are badly

CONCRETE POST

FIG. 10. *If rotting has occurred on a wooden post supporting a fence, it is often possible to strengthen the structure by fixing a concrete post at the base.*

which would otherwise bleed through the paint.

Before the first coat of paint is applied, a preparatory or priming coat should be given.

Woodwork which has been painted previously and, apart from being dirty, is in a firm, smooth condition, need only be washed down. Paintwork which is rough and in poor condition requires rubbing-down with pumice in order to produce a smooth surface.

For really good work all old wall-paper and ceiling paper should be stripped, the walls washed to remove scraps of paper, and sponged to free

BLOCKED DRAIN

FIG. 11. *Never allow the grates leading to drains to be clogged with leaves and rubbish. Although it is an unpleasant task, clearing by hand is most effective.*

cracked, or those which have been repeatedly repaired. It also gives a solid (opaque) base to stained plaster-work and affords a considerable saving in extra coats of distemper. Lining paper may also be used to advantage as a foundation for the subsequent application of expensive wallpaper, and a base for paint finishes.

All surfaces which are to be painted must be firm, and free from dust, dirt or grease. New woodwork should be examined and all splinters and loose knots removed. Knots which protrude should be cut down with glass-paper, or, better still, removed with a gouge. Other knots and resinous places must be given a good coat of knotting varnish. This material seals the resin

the wall of old paste. All plasterwork should be repaired with plaster or Keene's cement before the first coat of paint or distemper is applied. Distempered ceilings and walls should be well sponged if they have been finished with oil-bound distemper and washed clean if they have had size-bound dis-temper on their surfaces. Subsequent distempering or painting must not be attempted until such surfaces are dry.

All surfaces which are to be re-painted must be clean and free of grease. If large areas of Keene's cement are to be painted they should receive a coat of flat paint before the cement is dry to aid adhesion of the next coat.

It is true that preparation is the most important part of decorating. Not only does it save time in the long run, but it assures a workmanlike job. Often the only way to distinguish between the work of amateurs and experienced craftsmen is to compare the amount of the preparation, which is always obvious no matter how well the finishing of the work has been carried out.

Glass-paper is used for rubbing-down dry paintwork. Various grades, from fine o to coarse 2, are obtainable. Great pressure with glass-paper is unnecessary; undue force only results in scratching the surface of the paint. The function of glass-paper is to cut down a surface and not to plough

it with a series of minute furrows.

Stopping is the name given to the process of making good cracks, joints and holes with putty or similar sub-stances (Figs. 14-16). Putty used for stopping should be composed of whiting and pure linseed oil only. First-class stopping (known to the trade as hard stopping) is made with white-lead, whiting and japan gold-size. It becomes very hard indeed, and once applied should never fall out.

Work which has been stopped with putty may be painted immediately, but a surface which has been treated with hard stopping should be left until the stopping has hardened. Stopping should not be applied directly to un-painted woodwork. All such work should receive at least one coat of paint before stopping is attempted. In the case of a one-coat paint job, the places to be stopped should first be touched up with paint.

When walls have been washed or stripped of paper, it is usual to find many small damaged places and cracks in the plaster surface. These must be made good before any of the subsequent

CRACKED
DRAIN COVER

FIG. 12. *If cracks in the inspection covers of main drains cannot be repaired by bolting metal strips underneath or by welding the broken parts to-gether, a new cover should be fitted with the least possible delay.*

preparatory work can be undertaken.

The final preparations for plaster surfaces depend upon the finish desired. Painted surfaces which are to be papered should be rubbed-down with a strong solution of sugar soap. A waterproof abrasive should then be used to etch the surface and provide a key for the paper. On uneven surfaces a lining paper may be required.

Ceilings which, when washed of old distemper, are reasonably white need not be sized, but if the ceilings are discoloured a coat of clearcole is advised. To make clearcole, soak a little whiting in cold water and, when the whiting has settled, pour off the water. Add the remaining liquid whiting to the size and apply the mixture to the ceiling. It is used in the same manner as distemper.

Ceilings and walls cleaned of old size-bound distemper or previously coated with water-paint, must not be sized before the application of fresh water-paint. Trouble is bound to occur

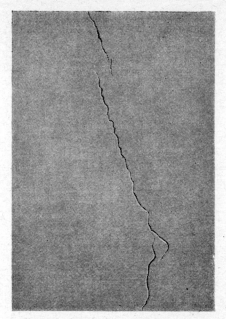

DAMAGED PLASTER

FIG. 14. *Cracks such as this must be made good before the surface is redecorated.*

if water-paint is applied to a sized surface. As soon as the water-paint hardens, and indeed often before, the material will shell and peel. Size may be applied with safety over an existing water-paint only if the surface is in good condition.

Ceilings and walls which are to be finished in plastic paint need no other preparation than that of cleaning and making good. If the plastic paint is to be finished in a texture pattern, a priming coat of paint or a coat of petrifying liquid is desirable. Some makes of plastic paint may be applied over a sized surface, but as other makes may not, it is as well to be on the safe side and to avoid the use of size, using petrifying liquid or a priming coat of oil paint as a preparation for the walls.

ECONOMY

FIG. 13. *If it is not possible to borrow a second pair of steps, a wooden box forms an excellent substitute for one pair.*

Plaster surfaces which have been painted and are then to be distempered should be washed down with a sugar-soap preparation. Places which have been repaired with Keene's cement should be painted to match the old paint and then be allowed to dry. If this is not done, the repair work will show through several coats of distemper.

Surfaces which have been decorated with plastic paint, and which are subsequently to be smooth, may sometimes be stripped in a dry state. The remaining plastic paint may then be washed off in similar manner to old distemper.

Existing plastic-painted surfaces which are unsatisfactory in relief or texture may be given another coat of the same material. If the textured surface has been painted, no preparation other than sponging with water is necessary, but if the old plastic paint has received no subsequent treatment, a thin coat of paint or a coat of petrifying liquid will be required to prevent the new material from being absorbed too quickly. A coarse texture may be made finer, or a fine texture coarser, by the application of another coat.

OLD PAINT

There are many preparations on the market which may be used to strip old paint. They are all effective, but the non-caustic variety is recommended to the home decorator. Caustic soda will also strip old paint with great speed, but it must be used with the greatest possible care. It is excellent for stripping old paint from marble, glass, or metal surfaces, and may be

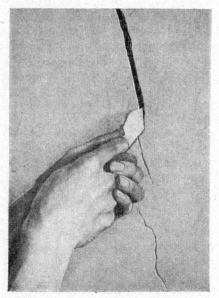

UNDER-CUTTING CRACKS

FIG. 15. *Cut away the under-surface edges of the cracks to provide a key for the application of new plaster.*

BEFORE FILLING

FIG. 16. *After the crack has been under-cut, wet the affected part with a brush, before filling it with plaster.*

used for stripping paint from walls and woodwork, but the surfaces must be washed down thoroughly with water.

Turpentine is not a solvent of dry paint. It is useless to stand hard paint brushes in turpentine in the hope that they will become soft again, or to brush turpentine on a wall or similar painted surface with the intention of softening the old paint, but turpentine or its substitute will remove greasy finger-marks from a painted surface to allow further painting to be carried out. Paint will not dry properly on a greasy surface. The grease may not be apparent, but may still be there. When lime water, soda, or sugar-soap preparations are brushed on old paintwork, the smell of ammonia proves that the grease is being broken down.

Do not mix lime and soda together; they produce caustic soda! Normal household cleaning materials are mostly harmless in themselves, but care should be taken not to mix them unless the result of such mixtures are known to be harmless.

POLISHED SURFACES

It is sometimes desirable to paint furniture which has been french-polished. Paint which is applied directly to the polished surface is satisfactory for a short time only. When the paint becomes hard, the slightest knock will cause the paint to chip from the polished surface.

All that is necessary for successful work is to produce a surface which will act as a key for the paint. This may be produced with glass-paper or a scraper, but a wash with ammonia is more effective and saves hard work.

When surfaces are prepared for painting there are usually many small holes, scratches and rough places which are far too small to be repaired with Keene's cement. Painters and decorators prepare surfaces until they are quite smooth with a preparation known as filling. There are several kinds of filling material, but the home decorator need only be concerned with the choice of either distemper filling or white-lead filling.

Distemper filling is suitable for interior work. Proprietary brands, which require the addition of cold water only, may be bought in powder form. Plastic paint may be used alone as a filling material, but some of the proprietary brands are improved by the addition of whiting.

FILLING

The process of filling should be carried out, with some exceptions, after the first coat of paint has been applied. The exceptions are prepared french-polished surfaces and plywoods with very coarse grain, which should be filled before painting. The dry filling is then cut down with glass-paper and the first paint coat applied.

White-lead filling which is required for exterior work may not be available ready made, but is made with one part of paste white-lead, two parts of gilders' whiting and a little japan gold-size. White-lead is poisonous and should be handled with care.

Thin paint, which contains plenty of oil, should be applied over distemper filling, but thin flat paint, with the normal oil content, should be used over lead filling.

No attempt has been made in this chapter to do more than give a summary of the work which should be carried out as a preliminary to decorating the whole house. All of the jobs are explained in detail elsewhere.

CHAPTER 14

DAMP-PROOFING

METHODS OF DEALING WITH FLOORS, WALLS AND ROOFS

WHERE dampness occurs on the walls of a cellar, or in a room where the outside wall cannot be treated, the dampness must be checked from the inside. The only effective method is to render the wall with a coat of waterproof cement. If dampness is coming from the floor as well as from the walls, the floor must first be covered with waterproof concrete.

If the old floor is of stone or concrete, it must be thoroughly cleaned and all loose material should be cleared away : joints between stone flags must be raked out and the old plaster, whitewash or paint removed from the lower part of the walls.

FLOOR AND WALLS

The new floor may then be put down. The concrete should be 4 in. thick and composed of special waterproof cement, good clean, sharp sand, and a non-porous aggregate such as granite chippings. The proportion of one part cement, two parts of sand and three parts of aggregate by volume will give a reliable mix. The cement, sand and granite chippings should be mixed dry until the mixture is uniform in colour and the water added by sprinkling as described later.

The mixture should not be sloppy, and when laid the floor must be protected from frost and the surface kept damp until the concrete is cured.

When the floor has set the walls may be treated. The whole surface must be cleaned-off down to the brick or stone and the joints between the bricks or stonework must be cleaned out to a depth of about ⅜ in. When the whole

RENDERING A WALL

FIG. 1. *Laths nailed at intervals of about 3 ft. enable a uniform thickness of cement rendering to be applied.*

surface is free from dirt and dust and the joints have been damped with an old brush, the wall should be covered with a mixture of one part waterproof cement and two parts clean, sharp sand.

Only a limited amount of cement should be mixed at one time, as it tends to stiffen before it can be applied. To ensure that a uniform thickness of cement rendering is put on, a series of laths about $1\frac{1}{2}$ in. wide by $\frac{1}{2}$ in. thick may be lightly nailed to the joints at intervals of about 3 ft. (Fig. 1). The cement is then applied up to the face of the laths, and when one panel is finished the lath may easily be pulled off and the space filled with cement. The cement is applied with a plasterer's float, and a small board with a handle underneath (known as a hawk) is needed to hold a quantity of the mixture close to the work. Internal

angles should be strengthened by rounding them, thus obtaining a thicker layer in the corner (Fig. 2).

It is not wise to use an oil-bound paint to colour the fresh cement as chemical action takes place and the paint becomes soapy. If the natural colour of cement is too drab, a coloured cement may be used. It is mixed with sand in the usual way. Alternatively, a special paint or distemper may be used which is not affected by the alkali in the cement. However, before an alkali-resisting primer is applied, ample time should be allowed for the surface to dry. There are various special preparations available for colouring cement surfaces.

As an alternative to waterproof cement, builders' merchants sell various brands of waterproofing compound which can be added to ordinary cement

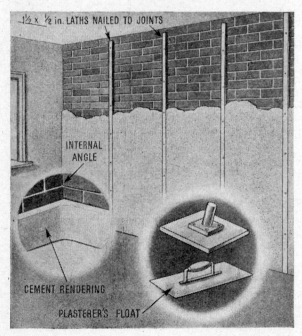

½ x ½ in. LATHS NAILED TO JOINTS

INTERNAL ANGLE

CEMENT RENDERING

PLASTERER'S FLOAT

WORKING TECHNIQUE

FIG. 2. *Cement is applied up to the face of the laths and when one panel is completed the lath can be pulled off and the space filled in. Internal angles should be rounded to give extra strength in the corners.*

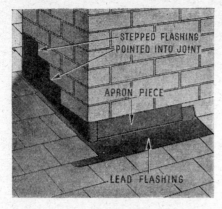

LEAD FLASHINGS

Fig. 3. *See that the apron piece is firmly wedged into the joints with pieces of lead and that the pointing is sound. If necessary, repoint with cement and sand.*

to make the mixture waterproof. These are supplied in either powder or liquid form and the maker's instructions should be followed when they are used. The liquid variety is generally more convenient, as it can be added to the water when preparing the mixture.

CAUSES OF DAMPNESS

In rooms, other than those below ground level, which have damp walls it is not recommended that the interior wall surface be treated. It is much better to seek the cause of dampness, and if possible to find a permanent cure.

In some cases, however, where only slight dampness occurs and the trouble cannot easily be traced to a fault in the exterior wall, the plaster surface on the inside may be treated with damp-proofing solution. Various solutions are available for both external and internal wall-surfaces, and those intended for internal use are applied with a clean, flat paint-brush; two or

three applications are usually needed.

It should be appreciated, however, that this treatment does not prevent dampness from entering the walls, although it may prevent the effects of dampness from showing on the inside surface and may stop the discolouring of distempered surfaces and the peeling of wallpaper.

The causes of dampness are numerous and it is not wise to jump to hasty

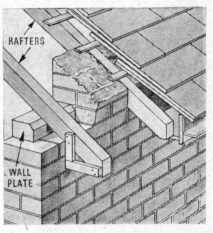

BEAM FILLING

Fig. 4. *The wall between the rafters and up to the underside of the slates should be extended, as shown, in order to prevent rain from entering under the eaves.*

conclusions after a brief inspection. The position of the damp patch on the inside wall is, however, usually a good indication as to the method of entry. If the damp patch is high up in a bedroom at the junction of the ceiling and wall, with dampness spreading on to the ceiling, the trouble is probably due to water penetrating the roof through a broken slate or tile. The water may be running down the roof timbers and into the wall where roof and wall join.

267

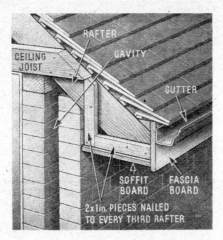

SOFFIT BOARD

FIG. 5. *This method of fixing a soffit board, which also serves to prevent rain from being driven in under the eaves of a roof, is much simpler than beam filling.*

The underfelt below the slates or tiles may be torn, so that rain, blown between the slates, runs down the felt and out of the tear, down the roof to the wall. If felt has not been used, the torching or pointing on the under side of the slates may be loose and have dropped off in places, allowing rain to be driven in under the slates.

The pointing between the ridge tiles or hip tiles may have cracked and worked loose. If this is the case, the old pointing should be picked out and the joints wetted and repointed with a mixture of one part cement and two parts sand.

Gutters and fall pipes must be inspected to make certain that rainwater is running away and not overflowing down the back of the gutter into the wall immediately below.

The pointing between the gable end of the house and the slates or tiles should be checked and made good if

defective, otherwise rain may be driven in between the slates and the wall, so that it passes down the wall and shows as a damp patch at the junction of wall and ceiling in the room below.

The lead flashing where the chimney joins the roof must be examined; see that the apron piece and flashing are properly pointed. The apron piece

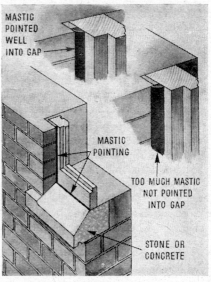

MASTIC POINTING

FIG. 6. *Mastic should always be pointed well into the gap between the frame and the wall. The joint should be filled flush. Avoid any excess of mastic in this position.*

should be wedged firmly into the joint with pieces of lead and repointed with cement and sand (Fig. 3). The lead gutter behind the chimney should be kept clear of leaves and rubbish and the gutter itself should be examined to make sure that the lead has not worn through.

Valleys occurring between two roof

slopes should be examined and the gutter kept clear of leaves and rubbish.

About the only other entry for rain is under the eaves. This is not a likely entry, but sometimes, owing to insufficient overhang of the roof or faulty beam-filling between the wall and the rafters, it is possible for driving rain to enter and show a damp place at the ceiling level in the room below.

To remedy this fault, the wall between the rafters and up to the underside of the slates should be filled up

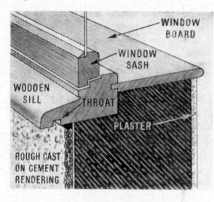

WINDOW-SILLS

FIG. 7. *It is suggested that the rough-cast immediately under the sill be chipped away and that the gap be pointed with mastic compound. Note the throat.*

(Fig. 4); this is an awkward job because of the difficulty of working in a confined space between the ceiling and roof. Alternatively, a soffit board may be fixed from the outside. This is most effective if placed horizontally, and in order to nail it in this position it is necessary to fix supports to the rafters (Fig. 5). The supports need not be fitted to every rafter, one on every third rafter should be sufficient.

If dampness shows high up on a

chimney breast, it may generally be assumed that water is entering near the chimney. It is, therefore, advisable to check the lead flashing and lead gutter behind the chimney for faults as previously described.

A very frequent cause of dampness in this position is faulty pointing of the chimney. A chimney, especially one built on an outside wall, receives the full force of wind-driven rain and any faulty pointing will allow rain to enter. The water may soak down the dry mortar joints and spread out on the chimney breast and possibly on the ceiling in the room. If there is any sign of general deterioration of the chimney pointing, all the old pointing should be raked out to a depth of $\frac{3}{8}$ in. and, after wetting, the joints should be repointed with one part cement to two parts sand. Yet another cause of damp-

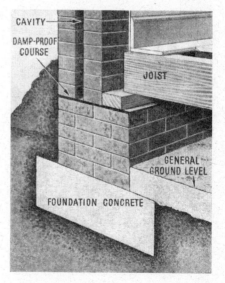

CAUSE OF DAMPNESS

FIG. 8. *Soil piled up against a wall and above the damp-proof course is a potential cause of dampness in the house.*

269

ness may be the porosity of the stone-work or brickwork of the chimney itself, owing to the inclusion of unsuitable material when the house was built. This condition may also be applicable to other parts of the wall and it will be referred to later.

If dampness occurs near a window or door, it can reasonably be expected to be entering from the junction between the wall and the window or door frame. First check the mastic pointing between the wall and the frame (Fig. 6). Sometimes the sun cracks the mastic with the result that water can enter. Any faulty pointing should be cleaned out with an old knife and the joint painted with boiled linseed oil. A small quantity, about two handfuls of powdered mastic, should be mixed thoroughly with boiled linseed oil into a stiff, almost crumbly, paste. This mixture is pointed between the window and the wall, using an old table-knife as a pointing trowel. When pointing the vertical sides of the door or window frame, less of the mastic will fall off the knife if it is held with the handle to the top and the pointing worked upwards. An excessive amount of mastic tends to crack and peel off, so the joint should be filled flush (Fig. 6).

There are several designs of window-sill in common use, but generally the joint between the wall and the sill is a likely place for damp to enter and this usually shows on the interior wall just below the window board. If a stone sill is used, the joint between the wall and sill must be cement pointed. If a concrete sill is used, the same procedure should be followed; the pointing must be checked and replaced if it appears to be defective. Where a wooden sill joins a stone or concrete sill, the pointing must be of mastic.

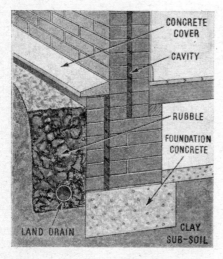

A COMMON FAULT

In the case of houses with a rough-cast exterior finish, the wooden sill often overhangs and the rough-cast is finished up to the underside of the sill. This covering usually serves for a time, but the cement does not adhere to the wood and eventually a crack may appear. As a result, the water running off the sill is driven into the crack and patches of damp appear on the interior wall.

The rough-cast should be chipped away with a narrow chisel and the cement beneath removed to a depth of about $\frac{3}{8}$ in. This gap is then painted with boiled oil and pointed with mastic. In the case of any type of sill which projects beyond the face of the

TRENCH DRAIN

FIG. 9. *If possible the soil, shown in Fig. 8, should be removed and a path laid in its place. In severe cases a low wall and a trench filled with rubble should be constructed in order to allow any water to drain away.*

MIXING CONCRETE—FIRST STAGE

FIG. 10. *First the cement and sand should be mixed dry. Coarse aggregate-gravel, broken stone or granite chippings is included if concrete rather than cement mortar is required. For waterproof concrete, the aggregate must be non-absorbent.*

wall, water will be thrown clear of the wall if the under edge of the sill is throated (Fig. 7). In first-class work a throat is usually included, but in cheaper work it is often omitted. Where possible it is wise to cut a throat in wooden sills about $\frac{1}{4} \times \frac{1}{4}$ in. With a chisel, make sure that the edges of the groove are straight and square, so that water is thrown clear. The joints between the bricks or stones which form the window opening must also be checked for defective pointing; similarly, the joints round a stone head or concrete lintel should have sound cement pointing to prevent the ingress of water.

In some cases, especially where concrete sills and lintels have been used, the sill or head is porous and allows damp to soak through. Treatment for

this type of fault is dealt with later.

Dampness which spreads upwards from the skirting may be the most difficult to trace and to cure. In old houses it is often due to the omission of a damp-proof course, which should be laid below the ground-floor joists to prevent dampness rising from the foundations. To introduce a damp-proof course into an existing house involves a major structural problem and the work should be carried out under the direction of an architect. However, the whole of the pointing should be examined and, if necessary, the whole exterior of the damp wall should be repointed.

The presence of soil next to a wall is often a cause of dampness (Fig. 8), and if possible the soil should be removed and a concrete path laid in its place.

The concrete should be given a gradual slope away from the adjacent wall.

Faulty gutters and fall pipes which do not conduct the roof water clear of the building are another cause of dampness at the foot of a wall. Remedies are obvious.

Sometimes water from high ground drains into the foundations of a house. This condition is generally caused by a clay sub-soil, below a lighter soil. Rain-water permeates the upper layers of soil and then runs with the fall of the ground on top of the clay sub-soil. Obviously, if this sub-soil level is at or about the same level as the founda-tions, the house is in the direct path of a considerable amount of water, drain-ing possibly from quite a large area. If this trouble should be suspected, a short trench should be dug close to the damp wall and down to the foundation concrete. This trench can be inspected from time to time to see whether water collects into it from higher ground. If water does collect, the trench must be dug for the whole length of the wall and extended at the lower end beyond the house. Land drain pipes can then be laid to take the water some distance away from the house.

The part of the wall which is below

MIXING CEMENT MORTAR

FIG. 11. *After making a hole in the centre of the mixture as illustrated, water should be sprinkled slowly over it from the rose of a watering can.*

FANNING OUT AFTER MIXING

FIG. 12. *Keep the mixture plastic and work it to a uniform consistency. Turn it at least three times. If it is used too wet, the work will be weak and porous.*

ground level should then be cleared of all soil and loose mortar and the joints raked out preparatory to rendering the surface with a $\frac{3}{4}$-in. coat of cement and sand. The cement must have a reliable waterproofer added. The trench is then filled in with loose stones, broken bricks or ashes, so that the water can drain away.

In severe cases it may be necessary to build a low wall to contain the rubble and broken brick in the trench. This wall should be cement pointed and should be three or four inches away from the house wall in order to leave an air space, which is the best insulation against damp. A concrete cover is then required to cover the cavity (Fig. 9).

Theoretically, concrete may be made absolutely waterproof, but builders know from experience that the addi-

tion of a waterproofer is usually essential. Thus concrete lintels and sills often allow dampness to pass through them and they may be the means of introducing damp into the house.

There are two general methods of remedying any excessive porosity. The first is to cover the whole of the affected area with a rendering of cement and sand. The cement should be of the waterproof variety or should be mixed with a reliable waterproofing additive. This method may not be desirable, since it covers the brick or stone on the affected wall, which is then noticeably different from the rest of the house. The alternative is to treat the whole house. The cement may be obtained in a variety of colours, and a suitable shade can, therefore, be chosen for mixing as shown in Figs. 10-12.

Porous brick or stone in a chimney

is often treated in this way and, being an isolated structure, it is not conspicuous if rendered in cement. The second method is to apply a waterproofing solution to the affected wall.

There are several makes of good waterproofing liquid on the market. In general, the best procedure is to buy from a builders' merchant rather than from an oil and colourman, as the merchant can usually offer advice as to which variety to use; solutions known as petrifying liquids penetrate the surface and harden the face, so making the stone or brick more durable as well as less porous.

Petrifying liquids are applied with an ordinary flat brush and do not usually discolour the wall. One, two or three applications may be needed. With some varieties they must be applied when the wall is dry and only on a warm day in spring or summer. Other brands may be applied at any time of the year provided that it is not raining. In general, however, best results are obtained when the wall is as dry as possible. Before treatment, the wall should be brushed clean of all dirt and the pointing must be sound.

The application of these waterproofing liquids is simpler and considerably cheaper than cement rendering, and in many cases this simple treatment proves equally effective.

CONDENSATION

A frequent cause of damp walls is condensation. Normally there should be little trouble in identifying this form of moisture, but occasionally it is so heavy that it is attributed to penetration from outside.

The appearance of the beads cannot be easily mistaken, but if the condensation is so heavy that the beads run together, there may be some doubt as to their origin. Dampness due to penetration affects the whole thickness of the wall and is, as a rule, more localized : condensation affects only the surface and is more evenly distributed. The appearance of plaster stripped of its decoration, or an examination of the back of any wallpaper which has been used, should therefore provide a positive means of identification.

The most effective cure is to provide better ventilation, because air which circulates freely does not give up its moisture so readily.

An impervious surface will show the effects of condensation more than one which has a certain amount of suction. Thus, condensation will be more in evidence on a wall finished in gloss paint or enamel than on one which has been distempered.

OTHER REMEDIES

The use of an embossed wallpaper is sometimes effective in overcoming condensation, largely because the raised portions are separated from the plaster by pockets of air, which is itself one of the best non-conductors of heat.

In mild cases the choice of a plastic-paint finish may help, particularly if this is one of the self-coloured variety and is not finished by painting or glazing. Plastic paint has some degree of suction, it is usually applied in a thicker coating than ordinary paints and if the texture is at all pronounced it assists in setting up air currents.

Special anti-condensation paints are also available. Some of these owe their efficiency to particles of cork in the mixture and cork is an excellent non-conductor of heat, but surface treatment prevents only light condensation.

CHAPTER 15

RENOVATING HARDWOOD FLOORS

TREATMENT OF OAK AND PARQUET

PLAIN hardwood and parquetry floor-ing may be laid by one of several processes and before attempting any replacements of worn or damaged parts it is advisable to find out which particular method has been used.

The usual construction for a first-class floor consists of softwood floor boards laid diagonally across the floor joists and nailed to them (Fig. 1). These nails are punched below the surface, and after the surface has been cleaned off flush, the hardwood boards of oak, maple, teak, or other suitable hardwoods, are laid on top of the under floor and secret-nailed to it. The nails are put through the lower part of the groove or through the tongue as detailed in Fig. 1 below.

This type of flooring is usually tongued and grooved at the ends as well as at the edges. It is often made up of short lengths which are seldom more than 3 in. wide and from $\frac{5}{8}$ to $\frac{7}{8}$ in. thick.

A cheaper method of construction is to lay the hardwood flooring directly on to the floor joists and thus to dispense with the underboards.

A hardwood-strip overlay floor is shown in Fig. 2. This type of floor is widely used and consists of hardwood strips $\frac{1}{4}$ or $\frac{5}{16}$ in. thick and 3 in. wide with square edges. These strips are laid on an existing wooden floor, set in glue, and nailed with fine panel pins punched well in.

Parquetry floors are similar, but the

FIRST-CLASS FLOOR

FIG. 1. *A good-quality floor would comprise a softwood sub-floor nailed to the joists, with hard-wood boards of oak, maple or teak above. The top boards would be secret-nailed as shown.*

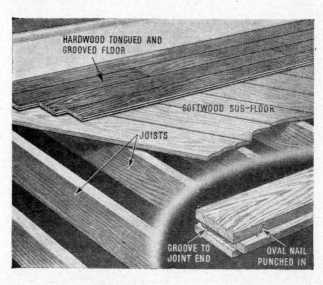

HARDWOOD TONGUED AND GROOVED FLOOR

SOFTWOOD SUB-FLOOR

JOISTS

GROOVE TO JOINT END

OVAL NAIL PUNCHED IN

strip overlay is built up to a pattern (Fig. 3). Frequently, however, the units of the pattern are assembled on and glued to sheet plywood. Manufacturers supply these units in squares of about 18 in. upwards; they are glued and fixed with panel pins to the under-floor. The edges of the squares are often grooved so that they may be fixed by secret nailing in the same way as the boards in Fig. 1.

OTHER TYPES OF FLOOR

In a well-laid floor it is impossible to tell whether the strips have been laid singly or in squares on plywood. In many cases, however, the difference can be recognized by the fact that the joints between the squares are not as close as the joints between the individual strips which make up the squares.

Units of plywood are often used in a similar manner to parquetry. These are simply glued and nailed to a deal under-floor. The thickness of the upper veneer of the plywood is insufficient to stand up to much wear, but the method is often used for surrounds to carpets and if the surface is well protected with polish, it proves a satisfactory and economical method of flooring.

The blocks of wood-block floors are usually 9 in. long, 3 in. wide and from 1 to $1\frac{1}{4}$ in. thick; they are generally laid on concrete. The edges are often grooved so that the special mastic, in which the blocks are bedded, runs into the groove and helps to secure the blocks more firmly. They are usually laid in either squares or in a herring-bone pattern, as shown in Fig. 4.

A floor constructed as shown in Fig. 1 should last a lifetime, but if a board should be damaged by accident it may be replaced. No attempt should be

made to lever out the damaged board, as this will only split portions away from other boards tongued to it. The ends of the boards are often tongued and grooved, and careless levering out of a board may damage the boards which join end-on as well as edge-on. The part to be removed should be marked out and then a series of holes should be bored as close together as possible across the width of the board. The hardwood can then be cut through with a chisel and the damaged part split out as shown in Fig. 5.

Care must be taken not to bore through the sub-floor. If the hardwood floor is fixed directly to the joists

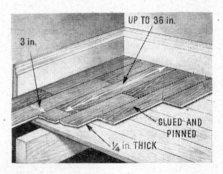

HARDWOOD-STRIP OVERLAY FLOOR

FIG. 2. *This type of floor consists of hardwood strips with square edges glued and pinned to the sub-floor. This method of construction is reliable and popular.*

without a sub-floor, the damaged part is removed as previously described, but after removal a further portion must be cut out so that the new board may rest on a joist at each end. The new board will need to have its tongue planed off and the tongue on the board at the edge of the opening will also need to be removed with a chisel, so that the new board will fit tightly,

PARQUETRY FLOOR

FIG. 3. *Similar floor to that shown in Fig. 2 except that the strip overlay is built up to form a pattern. Square units of various sizes are obtainable as shown.*

square into the new opening provided.

This new board cannot be secret-nailed, it will have to be nailed from the face with fine nails. The heads of the nails should be punched in and the holes filled up with beeswax. If several boards have to be replaced, only the last one will need fixing in the manner described; the others may be secret-nailed.

Where hardwood strips are used as an overlay, any badly worn or damaged strips may easily be replaced. One strip is first split with a chisel and levered out; others in the immediate vicinity may then be prised up.

Before fitting in the new strips, the old glue must be scraped off the under-floor and off the edges of surrounding strips. The new strips are then fitted

taken out, glued, and finally nailed with panel pins which are punched in.

The procedure for a parquetry floor is similar, but care must be taken to find out whether the units which make up the pattern are of single, separate strips or consist of units built up on squares of plywood. In the latter case the whole unit of plywood will have to be prised up and replaced.

Block floors will stand up to extremely hard wear. When badly worn, a block floor will probably need to be replaced throughout. Occasionally, however, individual blocks come loose; in some cases dampness causes a portion of the floor to swell and lift.

These blocks are usually set in a mastic compound consisting of a mixture of pitch and tar which is melted by heating. The blocks are dipped in this compound up to the groove and then rubbed together. When an individual block becomes loose, it may be fixed by bedding it in a cold-water glue. First the old mastic

BLOCK FLOOR

FIG. 4. *The blocks are usually laid on concrete and bedded with a special mastic. Grooves in the edges of the blocks help to provide good adhesion.*

must be removed, then the opening must be cleaned and the block fitted in to make sure that it is level. If so, it should be well glued and replaced.

When a number of blocks have been lifted it is best to clean them and the concrete below, and to replace the blocks by dipping them in mastic. This may be bought from a builders' merchant and heated in an old saucepan until it melts. The liquid is inflammable and care should be taken that the mastic does not run down the sides of the pan and catch fire.

If the blocks have lifted owing to dampness, this fault must be cured and the blocks must be thoroughly dried before they are replaced.

BLOCK FLOORS

If two or three blocks in a doorway are badly worn, they may be brought to the level of the rest of the floor by letting in a suitable piece of wood. This method may be more convenient than lifting the blocks and replacing them with new ones. The old blocks should be pared away for at least $\frac{1}{2}$ in.

to form a clean, level surface. Pieces of wood the same length and width as blocks are then made a suitable thickness. The pieces should be about $\frac{1}{8}$ in. thicker than required so that they may be cleaned off level with the floor after they have been fixed.

These pieces are fitted tightly into place and are bedded in good glue. If the fit is not as good as it should be, the inlaid pieces may be nailed as well as glued and the nails punched in. When the glue has set the pieces may be planed off flush, scraped and glass-papered.

At the same time as the floor is being repaired, the fitting of the skirting to the floor should be examined. The appearance of a well-kept floor is frequently spoiled by a gap between the skirting and floor. This gap may be caused by shrinking of skirting board or floor joists, bringing the floor away from the skirting.

To lower the skirting is impracticable and the quickest and neatest remedy is to fix a small quarter-round fillet in the angle between the

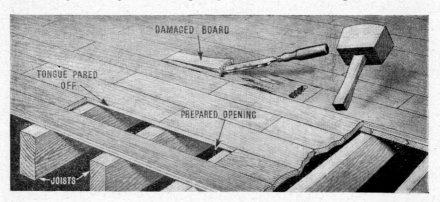

REMOVING A DAMAGED BOARD

FIG. 5. *After marking out the part to be removed, several holes are bored as close together as possible across the board. The defective part can then be removed with a chisel. Care should be taken not to bore through any sub-floor.*

GAP BETWEEN FLOOR AND SKIRTING

FIG. 6. *The appearance of a room can be spoiled by gaps between the floor and the skirting. The simplest way to remedy this defect is to fix a quarter-round fillet over the gap. Cut internal and external angles at 45 deg. to ensure a good fit.*

floor and skirting. The fillet should be about $\frac{3}{4} \times \frac{3}{4}$ in. and fixed with fine nails to the floor. The internal and external angles need cutting at 45 deg. to make them fit properly, and where the quarter-round fillet finishes in a doorway the end may need to be rounded; this is known as a returned end (Fig. 6).

When a hardwood floor has been neglected, the dirt and grease discolour the floor and make it patchy. If an unsuitable stain has been used, it may wear lighter in places and produce a patchy unpleasant appearance. The only real cure in such cases is to start with a clean floor. The floor should be scrubbed clean, using a fine abrasive to remove particles of grit which will have been trodden into the surface. After scrubbing a small area, the floor should be dried with a cloth to prevent swelling of the floor boards. A small quantity of soda may be used in the water to help in removing the grease, but if a strong solution of soda is used it may stain the oak flooring. It is best, therefore, to rely on pumice powder and vigorous scrubbing.

After the floor has dried and the grease and dirt have been removed, the surface of the floor should be scraped so that it presents a uniform appearance. This is a long and tiresome job. There are two or three makes of scraper on the market. These all work on the same principle and consist of a fine, sharp, curved blade held in a shaped handle (Fig. 7). The difficulty about using these tools is that they are difficult to sharpen and they soon lose their edge after some use. They are usually sharpened with a saw file and instructions for sharpening them are given by the manufacturers. It is best to obtain a scraper with at least a 3-in. blade, otherwise there is a risk of the edges leaving marks on the floor surface.

SCRAPING FLOORS

Many flooring specialists still prefer to use a plain, rectangular piece of steel known as a cabinet scraper. This may be held in a suitably shaped piece of wood rather like a hambone, with a saw-cut into which the scraper fits (Fig. 7). Alternatively, a metal holder, with a screw for adjusting the amount of curve on the scraper, may be used.

To be effective, the scraper should be capable of removing fine shavings from the surface of the hardwood. The scraper is worked along the grain of the wood, but where an awkward, rough piece of grain occurs it may be worked diagonally, in either direction, to make a smooth surface. Often a piece of board is easier to work in one direction than another and, if the surface is not as smooth as desired, it is advisable to try scraping in the opposite direction to the previous work.

SHARPENING THE SCRAPER

After five or ten minutes' work the scraper will need resharpening. First remove the scraper from the holder and take off the old, blunt and worn edge. This is done by laying the scraper flat on a table or bench and running the blade of a gouge or steel scriber backwards and forwards along the wide surface, so that the burr which projects on that side is removed. This action is repeated on both sides of the tool, so that the burr is removed on all four edges. The scraper is then held as shown in Fig. 8 and the round part of the gouge drawn smartly along the edge of the scraper at the angle shown, so that after three or four strokes the edge has been turned over to form the cutting edge. This procedure should be repeated on the other edges in order to make four cutting edges.

If a vice is available for holding the scraper, both hands can be used on the gouge or scriber; more weight can then be exerted and a sharp edge is formed more quickly.

After resharpening several times, the edge of the scraper becomes worn,

and before attempting to put on a new burr the edge of the scraper must be filed straight and square.

After a thorough scraping, the floor should be rubbed smooth with glass-paper. If the boards run in one direction only, the glass-paper should be used in the direction of the grain. Grade fine 2 is suitable. When dealing with a parquetry floor it will be found that the boards change direction frequently and it is best to use the glass-paper diagonally in the same direction. It is best to fold the glass-paper into three and to wrap it round a fairly thick block of soft wood, so that both hands may be used to grip glass-paper and block together. Any small cracks or

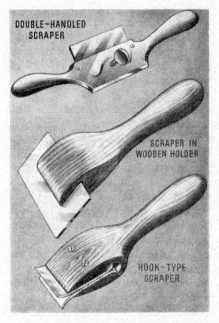

DOUBLE-HANDLED SCRAPER

SCRAPER IN WOODEN HOLDER

HOOK-TYPE SCRAPER

TYPES OF SCRAPER

Fig. 7. *Experienced craftsmen prefer a rectangular piece of steel known as a cabinet scraper, but one of the above tools, fitted with a handle, is more convenient.*

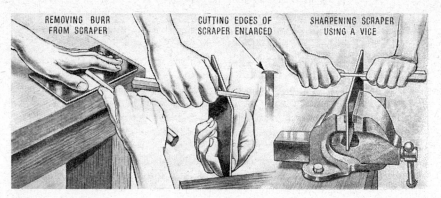

| REMOVING BURR FROM SCRAPER | CUTTING EDGES OF SCRAPER ENLARGED | SHARPENING SCRAPER USING A VICE |

SHARPENING A SCRAPER

FIG. 8. *First, lay the scraper flat and run a gouge or steel scriber over the edge to remove the burr. Then, hold the scraper against the edge of a bench, or in a vice.*

bad joints, nail holes or other defects should be filled up with beeswax. Heat an old knife and hold it against a lump of beeswax to melt small portions off and to press the wax into the holes. The excess beeswax may be scraped off the floor later.

After glass-papering the floor should be swept, and after the dust has settled the surface should be dusted. It is then ready for either staining or finishing without stain, in so-called natural finish.

The idea of a natural finish is to retain the colour of the wood and to protect the surface as far as possible from being damaged by dust, dirt and normal wear. Some authorities advocate the use of raw linseed oil, rubbed well into the wood before any wax polish is applied. This treatment undoubtedly brings out the richness of the grain, especially in oak and beech floors, and helps not only to preserve the wood, but also to improve the way it wears. If, however, too much linseed oil is used, it makes the floor greasy and liable to collect dust and dirt, because it prevents the wax polish

from hardening and giving a good gloss. If the floor is rubbed in an attempt to improve its appearance, the dirt is rubbed into the polish and the floor soon looks unattractive. If raw linseed oil is used, it must be used sparingly and rubbed well into the grain. The floor should be left to dry until the surface is non-greasy before any wax polish is applied.

Any risk of greasiness will be avoided if the floor is treated, immediately after scraping and glass-papering, with shellac varnish or french-polish.

POLISHING

The polish may be either white or brown, the white is practically transparent and allows the natural colour of the wood to be shown, while the brown is not quite clear and makes the wood appear to be very slightly darker. The method of application will be the same for either material.

The presence of damp, either in the atmosphere or on the floor, must be avoided or the shellac will turn cloudy. If the room cannot be thoroughly warmed artificially, it is best to choose

281

a warm, dry day in summer. The polish is applied with a camel-hair mop (brush) in the direction of the grain and one board should be covered at a time, using light strokes and not brushing the polish well into the grain nor going back to touch up any patch which has been treated previously.

In the case of parquetry floors, a line of units should be done at a time, so that the joins occur between successive strips on a joint between one line of units and the next. When the polish is dry, the whole floor should be rubbed down with fine glass-paper. No. o is the most suitable. The dust formed by the rubbing-down should be removed before a second coat of polish is applied in the same manner as the first. When this next coat is dry, the surface should be lightly rubbed down with grade o glass-paper once again. A hard surface should now have been formed with the grain filled with polish. This is an ideal base for finishing the floor with wax polish. There is no short cut to wax polishing. Vigorous rubbing after the polish has been applied is the only way to form a hard, non-greasy surface.

HOME-MADE POLISH

Proprietary wax polishes which never set hard must be avoided, these may be easy to apply, but if the surface remains greasy they are not effective. A good wax polish may be made by shredding beeswax into a tin containing turpentine. The mixture is warmed by placing the tin in a saucepan of boiling water, and more wax is then added until the mixture has the consistency of melted butter. The wax is then put on one side to harden ready for use. It should be applied with a soft cloth and vigorously rubbed off with a piece of canvas. Frequent applications, well rubbed in to produce a hard finish, will give a good wearing surface and a beautiful finish.

If a natural finish is considered to be too light in colour, then, after scraping and glass-papering, the floor may be stained to the desired shade.

The stain must be of a type which penetrates the surface and goes some distance into the wood. Of the three types in general use—water, spirit and oil—oil stain is to be preferred. Water stain is apt to raise the grain and the floor may need glass-papering after staining; furthermore, on a larger surface water stain is often patchy, lighter in some places than others; spirit stain dries very quickly and is difficult to apply without showing joins. Further instructions on the using of stains are given in Chapter 4.

FILLING AND STAINING

When the stain is dry, any defects caused by bad joints or nail holes should be filled with beeswax.

If the floor is darker than the colour of beeswax, a little brown-umber powder may be added to the melted beeswax in order to match the floor stain. The umber must be well stirred into the melted wax to obtain a uniform shade. When set, the mixture can be used as previously described for filling up any holes.

When a parquetry floor has been scraped and smoothed, and it is desired to stain alternate strips darker and to leave the rest a natural shade, the areas to be left natural should first be given two coats of clear french-polish. This will prevent the stain used on the remaining pieces from soaking into the strips which have already been treated.

CHAPTER 16

PELMETS AND CURTAIN RAILS

THEIR DESIGN AND CONSTRUCTION FOR
VARIOUS TYPES OF WINDOW

THE purpose of a pelmet is to cover the curtain track or rail from which the curtains are suspended, to prevent dust from settling on the fittings by which the curtains are pulled, and to improve the general appearance of a room. Pelmets may be either of wood, painted or stained to match the picture rail and architrave, or they may be of the same fabric as the curtains.

Wooden pelmets, being permanent, require the minimum of attention. They need only to be painted with the rest of the woodwork in the room. A selection of simple wooden pelmets is shown in Fig. 1.

Fabric pelmets may be preferred on account of their appearance, but they harbour dust and need to be taken down from time to time for washing or cleaning. Furthermore, it is not a simple matter to construct a fabric pelmet which can be taken down easily; the trouble of removing, wash-

INTERESTING DESIGNS

FIG. 1. *Selection of a pelmet must always depend on the width, height and position of the window for which it is intended. Most of the examples shown are made of wood. Fabric pelmets harbour dust and appear to be less popular in modern homes.*

ing and replacing is a point to be considered when choosing between a fabric and a wooden pelmet.

The construction of a pelmet depends mainly on the type of window for which it is intended, the position of the window in the wall and its distance from the ceiling. Many windows are surrounded by a wooden architrave from 2–4 in. wide, and with this design little difficulty should be experienced in making and fitting a suitable form of pelmet.

FIXING THE CURTAIN TRACK

The curtain track is most easily fixed to the face of the architrave and this work should be completed before the pelmet is made. The brackets to support the track should be screwed at intervals of about 18 in. to the face of the architrave. A bracket is needed at each end and the track is then bent so that the curtains overlap. If a special bracket is not available to support the end of the bent track, a small piece of tubing and a long screw should be used so that the end of the track is supported (Fig. 2).

The proportions of the pelmet are decided by the size of the window. A tall, narrow window requires a deep pelmet, whereas a long, low window looks better with a shallow pelmet. The pelmet should not stand out from the face of the curtains any farther than is necessary to allow freedom of movement for the curtains. If the curtain track is fixed first, the inside edge of the pelmet need only be just clear of the track.

The dimensions given for the construction of the pelmets shown are for guidance only and should be adapted to suit the thickness of architraves, the size of brackets used and the amount

the track projects from the face of the architrave.

Almost all the simple pelmets shown in Fig. 1 are made from wood $\frac{3}{4}$ in. thick with a plywood front. They are all of similar construction and intended for fitting to the architrave round the window opening. The top board should be 3–6 in. longer at each end than the distance across the architraves; a suitable width is $3\frac{1}{2}$–$4\frac{1}{2}$ in., and the ends may be rounded or square, as preferred. Two small metal brackets, screwed to the face of the architrave, support the top board. The top board can be tried in position, but it should not be screwed to the brackets until the front of the

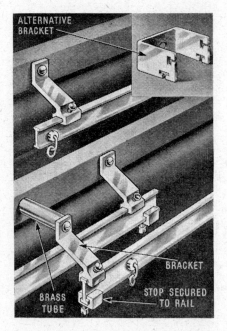

CURTAIN TRACK

FIG. 2. *Brackets to support the track are fitted at 18-in. intervals. A piece of tube and a long screw may be used to bring the track away from the wall at the overlap.*

pelmet has been attached, as it is easier to fix the front board while the pelmet is on a bench or on the floor.

If the end of the pelmet is to be curved, the plywood will bend round the curve more readily if the grain on the outside layers is vertical. It is not essential to use plywood and good

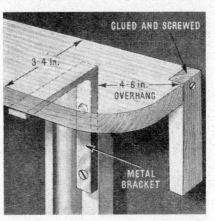

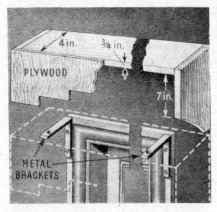

WOODEN PELMET

FIG. 3. *Suitable form of construction for a wooden pelmet supported by two metal brackets. The pelmet itself has a box form of construction and can be completed before fixing.*

results may be obtained by using thick cardboard, strips of linoleum or plywood substitutes, provided that the pelmet is to be painted and not stained.

The appearance of a long pelmet may be improved by fitting a decorative piece in the centre. This piece can also serve to cover a joint between two pieces of plywood in the front, if one long piece is not available. When stiff cardboard or linoleum is used it should be fixed to the top board with flat-headed nails. A method of hiding the nails and of relieving the appearance of a large flat surface is to fix a $\frac{1}{2}$

ROUNDED ENDS

FIG. 4. *To make a pelmet with rounded ends, cut the top board to shape and let in a piece of wood at the end to secure the front, which is best made of plywood.*

or $\frac{3}{4}$ in. wide half-round mould with fine panel-pins and glue (Fig. 5). Alternatively, a second piece of plywood or thick cardboard may be glued and pinned on top of the first piece so as to leave a margin and relieve the flat surface.

The general construction of a wooden pelmet, supported by two metal brackets, is shown in Fig. 3. The top board is first cut to length, and shaped to fit any irregularities in the wall. The ends are next shaped and nailed on, and finally the plywood front is fitted after it has been cut to the desired shape. The edges and corners should be smoothed and rounded with glass-paper, the nails punched in and the nail holes filled with putty.

If the end of the pelmet is to be rounded, the top board should be rounded first and then a piece of wood about $1\frac{1}{4}$ by $\frac{3}{4}$ in. let in to the end of the top piece and screwed to it (Fig. 4). The plywood front is then bent

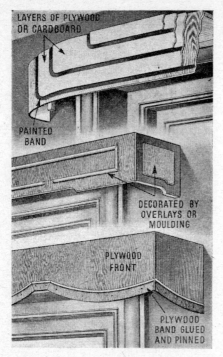

LAYERS OF PLYWOOD OR CARDBOARD

PAINTED BAND

DECORATED BY OVERLAYS OR MOULDING

PLYWOOD FRONT

PLYWOOD BAND GLUED AND PINNED

DECORATIVE NOTE

Fig. 5. *Some interesting designs for relieving the flat surface of very long pelmets. Some of the colouring in the curtains may be used on the front surface.*

round the top board and nailed to both the top and end pieces. The grain of the plywood should be vertical on the two outside layers and it is easiest to begin nailing in the middle and to work towards the ends, cutting off any excess at each end.

For comparatively narrow windows, fancy pelmets look particularly attractive and are simple to make. For wider windows, however, simple shapes are to be preferred. If a sufficient length of plywood is not available in one piece for a wide window, two pieces may be joined behind a centre block and screwed to it. Next the

shaped overlay should be fitted tightly to the centre block and glued and nailed to the plywood front. Further decoration may be added by painting contrasting coloured bands along the front of the pelmet.

Further suggestions for relieving the long flat surface of pelmets over wide windows are provided in Fig. 5. Several layers of cardboard glued to a plywood front board give the appearance of layers of cloth and can be made to match the curtains. A border of suitably shaped plywood $1\frac{1}{2}$–2 in. wide fixed to the lower edge gives the effect of a fringe. Half-round beading may also be fitted on the plywood frontboard to form panels. Alternatively, the flat surface of a plain pelmet may be decorated with transfers, stencils or wallpaper friezes applied after the pelmet has been stained or painted; finally it will be found that varnishing

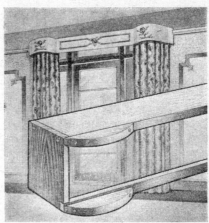

LARGE PELMET

Fig. 6. *Pelmet suitable for a large window decorated with a floral design to match the curtains. The side curves look very attractive when the curtains are drawn back, as shown.*

over the whole surface will help to protect the design.

A pelmet suitable for a large window and decorated by stencils with a floral design to match the pattern on the curtain is shown in Fig. 6. The design includes a curve which fits in well with the curtains when they are not closed. Two pieces of plywood are first bent round the shaped pieces and nailed to

FIG. 8. *If the picture rail is at about the required height, the length of the end-pieces may be adjusted to allow the pelmet to be rested on the rail.*

AWKWARD PICTURE RAIL

FIG. 7. *It is sometimes necessary either to remove a part of the picture rail or to cut the end-pieces to shape. Another solution to the problem is shown in Fig. 8.*

them and next the straight piece is fitted tightly between the two curves.

The picture rail sometimes makes the fitting of a pelmet rather more complicated. When the picture rail is above the window the problem will not arise, but if it is level with the top architrave, or 2–3 in. below, it may be necessary to fit the end-pieces over it. The picture rail could be cut and a suitable section of it removed, but this

is difficult without scratching the plaster above and below it. Since the picture rail is often partly set in the plaster, the removal of a portion may necessitate making good the plaster.

The quickest and best solution to the problem is shown in Fig. 7. Two saw-cuts are made in the side-pieces and the curved part of the rail is removed so that only the flat part remains. It is then a simple matter to cut out a piece of the pelmet end-piece to fit over the picture rail. Alternatively, a piece of card may be cut to fit the shape of the picture rail. When the correct shape has been obtained, the card is used to mark out the end-pieces, which can then be cut with a fret-saw or gouges.

If the picture rail is at about the

FIG. 9. *If a window is not surrounded by an architrave, a board must be fitted above the window opening. Sometimes this board is nailed to a wooden lintel.*

right height, the length of the end-piece may be adjusted in order to allow it to rest on the rail (Fig. 8). A light pelmet with its ends resting on the picture rail may be fixed by two screws in the top edge of the architrave without using metal brackets.

NEED FOR A BACK BOARD

In many houses the windows are not surrounded by architraves, but finished with plaster linings. The edges may be finished in hard plaster without the wooden angle-bead. In either case, it will be necessary to fasten a board 3–4 in. wide and $\frac{3}{4}$ in. thick to the wall. This board should be long enough to allow the curtains to be pulled back to the edge of the window opening; an allowance of 6–9 in. at each end should be sufficient for the purpose. The board should be held in position about 3 in. above the window head, and while in this position a pencil mark should be made all round it. Any plugging which is necessary should then be kept within these lines, so as to avoid the need for repairing cracked and broken plaster after the board has been fixed.

Sometimes a wooden lintel will be found over the window head to support the inside brickwork. It may be covered with plaster, but by driving a nail between the lines marked on the wall its position can readily be found. If a wooden lintel has been used, it will be a simple matter to nail the board through the plaster into the lintel (Fig. 9). The pelmet can then be supported by two metal brackets.

If preferred, the pelmet may be constructed as shown in Fig. 10. Firstly, the end-pieces are nailed to the

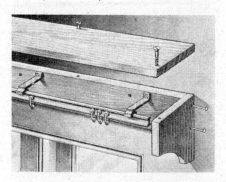

FIG. 10. *If preferred, the pelmet, complete with curtain track, may be assembled for fitting as a unit, the front being nailed on after fitting the frame.*

wall-piece, the top is then screwed to the structure, and the front-piece is then nailed on. If there is a wooden lintel, the pelmet may be constructed on the floor or bench by nailing the back, top and ends together and fitting, but not nailing, the front. The pelmet without the front may then be nailed or screwed to the lintel, the track is then fastened to the back board. Finally, the front may be nailed on.

If the nails will not pass through the plaster, the lintel is almost certain to be of concrete, in which case the concrete must be drilled and wooden plugs inserted, so that the back board may be

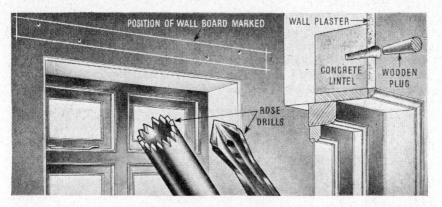

POSITION OF WALL BOARD MARKED   WALL PLASTER →

CONCRETE LINTEL   WOODEN PLUG

ROSE DRILLS

USE OF ROSE DRILLS

FIG. 11. *If the wall board is to be fitted to a concrete lintel, holes will need to be made with a rose drill for wooden plugs to be inserted as detailed top right.*

nailed to the plugs. A rose drill and a heavy hammer should be used to make the holes, which should be arranged as shown in Fig. 11; the drill should be turned repeatedly as it is being driven in. The holes need to be about 2 in. deep and the softwood plugs must fit the hole at the start; if given a slight taper the plugs will then fit tightly for the whole length of the hole. The plugs should be cut flush with the wall and the back board nailed to them. The position of the plugs must be carefully marked on the back board so that the nails hit the plugs. The rest of the pelmet may then be fixed to the back board as previously described.

FABRIC PELMETS

Small windows look bright and attractive when finished off with a pelmet made of the same material as the curtains. Such a pelmet should be 6–7 in. deep and well pleated; in estimating the amount of material required, the length of the window opening should be doubled, in order to make sufficient pleats. The pelmet may be fixed to either a shaped top board or a metal valance-rail.

If a top board is used it should be fixed to the top of the architrave either by two metal brackets or by screws passed through the back edge of the board down into the architrave. If the window has no architrave, a back board must be fixed to the wall and the top board fastened to it with two metal brackets as for wooden pelmets.

A cloth pelmet may be pleated by stitching a curtain tape to the top edge. The cords in the curtain tape may then be pulled up sufficiently to draw the pelmet to the required length. The pleated pelmet may then be fastened to the wooden top board by pushing drawing pins through the material into the wood edge. Alternatively, a length of gimp may be sewn along the top edge of the material, and drawing pins or tacks put in underneath the gimp.

Another method, which allows the pelmet to be removed most easily (Fig. 12) for washing purposes, is to sew a length of strong tape near to the top edge of the pelmet. The tape is folded over the edge and fixed on the top board by drawing pins, or by leaving loops on the tape and passing the loops over a series of nails, which cannot be seen from the floor of the room. The tape should be sewn to the pelmet usually lined, a stiffened cloth pelmet of the same material as the curtains is often used. It is not pleated, but is frequently cut to a decorative shape with braid on the lower edge. This type of pelmet should be fixed to a wooden

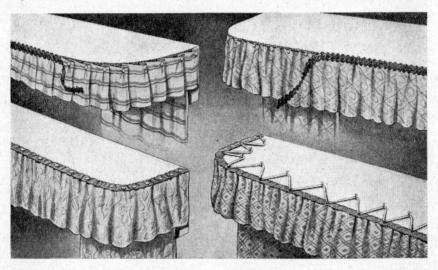

FABRIC PELMETS

FIG. 12. *Four methods of fitting a pleated pelmet to a wooden top board. Perhaps the most interesting idea is that in the lower right corner, where nails and loops are used.*

before it is pleated so that the tape and the material are pleated together.

Instead of using a board to support the pelmet, a metal rail can be used. This may be made from iron rod $\frac{3}{16}$ or $\frac{1}{4}$ in. in diameter, bent as shown in Fig. 13, and fitted into a screw eye fastened to the architrave. Another method is to use $\frac{1}{2}$ by $\frac{1}{8}$ in. strip iron. In either case, a hem is required on the top edge of the pelmet cloth, so that the rod or strip will slide through it. If no architrave is used on the window, the metal rod may be fixed to the back board which will have been fixed to support the curtain track.

For large, heavy curtains, which are

top board. After the top board has been fitted, the exact length of the pelmet can be measured; do not forget to allow for the returned ends, so that the pelmet finishes close to the wall. When cutting the material allowance should be made for turning in the edges.

The material is stiffened by backing it with buckram; the pelmet is subsequently lined with similar material to that used for lining the curtains. Any decorative braid or fringe may then be added and the finished pelmet may be fixed to the top board by any of the methods already suggested.

To ensure that the shape of the pel-

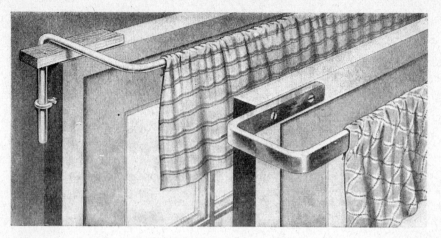

FIG. 13. *As an alternative support for a fabric pelmet, a metal rail or rod may be employed. In such cases a hem, wide enough to allow the support to be passed through it, must be made at the top of the material; the fitting may then be shaped.*

met is symmetrical, it is best to draw the required shape on the back of a roll of old wallpaper or lining paper; this can then be laid on the material as a pattern.

The ceiling above a bay window is usually level with the top of the window frame, and there may be no wall above the window to which a pelmet may be fixed. Furthermore, if there is a wide window-sill and the curtain track is fixed to the top rail of the window frame, then the curtains should finish at the sill level if they are to look neat.

In order to fix a pelmet of either the wooden or cloth type, it is necessary to fix a top board to the ceiling. This board should be 3–4 in. wide and $\frac{3}{4}$ in. thick. The pieces of wood do not need to be jointed at the angles, but merely butt against each other (Fig. 14). The top boards will, of course, be hidden by the pelmet and curtains when these are finally put up over the window area.

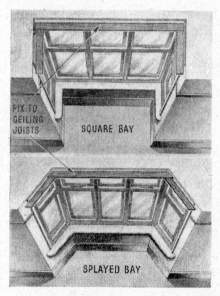

BAY WINDOWS

FIG. 14. *To fit a pelmet above a bay window, top boards 3-4 in. wide may require to be fixed to the ceiling. The wood need not be jointed at the angles.*

CHAPTER 17

TILED WALLS AND FLOORS

SIMPLE REPAIRS AND RENOVATION

UNDOUBTEDLY a better understanding will be gained of how to replace broken, loose or cracked tiles, if a short description is given first of how a simple piece of tiling is carried out.

For example, a small tiled lining to a wash-basin is a job which is straightforward and can well be carried out by the amateur. The advantages of a tiled surface over a painted or distempered surface in such a position are obvious. The area to be tiled should be marked out in pencil on the wall surface. The size will be arranged to suit the size of tiles which are to be used. The most common sizes are in squares of 2 by 2 in.; 3 by 3 in.; 4 by 4 or 6 by 6 in. It is proposed to use three courses of 6-by-6-in. plain tiles by way of an example (Fig. 1).

SIMPLE TILED LINING

Rectangular tiles may be used if preferred, and common sizes in this shape are 6 by 3, 6 by 2 and 6 by $1\frac{1}{2}$ in. The tiles may be arranged by bonding the joints, as in brickwork, but it is more usual to arrange all the vertical joints over each other.

The first job is to cut away the plaster with a cold chisel, or with an old wood chisel, down to the brick or stone wall. This area must then be rendered with a perfectly flat surface of cement mortar about $\frac{1}{2}$ in. thick. Before mixing the mortar it is useful to nail a $\frac{1}{2}$ in. thick lath to the wall by hammering the nails through the wood into the brick seam. The lath should be fixed near the top of the area to be tiled and a second lath fixed similarly near the bottom. A plumb rule should be used to ensure that these two laths are vertical and in one plane.

These laths act as guides to obtaining a true rendering of cement mortar. The face of the brick or stone wall should then be well wetted with a whitewash brush. If this damping is omitted, the moisture from the cement mortar is taken into the wall too rapidly and the setting of the cement

THREE-COURSE TILE LINING

FIG. 1. *The work of fixing three courses of 6-by-6-in. plain tiles to form a tile lining behind a kitchen sink should be within the capability of the handyman.*

is liable to be seriously impaired.
The cement mortar is made by
mixing three parts by volume of fine
sand to one of cement. The cement and
sand should be thoroughly mixed while
dry until a uniform colour is obtained,
water should then be added until the
mixture is the consistency of a stiff

LEVELLING THE MORTAR

FIG. 3. *When the area between the laths
has been covered with the mortar, a
straight-edge is drawn across the area
in order to level the surface.*

APPLYING THE MORTAR

FIG. 2. *A plasterer's float should be
employed to apply the mortar which is
taken from the hawk. Note the two laths
by which the rendering is levelled.*

paste. The mortar is then applied to
the wall with a plasterer's float. This
operation is simplified if a board about
9 in. square, with a handle underneath,
known as a hawk, is used (Fig. 2).
The hawk should be held close up to
the wall in the left hand so that suitable
amounts of mortar can be pushed off
and spread evenly over the wall with
the float. After the area between the
laths has been covered, a straight-edge

should be drawn across the face of the
two laths to ensure that the surface is
perfectly plane between them (Fig. 3).
After this rendering has stiffened for
about an hour, the wood laths may be
pulled off and the gaps filled in with
the mortar. The larger surface should
be stiff enough to be used as a guide
so that the two narrow strips can be
rendered flush with the main surface.
Before the surface has hardened it
should be scratched with a nail in order
to provide a key for the fixing of the
tiles. The cement rendering is best left
for a week before the tiles are fixed to
it.

Before the tiles are fixed they must
be well soaked in water. They cannot
be soaked too long, so it is best to leave
them overnight to ensure that they
cannot absorb any of the moisture from
the mortar used to fix them.

The fixing mortar is made by mixing
equal parts of very fine sand and

cement to a stiff paste. Only a small amount should be mixed at a time (Fig. 4), as it may harden before it can be used and consequently be wasted.

Start at the bottom to lay the first course. Spread a liberal amount of mortar over the back surface of each tile with a small trowel. Press the tiles to the wall and give each one a tap with the trowel handle. There should be a gap of about $\frac{1}{16}$ in. between each tile. When the first course has been completed, a wooden straight-edge should be laid across the face of the tiles and any tiles which project should be tapped back into line with the rest. Any cement left on the face of the tile should be removed with a damp cloth before it has had time to harden.

MIXING CEMENT MORTAR

FIG. 4. *Small quantities of cement mortar may be mixed on the hawk. The handle of the trowel is used to form a ring into which water should be sprinkled.*

In the example of tiling shown in Fig. 1, it would be an advantage for all exposed edges and corners to be rounded. Special tiles for this purpose, along with several other shaped varieties for internal and external angles, are illustrated in Fig. 5.

The joints between the tiles should be pointed with a rather creamy mixture of sand and cement in equal parts. It may be applied to the joints with a small trowel or, more easily, by using a brush across the joints to force the cement mortar into the joints. The excess mortar should be wiped off with a piece of paper, followed by a damp cloth, in order to clean the tiles thoroughly.

Where the tiles finish, it is usually necessary to make good the plaster which has been chipped away.

The plaster should be cut cleanly with a trowel edge or old knife so that the edge is undercut. Next the gap should be very thoroughly wetted with an old brush and filled up flush with plaster of paris or Keene's cement. If plaster of paris is used, it should be mixed with an equal volume of slaked lime.

CUTTING TILES

If it is required to fit a tile round taps or pipes, a semicircular hole on the edge of the tile should be marked so that small pieces can be nipped out with the corner of a pair of pincers. The edges can be smoothed by rubbing them with a piece of carborundum stone.

If a hole is to be made in the centre of a tile, it must first be cut into halves so that a semicircle may be cut out of each piece (Fig 6).

It is not easy to cut tiles, so that if this can be avoided by using a smaller

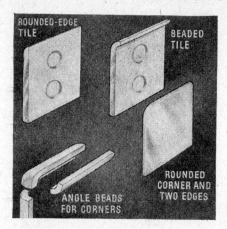

SPECIAL SHAPES

FIG. 5. *Selection of specially shaped tiles which are available for rounding exposed edges and corners. They are fixed in the same way as ordinary tiles.*

standard tile in certain places it is worth while. The best way to cut a tile is to use a glass cutter and straight-edge, making a firm incision across the glazed surface (Fig. 7). Mark across the back surface with the edge of the chisel, then, holding the tile as shown in Fig. 8, tap it smartly with a small hammer along the line marked on the back.

If a tile is loose or broken it may be levered out with the point of a trowel. To refix it correctly will mean that the old mortar used to fix the tile to the rendering must be chipped out of the opening.

A very narrow, sharp chisel should be used so as to chip a very small portion away at a time. Excessive vibration may loosen other tiles and more damage than good may result. When the opening is clean and the edges of the loose tile have been cleaned, the rendering should be wetted, the back of the tile spread with

cement mortar and the tile replaced If a new tile is used, it must be soaked in water for at least two hours. The joints may then be pointed as pre-viously described. The new pointing will, however, look brighter than the rest of the pointing, and the finished work will look patchy.

When replacements are made it is, therefore, a good ·plan to repoint the whole surface and thus to prevent a

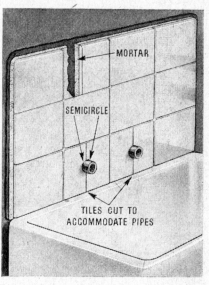

HOLES FOR WATER PIPES

FIG. 6. *To cut a hole for a water pipe, cut the tile in two and nip a semicircle out of each half, as illustrated, with the corner of a pair of pincers.*

patched-up appearance. Pleasing effects may be obtained by using coloured cement, so that the fine lines of pointing contrast with the colour of the tile.

Before repointing, the old cement must be raked out of the joints with an old penknife. The joints should also be washed out with an old brush before the repointing is carried out.

Work pointed with plaster or Keene's cement shows a white line which soon washes out and becomes dirty. In such cases it is worth while to rake out the joints and to repoint with a coloured cement.

To replace a loose tile, it may simply be glued into place. It is unnecessary to chip out the cement mortar from the opening, but the loose tile should be cleaned and the edges scraped. The back may then be liberally coated with glue, preferably waterproof glue, and the tile replaced. Plaster of paris may be used to point the gaps.

This rather unprofessional method is only suitable for replacing an isolated tile which has come loose. If two or three tiles need replacing, it is advisable to use cement mortar as the adhesive.

Tiles in fireplaces and hearths are frequently thinner than wall tiles, but they are fixed to their ground in exactly the same way. In many tiled fireplaces the rendering is merely a 3- or 4-in.-thick slab of concrete cast to the required shape. The tiles are fixed with cement mortar and the joints are pointed later. If, therefore, any tiles become loose or broken they may be replaced in exactly the same way as wall tiles.

Similarly, if an occasional tile comes loose it can be very quickly replaced by gluing. This method is more successful on fireplace surrounds than on walls, since there is seldom any damp-

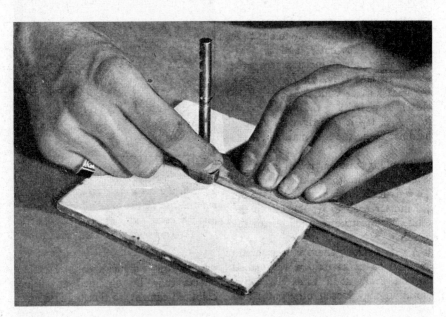

CUTTING A TILE WITH A GLASS CUTTER

FIG. 7. *The easiest way to cut a tile is to use a glass cutter and straight-edge, making a firm incision across the surface. Diamond glass cutters are held at an angle of about 45 deg., but the steel-wheel type is used in an upright position.*

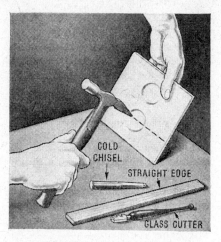

BREAKING AFTER CUTTING

FIG. 8. *After scratching the surface of the tile with a glass cutter, mark it across the back with the edge of a chisel before attempting to break it as illustrated.*

ness near the fire and any good quality glue will prove quite effective. The pointing may be done with plaster of paris, cement or linseed-oil putty.

A tiled hearth often becomes unsightly with cracked, worn and broken tiles long before the vertical surfaces show any signs of age. A new set of hearth tiles can easily be laid and the whole appearance of the fireplace will be considerably improved.

TILING A HEARTH

The old tiles and the cement mortar in which they are laid should be chipped away with an old screwdriver or chisel down to the rough concrete beneath. This cement mortar may be thicker than the $\frac{1}{4}$ in. put on the back of wall tiles, but it is easy to tell when the concrete has been reached.

After an even surface has been made of at least the thickness of the new tiles and $\frac{1}{4}$ in. below floor level, the hearth is ready for relaying. The tiles should be soaked and the concrete well wetted and cleared of dust and loose particles.

A cement mortar of equal parts fine sand and cement should be mixed and laid evenly into the hearth. A board shaped as shown in Fig. 9 can be used to make certain that the cement mortar is level. The tiles are then laid on the mortar and each one is tapped with the trowel handle to bed it. A straight-edge is used to test each course as it is laid and to make sure that the tiles are level.

Wipe any cement from the face of the tiles with a damp cloth. Later the joints may be pointed in a similar manner to that already described for wall tiling. Do not light the fire for a day or two after the work has been finished, so that the hearth may dry slowly.

Raised hearths may be re-tiled in a similar manner after stripping the old tiles and cement mortar from both top and edges. The new edge tiles should be put on first. When these are set, the top edge may be used to level the mortar for the remainder of the tiles.

TILED FLOORS

Floor tiles vary in thickness from $\frac{1}{4}$-$\frac{1}{2}$ in. and may be obtained in various colours and shapes. Unlike wall tiles, they have not a glazed surface. They must be laid on a firm concrete base if the tiles are to remain free from cracks.

After the concrete has been laid to the correct level and a perfectly flat surface has been obtained, the concrete should be allowed to become semi-stiff before it is scratched to form a key for the cement mortar. After a week or so when the concrete is cured, the surface is wetted and the tiles may

be laid without any further preparation.

Like wall tiles, the floor tiles must be
soaked until they are saturated. A mixture of cement mortar made from
equal volumes of sand and cement is
then used to set the tiles.

The floor tiles should have a liberal
amount of mortar spread over the back
of them with a small trowel and may
then be laid in place and tapped down
to the required level with the wooden
handle of the trowel.

Floor tiles should have a good $\frac{1}{8}$-in.
space between each. After laying the
joints should be grouted, by brushing
a creamy paste of cement mortar across
the face of the tiles so that the joints
are all flush. Surplus mortar should be
wiped off with a damp cloth.

DAMAGED TILES

A loose or broken tile must be prised
out and the opening cleared of cement
mortar. To avoid breaking other tiles
or making them loose, the mortar
should be chipped out by using a very
narrow chisel and a mallet in preference to a hammer. The edges must
be scraped clean and all dust and loose
particles washed out of the recess.
After the new tile has been soaked, it is
"buttered" on the back with cement
mortar, placed in position and tapped

down to the level of the rest of the
floor.

A stiff piece of card is useful to
scrape the mortar off the face of the
tile across the joints. The tiles must be
clean and free from mortar before they
are allowed to set. Damp sawdust
mixed with fine damp sand is useful to
clean the tiles.

The colour of floor tiles may be
brought out by the application of linseed oil.

First the tiles should be scrubbed
with hot soapy water and allowed to
dry. Linseed oil may then be applied
with either a stiff brush or a cloth. If
too much oil is used, it will stay on the
surface of the tile, make it greasy and
dirt will be collected.

Only sufficient oil should be used to
fill the pores; any surplus must be
wiped off so that the face of the tile is
dry. When the oil has soaked into the
tile and before the floor has had time
to become dirty, a good wax polish
should be applied. Subsequent wax
polishing at frequent intervals will
give a good finish.

If a tiled floor receives a lot of wear,
the upkeep of a waxed finish with a
high polish will entail a lot of hard
work. For this reason such floors are
simply scrubbed with soap and
water to clean and preserve them.

RENDERING A
HEARTH

FIG. 9. *To ensure that
the cement mortar on a
hearth is level, a suitably
shaped board should be
drawn over the surface
while the rendering is
still relatively soft.*

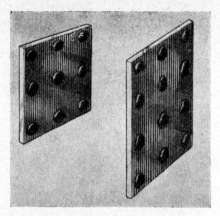

MASTIC ON GLASS TILES

FIG. 10. *Blobs of special mastic applied to the back of two different sizes of glass tile. The material should be worked up by hand until it is soft enough to be spread.*

Opaque-glass wall tiles may be obtained in a wide variety of colours. They are made in large sizes so that not many units are needed to cover a wall. Tiles 12 by 12 in. and 12 by 18 in. are sizes which are in common use.

FIXING GLASS TILES

The wall needs to be stripped of plaster and a $\frac{1}{2}$ in. thick rendering of cement mortar applied just as for ordinary, glazed wall tiles. After the rendering has set, it should be painted with a liquid specially prepared by the manufacturers of the glass tiles. This substance is called a sealer and serves to prevent the cement mortar from taking the oil out of the mastic which is used for fixing the tiles. It is usual to give the wall two coats of this sealer.

The manufacturers of the tiles and the sealer also supply the special mastic, which is very similar in appearance to linseed-oil putty.

The mastic is worked up by hand until it is soft, and the back of each tile is then covered with small blobs about 2 in. in diameter. The number of blobs will vary according to the size of the tile; for a 12 by 12 in. tile less blobs would be required than for a 12 by 18 in. tile (Fig. 10).

The tile should be placed into position and pressed against the wall by running the fingers round the edges of the tile so that it is left only about $\frac{3}{16}$ in. from the wall. Two thin pieces of card should be placed against the edge and the next tile fixed in the same way up to the card, so that the joints are equal to the thickness of the card. The mastic can also be used for pointing the joints after the tiling is finished.

These glass tiles are most suitable for use behind the taps on a pedestal wash basin to provide an anti-splash surface. Narrower tiles in contrasting colour may be used on the edges. The tiles may be cut with a glass cutter if necessary but, if possible, it is better to plan a job so that cutting is avoided.

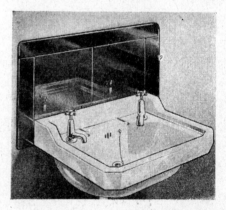

GLASS-TILE SURROUND

FIG. 11. *A glass-tile surround in position behind a wash basin. Narrower tiles in a contrasting colour make an attractive margin. Mirror glass may also be used.*

CHAPTER 18

GENERAL REPAIRS

RENOVATING DOORS, WINDOWS, GUTTERS, ROOFS
AND CONCRETE: LAYING LINOLEUM

THE first sign of rot in door frames is usually to be found at the foot where the frame meets the stone or concrete sill. The rot spreads upwards and when it reaches a certain point the nails may no longer hold and the door frame becomes loose. If the door frame has been surrounded by concrete at the foot this accelerates any tendency to rot, and therefore this method of securing the foot of the frame is not recommended. If the frame is securely nailed and the rot occurs only in the lower 4 in. or so, the defective part should be sawn through as far as is possible. The rotten part may be removed with a chisel as far as the depth of the saw-cut, but the rest of the decayed part will have to be cut through with the help of a chisel.

A second saw-cut should then be made about 4 in. higher up, and half-way into the thickness; this portion is removed with a chisel so as to make a half-lap joint (Fig. 1). A new piece of wood is prepared and well painted where the joint occurs. The back and the lower end should be creosoted. While the paint is still wet the new piece is fixed with four screws.

An alternative method, also shown in Fig. 1, may be found easier, as the rebate in the new piece of wood is formed by nailing on a lath instead of by cutting a rebate out of the solid. As the lath crosses both joints it strengthens the tie between the door frame and the new piece. After priming the new piece, the mastic on the outside will need to be renewed and the plaster

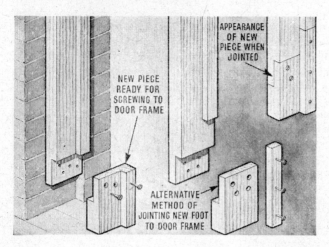

NEW PIECE READY FOR SCREWING TO DOOR FRAME

APPEARANCE OF NEW PIECE WHEN JOINTED

ALTERNATIVE METHOD OF JOINTING NEW FOOT TO DOOR FRAME

DOOR-FRAME REPAIR

FIG. 1. *Two methods of replacing the rotten wood at the foot of a door frame. The alternative method (right) is easier and just as satisfactory as that on the left.*

on the inside of the door frame may need to be made good. Any cracks or holes should also be filled while the work is in progress.

If the rot has spread above the lowest plug and the door frame is loose in consequence, the frame should be cut away as previously described and a new piece fitted. Before this piece is screwed fast, the seam in the brickwork which held the plug must be cleaned out and a new plug made and driven in.

To make the plug as tight as possible it should have a very gradual taper and be made to fit the hole before being driven in, so that it drives tightly for the whole of its length. The plug is then cut off with a hand saw and, after creosoting the back of the new piece and painting the joint, the new piece is screwed fast and nailed to the plug. The method is shown in Fig. 2.

With constant use over a period of years, the frames of both internal and external doors may work loose. As a result, bits of plaster may fall away, or the door frame may move and cause the door to stick. To remove the frame and fix new plugs is a difficult job and afterwards it would be necessary to replaster up to the door frame. Before resorting to such drastic measures it may be possible to cure the fault by one of the following methods.

LOOSE DOOR FRAMES

Sometimes, if the nails which fix the frame to the plugs are punched in with a nail punch and heavy hammer, the frame will be firm once more. If the wooden floor is sound, the foot of the frame may be secured by either nailing a wooden fillet into the angle or by letting in a metal angle-bracket (Fig. 3). Where the frame rests on a

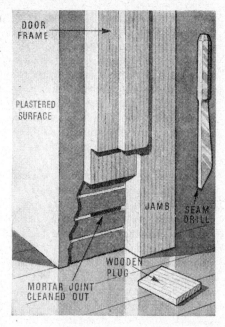

FITTING A PLUG

FIG. 2. *The wooden plug should have a very gradual taper and be made to fit the previously prepared hole between the bricks as tightly as possible. Any surplus wood may be removed with a hand saw.*

stone or concrete floor, a hardwood wedge may be driven between the frame and the floor, or a metal plate, shaped as shown, may be sunk into a hole drilled in the floor and screwed to the face of the door frame.

There are three types of wood-framed windows in common use, and these will be considered in turn. They are known as stand-sheet, solid-frame and bow windows.

For small windows and inexpensive types of larger window a stand sheet is used. This consists of a single frame which is fixed by wedging it into the opening. Where the wooden frame meets the wall the joint is pointed with mastic (Fig. 4). Rot usually begins in the bottom rail and spreads up the stiles. If the bottom rail is badly rotted, it will not be worth while to replace it, as in all probability the joint on the stile will also be defective and the glass would have to be taken out before a new bottom rail could be fitted. In such cases a new window is necessary.

If on testing with a knife, however, it is found that only the lower part of the bottom rail is decayed, this part may be removed either with a sharp chisel or by making a slot in the centre to insert a hand saw. The holes should be bored with a $\frac{1}{2}$-in. bit and the slot cleaned out with a chisel. A hand saw may then be inserted and the rail sawn in two. The ends need to be cleaned out with a chisel. A new piece is then prepared and fitted. If there is no window board the piece may be inserted from inside and the plaster patched up afterwards; otherwise it will have to be put in from the outside (Fig. 5).

The new piece should be about $1\frac{1}{2}$ in. longer than the distance between the reveals, pushed in at one end as far as it will go into the recess and then forced back so that it lies about $\frac{3}{4}$ in. behind each reveal. It should be well painted before insertion, as should the underside of the part to which it fits. It may be held in position by driving wedges underneath it to make a good joint with the old piece. After priming, the joint should be filled in with putty and later the joint between the bottom rail and the sill will need to be pointed with mastic.

The work involved in replacing a defective bottom rail on solid frame and box windows is somewhat complicated and is therefore outside the scope of this book. The most that could be done, if it were found that the rot had not spread too far, would be to chisel away the outer portion which projects beyond the face of the sash. A new piece may then be fitted.

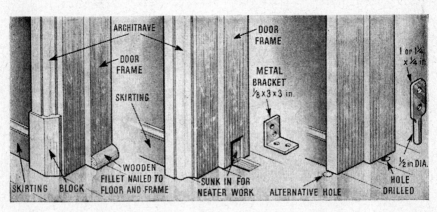

SECURING THE FOOT OF A DOOR FRAME

FIG. 3. *There are several ways of securing the foot of a door frame to the floor. A wooden fillet may be nailed into the angle, a metal angle bracket may be let in, or a metal plate, shaped as shown, may be sunk into a hole drilled in the floor and screwed to the architrave. The use of a metal bracket (centre) is to be preferred.*

Wooden gutters, which are kept clear of leaves and given sufficient fall, will last longer than cast-iron gutters, provided that they are kept well painted inside with a good waterproof paint, such as black bitumen.

REPAIRS TO GUTTERS

Rot may occur at one end, possibly where water has been standing owing to the gutter not having sufficient fall. If it is desired to add a new piece

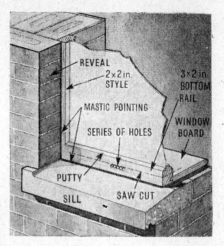

REPAIR TO WINDOW RAIL

FIG. 5. *If only the lower part of the bottom rail is decayed, bore a series of holes as shown and insert a hand saw to cut away the affected parts. A new piece of wood is fitted in the cavity.*

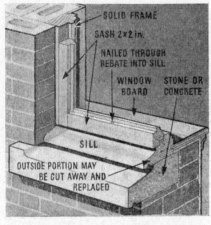

WINDOW CONSTRUCTION

FIG. 4. *This type of window is wedged into the wall and the joints are pointed with mastic. Decay, which usually starts in the bottom rail, should be dealt with promptly to prevent it from spreading.*

rather than to replace the whole length, the gutter should be carefully removed and brought down to the ground. This job usually requires two persons with a ladder each. The wooden gutter may be fixed by one of three methods : it may rest on stone or brick corbels and be fastened to the wall by a holdfast and screw; it may rest on iron holdfasts driven into the seams of the stone or brickwork; or it

may rest on metal brackets which are screwed to the fascia board. These supports are shown in Fig. 6.

After the gutter has been lifted down, the rotten end is cut off to where the wood is sound, and a new piece of similar section is jointed on. The thickness of the wood below the hollow is halved for 12–15 in. (Fig. 7) : a similar piece is also removed from the new length. These two parts should fit neatly together, the joints should be well painted with white lead and the gutter should be lined up so that it is straight. If necessary, the gutter should be packed up from below to ensure that it is not hollow where the joint has been made. The two pieces should be securely screwed together with heavy-gauge screws. Care should be taken to support the gutter at the joint while it is being lifted back.

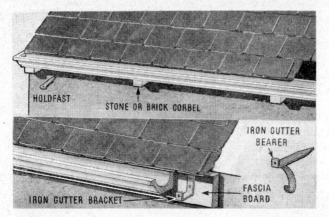

FIG. 6. *Gutters may be supported on stone or brick corbels, on holdfasts, on bearers, or on metal brackets screwed to the fascia board.*

The end of the new piece may need a stop fixing in it. This is done by gauging a line about 1 in. from the end. The wood is cut for about $\frac{3}{8}$ in. deep and split out from the end to form a recess (Fig. 8). A piece of 1-in. wood is then fitted into the recess and, after being well bedded in with white lead, putty or bitumen paint, it is nailed from the outside.

If it is necessary to fit an outlet pipe or lead socket leading into the down pipe, a suitable position should be marked on the wooden gutter. The hole should be bored through the gutter with an expansion bit; the socket pipe may then be pushed through and a

pencil line marked round the head of the lead socket. This is let in with a narrow chisel. When it is flush or slightly below the surface, it can be bedded in white lead or thin putty and fixed with three clout nails (Fig. 9).

It is not a difficult matter to repair

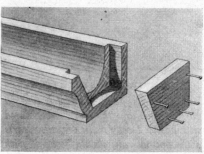

FIXING GUTTER STOP

FIG. 8. *To fit a new stop at the end of a gutter, cut the wood away to form a recess as shown, bed in the new piece with putty and secure it with nails.*

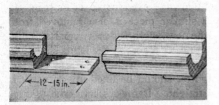

NEW END PIECE

FIG. 7. *To repair the end of a gutter, cut off to where the wood is sound and joint on a new piece as described in the text. This job should be done while the gutter is down on the ground.*

gutters which have a decayed or damaged front or back edge provided that the gutter can be readily unscrewed and lifted down and that the bottom of the gutter is sound. The defective part is cut away with a saw and chisel, and a recess made into which the new piece fits tightly. The new piece and the cut portion of the old gutter should be well painted. When the paint has dried the new piece should be bedded in white lead and fixed with screws or nails. Any trimming which is necessary to make the hollow coincide with the rest of the gutter should be done after the new piece has been fixed. Similarly, a new front piece may be shaped to fit the mould on the front after it has been fixed as illustrated in Fig. 10.

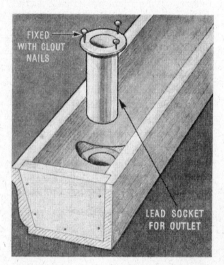

FIXED WITH CLOUT NAILS

LEAD SOCKET FOR OUTLET

SOCKET FOR DOWN PIPE

Fig. 9. *First bore a hole through the gutter with an expansion bit, fit the socket pipe flush or slightly below the surface and fasten it with clout nails.*

It is sometimes necessary to bring a wooden gutter round a corner. This practice should be avoided, but where there is not a suitable down pipe it is often necessary. The joint should be carefully made with the thickness of the base halved and the moulded, upper part mitred as shown in Fig. 11.

After fitting the two pieces together and boring holes for the screws, the two parts at right-angles should be painted, bedded in white lead and screwed together when the gutters are in position at the eaves of the roof. This job should not be done on the ground as the parts become unmanageable and it is difficult to arrange a suitable fall.

Before replacing any gutters it is wise to repaint the front of the fascia board and to treat the back of the gutters with a good preservative such as creosote. The inside, which is also easier to treat while it is on the ground, should be given a liberal coat of tar, black bitumen or some substance which allows the water to run off it.

The life of a gutter will be greatly prolonged if the slope or fall is carefully checked after replacement. Fix the end farthest from the outlet as high as possible and allow the lower end to be $1\frac{1}{2}$ in.–2 in. lower for every 20 ft.

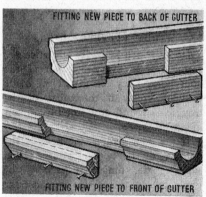

FITTING NEW PIECE TO BACK OF GUTTER

FITTING NEW PIECE TO FRONT OF GUTTER

NEW SIDES

Fig. 10. *A new piece for the front or back of a gutter should be cut roughly to size and shaped to the rest of the gutter after being nailed in position. In this way a very neat job is produced.*

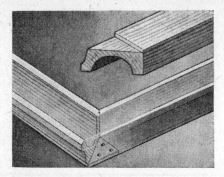

TURNING A CORNER

FIG. 11. *To bring a wooden gutter round a corner, the thickness of the base should be halved and the moulded upper part mitred. The two pieces are most easily fitted together when they are in position.*

ot length. Finally, look for hollow places where the gutter may be sagging and fix the gutter so that it is perfectly straight along its whole length. When testing the fall with water, do not use more than a basinful, see that it runs reely from one end to the other, and that it leaves the gutter quite dry.

BADLY FITTING DOORS

Doors which fit badly and stick are a nuisance to every member of the household. They can usually be made to work freely if the cause of the trouble is found and suitable adjustments are made.

If the door scrapes the floor at the bottom of the opening stile, first examine the hinges, especially the upper one. If the screws are loose the weight of the door will pull the hinge out and cause the door to drop at the nose. Open the door at right-angles and wedge a chisel, axe or wedge-shaped piece of wood under the nose of the door; while the door is in this position the screws may be tightened.

If the screws are slack in the door frame, a peg of soft wood can be driven into the holes so that the screws will hold tightly. If the hinge is firmly attached to both the door and the frame, joints have probably worked loose and allowed the door to drop at the nose.

The best method of curing this defect is to take the screws out of the hinges and to cramp the door square again with joiner's cramps, wedging the tenons and gluing the wedges before driving them in. After cleaning off the wedges when the glue has set, the door may be rehung. When joiner's cramps are not available, the following method is recommended.

Open the door at right-angles and drive a wedge under the nose to lift it, if possible, higher than it should be finally. While in this position glued wedges are driven into all the tenons. If there is not a space in which to start the wedge, make a space with a chisel equal in width to the tenon. The door should be left in this position until the

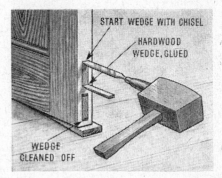

LOOSE DOOR FRAME

FIG. 12. *How glued wedges may be driven into the tenons of a door, the nose of which has dropped owing to the frame having worked loose. The wedges will serve to secure the joint.*

FIG. 13. *A suitable thickness of card-board fixed between the lower hinge and the frame will often lift the nose of a door and prevent it from scraping on the floor. Try this easy remedy first.*

glue has set hard, usually about twenty-four hours; the wedges may then be cleaned off flush with the edges as illustrated in Fig. 12.

PACKING THE HINGE

If the door has dropped only slightly and the joints appear to be firm, it may be possible to lift the nose of the door slightly by packing out the lower hinge. The screws should be loosened, the hinge pulled out a little and one or two thicknesses of cardboard placed behind the hinge flap before it is screwed back to the frame (Fig. 13). The screws are then tightened up again and the door tested.

If too great a thickness of cardboard is added the lower part of the door will bind against the rebate. If the methods described will not stop the door from scraping on the floor, a suitable amount of wood will have to be sawn or planed from the bottom edge of the door.

In the case of outhouse doors, which are frequently made from floor boards fixed to battens, it is a common occurrence for the door to sag at the nose owing to the nails being unable to carry the weight of the boards. To cure this trouble, the door should be wedged under the nose until it returns to its original position. Two diagonal braces of 3 by 1 in. or 4 by 1 in. material should then be fitted between the bars and the boards should be nailed to

BRACES ADDED

SAGGING OUTHOUSE DOOR

FIG. 14. *Two diagonal braces have been added to the door of this outhouse in order to help carry the weight of the boards and so prevent the lower edge from scraping along the ground.*

these braces. The braces should have their lower ends on the hanging edge and their upper ends on the opening edge (Fig. 14). The remainder of the nails in the door should be punched in and a few extra nails should be added.

EFFECT OF HUMIDITY

New doors, which may have been accurately fitted, often swell owing to their absorbing dampness from the atmosphere. Do not be too ready to plane off a large amount in order to make the door close. Often the door will dry out later and shrink, leaving a large gap. Remove as little as possible so that the door only closes with difficulty.

If after three or four months the door has not shrunk, a little more may be taken off. Sometimes a door will work satisfactorily in dry weather and stick when a damp spell occurs. The fact that the door will dry out again

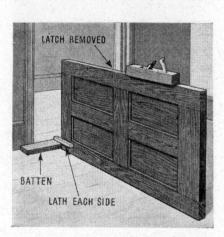

LATCH REMOVED

BATTEN

LATH EACH SIDE

EASING A DOOR

FIG. 15. *After unscrewing the hinges from the frame, the door may be laid on its side and held as shown while wood is removed from either edge with a plane.*

must be borne in mind and only sufficient wood should be removed to make it work freely under damp conditions.

Painting the edge of a door after it has been eased will not prevent the absorption of moisture entirely, but it will slow the process down, and the door may not have time to swell before the drier weather conditions return. Painting the edges, therefore, tends to make the door less liable to excessive expansion or contraction.

This point should not be overlooked when considering the top and bottom edges which, being out of sight, are frequently left unpainted. These surfaces should receive the same treatment as the rest of the door.

To plane the opening edge of a door along the whole of its length, it is necessary to take out the latch or lock and to unscrew the hinges from the door frame. The door may then be laid on its hanging edge and planed in a similar position to that shown in Fig. 15.

Owing to the use of unseasoned timber, or to the door being thin, it often happens that the top meets the frame before the bottom, or vice versa. The latch or lock is then difficult to work and the door has to be deliberately pushed in the appropriate place before it can be latched (Fig. 16).

CORRECTING TWIST

If the amount of twist is slight, the simplest and quickest method of making the door close easily is to pare off the rebate with a chisel so that it fits the door. The door is closed and a line drawn on the door frame parallel to the twisted door. The rebate may then be cut away to this line. The fact that the door will move farther in prob-

TWISTED DOOR

FIG. 16. *A very simple way of making a twisted door close easily is to pare off the rebate with a chisel so that it fits the door. The part which requires to be removed is indicated (in exaggerated form) by a broken line. After making this adjustment, however, the position of the keep may need to be altered.*

ably means that the keep, into which the latch or lock shoots, will have to be moved inwards.

If the door is badly twisted, it should be unscrewed from its hinges and laid on the floor. It should then be weighted or fastened down by a lath across the twisted corners; the opposite corners should be propped up by about 1 in. so that the door is now slightly twisted in the opposite direction. While in this position, the tenons should be tightened by driving a glued wedge into them. The tenons may be split with a chisel in order to make a start for each wedge.

The door should be left in this position for as long as possible before cleaning off the wedges and rehanging it. If the door has been put together with dowels there will be no evidence of these on the edges; they are usually arranged as shown in Fig. 17. After

weighting the door as previously described, a new dowel may be put in from the outside, driving it through the stile and well into the rail. This treatment helps to prevent the door from springing back to its original twisted position.

With the door on the floor it will be difficult to bore the hole for the dowel, and this operation is facilitated if the door is weighted down on a bench or table. The dowels should be grooved, or have a spiral cut made in them, so that when they are glued some of the glue will reach the framework.

REPAIRS TO WINDOWS

There are two types of window in common use : casements which are hinged at the top or the side and open either inwards or outwards, and box windows which have sliding sashes.

A frequent cause of trouble on casement windows is the opening sash sticking owing to coats of paint which fill up the rebate and make the sash so much larger that it is too tight. To remedy this defect, the paint in the rebates and on the edges of the sashes must be either burnt or scraped off. The window should then be tested for easy opening before giving the parts a thin coat of paint. The window must be left partly open until the new paint is absolutely dry.

Windows, like external doors, may fit well in dry weather, and swell in damp weather. When easing a tight window remember that if too much material is removed, there is a danger of having too large a clearance in dry weather. If the sash sticks in one particular spot, a shaving may be pared off with a sharp chisel, but if it is necessary to remove a shaving from the whole length of the frame, it will generally be quicker to unscrew the hinges from the frame and to take off a shaving with the frame in a more convenient position, either in a vice or as shown in Fig. 18.

When planing the edges where the end grain of the stiles occurs, it is safest to plane from the ends to the

EASING A WINDOW

FIG. 18. *If it is necessary to remove a shaving from the whole length of a window frame, it is usually quicker to remove the frame and to do the job either on the ground, as shown, or in a vice.*

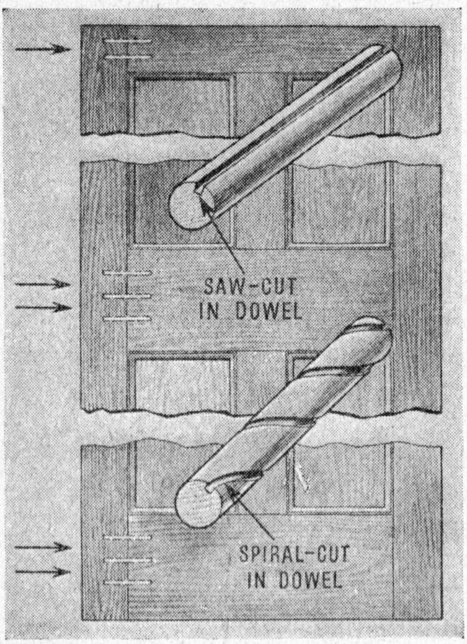

middle to prevent splitting off the corners. In good-class work the edges are rebated and in order to clean a little off the rebate it is necessary to use a square plane; that is, a plane with its blade the full width of the sole.

Modern, wooden casement windows constructed of the latest standard joinery sections have quite a considerable clearance; they do not depend on a tight edge-to-edge fitting to keep out wind and rain. The casement window shown in Fig. 19 is of the older type

SAW-CUT IN DOWEL

SPIRAL-CUT IN DOWEL

FIXING NEW DOWELS

FIG. 17. *New dowels, which should have a saw-cut or a spiral groove cut in them, should be fixed between the existing dowels as indicated by arrows.*

which may be given more clearance for opening purposes and yet be made more weatherproof, by the addition of laths nailed on to cover the joints between the sashes and the frames in the same manner as the modern type, which is worked from the solid. The addition of these laths is most effective when the sash is hinged along the top edge as shown in Fig. 20.

A lath cannot be fixed along the side which is hinged, but a weather bar may be fixed above it to throw the water clear. When the sash is hinged down the edge, laths may be put on three edges only and the hanging edge cannot be protected by a weather bar. Special hinges are used in the modern standard casement so that a lip may be carried over every edge.

SASH WINDOWS

Sliding sashes are often prevented from working properly by the amount of paint on the pulley stiles. The bottom inside sash is prevented from sliding up and the top outside sash from sliding down.

Paint which has been carelessly applied, put on too thickly and allowed to run in the joints between the staff bead and the sash, or between the meeting rails and the parting lath and sashes, may also cause trouble. When this paint dries, the sash is held firmly to the casing and, even if the sash can be forced open, the fatty edges which remain may cause the sash to stick every time it is opened. If the fatty edges are the cause of the sashes sticking, they should be scraped off with a knife and smoothed with glass-paper.

Sticking may also occur if the parting lath works loose and binds on the end of the meeting rail (Fig. 21). In this case the parting lath should be

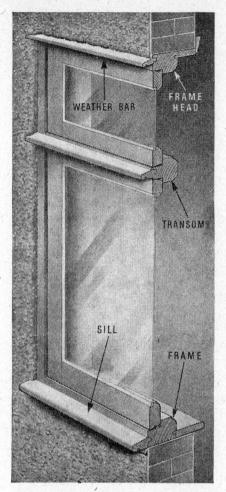

CLEARANCE FOR OPENING

FIG. 19. *If more clearance is provided for opening purposes on this older type of casement window, laths may be added as in Fig. 20 to keep it waterproof.*

secured with fine panel pins. The inner, lower sash sometimes sticks because the staff bead has been fixed too tightly up to the sash. The remedy is to prise off the staff bead, and to nail it back in such a position as to give

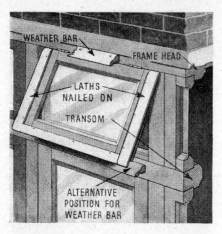

LATHS AND WEATHER BARS

FIG. 20. *Laths nailed on to cover the joints between the sashes and the frame as on modern windows. Weather bars may be added, as shown, in order to throw water clear of the hanging edges.*

proper clearance without looseness.

If one of the sash cords, which are attached to weights, happens to break, the sash will stick and the cord will have to be replaced. If the metal pulleys are kept oiled, the windows will work more easily.

BROKEN SLATES OR TILES

Slates are fixed to the battens on the roof by copper or zinc nails fixed through the centre or at the head of each slate (Fig. 22). Tiles are usually nailed at the head, but often they have nibs which hang over the batten. When fixed in this way every tile is not nailed, but only every third or fourth course. It will be obvious that if a slate is broken or has worked loose, it is not possible to nail it because the slates higher up cover the nail holes.

Probably the simplest way to fix a new slate is to bed it in a cement

mortar. First the old broken part should be removed. A slater uses a ripper for this purpose, but a long, thin piece of metal will serve quite well to push up between the slates, to rip the nail in half, and to loosen the upper half of the slate so that it may be worked out.

A mixture of cement and sand in the proportion of one part cement to two parts sand will be required. This mixture is bedded into the recess and the new slate pushed up into position. Any excess mortar should be cleaned off with a trowel. Tiles may be replaced in a similar manner, but if they have nibs these should be broken off with a hammer, otherwise it will be impossible to push the tile up into position.

If the underside of the slates and battens can be seen from inside the

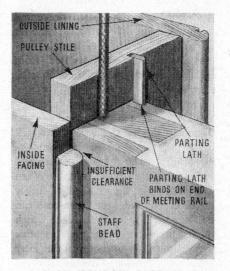

SASH-WINDOW DEFECTS

FIG. 21. *Sticking may occur on a sash window if the parting lath works loose or if the staff bead is fixed too tightly up to the sash. The remedy for both of these defects is given in the text.*

roof, it means that felt or boarding has not been used, but that the joints on the underside have been pointed or torched with mortar. In such cases it is possible to push a thin strip of copper or lead up the centre of the opening left by the broken slate. This strip must be long enough to go past the head of the slate on which it rests and to be bent down behind the lath (Fig. 23). The new slate is then pushed up into position and the bottom end of the copper or lead strip is cut off to a suitable length, so that it can be bent up in order to prevent the slate from dropping out after it is fitted.

FLOOR TILES

Earthenware floor tiles and glazed tiles used in fireplaces, hearths and walls are all bedded in a mixture of cement and sand. This bedding mortar is usually mixed to a fairly stiff paste by using one part of cement to two parts of sand, by volume. When a tile becomes loose or is broken, it usually comes away, leaving the cement mortar firmly attached to the ground. It is therefore useless simply to replace the loose tile with a bedding of cement mortar as unless space is made for the new cement the tile will stand up above the level of the rest of the tiled surface.

It is necessary to chip out the old bedding mortar with a chisel. A sharp, narrow chisel should be used so as to prevent excessive vibration which might loosen the surrounding tiles. When a thickness of about $\frac{1}{4}$ in. has been removed and the edges have been cleaned, the opening should be well damped. The tile should also be damped and the back well "buttered" with the cement mortar; it may then be tapped gently into place, flush with the

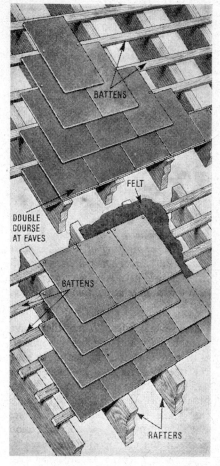

ROOF TILES

FIG. 22. *Slates may be fixed to the battens on the roof by nails through the centre or at the head of each slate. Tiles are usually nailed at the head, but they may have nibs, as shown in Fig. 23, which overhang the battens.*

rest. Use the wooden handle of the trowel for this purpose.

In view of the serious risk of loosening other tiles by chipping out the cement, this method is not recommended unless it is necessary to re-

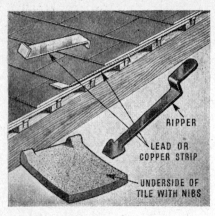

BROKEN SLATES

FIG. 23. *The ripper is employed to loosen the upper part of a broken slate and to cut through the nails. A metal strip, shaped as shown, may be used to hold a new slate in position on the roof.*

place several tiles. When tiles have been broken and are being replaced with new ones it is necessary to soak the new tiles for two hours in water before applying the cement mortar, otherwise the tile will quickly absorb the water from the cement mortar; this will prevent proper adhesion between the mortar and the tile.

In the case of a single loose tile, in a fireplace or on a wall, it is quicker and simpler to fasten the tile in position with glue. There is no risk of loosening other tiles since the cement mortar does not require chipping out, and only the loose pieces need to be removed. The edges of the tile should be scraped clean and the back and edges should be well glued; glue must also be smeared in the recess. The tile is then pressed in until it is level with the rest. Any excess glue must be wiped off with a damp cloth. A good quality cold-water glue is better than

the old, rather brittle scotch glue.

Glazed wall tiles require little more than washing with hot water and fine pumice-powder sprinkled on a cloth to keep them clean. Earthenware floor tiles, however, which are not glazed, soon show the effects of dirt. They should be well scrubbed and, when clean and dry, may be rubbed with a suitably coloured floor polish which is specially prepared for tiled floors.

These polishes make the surface less absorbent and the tiles do not collect the dirt as readily. To remove stains from earthenware tiles, ordinary household bleach, used at full strength and allowed to dry on the stained part, will lighten the stain very considerably, if not remove it. Greasy floor tiles should be well scrubbed and washed with hot water and soda, before repolishing with the special coloured polish for tiled floors. Paraffin is also an excellent cleaner for dirty and greasy floor tiles.

Sometimes a tiled surface begins to look shabby, not because the tiles are worn but because the pointing is dirty or has become loose and dropped out. The appearance of a tiled wall surface can be improved considerably, if a clean, white pointing line is visible between each tile.

REPOINTING

To repoint tiles on hearths, fireplaces and walls, it is necessary to scrape out the existing pointing to a depth of about $\frac{1}{8}$ in. with an old knife. The dust should be removed by wiping over the surface with a damp cloth.

A thin mixture of Keene's cement, or ordinary cement mixed with whiting, or a coloured cement, is required. This mixture is applied with a stiff brush across the joints so that the crevices are filled. The surface of the tiles is then worked over with a stiff piece of cardboard or a rubber squeegee. This procedure leaves the mixture in the joints and removes any excess from the face of the tiles. A few days later the surface should be cleaned to remove any traces of the pointing left on the face of the tiles.

LAYING LINOLEUM

If linoleum is to be laid on a wooden floor the surface should be regular and smooth. All nail heads should be punched down and loose boards firmly nailed. If any of the boards have warped, the sharp edges should be removed with a plane or chisel. When laying linoleum on a stone floor, the edges of any flag which

is higher than the rest should be levelled to the rest of the floor by filling with a mixture of one part of cement to three parts of sand, so that there is no sudden break. A layer of builders' waterproof paper will also help to even out irregularities and to prevent dampness from affecting the back of the linoleum.

Before purchasing linoleum it is wise to draw a rough plan of the room to be covered and to mark the principal dimensions on it. The salesman can then look at this plan and cut the material economically, according to the width of the roll.

It is best to fit the most difficult piece first, which may be at a bay window, round a chimney breast or up to a door opening. Where the linoleum must fit square up to a skirting board,

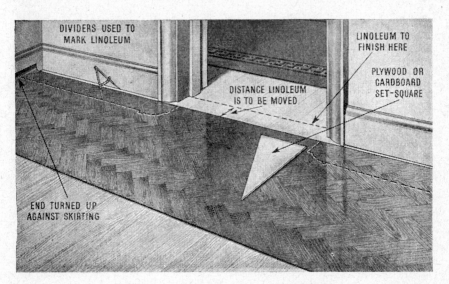

FITTING LINOLEUM IN A DOORWAY

FIG. 24. *To lay linoleum so that it fits a doorway and finishes under the door, measure the greatest distance which the linoleum has to move and mark this distance and the shape for cutting, as shown. A pair of dividers and a set-square will be required. The ends of the length may be turned up against the skirting.*

the trimming should be left until after the more complicated work has been completed.

The best method of marking out is to lay the linoleum as close as possible to where it has to fit along one side, allowing it to turn up at the ends against the skirting or against any obstruction such as a chimney breast. Lines should then be drawn on the linoleum opposite the shape to be fitted. This job is best done with a set square, try square, or with a piece of stiff cardboard or plywood cut to a right-angle.

Measure the greatest distance the linoleum has to move in order to reach its final position and transfer this distance to the linoleum. This may be done with a pair of dividers or with a thin lath cut to the required length. The various points are then joined up and the exact shape is obtained for cutting. This plan is clearly shown in Fig. 24; in this case the linoleum fits a doorway and finishes under the door.

CUTTING TO SHAPE

The cut is made with a thin knife shaped as shown in Fig. 25, but a good sharp penknife serves as a good substitute. Assume now that at one end the piece of linoleum has to fit up to the skirting. Previously it will have been cut roughly to length and will turn up some distance against the skirting. With thin material it is possible to cut along the skirting edge as the linoleum fits the angle, but with thick material it is not always possible to be sure of cutting it in the right place. A very convenient method of obtaining the correct length is shown in Fig. 26. A line is marked on the linoleum and on the skirting as at *A*, while another line is marked on the

linoleum and on the floor as at *B*. The distance from these two points to the face of the skirting is measured and when the material is laid flat this distance can be transferred to the linoleum to indicate a cutting line.

When linoleum has been laid for some time it spreads out. If it has been fitted tightly it may buckle and need to be refitted. To save this trouble it is advisable to leave the fitting $\frac{1}{8}$ in. short, so that after a time the material will spread out and fit the floor exactly. If more than one width of linoleum is used, it is a good plan to make the linoleum fit exactly on the long side, and to leave it $\frac{1}{8}$ in. short at each end, allowing it to overlap

CUTTING LINOLEUM

FIG. 25. *A specially shaped knife, as shown, is convenient, but by no means essential, for cutting linoleum. A sharp penknife serves quite well.*

slightly down the joins between the widths.

After a week or two when the linoleum has spread out, the centre joins can be made to fit exactly by using the edge of the uppermost piece as a guide and cutting through the lower piece.

Well-fitted linoleum should not need to be fastened down, but if it

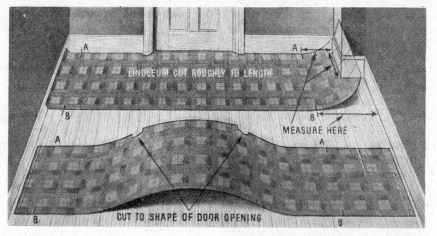

LINOLEUM CUT ROUGHLY TO LENGTH

MEASURE HERE

CUT TO SHAPE OF DOOR OPENING

HOW TO FIND THE CORRECT LENGTH

FIG. 26. *A convenient method of obtaining the correct length for linoleum is to mark a line on the material and on the skirting (A) and another line on the linoleum and on the floor (B). The distances from the face of the skirting to these marks are then transferred to the linoleum.*

curls at the edges it may be secured with fine panel pins—not tacks. The head of a panel pin sinks just below the surface and is not noticeable.

Fig. 27 shows the method of fitting linoleum around a pedestal-type water-closet and a wash-basin pedestal. This illustration shows how the fitting of linoleum around awkward shapes can be made comparatively simple. Each corner of the object is marked out on the linoleum and the distance X is marked from each corner of the object so as to give the shapes for cutting. The cut should be made just outside the lines to allow for the subsequent spread.

It is important that patterned linoleum should be matched where the several widths join. A certain amount of waste is inevitable and when buying such material due allowance must be made. The maximum amount of waste from each length used cannot be more

than the length of one of the units which make up the design. With a small pattern the amount wasted at the end of each length will be small,

DISTANCE LINOLEUM IS TO BE MOVED FORWARD (MARKED X)

ODD SHAPES

FIG. 27. *Fitting linoleum around obstructions involves marking the shape of the objects at suitable distances from the edge before the material is fitted.*

but with a large pattern, which repeats itself say every 18 in., it may be necessary to cut about 18 in. off the beginning of the second length, in order to match the pattern on the first length.

The method of fitting is the same as for plain linoleum, except that the

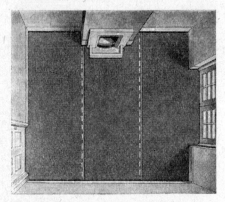

ALLOWANCE FOR SPREADING

FIG. 28. *To allow for linoleum spreading after it has been laid, some workers allow an overlap of about ⅛ in. at the joins (shown dotted) and trim off the surplus after an interval of a few weeks.*

inlaid variety is often brittle and may be easily cracked. The method of allowing widths to overlap, and then fitting them exactly when the linoleum has spread (Fig. 28) is useless if the pattern has to be matched. The widths must fit up to each other and ⅛ in. must be left round the edges for swelling.

Sometimes one piece of linoleum receives more wear than the rest and if a neat patch can be inlaid the life of the floor-covering may be prolonged. A piece of linoleum large enough to cover the damaged or worn part will be required. If the linoleum has a pattern,

the patch should be cut to match it. The patch is then placed over the damaged part and held in place by four panel pins driven partly in, then, using the patch as a guide, the linoleum knife is used to cut round the patch. This ensures a good fit.

The edge of the linoleum in a doorway may be kicked up and torn. To overcome this difficulty a thin lath may be fitted over the edge of the linoleum and tapered a little on the opposite edge. The lath is nailed to the floor and stained to match the surround as shown in Fig. 29.

REHANGING GARDEN GATES

The four principal types of hinge used for garden gates are shown in Fig. 30. Sometimes a tee hinge is used on a gate which is too heavy for it, with the result that either the screws are pulled out of the gate post or the hinge breaks at the knuckle.

Unless the gate is of light construction it will be best to fit the single strap type of hinge. The strap should be screwed and bolted to a rail on the

PROTECTION FOR LINO

FIG. 29. *A thin lath, stained to match the surround, may be nailed over the edge of the linoleum in a doorway to prevent the edge from being kicked up and torn. The lath should be tapered.*

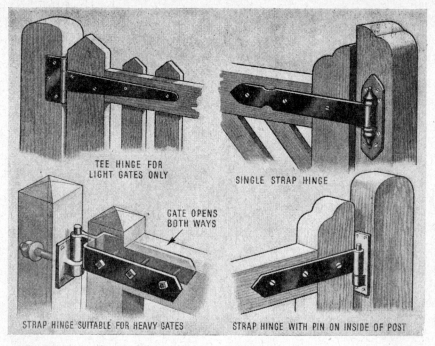

TEE HINGE FOR
LIGHT GATES ONLY

SINGLE STRAP HINGE

GATE OPENS
BOTH WAYS

STRAP HINGE SUITABLE FOR HEAVY GATES

STRAP HINGE WITH PIN ON INSIDE OF POST

HINGES FOR GARDEN GATES

FIG. 30. *These are the four main types of hinge used for garden gates. The single strap hinge is suitable for gates which, on account of their weight, should not be fitted with a tee hinge. General recommendations and instructions for fitting are given in the text. Avoid putting too much weight on hinges of light construction.*

gate so that the knuckle lies well on to the face of the gate-post. The gate should then be propped up with a piece of wood so that the gate has ample clearance, and the pin fitted into the socket and screwed or bolted in position. Note that when fixed in this way the hinge allows the gate to open one way only, but allows it to swing through 180 deg. (Fig. 31).

If the gate-post is wider than the thickness of the gate it may be preferred to hang the gate in the centre of the post. The gate should be propped in position leaving at least 1 in. of clearance between the gate and the

hanging post. The complete hinge is then held in position, the location of the pin plate is marked on the gate-post and the fitting is bolted or screwed in position. The strap is next fitted on the pin and, after checking the position of the gate, the strap may be screwed to the rail of the gate. With this method of hanging the gate only opens on one side and not more than 90 deg.

For heavier gates and for gates which are required to open in both directions a double strap hinge is used. First the pin is fixed at a suitable height in the centre of the gate-post, so that, when the strap is put on, it falls along the top or bottom rail. With the gate propped in position to give suitable clearance, the strap may be bolted in position.

REPAIRING CONCRETE

Cracks and hollow places in the surface of concrete cannot be repaired merely by covering the affected parts with a thin skimming of cement mortar. Concrete which has been worked out to a feather edge in order to level up a hollow place will crumble away on the edges and rapidly break up. The minimum thickness must not be less than 1 in. if this trouble is to be avoided.

A crack needs to be made at least 1 in. wide and preferably $1\frac{1}{2}$–2 in. deep. The edges need to be tapered with a sharp cold chisel, bolster or old wood chisel. It is best to cut out the concrete on each side of the crack roughly (Fig. 32) to a line on the concrete and then to work accurately up to the line with a broad chisel.

Sharp decisive blows are needed to cut the concrete cleanly without crumbling the edge. The cavity, thus prepared, should then be cleared out

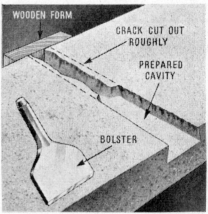

CUTTING OUT CRACKS

FIG. 32. *Cracks in a path should be cut out with a sharp cold chisel or bolster to a depth of $1\frac{1}{2}$–2 in. and the edges tapered before filling in with mortar.*

and well damped: the new cement mortar should be tamped into the cavity and the surface levelled off.

Hollow places, where water stands in pools, may be repaired in a similar fashion. The hollow spot should be marked out and the cavity roughly prepared. The edges should then be cut clean and slightly undercut to a suitable depth. When the new concrete has been well tamped down to squeeze out the air and ensure that the mixture is worked into the edges, the patch may be levelled up to the rest of

GATE OPENING

FIG. 31. *This gate is fitted with a single strap hinge attached to the back of the post so that it is possible for the gate to swing through 180 deg. Note, however, that the gate can be opened one way only.*

the surface by using a wooden straight-edge. This float should be used with a chopping action in order to level up the patch and make the surface smooth (Fig. 33).

Broken edges should be repaired in a similar manner by preparing a suitable cavity, undercut on the edges, and the full depth of the concrete. A length of board (Fig. 34) is required on the edge as a form for the new concrete and to hold it in position until it has

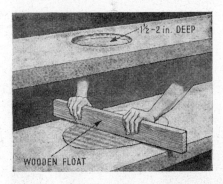

FILLING IN HOLLOWS

FIG. 33. *Hollows where water collects should be cut out to a depth of 1½-2 in. before filling them with cement mixture, which should be tamped well down*

set. The top edge of the form should be level with the path, so that the form may be used as a guide for the float when finally levelling the surface of the work.

For repairing relatively small areas, a mixture of one part of cement to two parts of sharp, clean sand (by volume) is suitable. For larger areas one part of cement, two parts of sand and three parts of coarse aggregate provide a strong mix.

To obtain a non-dusty and water-tight concrete use a non-porous aggregate such as granite chippings. The ingredients must be thoroughly mixed together dry, until when turned over with a spade the heap is uniform in colour. Clean water should be sprinkled on sparingly from the rose of a watering can so that a fairly stiff mix is obtained. Never mix more than the quantity of cement mortar required or more than can be laid in about twenty minutes.

Damp the cavity well and place the mixture as quickly as possible after it has been prepared. Tamp it well down into the cavity with the end of a board, well up to the edges of the cavity, so that the coarse aggregate is forced back and the mortar is allowed to flush in. Excessive trowelling or floating of the surface to obtain a smooth finish only causes cracks to develop.

OUTSIDE EDGES

FIG. 34. *Broken edges should be cut out as illustrated. A length of board will be required as a form to hold the new concrete in position until it has set.*

EXAMPLES OF DECAYED TIMBER

The upper photographs show decay caused by dry rot (left) and by excessive heat (right). Below, the fruit body of the commonest form of dry rot (right) and the effect of damage to previously decayed wood by the death-watch beetle (left) are shown.

CHAPTER 19

PRESERVING WOODWORK

HOW TO PREVENT AND TREAT DECAY AND ROT IN TIMBERS

BEFORE dealing with the application of suitable preservatives to existing fences, gates or wooden buildings, it is advisable to consider the various types of preservative in use, their advantages and disadvantages. It will also be an advantage to know the best possible treatment for fences, gates and the like, when they are erected or about to be erected. This first treatment is vital if the timber is to be preserved, as no amount of treatment after rot and decay have set in can be effective.

In many cases the timber is inaccessible after it has been fixed and the application of a preservative to that part of a fencing post which is in the ground, to the back of a gate-post against a wall, or to joists and sleepers of wood buildings, is impracticable once the members are in position (Fig. 1). The first essential, therefore, is correct treatment before erection.

QUESTION OF COST

It may be thought that the expense in labour and materials in applying preservatives is scarcely worth while and that in any case the life of, say, a wooden fencing post is so short that the treatment is not justified. Evidence to the contrary is generally obtained from material which has not been correctly preserved. With suitable treatment a piece of timber will last many times longer than if it is untreated. Softwood sleepers, as used on the railway, treated in the first instance by forcing creosote into them under pressure, last for twenty years and even at the end of this time they are suitable for making temporary roads, foot-bridges and the like. Softwood timbers which are, in general, not so durable as the more expensive hardwoods, may be preserved for a considerable time, and undoubtedly the treatment is always economical in the long run.

RESISTANCE TO DECAY

Different timbers vary in their ability to resist decay. English oak, larch and sweet chestnut are woods which naturally resist decay. Birch and beech, although hardwoods, are considerably less resistant and should not be used for outside work. Ash, Scotch fir and Douglas fir are not particularly resistant to alternations of wet and dry weather, but with suitable treatment they last well.

In all cases the bark should be removed from the timber before it is used, and if the wood has been well seasoned it is not so liable to be attacked by disease.

Timber which is exposed to the weather or which is fixed where there is excessive moisture, is bound to be attacked by fungi. The spores of the fungi alight on the wood and, if the conditions are suitable, the fungi feed

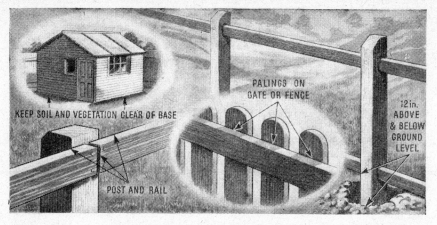

KEEP SOIL AND VEGETATION CLEAR OF BASE

POST AND RAIL

PALINGS ON
GATE OR FENCE

12 in.
ABOVE
& BELOW
GROUND
LEVEL

WHERE DECAY IS LIKELY TO OCCUR

FIG. 1. *It is recommended that all outside woodwork be treated with a preservative before it is erected, as many parts of a structure may be inaccessible later. Those parts indicated by arrows are most likely to decay and require special attention.*

on the timber and quickly eat it away. Timber may also be attacked by insects. Preservatives for timber are, therefore, intended to be poisonous to both fungi and insects.

A good preservative must also penetrate the surface of the wood, because it shrinks a little in dry weather and swells when the air is damp.

It is this continuous working of the wood which causes the surface to crack, and when the spores of fungi alight in these cracks decay follows quickly. A preservative must, therefore, penetrate deeply enough to prevent the attack of fungi when the surface is cracked.

The reason why a fencing post usually decays first at, or about, ground level is because there is an excess of moisture at this point. The part of the post above ground dries in the air fairly quickly after a spell of wet weather.

At the base of the post the ground may be wet, but there is insufficient

air for the fungus to live, so the foot of the post usually remains sound. A little above and below ground level, where there are air and dampness, the spores of the fungus find conditions to be ideal, and quickly consume the wood. The post normally breaks off at this point.

Similar conditions occur where pieces of wood are joined, for example where the rail is nailed to the post. It is therefore important, when treating either new timber or existing fences and gates, to pay special attention to the places where rot is likely to occur.

CHOICE OF A PRESERVATIVE

There are two types of preservative in common use which can be most effective if correctly applied.

One type is obtained by the distillation of coal-tar and in its commonest form is known as creosote. It is sold by the gallon and may be obtained from the local gas works, paint shops or builders' merchants. There are also different brands of refined creosote sold under trade names: these are more expensive than creosote and may be obtained in either brown or green shades. They are usually thinner than creosote, but are said to have better penetrating powers and to be more effective in preventing decay.

Creosoted timber cannot be painted successfully and it has a strong smell which largely prohibits its use for interior work. While being poisonous to fungi and insects, creosote is also poisonous to plants and should not be used for seed-boxes, greenhouse interiors, trellis-work and the like. If used on woodwork which is in contact with plaster, the creosote runs into the plaster and an ugly stain spreads over the plaster surface. Creosote is, however, the cheapest and most widely used of all preservatives.

HOT AND COLD TANKS

To obtain the best results, all new timber should be pressure-treated. This means that the wood has been impregnated with creosote forced into it under pressure. This treatment, of course, is practicable only where a considerable amount of new work is in hand. An alternative method, which gives very good penetration, is the hot-and-cold tank system. An old oil drum is half filled with creosote and heated over a fire until the creosote is about 200 deg. F. The timbers to be impregnated are placed in the hot creosote for half an hour and then put into a tank of cold creosote (Fig. 2). This treatment causes the creosote to be sucked into the wood, which is then allowed to stand so that the excess creosote drains away. When new fences are being erected this method is particularly useful. Creosote is inflammable and should not be allowed to run down the side of the drum and catch fire.

The wood to be preserved may also be immersed in a tank or drum of creosote and then taken out to drain off the excess. This method is better than brushing on the creosote, but not so effective as the pressure treatment.

The application of creosote to existing structures is best carried out with a brush, but where a considerable area

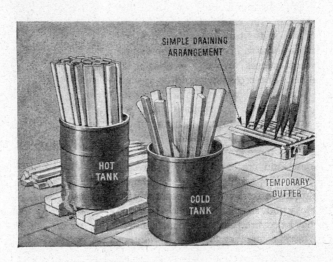

PRESERVATIVE
TREATMENT

Fig. 2. *After putting the timber to be impregnated in the tank of hot creosote, it is transferred to the cold tank and finally left to drain as illustrated.*

SIMPLE DRAINING ARRANGEMENT

HOT TANK

COLD TANK

TEMPORARY GUTTER

WIRE-BRUSH TREATMENT

FIG. 3. *Before treating a fence with pre-servative, it is recommended that all dirt and dust on the surface should be removed with a strong wire brush.*

of air is highly desirable and sheds or huts should be raised clear of the ground so as to keep the timber as dry as possible. If the timber is sound, it is best to apply creosote to all fence gates and wooden outbuildings every two years.

Another good preservative includes naphthalene as a solvent and contains the metallic salts of copper or zinc. Ultimately the naphthalene evaporates, leaving the poisonous metallic

SPRAYING CREOSOTE

FIG. 4. *Where a considerable area has to be covered, creosote may be applied with a spray, but a liberal coat should be given and the material should be spread as thickly as when using a brush.*

has to be covered a spray may be quicker (Figs. 3 and 4). Try to choose a day during a spell of warm dry weather for the work, when the shakes in the timber will be open and when there will be no trace of moisture where pieces of wood overlap each other. The creosote should be applied liberally, and where the wood seems to soak up the preservative and the surface appears to be dry, more of the material should be applied.

It is more important to cover the joints and cracks than the plain surfaces. If possible soil or vegetation should be removed from contact with the wood so that the whole surface may be covered and dampness avoided. Always remember that free circulation

salts in the wood. This type of preservative is sold under various trade names, and may be recognized by its very strong smell. There are only a few brands on the market, so that by asking the builder's merchant for a good preservative with a naphthalene solvent a suitable preparation will be recommended. This type of preservative is more expensive than creosote, but a gallon will cover a much larger area than the corresponding quantity of creosote. It penetrates somewhat more readily than does creosote, and, for application by brush to existing fences and the like, probably provides the best form of treatment. Such preservative has the great advantage of taking paint after the surface has dried. It is usually obtainable in shades of brown or green and may be applied liberally with a brush or spray as previously described for creosote. Wood may also be immersed in a tank of the cold mixture. This preservative must not be used hot, as it is too highly inflammable to be heated. Similar types of preservative, but with water as a solvent, are obtainable. They are used in the same general manner, but are perhaps not quite as effective.

PREVENTION OF FUNGUS

The first stages of decay in exterior timber work is difficult to detect. If the surface has been protected with creosote or other preservatives, the spores of the fungus cannot feed on the surface of the wood (Fig. 5). The fungus makes its attack through the small cracks which appear on the wood owing to alternate swelling and shrinking; thus the inside of the wood decays but the outside shows no signs until the decay has reached an advanced stage. The most likely places for the

FUNGOID GROWTHS

FIG. 5. *If timber is protected with creosote or other preservative, fungus cannot feed on the surface of the wood. Growths, such as are shown, provide an indication that preservative treatment is needed.*

DEATH-WATCH BEETLE

FIG. 6. *A piece of deal attacked by the death-watch beetle. The work of this insect may be easily recognized by the large size of its exit holes. It has seldom been known to attack sound timber.*

fungus to attack should be closely examined once a year. The parts to inspect are where pieces of wood join, where the rail of a fence is nailed to the post and where a post is in contact with the earth. On a dry, warm day these parts should be flushed with creosote or one of the other preservatives described.

At the foot of gate and fencing posts the soil should be removed to a depth of about 12 in. and any defective wood chopped away. The post should then be well soaked in preservative. It is also an advantage to pour some creosote on the soil which surrounds the post. Posts for gates, which are often large and therefore valuable, should be removed: any rotten wood may then be chopped away, the exposed part well charred with a painter's blow-lamp and then liberally creosoted. Creosote should also be poured over the soil which has to be replaced at the foot of the post.

PRESERVATIVES

Oak is naturally resistant to decay; it also has a pleasing appearance and it is generally preferred to retain the natural appearance of the wood than to cover up the beauty of its surface with dark-coloured preservatives. Linseed oil rubbed well into the wood brings out the grain, and preserves it from the weather to a limited extent. If too much oil is used, the surface becomes greasy and collects dirt, and the effect is not so pleasing.

A better method is to scrape the surface quite clean, to rub it down with glass-paper and to apply linseed oil rather sparingly, rubbing it well into the grain so that the wood does not feel greasy to the touch.

After a week or so, when the surface is perfectly dry, the natural colour may be preserved by one or two coats of clear outside varnish.

An excellent alternative method is to apply one or two coats of a preservative containing naphthalene. This preservative is available in clear form if a natural colour is preferred or may be bought in light, medium or dark brown colour, if required. The surface must, of course, be cleaned by scraping and glass-papering before treatment.

When the preservative has dried, the surface will be dull, but a coat of clear varnish may be used to give a glossy finish. This method gives excellent results, as the metallic salts left in the wood after the naphthalene has evaporated prevent most forms of decay, while the varnish finish usually protects the surface from the weather. From time to time, say every two or three years, the varnish should be rubbed down and another coat should be applied.

The value of paint as a preservative lies solely in its ability to form a hard protective surface. It does not penetrate the surface of the wood and once the spores of fungi have found a crack in the painted surface they live and feed on the wood underneath the paint. If it is preferred to paint wooden railings and fences, it should be done with the idea of producing a pleasing finish rather than to prevent decay. If paint is used as the sole protection, the surface will need to be re-painted as soon as blisters or cracks appear.

If a painted finish is desired, it is by far the best plan to apply a coat of preservative of the second type described before any paint is put on. If the woodwork has previously been painted, the old paint must be burnt off, scraped and rubbed down. The wood must be perfectly dry before the

FURNITURE BEETLE
FIG. 7. *Chair leg damaged by the common furniture beetle which bores directly into the wood. Infested areas need special treatment, but regular polishing with wax and aromatic oils acts as a deterrent to this troublesome pest.*

HDR—L*

preservative is applied and a liberal coat should be given. After a week or two the wood should be given a priming coat, followed by an under-coat and a gloss coat, using paint intended for outdoor use.

Such a surface will resist the weather and be less liable to crack, while the preservative will be poisonous to any attacks by fungi if they find a way through the cracks in the paint. The metallic salts remain permanently in the wood and it is only necessary to re-paint the surface when it deteriorates.

INSECT ATTACK

Complete immunity from insect attack is difficult to guarantee by any method of timber preservation, but if conditions which lead to fungal attack are avoided, the danger from common wood-boring insects is very remote. In many cases, fungal attack prepares the way for insects, which seldom enter sound timber (Figs. 6 and 7).

Provided that the moisture content of interior woodwork is low and the use of unseasoned timber is avoided, regular treatment with a good wax polish, or the application of the pre-servatives already mentioned to ex-terior timber, should be all that is required.

The bore-holes and wood dust which are made by different types of insect when they attack timber are easily recognized. Beetles which attack both seasoned and unseasoned timber include the notorious death-watch beetle and furniture beetle. Wood wasps cause relatively little damage, but there are, of course, certain species of moth and butterfly which do harm to growing trees.

Certain timbers are naturally resis-tant to decay. Of the softwoods, yellow cedar, southern cypress, and western red cedar, which contains a natural preservative oil, are particu-larly resistant. Under the heading of hardwoods, certain types of oak, teak and mahogany may be selected which are very resistant.

Perhaps the only occasion on which the average householder will need to consider an attack by wood-boring insects is when furniture, which has been stored for some time in a ware-house or disused room, is put back into service. Care should then be taken to examine any cracks or crevices, as well as the unpolished parts of drawers and the undersides of chairs and cabinets. The application of paraffin followed by a good pro-prietary insecticide to these parts, and the regular treatment of the exterior with wax polish, should preserve the

SLEEPER WALLS

FIG. 8. *To permit of free air circulation sleeper walls should be honey-combed as illustrated. Bricks should be removed at suitable intervals if this has not been done.*

wood from most wood-boring insects.

Dry rot is caused by a fungus which, although it requires damp to start it, once it has developed can spread across walls or girders.

This fungus spreads to sound timber which may be quite dry, because once dry rot is established it obtains sufficient moisture from the air. Eventually the wood becomes extremely dry, brittle and very light, thus the term dry rot refers to the final stage of decay. In view of its ability to spread from basement to roof, dry rot is by far the most serious form of decay. If timbers are not allowed to remain damp there is little fear of decay starting due to attacks by other **fungi.**

PROBABLE CAUSES

Dry rot usually begins in the basement or ground-floor timbers where conditions are suitable for its development. Briefly, the conditions necessary for dry rot to attack the timbers of a house are as follows:

(1) Use of improperly seasoned wood.

(2) Dampness under floors due to earth being piled above the damp course or to damp penetrating the walls.

(3) Lack of air circulation under the flooring (Figs. 8 and 9).

(4) Surface of the building site not being covered with a layer of concrete or asphalt to prevent the growth of vegetation.

(5) Pieces of wood and shavings being left on the concrete under the flooring.

Dry rot can be detected by a musty smell, or by the dull sound, instead of a hard ringing sound, which is heard when the timber is tapped with a hammer. If the point of a knife can easily be pushed into the wood and a brownish, red powder is noticed, dry rot is almost a certainty. In some cases a white fluffy growth is seen on the surface of the wood (Fig. 10).

As a remedy, all the affected wood must be cut out and burnt: the rest of the timber, if it is sound, should be given a coat of preservative. Walls in the affected area should be treated with a blow-lamp to destroy the spores of the fungus. New timber, which replaces the old, should have a good preservative applied to it. Creosote is suitable if there is no objection to the smell.

The type of preservative which consists of metallic salts in naphthalene is excellent, the strong smell quickly disappears and the wood may be painted afterwards if desired.

An excellent preservative may be made by dissolving $1\frac{1}{2}$ oz. of sodium fluoride in a quart of water. The mix-

AIR GRATES

FIG. 9. *Make sure that air grates are clear of any obstruction. Push a wire rod through the opening to check that the inside brick has been removed. Earth should not be piled above the damp course, or over the air grate.*

SERIOUS EXAMPLE OF DRY ROT

FIG. 10. *Severe attack of dry rot as caused by the flooding of a basement and delayed drying out. Once this form of decay has started, the application of preservatives is of little value; all the affected wood must be completely cut out and burnt.*

ture should be applied liberally with a brush. This preservative may also be painted over after the wood has dried. In the case of dry rot, prevention is better than cure. The first essential is to keep all woodwork dry, and the second, to ensure a free circulation of air around timber which is below ground level so as to preserve it.

ASBESTOS PANELS

The asbestos panels used in garages and outbuildings do not require a preservative. They will last indefinitely. Their appearance, however, may not harmonize with the rest of the house. If ordinary oil-paint is applied directly on to asbestos sheeting, a chemical reaction prevents good adhesion and the paint is liable to bleach and change colour.

The panels should be treated first by giving them a coat of a good cement primer. If the cement primer can be obtained in a suitable shade it will be sufficient to use this alone, applying two or three coats. Otherwise a suitably coloured oil-paint may be used on top of a single coat of primer to give the desired colour for the surroundings.

CHAPTER 20

ELECTRICAL REPAIRS

SIMPLE WIRING AND FAULT-TRACING

Perhaps the most common need which arises for electrical repairs in the home is the result of a sudden emergency: a light fails, a fuse blows, or an electrical appliance ceases to function. Such emergencies are so comparatively rare that the average householder does not trouble to find out about the intricacies of the electrical installation until the time for action arises; as a result, in the emergency it is often necessary to grope in the dark!

The source of electric light and power in the home usually appears as a cable coming up from the foundations. This cable from the mains supply into the house contains two copper wires which are heavily insulated and protected. Inside the house, the end of this cable terminates in a junction box, in which it is sealed. Each wire of the two mains leads is connected into a metal box containing a single fuse (Fig. 1).

These two fuses are commonly referred to as the company's fuses. They are fitted, on installation of the electricity service cable, by the local Electricity Board. When the fuses have been fitted the fuse boxes are closed and fastened with a lead seal by the Electricity Board's engineers. These seals should never be broken by the householder. The supply authority's ("company's") fuses are fitted to protect the supply cables and equipment. From these fuses the mains leads

are connected to the electricity meter. On the other side of the meter the two wires are led out which carry the electric light and power load of the house installation. All electric current used in the house must, therefore, pass through the meter for recording purposes.

The electricity meter indicates, usually by pointers which move around small dials, the total amount of electricity which has passed through it (Fig. 2). The number indicated represents Board of Trade units of electricity. By subtracting an earlier reading from a later reading the

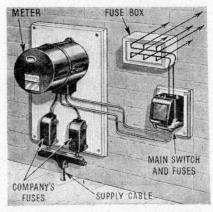

SUPPLY-CABLE CONNEXION

Fig. 1. *The supply cable terminates in a junction box from which leads are taken to the supply authority's fuses, meter, main switch and house fuses.*

333

amount of electricity which has been consumed during the period between the two readings can be assessed.

The Board of Trade unit is technically equal to one kilowatt-hour of electricity. A kilowatt is one thousand watts. Most electrical appliances or lamps are rated in watts or kilowatts, representing the amount of electrical energy they consume. The number of units, which will be indicated on the electricity meter by their use, can therefore be readily assessed. A 100-watt lamp, for example, burning for ten hours, would consume 1,000 watt-hours (100 watts multiplied by 10 hours), or one kilowatt-hour, and exactly one unit would be added to the total shown on the electricity meter if such a lamp were left burning con-

tinuously for a period of ten hours.

The larger the current consumption, of course, the shorter the time before one unit is recorded on the meter. A one-bar electric fire consuming 1 kW, or one thousand watts, could be switched on for one hour only before a unit would be recorded.

The wattage or energy consumption of any electrical device can be calculated by multiplying the pressure of the supply in volts by the current passing through the circuit in amperes. This subject is explained in further detail under fuses, which are always rated in amperes or current-carrying capacity.

It is a wise plan to turn off the main switch when leaving the house for any length of time. This precaution avoids

HOW TO READ THE METER

FIG. 2. *Starting with the dial on the left, the figures indicated by the pointers on the first four dials should be written down in sequence. Always take the lower of the two numbers adjacent to each pointer. By subtracting the previous reading from this total, the number of units consumed during the current period may be determined. The two dials with black faces and the disk below are for test purposes only.*

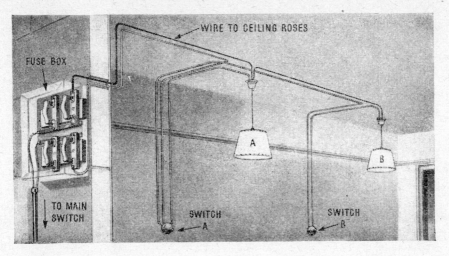

WIRING OF SEPARATE CIRCUITS

FIG. 3. *Leads from the main switch and fuses may be taken to a further fuse-box. Each pair of fuses protects one circuit with one or more lights and plug points. Note the wiring of lamps A and B which are controlled by separate switches.*

electric fires or lights being left on inadvertently and, incidentally, a heavy electricity bill, if nothing worse.

First let us consider how the tree of wiring, which forms the electrical installation for the average house, divides into branches to feed the various lighting and power points. In the wiring of a typical small house, the two wires from the main switch and fuses are taken first to a further set of fuses in a small fuse-box or distribution board (Fig. 3). In this fuse-box there may be several pairs of fuses, each pair protecting one branch or circuit of the house wiring system by providing a fuse in each separate lead. An individual circuit will consist of a few lights, with perhaps two or three 2-amp plug points. A larger installation may have separate circuits for hall, staircase and landing lights, with another circuit for garage and outside lights.

With this arrangement a defect in any part of the system will blow the branch fuses only. The remaining fuses will not be affected, and only a small group of lights or plug points will be affected.

Similarly, the circuits to the power points on the skirting boards (Fig. 5) must also be broken up into groups and protected by separate fuses.

PURPOSE OF FUSES

Fuses protect the electrical wiring of the home from overheating or damage in the event of overload, or a short-circuit developing in the wiring. Such defects are caused by the two electrical conductors being connected directly together, with the result that a heavy current flows momentarily along the wires. The fuse consists of a short piece of very thin wire, which will melt at a fairly low temperature. When

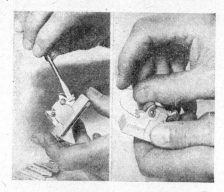

FUSE REPLACEMENT

FIG. 4. (*Left*) *Testing the fuse wire by gently pulling on the end with a screw-driver.* (*Right*) *Threading new wire through the cavity in the centre of the fuse. Only one strand should be employed.*

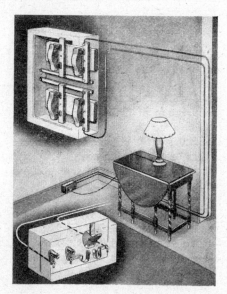

POWER POINTS

FIG. 5. *Circuits to the power points on the skirting are protected by fuses and a switch should be fitted as an integral part of the socket. An earth wire should be connected to the socket, as in Fig. 12.*

the heavy current resulting from an overload or short-circuit passes through this thin wire; it heats up, melts and disconnects the circuit.

It should, therefore, be realized how important it is to use a fuse with the correct type and size of fuse-wire. If the fuse-wire is too thick it will not heat up and blow; as a result, the house wiring itself may heat up, which may damage the insulation of the wiring and even cause a fire.

Electric current is measured in amperes, and fuse-wire is usually supplied on a card marked 5 amp., 10 amp., and 15 amp.; these three fuse-wire sizes covering all normal requirements. The 5-amp. size is generally suitable for lighting circuits, the 10-amp. size is for 2-kW circuits, and the 15-amp. wire is for heavy-current circuits to which large three-bar fires, immersion water-heaters, or electric wash-boilers may be connected. These figures are based on the assumption that the supply is at the pressure of 230 to 240 volts.

CURRENT CONSUMPTION

The power consumed by any electrical device is measured in watts. For example, it is common to speak of a 100-watt lamp or a 2-kW fire, kW standing for kilowatts, and one kilowatt equals one thousand watts, so that a 2-kW fire consumes 2,000 watts. To find the current in amperes, divide the wattage by the voltage. For example, a 1-kW fire taking 1,000 watts on a 240-volt supply would consume 1,000 ÷ 240 = just over 4 amp. A 5-amp. fuse, therefore, would safely carry this load. Some electrical appliances and the approximate current they consume on a 240-volt supply are given in the following list:

Electric lamp, 100 watts	$\frac{1}{2}$ amp. (approx.)
Small bowl fire, 500 watts	2 amp.
One-bar fire, 1 kW	4-5 amp.
Two-bar fire, 2 kW	9 amp.
Electric wash-boiler 3 kW	13 amp.
Vacuum-cleaner	1 amp.
Refrigerator	1-2 amp.
Kettle, 1,500 watts	$6\frac{1}{2}$ amp.
Electric iron, 400 to 750 watts	2-3 amp.
Radio	Less than $\frac{1}{2}$ amp.

It is, therefore, a simple matter to find out what load the house fuses are carrying and if they are likely to be overloaded, by adding together those items which may be switched on at one time on the same circuit, finding the total load in watts, and then dividing by the supply voltage figure to obtain the current in amperes.

For safety reasons, it is advisable to switch off the electricity supply at the

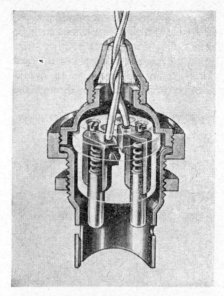

LAMP-HOLDER CONSTRUCTION

FIG. 7. *In this cut-away view, the general construction of a typical lamp holder may be seen. The exterior may be of metal or plastics; the interior fittings being separate units. It is particularly important to make use of the cord grips, when these are provided.*

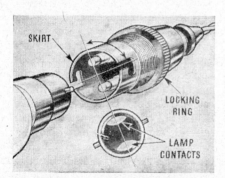

LAMP-SOCKET DETAILS

FIG. 6. *The correct position of the skirt in relation to the spring plungers in a lamp holder is with the bayonet slots at right-angles to the plungers. Never let the skirt work loose and twist round.*

main switch before attempting to replace a blown fuse. An electric shock may not only be dangerous, but there is also the risk of falling off a chair or

steps which may have been used to reach the fuse-box, as a result of the muscular reaction to the shock.

A card of fuse-wire should always be kept near the fuse-box. A blown, open-type fuse can easily be found by withdrawing each fuse in turn and looking for the absence of the fuse-wire itself. An enclosed fuse should be checked by pulling gently on the end of the wire which is clamped under the terminal screws, as shown on the left in Fig. 4. Sometimes an enclosed fuse, which has blown, will be warm owing to the heat generated by the fuse-wire before it finally melts.

To replace a fuse, the two end

terminals should be unscrewed and the remnants of the old fuse-wire should be removed. A length of the new fuse-wire of the correct size as shown on the card for 5-, 10- or 15-amp. circuits, should then be threaded along or through the

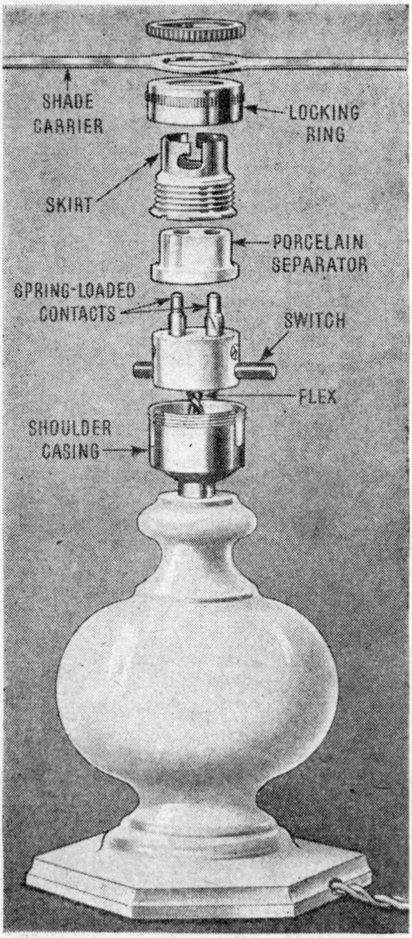

fuse (Fig. 4, right-hand picture) and clamped under the washer and screw at each end. In tightening the screw again be careful not to wind the wire around the thread of the screw and break the fuse between the terminals. It is important to trim off neatly the ends of the fuse-wire after clamping it so that there is no possibility of the fuse-wire making contact with any metal part on the fuse-box.

THE WEAK LINK

Never re-wire a fuse with odd bits of wire or flex. The fuse is intended to protect the electrical wiring from over-loading, overheating or fire risk by being the weak link in the chain. It must be kept weak by re-wiring only with the fine low-current-carrying types of special fuse-wires, which are readily obtainable from any electrical dealer.

When the fuse or fuses have been re-wired and replaced, the mains switch may be returned to the ON position. If the fuses blow again, it will be necessary to locate the fault in the circuit. In some cases a fault may indicate itself. For example, a defective light-bulb which has developed an internal short-circuit may show a bright flash at the moment the fuse blows, or a spark or smouldering may be noticed on a length of flex; even smoke from a defective plug may indicate the cause of the trouble.

Before the fuses are re-wired and replaced a second time, all parts of the circuit protected by these fuses should be switched off, and flexible leads to lamps or appliances should be removed from the sockets. The fuses may then be replaced, the mains switch re-closed, and the switches tried one at a time. If the fuses blow when a certain

TABLE LAMPS

FIG. 8. *The electrical parts of a table lamp must be assembled in the correct order. When re-wiring, the manner in which the parts are removed and the way in which they fit should be noted.*

switch is operated, or a lamp or appliance is plugged into a socket, the fault will obviously be on that part of the circuit or appliance, which should be disconnected. The fuses may then be replaced, and should not blow again.

Lamp holders seldom cause the fuses to blow, but attempts to adjust them, while the switch is on, frequently result in blowing the fuses. A common fault in metal lamp holders is for the locking ring, which holds the skirt, to become loose, with the result that this skirt twists round. It should only be replaced after the current has been switched off. The correct position of the skirt relative to the spring plungers is with the bayonet slots at right angles to the line through the plungers (Fig. 6).

WHY FUSES BLOW

Probably the most common cause of blown fuses is the fraying or wearing of flexible leads. The two bare wires are exposed and touch each other. With hanging lamps and fittings this fault often occurs just above the lamp holder, where continual heat from the lamp dries out the cotton or silk covering and hardens the rubber insulation. Occasionally it may occur just inside the cord grip, where the flex is held tightly between two pieces of hard wood or insulating material. The defect may also happen if cord grips have not been fitted or have been lost and the sharp edge of the ferrule rubs against the flexible lead. The interior of a lamp holder and the cord grips are shown in Fig. 7.

The only certain way of avoiding trouble for some time to come is to replace the flexible lead. First the old lead will have to be removed, after

RE-WIRING A TABLE LAMP

FIG. 9. *It is a good plan to tie a piece of string on to the end of the old flex before it is withdrawn, to facilitate threading the new flex into the base.*

switching off at the main switch. In the case of a hanging lamp, the bulb and shade should be removed first, and the flex disconnected at the ceiling rose, where it is usually connected either by clamping the two bared ends under screws and washers, or in two holes with pinch screws at the sides.

After withdrawing the plug from the skirting-board socket, the holder on floor and table lamps may be detached by loosening the clamping ring, lifting off the lamp-holder skirt, and detaching the interior (Fig. 8). It is a good plan to tie a piece of string or flexible wire to the end of the flex on the lamp holder before withdrawing the lead, so as to leave the string threaded through the stand to help draw in the new flex (Fig. 9). It is also advisable to avoid removing the small pinch-screws from lamp holders and other electrical fittings. Loosening them sufficiently to release the old flex is all that is necessary and time will be saved in replacing these small screws in the awkwardly placed threaded holes.

The new flex may be stripped most easily by cutting the end level with a pair of pliers, separating the two leads, and pushing back the outer covering for about an inch. About half an inch of the rubber should then be stripped (Fig. 10). The plastic type of flex with a tough outer covering may be stripped by holding each lead on the edge of a bench or table and rolling it round while applying a sharp knife or razor-blade about half an inch from the end. Just sufficient pressure should be applied to nick the insulation without cutting through to the wire. The end can then be slid off neatly with the pliers or finger-nail.

After stripping, all of the wire strands should be twisted together quite tightly, and then folded back to give an exposed end about a quarter of

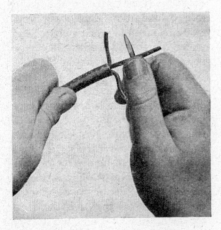

PREPARING NEW LEAD

FIG. 10. *About half an inch of the outer rubber covering is being removed from each lead with a penknife, preferably one which is not too sharp, ready for making the terminal connexions.*

an inch long, with no loose strands. The stripped ends of the wire should then be connected to the lamp holder, making sure that they go through far enough for the pinch screw to obtain a good grip. Make sure that no stray ends are left loose. In the case of a hanging lamp, the holder may be reassembled by fitting the skirt and screwing the locking ring in position. The cord grips should also be replaced and clamped in position by the top screwed ferrule, so that the weight of the lampshade and fitting is not carried on the wires.

From time to time it is wise to test the spring plungers on the lamp holder by pressing them in and making sure they spring back as illustrated in Fig. 11. If the lamp holder has been in use some time the springs may have become weak; in this event it is advisable to fit a new lamp holder if future troubles from intermittent contact and flickering lights are to be avoided.

In the case of a stand or table lamp, after the lamp-holder interior has been fitted, the free end of the flexible lead may be attached to the lead-in string, which has been left threaded through the lamp stand, and the new flex may be drawn in very easily.

METHODS OF WIRING

For a hanging lamp the flex should be cut off to the required length, allowing about 3 in. extra for the connexions into the ceiling rose. The ceiling-rose end of the flex should then be stripped, allowing about ½ in. of tightly twisted wire to clamp under the screw-heads.

The wire should be doubled back for fitting into connexion blocks. Do not forget to thread the cover of the

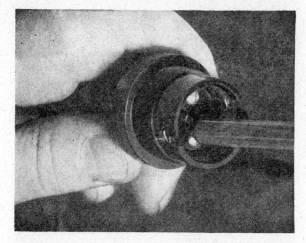

SPRING PLUNGERS

FIG. 11. *A good method of testing the spring plungers in a lamp holder is to press them in with the end of a pencil. When released, the plungers should spring back to the extended position.*

ceiling rose on to the flex the right way round before making the ceiling-rose connexions.

There are many different types of plug, and various methods of wiring them. Where there are slots or grooves provided, the flex should be tucked in neatly and tidily, so that the top, which must always be fitted, can be screwed home tightly and securely.

Although most modern plugs are made to standard specification in definite sizes, for many years manufacturers have produced a confusing variety of shapes, sizes, pin diameters and pitch. For an old installation, therefore, it is usually advisable to take one of the old plugs as a pattern when buying a new one.

Plugs for lighting, radio sets, vacuum-

THREE-PINS

FIG. 12. *A three-pin plug and socket showing how the earth point is connected to the conduit in which the mains leads are run. The largest pin on the plug and the corresponding hole in the socket are always used for the earth connexion.*

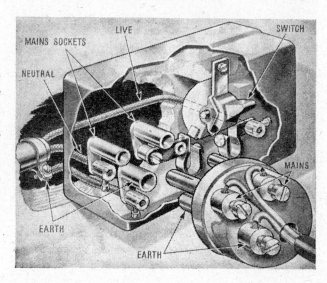

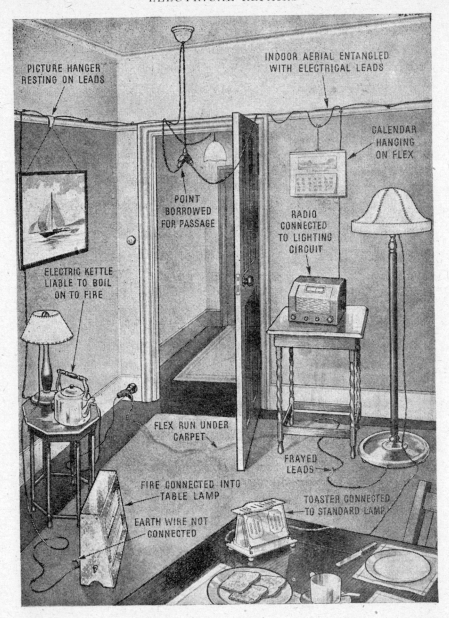

PICTURE HANGER
RESTING ON LEADS

INDOOR AERIAL ENTANGLED
WITH ELECTRICAL LEADS

CALENDAR
HANGING
ON FLEX

POINT
BORROWED
FOR PASSAGE

RADIO
CONNECTED
TO LIGHTING
CIRCUIT

ELECTRIC KETTLE
LIABLE TO BOIL
ON TO FIRE

FLEX RUN UNDER
CARPET

FIRE CONNECTED INTO
TABLE LAMP

FRAYED
LEADS

EARTH WIRE NOT
CONNECTED

TOASTER CONNECTED
TO STANDARD LAMP

WHAT TO AVOID

FIG. 13. *One or more of the faults illustrated can be found in most homes. Although
there may be no immediate danger from any of the wiring or appliances as shown,
the chances of an accident are increased if good electrical practice is ignored.*

342

cleaners and similar light-current loads are usually of the 5-amp. two-pin variety, which means that it is provided with two connexion pins, one for each wire in the flexible lead. In some cases, however, it may be found that three-pin plugs and corresponding sockets are installed. The third pin in these plugs is for earthing purposes. The third, larger hole in the socket leads to an earth connexion, usually a water pipe or cold-water main (Fig.12).

EARTH PIN

It should be explained that one side of the electrical supply is earthed, and is called the "neutral" in the A.C. or alternating-current type of power now supplied to the majority of homes in Britain. The other side, or "line," as it is called, is the live conductor, at a potential of usually 230 to 240 volts above earth. All fuses and switches should be fitted in this live side of the circuit, so that if a switch is off or a fuse withdrawn, the line will be dead and safe to handle.

If, however, a fault develops on an electrical appliance which is normally handled in use, so that a connexion is made internally to the live side of the circuit, any external metal components will also become alive. If these metal parts are touched, an electrical circuit will be completed through the human body down to earth, causing a shock, which may be severe if the recipient is standing on a wet floor, concrete, tiles or on any other well-earthed material.

The earth pin is provided on the three-pin type of plug and socket, so that a third lead may be included in the flex, to earth the outer metal parts. This third lead is connected to the appliance by clamping it under a washer and screw against a cleaned part of the metallic surface, so as to provide good electrical contact. At the plug end it is connected to the earth pin and from there to the third hole in the socket, to earth.

If an internal fault develops on the appliance, and connexion is made to the live side of the circuit, the current, instead of passing through the human body to earth, will take the short cut through the path of lower resistance, through the earth lead in the flex, to the earthed pin at the plug. This heavy current will invariably blow the fuse in the line side of the circuit, giving warning of a defective condition in the appliance.

Such items as stand and table lamps, which are made of wood, may not be fitted with earth wires, and these accessories are often wired with twin flex connected to the two mains pins of the usual 2- or 5-amp. plug.

TRACING FAULTS

Many plug troubles are due to rough handling and mechanical damage; the pins may become overheated if they are used for connecting appliances beyond their normal current-carrying capacity, as, for example, the connexion of a 2-kW electric fire to a 5-amp. plug and socket (Fig. 13). A bad connexion at the plug may cause lamps to flicker, or crackling noises to be heard in radio sets. Plug pins which are loose in the sockets may sometimes be tightened by inserting a screwdriver in the slit of the pin and carefully prising the two sides open.

In older houses the sockets into which the plugs are inserted, usually fitted on the skirting boards, may be different shapes and sizes. In modern homes the smaller 5-amp. size of two- or three-pin socket is usually provided for

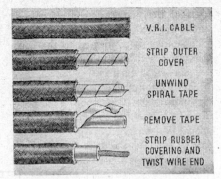

V.R.I. CABLE

STRIP OUTER COVER

UNWIND SPIRAL TAPE

REMOVE TAPE

STRIP RUBBER COVERING AND TWIST WIRE END

STRIPPING CABLE

FIG. 14. *How to remove the covering from vulcanized-rubber-insulated cable. A sharp knife and a pair of pliers will be needed for the job.*

lighting circuits, and larger 15-amp. three-pin types for power circuits. Some sockets are provided with switches.

If there seems to be no current supply to a lamp or appliance from a plug and socket connexion, a lamp or appliance, which is known to be in good working order, should first be plugged in to check that the connexion is not defective.

Next, the plug from the lamp or appliance should be checked by removing the plug cover, examining the connexions to the flexible lead, and making sure that the screws are tight.

If still no supply can be obtained, and perhaps another socket which is also on the same circuit is "dead," the fuses should be checked. If all the fuses are in order, a defective socket may be suspected.

Before carrying out any examination or repairs to the socket it is important to switch off the supply at the mains switch, after which the cover of the socket may be removed. If a switch is included, it may be found that the switch contacts, into which the blades snap as the switch operates, are loose and that good firm contact is not being made. If so, they may be bent gently together with the end of a screwdriver, so that when the blades spring between them they make good contact. If the contacts are bent, broken or worn due to arcing, the complete switch and socket may have to be replaced.

Failure of supply at a socket may occasionally be due to loose connexions at the socket terminals, in which case the screws at the terminals should be tightened. If the wiring into the socket has broken off behind the connexion blocks, the socket will have to be removed from the skirting-board, and from the wiring by unscrewing the screw holding it to the unbroken lead.

V.R.I. CABLE

Sufficient spare wire should have been left behind the socket on installation to allow for an inch or two to be pulled through to re-make the connexions, and the ends of both wires should be stripped. The wires which protrude will be part of the house wiring, usually what is called V.R.I. cable (vulcanized rubber insulated), run in steel conduit, or covered with a lead sheathing.

If lead-covered cable has been used, it may be necessary to remove an extra inch or so of the sheathing to allow the wires to reach the socket connexions. This lead sheathing may be easily removed by nicking round the outer cover with a penknife, bending it backwards and forwards once or twice at the cutting mark and then sliding off the broken piece.

The ends of the conductors should then be stripped by finding the edge of the spiral tape covering which is laid round the rubber insulation, pulling it back from the rubber for about an inch and tearing it off neatly. About half an inch of the rubber should then be stripped from the wire.

In the case of V.R.I. cable run in conduit, there is an outer waxed sleeve around the spiral tape, which should be stripped off with a penknife (Fig. 14).

The wire should be twisted together if necessary and bent back about a quarter of an inch at the end to give additional thickness for the connexion screw to hold.

DEFECTIVE CONTACTS

Ordinary lighting switches which have defective contacts may often be adjusted before the contacts are burned away due to arcing, by switching off the mains supply, removing the switch cover, and bending the contacts slightly together with the switch knob in the off position. If the contacts are already badly burned, or their springiness has been affected by much overheating, or if the switch mechanism is broken, it will be necessary to fit a new switch.

This job is similar to replacing a socket.

A special arrangement of switches is often found in hall-ways and landings, which makes it possible to control one light from two places. The switches are wired as shown in Fig. 15, so that in whatever position one switch is left, the other switch can open or close the circuit.

Defective contacts on one of these switches will affect the operation of the other switch, and both switches should be examined in the event of a failure.

Toggle switches are usually fitted in the bases of table lamps and on electrical appliances. If a table or standard lamp fails to light when switched

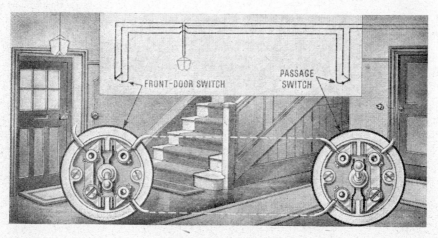

TWO-WAY SWITCHING

FIG. 15. *The arrangement of switches, as commonly fitted in hall-ways and landings, so that one light may be controlled from two positions in the house. In whatever position one switch may have been left, the other can open or close the circuit.*

on, the bulb should be replaced with a known good bulb, the lamp holder, flex and plug should be checked, and the socket tested by plugging in another table lamp or appliance. If the socket is alive and no other fault is discovered, the switch should be suspected. After disconnecting the lamp, the switch may be inspected, usually by unscrewing a base cover-plate or removing a baize cover.

Some small switches have soldered connexions, which must, of course, be unsoldered in order to remove the switch.

If a suitable replacement switch cannot be obtained, the lamp may be put into service by leaving out the switch in the circuit, connecting the flex and covering the join with insulating tape. Preferably new flex should be fitted throughout.

Special switches are available which may be fitted in the lead close to the lamp and look particularly neat.

The method of connecting this type of switch in the flexible lead is shown in Fig. 16. It will be noted that the flex must be separated before fitting this type of switch, as one wire of the flex should be passed through the hole in the centre without being cut; the two wires should then be wrapped neatly together with insulating tape before the covers are replaced.

WIRING EXTENSIONS

Another form of this switch has one end closed, and is used at the end of a length of flex, particularly for bedroom lights. It is connected by removing the cover of the ceiling rose, after switching off the mains switch, detaching one wire of the flex which leads to the lamp holder, and attaching one end of the switch flex to this ceiling-rose terminal after threading the flex through the hole in the ceiling-rose cover. The free ends of the flex should then be connected by a small porcelain

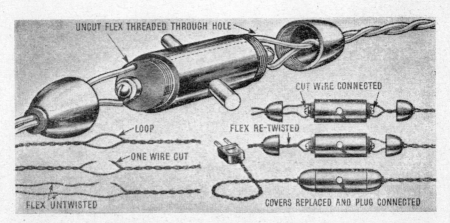

TORPEDO SWITCH FITTED IN FLEX

FIG. 16. *To fit this switch in a twin-flex lead close to an electrical appliance, one wire is cut and the two ends connected to the switch terminals. The other wire passes through, as indicated by dotted lines. Such switches should not be used to control heavy currents, as taken by electric irons and most heating equipment.*

connector and completely covered with insulating tape (Fig. 17). With this type of extension switch it is possible to switch the light off at the bed after it has been switched on at the door.

When fitting extension leads, the wire should never be fixed with drawing-pins, tacks or staples which may penetrate or pinch the wire. For holding flex neatly in position insulated screw-eyes should be used.

Flex extensions may also be run from ceiling roses for additional lights (Fig. 18) and light-current appliances such as electric razors and fans, but not for heavier current appliances such as electric irons, fires, heaters or toasters. Such flex extensions are wired in parallel with the existing lead to the lamp holder, by removing the ceiling-rose cover, after switching off at the mains switch, detaching the wires from under the terminal screws, pushing the extension wire through the hole in the cover and twisting one wire of each of the flexible leads together for each side of the circuit before re-connecting to the ceiling rose.

Flex extensions should be regarded as temporary arrangements only.

TWO-WAY ADAPTORS

With this arrangement, the switch which controls the original light or fitting will also switch the extension on and off. The only way to obtain selective switching is to fit a switch-lamp holder on the end of each lead.

Two-way adaptors are obtainable either with or without a switch controlling one side of the attachment. The flex extension previously described is an alternative arrangement which is particularly useful where a narrow lamp-shade or an enclosed fitting makes it inconvenient to fit a

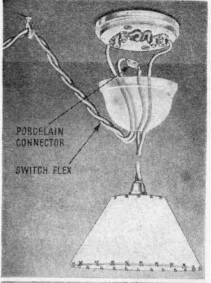

PORCELAIN CONNECTOR

SWITCH FLEX

REMOTE CONTROL

FIG. 17. *How to connect a length of flex into a ceiling rose so that a switch may be provided to control the light from a remote point, as in this bedroom.*

two-way adaptor as in Figs. 20–22.

If extensions are required from a single plug-point, a two-way or three-way adaptor may be obtained, fitted with pins which plug into the socket in the usual way. Several plugs may then be used on the same point. It

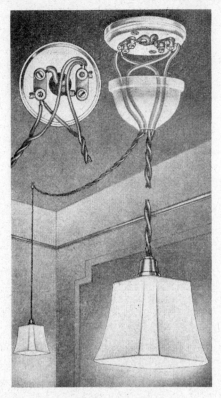

EXTENSIONS

FIG. 18. *An extension may be run off a ceiling rose by connecting a suitable length of flex to the terminals as shown; but avoid overloading the circuit.*

circuit and even a danger of fire.

When carrying out maintenance, repairs or alterations to house wiring, conductors of adequate size and insulation are essential. In the home, currents heavier than 15 amp. are seldom required, but for sockets to which heavy-current devices such as fires will be connected, cables of 15-amp. capacity should be employed, irrespective of the anticipated consumption. The system of running cables in conduit used by electrical contractors is very satisfactory, but lead-covered or tough, rubber-sheathed cables are easier for the amateur to manipulate and to erect.

Clips or saddles should always be used for fixing any cable not run in conduit; they give a neater finish to the work. The cable should be kept under slight tension during erection to prevent it from sagging.

Tough, rubber-sheathed cable is very suitable for domestic wiring and extensions. It provides better pro-

should, however, be remembered that the loading of the socket is determined by its size and the fuse which protects its wiring, and care should be taken not to overload the circuit.

It is best to avoid extending flex by making twisted joints covered with adhesive tape. Use proper flex connectors (Fig. 19).

Flexible extensions should never be run out of sight or tucked under carpets or rugs : if the insulating material wears away, there is a risk of a short-

PLUG AND SOCKET JOIN

FIG. 19. *Use a plug and socket for joining extension leads. Joins with insulated tape are never satisfactory. Fit the socket on the "live" side.*

tection against damage than lead-covered cable and, as the outer cover is not a conductor of electricity, the need for bonding and earthing is avoided. Such cable is made up with one, two or three insulated conductors in the one sheath.

In three-core flex, as fitted on portable appliances such as kettles, irons and fires, the conductors are usually covered with coloured insulation. The red wire should be connected to the live (un-earthed) side of the circuit, the black or grey to neutral and the green wire to earth.

Twisted flex should only be used for light current devices such as light fittings and household appliances consuming less than 5 amp.

To avoid spoiling the appearance of any type of room, it is desirable that

ADAPTOR WITHOUT SWITCH

FIG. 20. *The extension from this adaptor is controlled by the same switch as the lamp on the left of this illustration.*

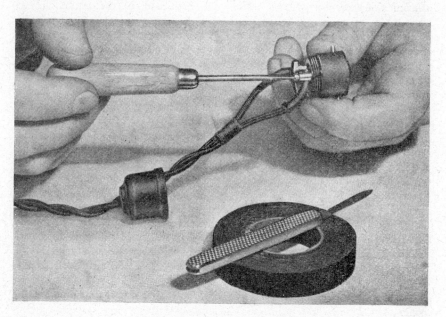

BAYONET-PLUG CONNEXION

FIG. 21. *Fitting a bayonet plug to an extension lead. The ends, which should have been cleaned, twisted and doubled back, are being connected to the terminals.*

ADAPTOR WITH SWITCH

FIG. 22. *The built-in switch on this two-way adaptor allows one socket to be switched independently of the other.*

all electrical wiring should be hidden under the floor boards, behind the skirting or in the wall. The professional conceals his wiring in various ways. Sometimes a channel is cut in the plaster, and a conduit, through which the cable is passed, is inserted and subsequently covered with Keene's cement or plaster. Floorboards may be taken up and the cables run along the floor joists. These methods, attractive as they may be, cannot be recommended to the amateur. All house wiring must comply with strict regulations laid down by the Institution of Electrical Engineers and the local Electricity Board. Unless some experience has been gained in this type of work such methods are best left alone.

Twisted fabric-covered or PVC-covered flexible lead is intended for lamps, radio sets, fans and similar light-current appliances. Extension leads of these types of cables should always be kept as short as possible, and should not be allowed to trail on the floor. For electric fires and portable appliances such as vacuum-cleaners, which must have long flexible leads, the heavy circular-section two-core, or preferably three-core, lead should be used. For portable inspection lamps, electric tools and other appliances used in garages, three-core flexible leads with a tough rubber outer covering are essential.

Most electric shocks and serious accidents occur in the bathroom. Anyone in contact with a damp floor runs a risk of a dangerous shock, even at ordinary domestic supply voltages, if contact is made with the live side of an electrical circuit. The metal taps, the bath and all the plumbing are earthed contacts, and condensation increases the chance of current leakages from electrical appliances.

DANGER OF SHOCKS

Portable electric fires should never be used in a bathroom unless they are mounted permanently high up on the wall and controlled by a cord-operated switch. Hair-driers and similar appliances are equally dangerous unless they are properly earthed.

Complaints of shocks, however slight, or tingling from any bathroom switch, should be investigated immediately, and if the trouble is due to an old metal-cover switch it should be replaced with a new switch of the all-insulated type.

The flexible lead and its plug are the most likely causes of trouble on a fire, as in other electrical appliances. An electric fire consumes a heavy current compared with an electric lamp, the smallest fire taking several times the current of the brightest domestic lamp. The flex which carries this heating current, therefore, should be of the thick, well-insulated variety specially supplied for the purpose, and of the three-core type. From time to time this lead should be carefully examined throughout its length for weak points, chafing or damaged insulation. It is also a good plan to remove the plug cover, to examine the connexions and to tighten the pinch screws or nuts and washers where necessary.

On the electric fire, the flex should be examined where it passes into the frame; an insulated grommet should always be located at this point to pro-

tect the rubber insulation from the sharp metal. The flex usually terminates inside the casing at a terminal block of heat-resisting material.

From the terminal block the wiring is continued to the switch, if fitted, and elements by thick copper wires which may not be insulated but which are securely fixed away from the casing. Alternatively, fireproof insulators may be fitted to withstand the considerable

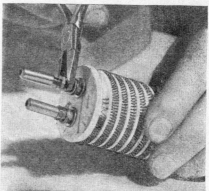

CAUSE OF ARCING

FIG. 24. *Loose terminal connexions or a bad fit of the split-pins in their sockets may cause arcing, recognized by blue sparks and sizzling noises. Tightening and cleaning eliminate the trouble.*

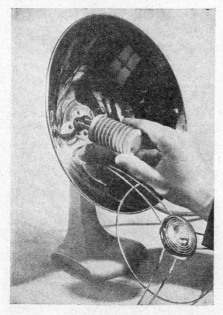

PLUG-IN ELEMENT

FIG. 23. *The heating element in this bowl fire plugs into a socket at the back of the reflector and may be very easily removed for repair and servicing.*

heat at the back of the elements. Terminals or connexions which may pass through the casing are insulated either with porcelain, or mica bushes and washers securely clamped in position.

To replace the flexible lead on a fire the back cover should be removed, but before removing the old lead make a note of the connexions.

The ends of the cable may be fitted into holes in a connexion block and held by pinch screws, or turned around

351

a bolt and held securely between two washers by a nut. The screws or nuts have probably been thoroughly tightened, and some force may be needed to unscrew them.

After the old flex has been removed, the new flex may be inserted through the casing grommet. Strip just sufficient of the insulation to pass the wires into the connexion block or to wrap one full turn around a bolt or screw. Twist all of the strands tightly together with the pliers, and make sure that there are no stray ends.

OBTAINING GOOD CONTACT

Before making a connexion to a bolt, make sure that the lock-nut holding the bolt is tight and that it clamps any mica washers below it securely in position. Next replace one of the metal terminal washers, then wrap the stripped end of the flex conductor round the bolt in the same direction as the top nut will be screwed down, fit the second washer over the wire loop, and tighten the top nut, making sure that the wire is firmly gripped between the two washers. If the clamp washers have been lost, suitable brass, not steel, washers should be substituted,

otherwise it will be difficult to make a firm connexion on the wire between the two nuts.

All connexions on electric fires must be firm and tight. Unless good contact is made, arcing will occur at loose joints when using heavy current.

LOOSE TERMINAL CONNEXIONS

Arcing, due to bad contact, will sometimes occur on small bowl fires of the plug-in element type (Fig. 23). Loose terminal connexions at the ends of the element wire, or a loose fit of the split-pins in their sockets, may be the cause of the arcing which may usually be noticed by the sizzling noises and small blue sparks. Tightening all connexions, as well as cleaning and opening the pins slightly, should eliminate this fault (Fig. 24).

Similar troubles may develop on fires with bar-type elements (Fig. 25), which consist of a length of nickel-chrome wire wound in close spiral turns on an insulated rod. The ends of the element wire are clamped to metal end-caps, which are provided with screwed studs and lock-nuts (Fig. 26) which fit into slotted strips. The connexions at these terminal screws

BAR-TYPE FIRE

FIG. 25. *The element on a bar-type fire is removed by loosening the retaining screws at each end and lifting the bar out of the mounting slots.*

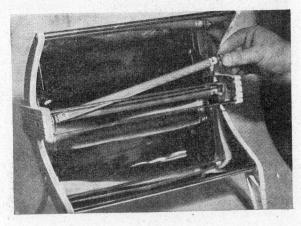

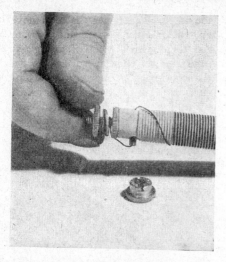

BAR-TYPE ELEMENT

FIG. 26. *The ends of the element wire should be tightly clamped under washers and nuts. If the fireclay is undamaged new wire may be wound on the bar.*

should be inspected and the contact surfaces cleaned with emery-cloth.

Electric-fire elements of all types should be replaced when they show signs of wear, and before they break or burn out. After long periods of service the element wire may stretch or sag. If light and dark patches are seen, instead of a uniform glow, some of the turns in the wire will have short-circuited together. A new element for a bowl fire is usually plugged in. A rod or tubular element, for reflector-type fires, requires to be fitted in the slots provided, and the locking nuts need to be tightened.

If in good condition, round or rectangular fire-bars may be retained, and a new spiral wire element fitted. See that the new element wire is stretched round the supports, that it lies neatly in the grooves with the turns uniformly

spaced and that adjacent turns are not touching. The ends of the element wire should be clamped tightly at each end under washers and nuts.

After repairing a fire fitted with a three-pin plug, remember to reconnect the earth wire, if it has been removed for any reason. Make a clean connexion to the frame or casing by scraping away the paint and clamping the lead tightly under a washer and screw. Before plugging in again, be sure that this earth lead is connected at the plug to the thickest of the three pins, and that it does not happen to be connected to a live pin.

VACUUM-CLEANER REPAIRS

Vacuum-cleaners, like other electrical appliances, are frequently put out of order by nothing more serious than a defective lead or plug. The flexible lead of the vacuum cleaner has to stand more handling than most other appliances, and when replaced, the correct type of heavy rubber- or fabric-covered flex should always be used.

Most vacuum-cleaners are driven by small high-speed motors, which operate on either A.C. or D.C. supply. These motors are fitted with small carbon brushes, which press on the commutator and conduct the current to the armature. Pressure is applied to the two brushes by small spiral springs, located with the brushes in the brush-holders. If these carbon brushes are excessively worn, or stuck in the holders, or if the springs are weak, there may be insufficient pressure on the brushes and motor commutator to pass the required current.

A vacuum-cleaner which has no other defects, but which refuses to operate, should be examined by removing the end caps of the brush-holders. These end caps are usually knurled insulated knobs located opposite each other at one end of the motor, and when removed will disclose the brush springs (Fig. 27). The springs and then the brushes should be withdrawn for examination and, if they are worn to short stubs, the brushes should be renewed.

If the brushes are not worn, they may have stuck in the holders, in which they should slide easily but not too freely. The remedy is to remove any oil or other deposit and then to rub them with a piece of fine glass-paper lightly on each surface except the working end. If necessary, the tension on the springs may be increased by pulling the coils out slightly at each end. When re-inserted in the holders the brushes should slide in easily and make good contact with the motor commutator. After the springs and end caps have been replaced, the vacuum-

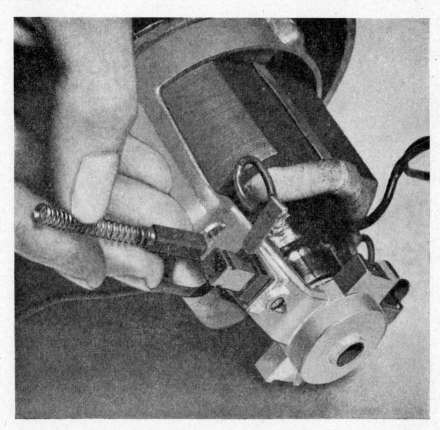

VACUUM-CLEANER BRUSHES

FIG. 27. *The springs and brushes may be removed for examination by removing the end caps. The brushes may require cleaning or renewing if they are worn down, and the tension on the springs may need to be increased.*

cleaner may be plugged in again. If the motor still does not start, the machine will need expert attention.

Incidentally, sparking and arcing inside the motor are often the cause of interference with radio reception.

IRONS AND KETTLES

Electric irons and toasters are basically electric fires in miniature, employing heater elements which operate at a lower temperature than an electric fire. In electric irons the heater element is wound on a flat heat-resisting mica former, clamped between two mica sheets to form an insulated sandwich. If an electric iron fails and the lead and connector (which sometimes embodies a switch) seem to be in order, the element may have burnt out. Non-thermostatic irons may usually be taken apart by removing the two nuts which hold the handle and the top casing of the iron to the lower sole-plate. The components may then be prised out and the old element can be removed by detaching two thin strip connectors which are attached to the plug pins in the body of the iron.

Electric-iron elements vary not only in size and shape, but also in wattage, from 450 to 750 watts or more. It is necessary, therefore, to obtain a new element which is identical with the defective one. When the element has been renewed it is most important to see that the mica sheets are correctly replaced and that the live parts of the element and the connector tags do not touch the interior of the casing at any point.

Electric kettles usually employ a heater element of an immersion type. Some makes embody an automatic device which prevents the kettle boil-

RENEWING THE ELEMENT

FIG. 28. *A new element for an electric kettle is inserted through the lid opening and held in position with a packing washer and retaining collar on the outside.*

ing dry. An excessive rise in element temperature causes a bi-metallic strip (a form of thermostat) to bend and release a spring-loaded plunger, which pushes out the lead connector and breaks the supply.

In the event of a failure of an element or its built-in protector, the complete unit must usually be replaced. The element is usually fixed by an external collar or large nut clamped through a hole which is sealed with fibre washers or similar jointing material. The new element unit, which must be obtained from the manufacturers or their agents to suit the particular type and make of kettle, is fitted by inserting it through the lid opening (Fig. 28) and re-fitting the clamp nut or collar. Particular care should always be taken to replace, and if necessary to renew, the washer.

CHAPTER 21

WATER AND GAS SERVICES

SIMPLE PLUMBING AND GAS-FITTING REPAIRS

ALMOST all failures with domestic water supplies are the result of neglect to carry out simple maintenance jobs or to take certain elementary precautions. Water, like its co-utility services gas and electricity, is a good servant but a bad master if it be allowed to get out of control. A burst pipe due to frost or a leaky tap left unattended may be the cause of serious damage involving costly repairs for the householder.

If the water in a pipe freezes the water will expand on freezing and may burst the pipe. There is, however, no indication that the pipe has burst until the thaw sets in and the water begins to leak from the fracture.

LAGGING

The parts of a water system most susceptible to frost are those exposed to icy draughts in frosty weather. Unfortunately, these parts are usually the least accessible, being up in the roof and often in the angle made by the roof and the floor of the loft. If the roof is not boarded or felted, the cold-water cistern and the service pipe which conveys water to it from the main are almost certain to be affected. The remedy is to lag them, that is, to protect them with a covering of material which will insulate them from the surrounding cold air. Not only will this lagging prevent the cold water from freezing in winter, but it will also keep the water cool in summer by insulating

it from the warm air inside the house.

The methods of insulating, or lagging, pipes to be described may be used on hot- or cold-water storage tanks and pipes. By lagging the hot-water tank and any long runs of hot-water pipe the temperature of the water will be maintained and fuel costs will be reduced. On current prices for gas and electricity, it is estimated that every foot of lagged pipe can save a penny a week in fuel costs.

The simplest method of lagging a pipe, shown in Fig. 1, consists of winding round the pipe a strip of hair felt which can be obtained in rolls ready for use. Begin by wrapping one end of the roll of felt around the pipe and bind the end tightly with string. Continue to wind on the felt, allowing

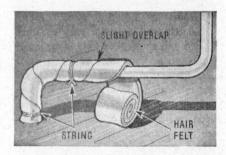

LAGGING WATER PIPES

FIG. 1. *The easiest method of lagging pipes is to wrap them with hair felt, which is obtainable in rolls ready for use. Each turn should overlap the previous one and the felt should be secured with string at regular intervals.*

each turn slightly to overlap the previous one. Keep the spare felt tightly rolled, because it is easier to manipulate a roll than a loose strip. On a long pipe it is desirable to bind the felt at intervals with two or three turns of string, tied tightly.

Although old rags or even several thicknesses of folded newspaper may be used as lagging, it is well to remember that the specially prepared hair

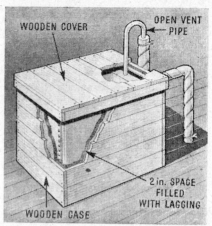

BOXING-IN A CISTERN

FIG. 3. *Perhaps the best method of protecting a cistern is to box it in. A space of about 2 in. should be left between the case and the tank and packed with suitable insulating material.*

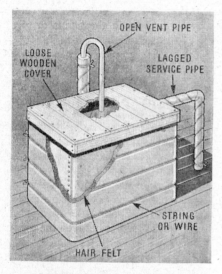

PROTECTING A CISTERN

FIG. 2. *The top of every cistern should be fitted with a loose wooden cover. The sides may be lagged with sheets of hair felt, kept in position by string or wire. Another method is shown in Fig. 3.*

felt is treated to make it vermin-free and it offers no attraction to rodents which can become a nuisance if newspaper is used.

If the top of the cold-water cistern is exposed, the first precaution is to provide it with a loose-fitting wooden cover. This cover will prevent icy

draughts from blowing on to the surface of the water. The sides of the cistern should be lagged next, preferably with sheets of hair felt which may be kept in position by string or wire (Fig. 2). Another excellent method is to box in the cistern completely (Fig. 3). The box should be made about 2 in. larger all round than the cistern. The intervening space can be filled with any of the following materials : lightly crumpled "silver" paper (aluminium foil), lightly crumpled newspaper, torn-up and lightly packed rags, sawdust, shavings, glass wool, or any fabric which will not pack too tightly. The object is to retain small cells in which air is imprisoned, because still air is an excellent insulator. If old rags or newspapers are used they should be sprinkled liberally with a dry insecticide.

If the pipes to be lagged are exposed

to moisture or steam, increased efficiency and a better appearance can be obtained by using hair felt and waterproof cardboard (Fig. 4). The roll of hair felt should be obtained in a width equal to the circumference of the pipe, and the cardboard should be in strips about 2 ft. long and about one and a half times as wide as the hair felt. Referring to Fig. 4, proceed as follows:

(1) Unroll the hair felt and cut it into strips of about 4 ft. This is the most convenient length to handle. The strips may have to be shorter, but do not make them longer than 4 ft. (A).

(2) Wrap the hair felt lengthways around the pipe and bind one end with string or wire. Then continue binding the whole length and tie it securely at the other end (B).

(3) Continue until the required length of pipe has been covered with hair felt.

(4) Take the strips of cardboard and roll them in the hands to give them a tubular shape (C).

(5) Begin wrapping the cardboard round the hair felt, aligning it so that the joints between the felt strips lie between the joints of the cardboard covers (D).

(6) Bind the first band of cardboard in the middle with adhesive tape.

(7) Arrange the next band of cardboard so that it butts neatly up to the first strip. Bind this second band of cardboard in the middle (E) and (F).

(8) Bind the joint between the cardboard bands (G).

The binding will occur at intervals of 1 ft. along the finished lagging.

The lagging may now be painted to match the surrounding decorations. If the cardboard has been neatly fitted with the edge towards the wall and the binding neatly applied, the finished job should look very neat.

Bends and tees can be effectively covered by carefully cutting the cardboard in small sections (Fig. 5).

If it is necessary to leave a house unheated for any appreciable period during frosty weather, for example, when going away for holidays, the only sure way to prevent freezing is to empty the system. This is done by

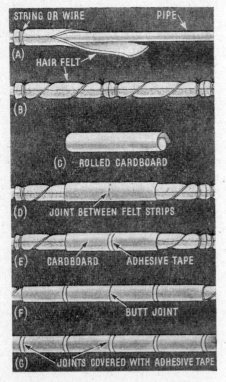

PIPES EXPOSED TO MOISTURE

FIG. 4. *A covering of hair felt and waterproof cardboard should be provided for pipes which are exposed to moisture or steam. The procedure to be followed in covering a pipe is illustrated step by step.*

turning off the stop-cock, known as the consumer's cóntrol, on the service pipe. Many houses have two such cocks on the water service pipe, one inside the house and the other usually in the footway outside. If there is one, the cock inside the house should be used. If not, it will be necessary to obtain a turn-key to shut off the cock outside the house.

Before shutting off the water, make sure that all sources of water heating are turned off, extinguish the fire and turn off the gas or electricity supply. Next open all taps and allow the water to drain away. Most gas and electric water-heaters have a drain tap or plug to enable them to be emptied. If the heater is not over a sink or bath it may be necessary to attach a short length of hose to the drain tap.

When refilling the system with water it is important to avoid the formation of air locks in the pipes. Before turning on the consumer's control make certain that all taps are open and that any drain plugs or taps on heaters are closed. Turn on the water and wait until it flows freely from the lowest tap, then close this tap. Repeat the procedure at the next higher tap and so on, through the house. Do not light the boiler fire or turn on the gas or electric heater until the whole system is fully charged with water.

FROST

A frozen cistern can easily be thawed by pouring boiling water into it. When all the ice has been melted the ball tap should move freely. If not, cloths dipped in very hot water should be placed around the valve until the ball and arm move freely and water issues when the arm is depressed. Do not apply a blow-lamp or any form of

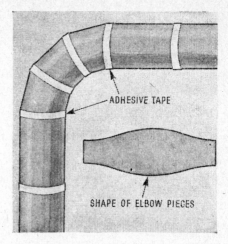

BENDS IN A PIPE

FIG. 5. *Bends and tees in a pipe may be covered very effectively by cutting the cardboard to the shape indicated. The joins between the elbow pieces should be secured with adhesive tape.*

flame to the ball tap, which may be damaged by excessive heat. Frozen pipes are best thawed by applying cloths which have been dipped in boiling or very hot water. Use plenty of hot water and several cloths. Obviously, if water flows at one tap and not at the next, the freezing is on the pipe between these two taps. If the source of the trouble is not so obvious, go first to the points most likely to be frozen on account of exposure to draught. If this fails, it will be necessary to work systematically along the pipes, applying hot cloths one after another.

Frozen waste pipes should be treated in a similar manner. Do not pour boiling water into a porcelain sink or basin to thaw a frozen waste pipe. The boiling water will almost certainly crack the porcelain and may fail to melt the ice on the drain side of the trap where it usually forms.

Many water authorities undertake to re-washer taps free of charge, and it is advisable to take advantage of any such service. If the job is the householder's responsibility, it is such a cheap and simple task that it pays to do it at the first sign of the tap not shutting off tightly. The work is illustrated in Figs. 6–10. First obtain the correct size of washer of the appropriate type. For cold-water taps, washers are made of specially treated leather or rubber-asbestos composition. For hot-water taps, fibre or rubber composition is used. In case of a leakage past the spindle, the gland packing may need to be renewed as shown in Fig. 11.

For most domestic water-taps, other than bath taps, $\frac{1}{2}$-in. washers are used, but, as the exact size may not be known until the tap is dismantled, it is desirable to have available a washer of

each size · $\frac{3}{8}$, $\frac{1}{2}$ and $\frac{3}{4}$ in. The only tools required are a smooth-jawed adjustable spanner and a pair of pliers.

If the tap to be re-washered is on the service pipe and, therefore, under mains pressure it will be necessary to shut off the supply at the control cock, situated either outside the house or just inside, adjacent to an exterior wall. If the tap is on a pipe fed from a cistern

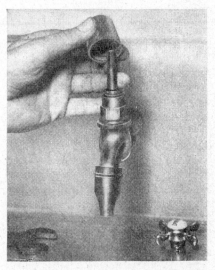

UNSCREWING THE DOME

FIG. 7. *After removing the handle, unscrew the dome by hand. It is not advisable to use a tool, as the metal is thin and may very easily be damaged or scratched. In some cases a wrench will be necessary to grip the dome.*

where there is no stop-cock, and the vertical distance between the cistern and the tap is more than 3 or 4 ft., it will still be necessary to shut off the supply, but the system will only need to be drained to the level of the tap to be re-washered. If the head of water (the vertical distance between the cistern and the tap) is less than about

PREPARATION FOR RE-WASHERING

FIG. 6. *It is usually necessary to remove the handle from the tap before a new washer can be fitted. The handle is retained by a small set-screw.*

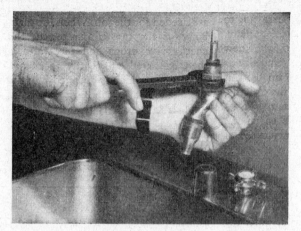

REMOVING COVER

FIG. 8. *Holding the base of the tap firmly in one hand, the cover is unscrewed with a spanner. All modern taps have a right-hand thread, but sometimes on older taps the thread is left-handed.*

4 it. the tap can be dismantled and quickly plugged with wet rag. The construction of the most common form of tap is shown in Fig. 12 and that of a modern tap of novel design in Fig. 13. First open the tap fully and unscrew the dome by hand. Do not use a tool, as the metal is thin and easily damaged. When unscrewed the dome can be lifted sufficiently to place the spanner on the hexagonal part of the cover. All modern taps have a normal right-hand thread and the cover is removed by turning to the left, but some older types of tap have left-hand threads and are unscrewed by turning to the right. If the cover will not turn, do not force it unduly, but try it in the opposite direction.

Removing the cover will reveal the jumper, which consists of a washer plate and stem, the washer being held to the plate by a nut. Some jumpers are merely a loose fit and drop out when the head of the tap is unscrewed. In others, the stem of the washer plate is a press fit and the nut must be gripped with the pliers and pulled in order to remove the jumper. In a third type a **pin passes through** the hole in the

WITHDRAWING THE JUMPER

FIG. 9. *When the cover has been removed, the jumper, consisting of a washer plate and stem, is withdrawn. The washer is usually attached to the plate by a nut which must be removed.*

spindle and secures the stem. All modern types of tap have jumpers secured in such a way that the washer plate rises and falls with the spindle

Loosen the nut, taking care not to damage the stem of the washer plate. Remove the old washer and fit the new one, which should be the same size as the washer plate. Tighten up the nut and refit the jumper to the spindle, making sure that the stem rotates freely. Finally, replace the cover and the dome. Some proprietary types of tap have jumpers with integral washers which cannot be removed. With such taps it is necessary to fit a complete new jumper of the same make as the tap.

Those who want an easier water tap to maintain may be interested in the unusual design shown in Fig. 13. The main advantages of this tap are that a new washer can be fitted to it in less than 30 seconds without shutting off the water supply and that no tools

are needed for the job. When the main body of the tap is unscrewed, the check valve drops and the water is then restricted sufficiently to change the washer, which is dropped into the top of the anti-splash device. Another important feature is that it is interchangeable with any standard water tap.

The method of maintaining a ball tap, or ball valve as it is more often

RENEWING THE PACKING

FIG. 11. *To remedy a leakage past the spindle, unscrew the gland nut, remove the old packing and press a short length of greased string into the recess between the spindle and the cover.*

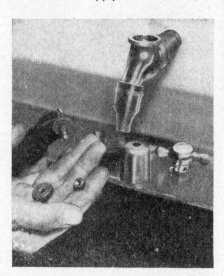

FITTING THE NEW WASHER

FIG. 10. *After the old washer and its retaining nut have been removed, a new washer may be fitted; this should be of the same size as the washer plate. Then tighten up the nut and refit the jumper.*

called by tradesmen, is quite different from that which applies to taps of the kinds already dealt with.

A ball tap (Fig. 14) is used to control the supply of water to the cold-feed cistern and to control the entry and level of the water in every flushing cistern. After a time the washer may wear and fail to fit firmly on the seating when the arm carrying the ball is fully raised. This defect will cause the water level to be raised and the excess water to discharge through the overflow pipe.

On the cold-feed cistern it is first necessary to shut off the stop-cock controlling the supply to the cistern. There is no need to empty the cistern, but care must be taken to avoid dropping any parts of the tap into it. If the size of the washer is not known it is advisable to obtain one of each of the common sizes. The correct size of rubber washer must be used and no attempt should be made to pare down a washer of larger size.

RE-WASHERING A BALL TAP

With a flushing cistern which is supplied from the cold-feed cistern and has no separate control cock, the water supply can be shut off temporarily by plugging the outlet from the cistern with a broomstick, the end of which has been sharpened and bound with rag to form a tapered stopper (Fig. 15). Alternatively, the ball tap of the feed cistern can be tied up with string (Fig. 16), and the system drained to the level of the ball tap of the flushing tank.

After shutting off the water to the defective ball tap, remove the cotter pin (Figs. 17 and 18) and, before withdrawing the lever, depress the arm in order to push out the piston so that its end can be gripped Withdraw the lever and ball and slide out the piston. The washer is held by a brass screw cap. Unscrew this cap with the pliers and remove the old washer (Fig. 19). After fitting the new washer and replacing the brass cap, it is worth while to polish the piston with grinding-in paste or metal polish; at the

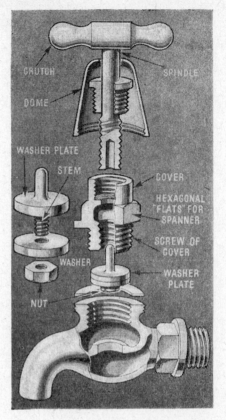

TAP COMPONENTS

FIG. 12. *The principal parts of a typical water tap. It will be found that after studying the appearance and function of the various components, most repairs to a tap will be comparatively simple.*

same time, make sure that the valve seating is clean and free from burrs or obstruction. Next replace the piston temporarily and, using a handle of the pliers as a lever, slide the piston up and down a few times to make sure that it is free and that it moves easily.

On some types of ball tap the piston operates vertically, but the method of replacing the washer is substantially

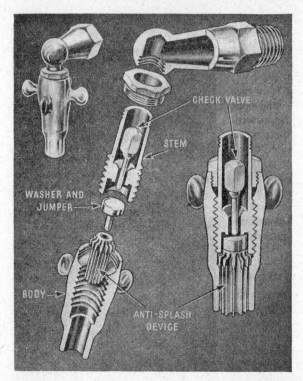

UNUSUAL WATER TAP

FIG. 13. *The particular advantage of this new water tap is that a new washer may be fitted in a minute or so without tools and without shutting off the water supply or draining the system. The built-in check valve cuts the water off automatically when the body is unscrewed. The washer and jumper fit into the anti-splash device.*

the same for all forms of ball tap.

If the lever arm carrying the ball is bent upwards, the water level will be too high and water will run to waste through the overflow pipe. Conversely, a lever arm bent downwards will cause the valve to close with the cistern level below normal. In a flushing tank this may cause difficulty in operation due to there being insufficient water to effect siphonage.

The arm is made of soft brass and is easily bent (Fig. 20). On no account should the ball be gripped when bending the arm. If two adjustable spanners are used the job can be done without removing the arm and ball, and there will be no possibility of damaging the ball. The spanners should be brought together to raise the

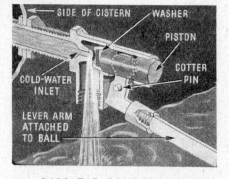

BALL-TAP COMPONENTS

FIG. 14. *This type of ball tap controls the supply of water to cold-feed cisterns and flushing tanks. The piston may operate horizontally or vertically. Only the main components and method of operation are shown. The complete assembly is illustrated later.*

water level and forced apart to give a lower water level.

When making adjustments to a high-level flushing tank, do not stand on the lavatory seat or put boards across the pan to stand on. A man's full weight puts too great a strain on the rigid waste-pipe joint and may cause a

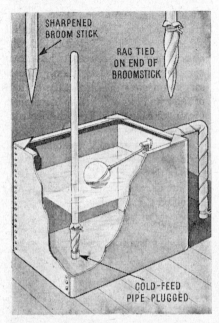

SHARPENED
BROOM STICK

RAG TIED
ON END OF
BROOMSTICK

COLD-FEED
PIPE PLUGGED

TEMPORARY MEASURE

FIG. 15. *During repair work, the outlet from a cold-water cistern may be temporarily plugged with a broomstick, the end of which has been sharpened and bound with rag to form a tapered stopper.*

leakage or a cracked pan. Steps should, therefore, be used and the pan should be covered to avoid damage in case any tools are dropped.

The old-fashioned rag-and-putty joint for connecting the flushing pipe to the pan is now being superseded by rubber and mechanical joints. By far

the simplest method of repairing a defective rag-and-putty joint is to remove all the old putty, thoroughly cleaning the end of the flushing pipe and the socket of the earthenware pan, and to remake the joint with a rubber connector (Fig. 21). Having cleaned off the old joint, remove the union nut at the cistern and remove the flushing pipe.

Slip the smaller end of the rubber connector over the lower end of the flushing pipe and push it back a few inches. It will slip on easily if both the pipe and the rubber are moistened with soapy water. Next reconnect the flushing pipe with the lower end loose in the socket of the pan and the upper union hand-tight. Slip the rubber connector forward and work the wider end

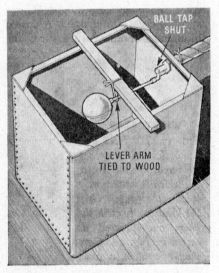

BALL TAP
SHUT

LEVER ARM
TIED TO WOOD

ALTERNATIVE PLAN

FIG. 16. *As an alternative to the method shown in Fig. 15, the ball tap on the feed cistern may be tied up with string, the water then being allowed to drain away before the repairs are started.*

over the socket of the pan. When a satisfactory fit has been obtained, tighten up the union at the cistern. A fairly large adjustable spanner will be required for this union. The type included in a car tool-kit should be satisfactory.

The flushing tank should be examined and overhauled at regular intervals or when it becomes necessary to pull the handle several times before satisfactory flushing is obtained. The most common fault, a low water level, is quickly remedied by bending the arm of the ball tap upwards until the tap shuts off with the water level just below the overflow pipe. Another cause of trouble may be rust in the well and under the bell (Fig. 22). The remedy is to shut off the water by tying up the lever of the ball tap and removing the bell. All rust should be removed and the surfaces cleaned and dried. A coat of bituminous or other corrosion-resisting

paint should be applied and this treatment will considerable prolong the life of the cistern.

The failure of a sink or basin to drain quickly indicates the presence of a partial stoppage in the U-trap (Fig. 23). This trap forms a water seal to prevent smell passing up from the drains into the house. Foreign matter, such as hair and shreds of cotton, gradually forms a mass to which other substances adhere. Neglect to clear the obstruction will eventually lead to a complete stoppage. It is only necessary to unscrew the plug at the bottom of the trap (Fig. 24) and to use a piece of wire or cane to hook out the obstruction.

In districts where the water is hard, scale deposits are formed in water-heaters. If the water is allowed to boil, the rate of scale formation can be rapid. Provided that hard water is not heated above about 140 deg. F., the produc-

FIRST STAGE

FIG. 17. *The lever arm and ball may be detached by removing the cotter pin which is immediately below the tap. Grip the head firmly with the pliers and proceed as shown in Fig. 18. Care should be taken to avoid damaging the hollow metal float during these operations.*

tion of scale is not serious. This is why the thermostats of gas and electric water-heaters are normally set to maintain the water at about 140 deg. F. The de-scaling of gas and electric water heaters calls for specialized knowledge and the method employed varies with each proprietary type of appliance. It is not, however, a job for the amateur.

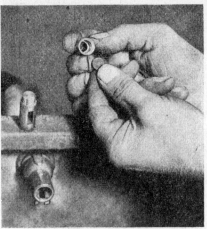

FITTING THE NEW WASHER

FIG. 19. *The cap which retains the washer may be unscrewed with the pliers. After the new washer has been fitted and the brass cap has been replaced, it is a good plan to clean the piston with metal polish.*

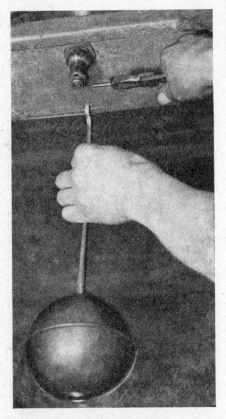

SECOND STAGE

FIG. 18. *As the cotter pin is withdrawn the lever arm should be carefully depressed in order to push the piston outwards, so that its end may be gripped and gently withdrawn. The washer is held by a brass screw cap.*

Work of this nature should always be carried out by experts.

The simple type of coke boiler, however, can be de-scaled quite easily should the need arise and this will be apparent when the efficiency falls off. The presence of scale reduces the efficiency by forming an insulating layer which restricts the passage of heat from the fuel to the water. Moreover, it results in the metal becoming overheated and, in bad cases, this may be burnt away and eventually cause a leak.

De-scaling may be carried out either by chipping out the scale manually or by dissolving the deposits with a suitable chemical solution.

The manual method necessitates removing the manhole of the boiler to obtain access to the interior waterways. With both methods the system must

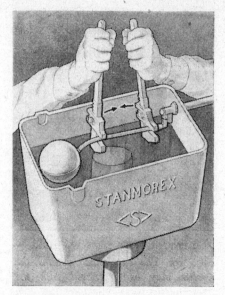

manhole cover. Any loose scale may be removed by hand, but the rest will have to be chipped out with a cold chisel. The outside of the boiler may be tapped lightly to crack off the scale, but this should be done carefully to avoid cracking the cast iron. Before the manhole cover is replaced the surfaces should be thoroughly cleaned. The rejointing of the manhole cover must be carefully done to avoid any leakage when the boiler is reconnected.

A chemical de-scalent contains strong acid which must be handled with care to avoid spilling or splashing it either on the person or on any painted or galvanized surface. After removing the boiler to a suitable place, mix the de-scalent with water, as instructed on

ADJUSTING THE WATER LEVEL

FIG. 20. *Two adjustable spanners should be used to bend the level arm of a ball tap. The water level is raised by bringing the spanners together and lowered by forcing them apart. Never touch the ball.*

be emptied and it is strongly recommended that the boiler be disconnected and removed. For manual de-scaling it is better to have the boiler in a good light, and it is preferable with either method to take the boiler out where any mess will not matter unduly.

If it is decided to chip out the scale, first examine the boiler and note the number of manholes. When re-assembling it will be necessary to use new washers for the manholes; these should therefore be obtained before beginning the work. When ordering it is important to state the make, type and size of boiler to obtain the correct washers.

After draining the boiler and removing it to a convenient place, unscrew the set-screws and remove the

LAVATORY-PEDESTAL CONNECTOR

FIG. 21. *By far the simplest and most satisfactory method of repairing a faulty rag-and-putty joint is to remake it with a rubber connector. Detailed instructions for fitting are given in the text.*

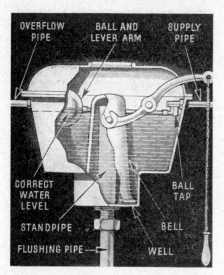

OVERFLOW PIPE — BALL AND LEVER ARM — SUPPLY PIPE

CORRECT WATER LEVEL — BALL TAP

STANDPIPE — BELL

FLUSHING PIPE — WELL

REMOVAL OF RUST

FIG. 22. *View of a cut-away flushing cistern. It is particularly important to remove any rust in the well and under the bell. There are few working parts and most adjustments are simple to make.*

the container, in an enamelled or porcelain jug or bucket. Never use a galvanized iron bucket, as the solution will remove the galvanizing.

By means of a vitreous-enamelled or glass funnel pour the solution carefully into one of the connecting pipes a little at a time. It will froth vigorously, so wait until the frothing ceases before pouring in more solution. Continue pouring slowly until liquid free from froth flows from the other pipe. Leave the solution in the boiler for about ten minutes, then drain it off and flush the equipment thoroughly with clean water until all trace of the solution and sludge has been removed. This washing out is best done with a hose.

Whichever method of de-scaling is

used, before re-connecting the boiler the ends of the flow and return pipes should be examined and any deposit should be removed by hammering and chipping.

The complete hot-water installation can be de-scaled chemically without disconnecting the boiler, but this should not be attempted without expert advice. It is really a job for the experienced heating engineer.

GAS APPLIANCES

If the house is to be left for any considerable time it is advisable to shut off the gas supply by the control cock at the meter. At the same time, all

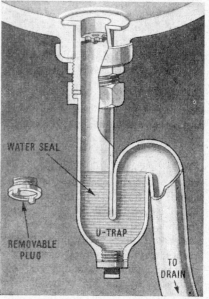

WATER SEAL

REMOVABLE PLUG

U-TRAP

TO DRAIN

CLEARING A BLOCKED U-TRAP

FIG. 23. *To clear a stoppage in the U-trap under a basin, it is necessary to unscrew the plug at the bottom of the trap. Plugs in common use have either a square nut or projecting shoulders at the base to engage a spanner or bar.*

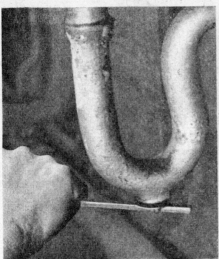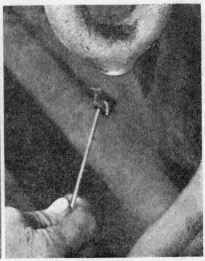

CLEARING AN OBSTRUCTION

FIG. 24. *With an adjustable spanner or a metal bar, engage the shoulders on the U-trap plug and unscrew it. A piece of wire with a hook at the end may then be inserted through the opening and moved about inside the bend to remove any obstruction. Replace the packing washer on the plug before screwing it back.*

appliances should be turned off. On returning to the house, and before turning the gas on again at the meter, it is advisable to ensure that all appliances are still turned off.

In the event of a serious escape of gas, the control cock at the meter should be turned off, the premises should be ventilated by opening the windows, and the local office of the Gas Board notified at once. Small escapes may be stopped temporarily with soap, putty, modelling clay or, preferably, by binding with adhesive tape; but such repairs must be regarded as a temporary expedient only. The Gas Board should be notified so that proper repairs can be made. The existence of a small escape can be definitely established only by a gauge test, but in cases of doubt the householder may try the following test.

Keep the control cock at the meter full on and turn off every appliance, being particularly careful to see that all pilot flames and by-passes are properly shut off. Observe the test dial of the meter, which is the single dial above the row of five dials used for measuring the gas consumption (Fig. 25). Against the pointer of this top dial stick a small piece of stamp paper to mark its position. Wait as long as possible and observe the dial again. If the pointer has not moved there should be no escape, but if in doubt the Gas Board should be notified. A smell of gas should always be reported, as, although the installation may be quite sound, gas may be entering the premises from elsewhere.

The control cock at the meter— known as the consumer's control— should be fitted with a key which should be kept in position on the cock. It is then to hand in an emergency. If the key is missing, ask the Gas Board to supply a new one. The consumer's control cock should turn easily, but it should not be loose. If it is either too tight or too loose the Gas Board should be notified. The consumer must not attempt to adjust this cock himself.

GAS TAPS

Many taps now used on gas appliances are of intricate construction, with spring loading, and require special tools and expert adjustment.

Such taps seldom need to be adjusted, but if they do it is desirable to obtain skilled attention. The ordinary type of gas tap, however, is simple enough to adjust. If too tight, the nut at the bottom should be loosened very slightly—only about a quarter of a turn, using a small spanner. Pliers should not be used, as they will damage the nut. Having loosened the nut, turn the tap on and off several times and adjust the nut until the best tension is obtained. A loose tap is adjusted in a similar manner. The tap should turn comfortably without bind-

HOW TO READ THE GAS METER

FIG. 25. Readings on the five small dials should be written down in sequence from the left. Take the lower of the two figures adjacent to each pointer. A nought should then be added to the total, as the last dial records tens. In this case, the reading would be taken as 000130, or 130 cubic feet. The large dial is for test purposes.

ing and should not be so loose that it can be turned accidentally, or that leakage occurs. If a tap binds even after being loosened, the control cock at the meter and all appliances should be shut off. The defective tap should then be serviced (Fig. 26).

SIMPLE ADJUSTMENTS

Before dealing with gas appliances it is convenient to consider gas burners. On all types of appliances, burners may be of either the simple luminous type or the aerated or bunsen type. With the former type no adjustment is possible or necessary. It is, however, desirable to clean them occasionally : Fig. 27 shows how to clean a luminous burner of a type now being used extensively on certain gas cookers and space-heating appliances. With aerated burners the method of adjustment varies with the particular make, but with the majority of types the essential adjustment is the opening or closing of the air supply (Figs. 28 and 29) to give a flame with a clearly defined inner cone, light blue in colour (Fig. 30).

Gas cookers require little attention beyond cleaning the oven, which is best done by wiping it out immediately after use while the greasy deposit is warm and easily removable. The hot-plate burners and bars should be taken out periodically and cleaned in hot water to which some common soda has been added.

Clear the holes in the burners as shown in Fig. 31. The rod of the thermostat which runs along the top of the oven should be cleaned, but it

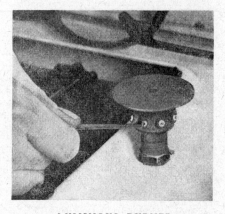

LUMINOUS BURNER

FIG. 27. *Clearing the holes in a luminous burner with a pricker as supplied for use with vacuum pressure stoves.*

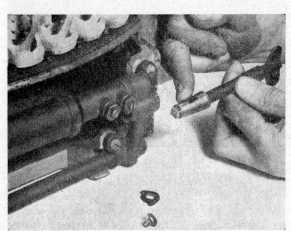

GAS TAPS

FIG. 26. *When a gas tap is dismantled for cleaning it is a good plan to polish all moving parts and to apply a film of grease before the tap is reassembled.*

GAS COOKER

FIG. 28. *The supply of air and gas on this cooker is controlled by the two screws below the taps. For maximum efficiency a light-blue flame with a clearly defined inner cone is required.*

should not be tampered with in any way. Satisfactory working of the thermostat may be checked in the following manner :

(1) Set the dial to a medium number (Mark 7 or H).

(2) Turn the oven tap full on and light the gas.

(3) Close the oven door and wait at least ten minutes.

(4) Open the oven door and turn the dial to its lowest setting.

If the flames diminish in size to small beads the thermostat is in good order. But if the flames are not reduced in size, or if they go out, the thermostat requires expert attention

If there is a battery-operated lighter it may require a fresh cell (No. U 2) (Fig. 32). If the lighter is flint-operated the flint should be exchanged when it becomes worn out. The consumer is, however, warned against buying alleged gas savers for use on the hot-

GAS FIRE

FIG. 29. *After removing the front of a gas fire the control for air and gas supply will be found just below the radiants in the form of an air ring, shutter, or screws as shown.*

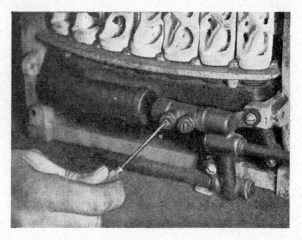

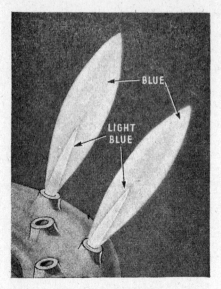

AERATED FLAME

FIG. 30. *When correctly adjusted, an aerated burner should give a light-blue flame with a clearly defined inner cone. If the flame is light yellow in colour, the air supply needs to be increased.*

plate. The burners and bars are designed to give maximum efficiency; most gadgets will impair their efficiency. The use of any tins in the oven other than those supplied with the cooker is also to be avoided. Tins of incorrect shape may upset the temperature zones and give poor cooking results. Lastly, never interfere with the thermostat or with the pressure governor if one is fitted on the gas-supply pipe to the cooker.

Broken radiants on gas fires should not be tolerated. Apart from the poor appearance, the heating efficiency is lowered. Before beginning to renovate a gas fire the required number of new radiants of correct type for the fire should be obtained. Radiants other than those designed for the particular make of fire should not be used, as each type of radiant is designed for use with its appropriate type of burner.

With a gas fire of the type that stands on the hearth in front of a surround, it is better to turn off the gas and to disconnect the supply at the union, using a small adjustable spanner. The fire can then be lifted away from the hearth to enable the back of the grate to be swept. There should be no soot, but there may be dust and dirt from the chimney. If the fire is built-in, it should not be removed, while great care must be taken not to disturb any of the cement luting which controls the draught to the fire.

With either type of fire the procedure for overhauling is as follows :

(1) Remove the radiants carefully

CLEANING THE BURNER

FIG. 31. *The holes in a burner are easily cleared with a stiff wire. Occasionally the burner should be washed in hot water to which some soda has been added.*

GAS LIGHTER

FIG. 32. *How to fit a new cell in a battery-operated lighter. It will be found that the battery case will corrode if the old cell is left in it for any length of time.*

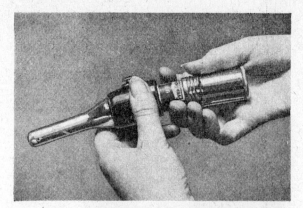

as shown in Figs. 33 and 34, and lay aside any which are unbroken.

(2) Remove the fender of the fire (some are held with screws, others can be lifted off).

(3) Cover the burner holes with rag or paper.

(4) Brush out dirt from inside the canopy, flue nozzle, and burners.

(5) Remove all dirt and dust from

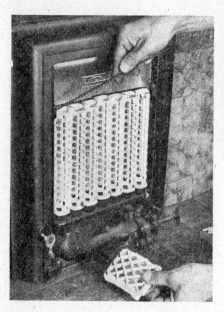

GAS-FIRE RADIANTS

FIG. 33. (*Left*) *After removing the top radiants, the bar which keeps the lower radiants in position may be lifted out.*

FIG. 34. (*Above*) *The lower radiants are removed by gripping the top as shown and lifting the radiant upwards to disengage the base from the jet.*

the burner. A vacuum-cleaner is best for this purpose, but the dirt may also be blown out with a length of tubing (Figs. 35 and 36). The holes in the clay disks or gauzes on each burner nozzle should be clean and undamaged (Fig. 38). A broken

CLEANING THE JETS

FIG. 35. *A short length of rubber tube may be used to blow away the accumulated deposits of dirt from the small perforated disks at the head of the burner.*

disk will cause the fire to pop when lighted or turned out, and to be noisy in use. If any disks are broken, replacements should be obtained.

(6) If the back of the fire is composed of firebrick and is discoloured, it should be painted with a wash made by mixing some fireclay (there are various proprietary makes) with water. This will dry white and make the firebrick as new. If the firebrick

is of asbestos, use a wash made by pounding up pieces of the broken radiants into a fine powder and mixing with water.

(7) Paint all the radiants—the new ones as well as the old—with the wash made from the old radiants. When dry, they will all look the same (Fig. 37).

(8) Re-fit the fire, if it has been removed.

(9) Carefully place the radiants in position. Light the gas and examine the fire to ensure that the radiants are evenly incandescent and that flames do not project beyond the top of the radiants.

From time to time it is necessary to

CLEANING THE BASE

FIG. 36. *The rubber tube employed for clearing the jets also serves to dust out the base of the fire and to dislodge any dirt from behind the grate.*

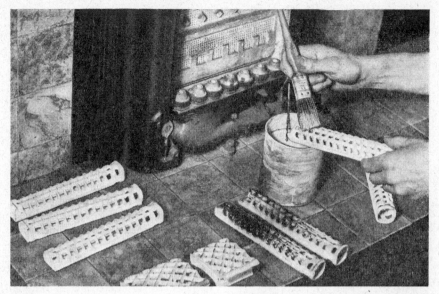

RENOVATING AN OLD GAS FIRE

FIG. 37. *Both the radiants and the back of the fire, if it is composed of firebrick, may be painted with a wash made by mixing fireclay and water. Various proprietary makes are also available. If new radiants have been fitted, these should be painted at the same time as the old ones so that all the radiants will look alike.*

clean the flue on a gas refrigerator, and a small wire brush is normally supplied with the refrigerator for this purpose. First turn off the gas at the tap under the cabinet. Then cover the burner with rag and withdraw the wire and spiral baffle from the flue. The flue brush should now be pushed down the flue and worked up and down a few times (Fig. 39). When the baffle has been replaced, the rag can be removed and the burner relighted. Cleaning and adjustment of the burner is best left to the gas service-men, but a clogged jet may often be cleared by unscrewing the burner (Fig. 40) and inserting a fine wire.

The cabinet should be defrosted at about fortnightly intervals to obtain the best results. A layer of frost acts as

BROKEN DISKS

FIG. 38. *The holes in the clay disks or gauzes on each burner nozzle should be clean and undamaged. If any disks are broken, the fire may tend to light back and will be noisy in use.*

CLEANING A REFRIGERATOR FLUE

FIG. 39. *Turn off the gas at the tap under the cabinet, cover the burner with rag, withdraw the baffle from the flue and work the flue brush up and down.*

an insulator and retards the cooling of the cabinet. When defrosting, the contents of the refrigerator should be removed. When the frost has melted the cabinet should be washed out with a weak soda solution, rinsed with cold water and thoroughly dried.

If a gas refrigerator is not operating well it should be ascertained that :

(1) The cabinet has been defrosted.
(2) The flue is clean.
(3) The cabinet is level.
(4) The wire mesh and cooling fins are unobstructed.
(5) The cabinet door fits tightly all round. (Test with a piece of paper which should be gripped at all points around the door.

(6) The thermostat or control-tap setting is correctly adjusted.

The ideal temperature for the storage of foodstuffs is between 40 and 45 deg. F. On almost every modern refrigerator the temperature inside the cabinet is controlled automatically by what is known as a thermostat. This device is normally fitted in the coldest part of the refrigerator, immediately above the cooling coils which surround the ice trays, and connected to a calibrated control knob in the cabinet.

If a layer of ice covers the thermostat, its sensitivity is reduced. As a result the efficiency of the temperature control system is affected.

If, after the refrigerator has been defrosted, the thermostatic control is thought to be defective, a simple check may be carried out with a thermometer. The temperature varies inside the cabinet, the space around the cooling coils being rather colder than

GAS REFRIGERATOR JET

FIG. 40. *Cleaning and adjusting the burner on a gas refrigerator is best left to an expert, but a clogged jet may sometimes be cleared by unscrewing the burner, as shown, and inserting a fine wire.*

the area below. To obtain an average reading put the thermometer on the middle shelf, close the outer door, and take a reading after ten minutes. Further readings should be taken at regular intervals of, say, a quarter of an hour. If the temperature falls uniformly and, after an hour or so, does should be on the fixed gas pipe and not on the appliance, so that, when out of use, the flexible tube is not charged with gas. A leaky flexible tube can be temporarily repaired with insulating tape or sticking plaster, but a new tube should be fitted as soon as possible.

Periodically gas water-heaters re-

MODERN GAS PLUG AND SOCKET

FIG. 41. *When the plug is inserted, the pins on the plug engage bayonet slots in the socket. As soon as the connexion is broken, the gas is turned off automatically.*

not fluctuate by more than a few degrees, it may be assumed that the thermostat is in good order. By this means also the temperatures corresponding to the calibrations on the control knob may be established.

Gas tubes with push-on rubber ends are not recommended : they should have screwed metal ends and be connected to the fixed gas-supply pipe by means of plug-and-socket connectors as shown in Fig. 41. The control cock quire expert servicing, but the householder can often improve their efficiency by cleaning the flue-pipes and burner. If the burner cannot be removed it should be covered with rag while the flue pipes are brushed. A small flue brush with a wire handle will be needed, while an old hacksaw blade may be useful for clearing any narrow passages. The burner should then be cleaned with a wet brush. If it can be removed, it should be held under a

WATER-HEATER BURNER

Fig. 42. *If the burner on a water heater can be removed, hold it under a running tap so that water flows through it.*

running tap so that the water flows through it (Fig. 42).

If the heater has a flue discharging to the outer air, the exit should be examined and brushed clear. If it is damaged or needs replacing, the Gas Board should be consulted.

USEFUL HINTS

The flames of a gas wash-boiler or washing machine should have clearly defined inner cones and should be adjusted with some water in the pan. After use the interior of the pan should be wiped with a rag dipped in paraffin. This will keep the inner surface of the pan clean and bright and prevent the washing from being discoloured.

A modern gas-ignited coke fire should require little attention. Its efficiency and the easy control of combustion depend on all extraneous points of air entry being sealed with

fireclay cement. Air for combustion can enter, therefore, only by way of the adjustable air shutter. If any of the fireclay luting has broken away, the remainder should be scraped out and neatly replaced with fresh cement (Fig. 43). Any good fireclay cement may be used, but it is preferable to use a brand which expands on setting.

When the blade of a gas poker burns out, it is a sign that the poker has been left in the fire after it has started to burn. Apart from overheating the blade, this oversight wastes gas. When a poker blade has been damaged it is economical to renew it immediately. The old blade may be unscrewed from the handle and taken to the shop as a pattern when buying a replacement.

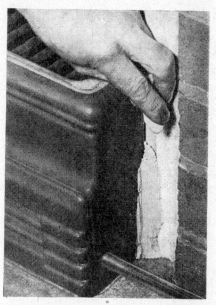

GAS-IGNITED COKE FIRE

Fig. 43. *If any of the luting has broken away, new fireclay cement should be applied without delay, as it is important that air should not enter through the side.*

INDEX

INDEX

ACKNOWLEDGEMENTS

The Publishers wish to thank the following for valuable help with the preparation of this book: The Aerograph Co., Ltd.; Alabastine Co. (British), Ltd.; F. H. Bourner & Co., Ltd.; British Electrical Development Association, Inc.; Cement and Concrete Association; The Cement Marketing Co., Ltd.; General Electric Co., Ltd.; Hamilton & Co. (London), Ltd.; The Controller, H.M.S.O. (Crown copyright photographs on pages 246, 248, 249, 251, 322, 328 and 329); Imperial Chemical Industries Ltd.; Richard Melhuish (London), Ltd.; North Thames Gas Board; Paint Research Station; Arthur Sanderson & Sons, Ltd.; Timber Development Association (photographs on pages 327, 332 by B. Alwyn Jay).